PSYCHOLOGY AND LOGIC

Psychology and Logic

J. R. KANTOR

VOLUME II

1950
THE PRINCIPIA PRESS
CHICAGO, ILLINOIS

ISBN 0-911188-36-3

Copyright 1950 by the Principia Press
5743 S. Kimbark Avenue
Chicago, Illinois 60637

First Reprinting 1976
Second Reprinting 1985

Printed in U.S.A.

CONTENTS

CHAPTER XV

CHAPTER XVI

CHAPTER XVII

CHAPTER XVIII

CHAPTER XIX

CHAPTER XX

CHAPTER XXI

CHAPTER XXIV

CHAPTER XXV

FOREWORD

This volume emphasizes the applied aspects of the relation between psychology and logic. Whereas in the first volume we were chiefly occupied with logical theory, we now investigate the ongoing processes and finished products of system building. Because theory and practice are continuous, the materials of the two volumes are, of course, intimately integrated. The topics of Volume II are treated on the basis of the principles worked out in Volume I; the results, therefore, in a significant way constitute illustrations and tests of interbehavioral theory.

Applying logical principles means for us in no sense exploiting them. Interbehavioral logic is not a unique logical system ready for use in annexing truth and reality. Logics of that type we reject, along with the various historical philosophies serving as their foundation. Specificity logic, in both its theoretical and applied aspects, constitutes a scientific study of systemizing situations. Its application, accordingly, consists in observing how well descriptions of system making fit when they are projected back into the fields from which they are drawn. Thus exploitation gives way to verification.

The chapters of the present volume demonstrate the essential place in various logical situations of (1) concrete specific operations and (2) the things, events, and relations which constitute the raw materials for (3) systemic products. In many instances, too, we clarify (4) the types of instruments employed in system construction. The indispensability of these four factors is amply exemplified in the investigation of system products (chap. 15), as well as in many other chapters.

It is only to be expected that the emphasis of the four factors varies with the specific topics treated. For example, in Chapters 13 and 14 in which we study abstracting, generalizing, defining, and classifying operations, the focal point of observation is the logician engaged in system building. By comparison, Chapter 16

describes the instruments necessary for constructing systems—
namely, models, schemata, and formulae. In the chapters on
categories (17) and universals (18) we show that these intellectual products constitute, on the one hand, system components
which may be analyzed out of, and separated from, given systems and, on the other, tools useful in logical construction.

The seven remaining chapters (19-25) comprise the more
strictly applied materials of the volume. These chapters serve
their verification function by displaying the contrast between the
conventional logical and interbehavioral approaches in the treatment of causation (19), laws of thought (20), probability (21-
22), measurement (23-24), and the perspectives of logic (25).
Outstanding are the differentiations revealed in logical and
scientific results when classical mentalistic psychology, which has
paralleled the transcendent philosophies of historical absolute and
universal logic, is set aside in favor of interbehavior with things
under specific circumstances.

As in Volume I, the frequent use of illustrative quotations is in
all cases exclusively intended to exemplify doctrines. It has not
been necessary, therefore, to inquire whether other writers share
some particular view, condemn it, or whether the quoted author
has retreated from the position specified.

I want to call attention to a change in style of footnote
references. A number of book titles, which in the first volume are
cited by two or more words, have been reduced to a single word,
usually the first.

Circumstances long delaying the completion of the present
volume have not been without compensations. The interval has
enabled me to consider several criticisms made of the first
volume. While I have no intention of defending the materials
presented beyond the arguments in the text, I prize the op-
portunity to sharpen a few points.

First, consider the criticism that the interbehavioral hypothesis
is contradictory. On the one hand, it is charged that I deny
generality to logic, but, on the other, claim generality for the interbehavioral hypothesis. My answer is simply to invoke the specificity

rule. The rejection of all absolute and general logical systems is in no way incompatible with the construction of a generalizing hypothesis. The assertion that there is no universal logic is not contradicted by demonstrating that *all* logical systems are specific creations of particular individuals under unique auspices. The charge here is reminiscent of Bradley's absolutistic argument about metaphysics. Deny metaphysics and you are a metaphysician, though a bad one; for to deny that reality is attainable by knowledge is to claim knowledge of an unknowable reality. Absolutists lack nothing except the appreciation that their universalism is but a specific kind of local creation.

The same critic objects to my attempt to separate both logic and psychology from traditional philosophy. On what ground? On nothing less than that presuppositions are inevitable and that presuppositions mean philosophy. Granted that philosophy is synonymous with presuppositions, one must still differentiate between types of presuppositions. Current philosophy concerned with the critical methods of science is vastly different from traditional metaphysics. I am thoroughly sympathetic with philosophy taken as a generalized science of science. But it is clear beyond a doubt that the development of an objective psychology makes possible the complete and final extrusion of all idealisms, nominalisms, and realisms from science and logic. As an independent branch of study logic is in no sense connected with the classic metaphysical systems called philosophy.

My suggestion that logic might profit from cooperation with an objective psychology has prompted another writer to raise the perennial cry: *psychologism*. Two comments are in order. First, the present epithet *psychologism* must be regarded as altogether different from the classic one used by Husserl and others. From the standpoint of interbehavioral psychology there are no psychic elements or essences such as are involved in classic psychologism. Specificity logicians, therefore, are farther removed from psychologism than are both the original antipsychologists and those they attacked. Interbehavioral system building is completely free from internal spiritistic entities. Supported by an objective psychology we are able to demonstrate how cosmic logic, whether psychologistic or nonpsychologistic, is primarily verbal creation and projection.

Moreover, it is precisely an operationally rooted psychology which can differentiate (a) the various types of human behavior, (b) the materials interbehaved with, and (c) the products of such behavior. On this basis the work of psychologists can be distinguished from that of logicians, scientists, and other workers, while full justice can be done to the interrelations of the diverse enterprises.

Considering that, unlike most logical theorists, I have formally set down my postulates, it is anomalous to find a critic asserting that I regard specificity logic as without presuppositions. The association with objective psychology of a logical theory lacking presuppositions is impossible. The point is precisely that interbehavioral presuppositions are *different*. What can be a more definite presupposition than the rejection of classical logical presuppositions? Because a disdain for autistic world systems is not pleasing to cosmologicians, they find such a presupposition unpalatable.

In another instance a writer who does associate postulates with presuppositions denies that most of the basic interbehavioral presuppositions are postulates. The assumption is that only classical-logical postulates are postulates. This criticism is made on the expressed ground that logic is an *a priori* discipline; and, since specificity logic is not such a discipline, it simply is beyond the pale. Strangely enough, the argument made for *a priori* logic concerns the existence of scientific contents—namely, events—which are independent of scientific work. But this is exactly the interbehavioral position. All authentic scientific work consists of interbehavior with events described *in situ*, manipulated in the laboratory, and counted and computed when possible. Descriptions and explanations can only be structured on such events as an indispensable foundation. Furthermore, all this activity goes on within the bounds of human interbehavior. If there is anything that one must call *a priori*, it belongs inside this system. No contact with scientific work or with scientific subject matter allows for any absolutes and transcendents, whether empiricistic or rationalistic.

Several writers criticize my proposed cooperation between logic and psychology on the ground that, if this cooperation is necessary for logic, it is likewise necessary for physics and other sciences.

To such critics it seems axiomatic that cooperation of physics and psychology is *not* necessary. But writings on physical theory show conclusively how an objective psychology can obviate the mysticism and metaphysics filling the pages written by physicists. Think only of the bifurcated universe of the classical physicists, of the indeterminism and reality puzzles of relativists and of quantum mechanists! This matter is amply treated in our chapters on probability and measurement.

Curious are the vagaries of reviewers. One writer indulged in considerable dispraise of objective psychology because, obviously, formal mathematical analysis cannot be replaced by psychological investigation. Missed altogether was the fundamental point that interbehavioral psychology not only marks the boundaries of human behavior, but also differentiates the various activities within these limits. For example, because of the variations in materials, I have stressed the specificities of system building in mathematics, in science and in everyday life. I have also pointed out the contrast between system building and other behavior—a contrast which should separate sharply, say, the mathematician's calculative and analytic behavior from the logician's structuring of operations and products. In addition, behavior analysis distinguishes clearly the work of the creative mathematician from that of the logician who builds symbol or word systems describing the products of such mathematical work.

Quite aside from the above, it is reprehensible to overlook the fact that, because of the continuity running through all intellectual activity, new developments in one domain are reflected in all the others. What science can escape the revolutionary consequences of the physicist's relativity and discontinuity? Thus the emergence of objective psychology cannot but leave its mark on other disciplines. Only at the risk of intellectual peril can one cavalierly wave it aside.

When Paul Valéry (Hadamard, an Essay on the Psychology of Invention in the Mathematical Field, p. 60) was asked about his reaction to his completed works, he replied, "It always turns out badly; *Je divorce*." I admit that I have been unable to grasp as high as I have reached. Still, the unfettered reader will be able to see that an objective psychological treatment of language, thought, and reasoning is of considerable consequence for logic.

Once more it is my pleasure to acknowledge the day-by-day collaboration of H. R. Kantor. I wish also to thank Mr. Ernest Lilienstein for his effective services while this book was being written and printed. Likewise I am indebted to Deans Payne and Thompson of the Graduate School of Indiana University for grants required for library and secretarial assistance. As in the case of Volume I, I want to acknowledge the help received from Dr. A. E. Kanter, and the Directors of the Principia Press who have generously contributed to publication costs.

J. R. K.

April 1950

CHAPTER XIII

ABSTRACTING AND GENERALIZING OPERATIONS

ALL logicians recognize that, in some form or other, abstracting and generalizing are indispensable operations in complex system making. Especially writers on mathematical theory have pointed out how vital for the evolution of mathematics and logic was the original achievement of abstracting numbers from things.[1] What is now required is to treat these operations as definite interbehavior in concrete fields. Such an objective treatment runs counter to the tradition that logical abstracting and generalizing comprise acts of "reason" or "mind," whether or not dependent on autonomous ontological entities.

Naturally, in conventional logic, which is universalistic and necessitarian, we can not expect abstracting and generalizing to be described as specific interbehavior of persons with stimulus objects. Logicians for whom the materials of system making are formal or verbal things automatically accept the interpretation that forms and propositions constitute autonomous entities. Thus they overlook the competing view that conventional logical materials consist of products of concrete operations (vol. I, p. 2f.). In this work we treat abstracting behavior as analytic operations upon a continuum, and generalizing as synthetic interbehavior with presented materials.

Failing to appreciate the field character of abstracting and generalizing operations, logicians tend to pay more attention to the products achieved than to the constructive processes by which products are obtained. Once obtained, products appear not only independent but established, and may easily conceal the specific operations through which they were produced. For instance, though it is quite proper to regard mathematical equations as purely formal and autonomous structures, they are nevertheless

---

[1] Russell, Introduction, p. 3; Whitehead, Science, p. 29f.; Bell, Development, p. 23f.

derived from interbehavioral field operations upon definite materials. That all equations must be accompanied by a text[2] points to two interbehavioral situations: (1) In applied mathematics no equation is valid unless it can be carried back to the original set of measuring operations from which it springs; (2) In pure or formal mathematics, equations go back to contacts with particular systems of relations.

The confusion of formal objects and systems with unproduced entities is an acute instance of the antigenetic fallacy. Because something exists in the fullness of its structure and use there is a tendency to ignore the elaborate processes of its evolution. Granted that the narrated history of a thing seldom suffices for its complete explication, there is still no warrant for assuming ingenetic essences among its properties.

Abstracting and generalizing operations are frequently overlooked because insufficient account is taken of their specific characteristics. Frege supports his belief that Platonic numbers inhabit a timeless realm of *Pure Being* on the ground that numbers, unlike color, are not abstracted from things.[3] But to grant this point is certainly not to sanction the view that numbers are not, in some way, constructed. The ontological argument that "nicht jeder Gegenstand ist raumlich"[4] proves nothing contrary to the theory that such objects and their nonspace are created by abstracting and generalizing operations upon concrete things.

The interbehavioral standpoint represented in this treatise implies that constructional operations may be either refined or crude depending upon the kind of materials operated upon. Whether the materials are concrete or abstract, and whatever the motivation, the abstracting analysis is definitely selective. By the same token, generalization is constantly subject to the materials and problems at hand.

Logical Forms as Products of A. and G. Operations

With the development in recent decades of mathematical or symbolic logic we might have hoped for an increased elucidation of abstracting and generalizing operations. Mathematical logic,

---

[2] Bridgman, Nature, chap. 6.
[3] Grundlagen, vol. I, p. 27.
[4] Ibid.

like mathematics itself, has steadily become pervaded by the twin characters of abstractness and generality.[5] Has not logic itself been claimed as the science of pure form, and mathematics as reducible to logic because it can be exhibited as a completely logical structure?[6] That logical proof or demonstration is independent of subject matter has become a greatly lauded principle.[7]

No appreciable clarification of abstracting and generalizing processes, however, has materialized. And why not? Probably because the early introduction of mathematical logic coincided with the resurgence of mystic doctrines and with the notion that logic is concerned with Platonic essences. But do not forms really constitute systems and organizations? Are not forms structures, and therefore products of (1) investigation, in the case of objects and events, and (2) constructed relations between things, when the latter are submerged in their relations?

However, the conventional doctrine of logical forms has its value for our present study. For one thing, the most extreme abstraction is replete with material suggesting the paradox that nothing is so full as the emptiness of a construct. The maxim maker may define mathematics "as the subject in which we never know what we are talking about, nor whether what we are saying is true,"[8] but obviously he cannot conceal his cap and bells.[9] Why should an eminent mathematician[10] confound visible and palpable things with things, or overlook the concreteness and actuality of relations?

Formalism in logic and mathematics openly flouts the fact that such creations as "zero," "number," and "successor" have been used to demonstrate the reduction of mathematics to arithmetic and arithmetic to logic. It seems highly anomalous to deal with structures, especially such obviously made and remade structures, only to forget about the effort and the plan responsible for their production. To assert that mathematics is structural is entirely different from saying it reaches out toward empty and eternal forms.

[5] Bell, Development, p. 153.
[6] Stebbing, Modern, chap. 10.
[7] Nicod, Foundations, Part I.
[8] Russell, Mysticism, p. 75.
[9] This definition appears in an article designed to be "as romantic as possible," ibid., Preface.
[10] Eddington, Space, p. 14 n.

In the former instance it is tacitly acknowledged that mathematical logic is system building, with sets of relations as the building material. Is it preferable to interpret mathematics as the science of forms instead of the science of quantities? Yes, and here again the work of formalization and system construction is evident. To describe or define mathematics as structure or system building, however, does not eradicate the difference between mathematical work and mathematical logic. The former involves many processes besides system building.

The proposition that mathematics is logic, or reduces to logic, is in itself an excellent illustration of abstracting and generalizing operations. Note that the constructor creates the proposition by abstracting all but a certain residue from the elaborate work and materials of mathematics, and then legislatively generalizing that the residue is the whole. The procedure in all respects is equivalent to the creation of frictionless surfaces, perfectly rigid bodies, genic determiners, sensations, and other such abstracted products.

Constructional Principles in
A. and G. Operations

In this work we are primarily concerned with abstracting and generalizing designed to produce system-building materials. These operations, of course, are only members of a general class. In all cases the constructive feature, the development of a product, is the outstanding characteristic. For objective psychology, abstracting and generalizing operations constitute instances of creative imagination.[11]

Basic abstracting and generalizing operations can be very effectively studied in considering the Euclidean dimensionless point, breadthless line, straight line, etc. Let us compare three interpretations of how abstracting and generalizing operated in the development of these materials for Euclidean geometry.

Mach. As a confirmed empiricist within traditional philosophical dualism, Mach stressed sensations as the basic factors of reality. Accordingly he attempted to derive all constructs (concepts) by a process of emptying out sensuous objects. Euclidean points and

---

[11] Cf. Kantor, Principles, vol. II, chap. 18.

lines, he argued,[12] were end results of eliminating all other content from actual things. Thus, geometry as the science of space must be concerned with bodies, but bodies from which all the properties and characteristics are removed, until only a point or a breadthless line is left. Geometry, therefore, is concerned with *ideal* objects produced by the schematization of *experiental objects*.[13]

Despite the fallacies inherent in Mach's philosophy of sensations, consciousness and mind, he hit, in a genuine way, upon the proper description of the evolution of the abstractive and generalized constructs of geometry. Undoubtedly he clearly understood the enormous cultural developments included in so elaborate a humanistic system as Euclidean or other sorts of geometry.

Poincaré. Armed with equipment obtained from a different type of philosophy—namely, Kantian conceptualism—Poincaré argued that a geometrical point is in no sense derived from evacuating concrete objects. Points are elementary and original ideal elements, derived from rationally constructed systems; the process of abstraction is the isolation of the point element from the remainder of the organization. The basic operation for the development of points consists of intuition.

What Poincaré especially stands for is freedom of invention and construction. For him, mathematical constructions are conventions and conveniences of systematic organization. What Poincaré especially inveighs against is the opposite extreme—namely, the purely formal and empty[14] structures made up of logical propositions and symbols.

Strong. Both of the above statements concerning the basic sources of geometric things, Strong believes, are derived from a theory concerning geometry, rather than from a study of actual geometric operations.[15] He suggests, that from the standpoint of actual mathematical operations, geometric points are relations (positions). In Book I of Euclid's *Elements*, he argues, points are consistently treated as positions, either indeterminate or determinate ones.

[12] Mach, Space, p. 48f.
[13] Ibid., p. 68.
[14] Foundations, pp. 413-485.
[15] Strong, Procedures, Appendix.

Most appealing in Strong's discussion is the emphasis upon locating Euclid's abstractional processes in his actual geometric work. This is tantamount to studying abstracting and generalizing as the behavior of persons in specific situations. Certainly it is important to study Euclid's points, lines, and other constructions as derived from his subject matter and procedures. Especially is this true when the system elements, as products of work, do not match those verbally and formally stated. But possibly Strong does not carry this valuable point far enough. When we study an individual at work, particularly when the work is of such giant proportions as the systemization of a geometry, the interbehavioral field cries out for analysis.

How incongruous is the system-building work of persons—their actual operations upon materials—with glib verbal or symbolic formulations. That there must be something in common between the structure of sentences and facts[16] is an extremely defective proposition. Notice Euclid's vacillation in his definitions; in the first, for example, he declares: "A point is that which has no part," while in the third he says: "The extremities of a line are points." As Heath[17] indicates, Euclid was influenced by the necessity both of organizing elements and refraining from violating the established principles of logic and science.

Now the difficulty with Mach's and Poincaré's discussions of the creation of points and lines is probably not that they establish meanings for these elements on the basis of their particular epistemologies, but that they attempt to make the latter valid for Euclid. What they accomplish, then, is the explanation of wrong epistemology. As creative workers, both Mach and Poincaré are operating upon the basis of their characteristic intellectual traits, and these traits inevitably show in their work and products. Similarly, Euclid's epistemology influenced his work. At the same time, however, he operated on a commonsense and objective basis. Nonspatial mental states (sensations) or organized faculties did not guide his constructions. Rather, he made his abstractions according to the geometric knowledge and traditions at hand, and in connection with the need to formalize and systematize them.

[16] Wittgenstein, Tractatus, 4.01, 5.05, 5.06, 5.12, et passim.
[17] Thirteen, vol. I, pp. 155, 165, et passim.

Envisaged in this way, the inaccuracies and inconsistencies of his abstractions and generalizations are easy to understand.

ABSTRACTING AND GENERALIZING LEVELS

Because all systems are specific it follows that particular abstracting and generalizing operations are influenced by the type of system being evolved. More important, we need to emphasize the work of particular individuals (vol. I), not only in a personal capacity, but also as agents in the cumulative historical evolution of cultural elements and systems.

Individual Operations. Individual abstracting and generalizing operations may be schematized as linking the crude data with which the worker begins and the constructional products representing the results of his action. This is indicated in the following schema.

| Construction (Product) | Constructional Operations | Material worked upon (Crude Data) |

The operations always may, and sometimes must, be organized in a hierarchical scale of stages or levels.

The first or most elementary stage is a simple form of selective reaction with respect to things, the assumption of an attitude, say, concerning some sort of material. Next in the series is the description of the selected event as a phase of the worker's orientation toward it. Then follows the fixation of this description in some linguistic or symbolic form. Obviously, the interbehavior becomes increasingly abstractive, in the sense that the selection and description may be regarded as definitely constructional.

As this abstractional process progresses it is possible to manipulate the descriptions, whether elementary protocols or highly formulated laws, with an increased independence of the original materials. To be sure, there are distinct limits to this increasing remoteness from original contacts with things. In system building, illimitable abstraction is a cardinal error leading to utter simplicity, mystic absolutes, tautology, and all the paradoxes of mathematical infinites. Again, the individual may construct generalizations by analogy or other techniques, and in diverse styles. At the same time, the worker, in proceeding, should check his generalizations by referring to the original data. These are propositions few will attempt to dispute, but the various attitudes toward the checking criterion are another matter. Within recent years, since the advent of relativity and quantum mechanics, even physical scientists question the existence of an objective world—that is, events independent of the scientist's descriptive and interpretative constructions (p. 312f). In paper after paper, in book after book, physicists discuss whether the events with which they deal are anything but sensations.[18] Such discussions always skirt the abyss of meaningless problems.

It is hoped that the interbehavioral position adhered to in this work may serve to illuminate the character of the criterion by which we check our constructions. Recall that the physicist, as well as every other intellectual worker, operates in a definite reference field. It is very easy, then, to determine whether or not he is influenced by presuppositions describable as cultural influences or simply by local school traditions. As pointed out in Volume I (chaps. 5, 6), any notion that things and events are reducible to sensations (psychic constructs), or that scientific propositions are based upon sensations, can be definitely traced to the dualism hampering scientific thinking. In this sense we can identify the influences leading such a physicist as Mach to build upon Hume's formulations, or the mathematician Poincaré to retain the conventional conceptualism derived from Kant.

Cultural Abstracting and Generalizing. The evolution of the number system provides the most effective sample of the pyramiding of individual abstracting and generalizing operations. The base of the pyramid, obviously, is the series of positive integers. Perhaps the next few levels should include the negative integers, ratios, fractions, irrational numbers, and zero. Disregarding exact chronology, we may point out another series of levels comprising literate numbers, complex numbers, and ideal numbers. At the apex, as of our time, we might place the numbers belonging to the transfinite domains (p. 23). Clearly, these levels represent not only possible temporal successions but also degrees of abstraction. Only the most elementary levels of numbers are abstracted from things. For the rest, abstractions and generalizations are produced

---

[18] Houston, Philosophy; Eddington, Philosophy; Dingle, Through; Lenzen, Nature; Bridgman, Nature.

by means of constructive procedures, occupying varying degrees of remoteness from original objects.[19]

Scientific and intellectual histories constitute, for the most part, narrations concerning the evolution of interrelated items forged through longer or shorter time periods; these items in their completed stages comprise cultural institutions. The history of logic consists primarily of instances of cumulative abstractions and generalization growths. A noteworthy example is the development and elaboration of mathematical and symbolic items in modern Formal Logic.

THE INTERRELATION OF A. AND G. OPERATIONS

Our exposition so far has indicated that abstracting involves the manipulation of concrete or abstract stimulus objects in order to analyze out certain factors. Generalizing, on the other hand, is primarily the creation of a product based upon concrete or abstract materials either previously analyzed out of a continuum or approached in their integral character.

Despite variations in detail these operations are often very closely interrelated, a fact well exemplified in the building of philosophic systems. For instance, by a series of abstractive procedures persons are separated on the ground of their varying-interbehavior with visually presented objects, say, variously colored or shaped things. Then, by similar techniques, variations are emphasized which are based upon differing relations between persons and objects. Other abstracting procedures yield sharp differentiations between the perceiving individuals and the objects perceived.

Next, a number of generalizing procedures are brought into play. First, the relativity of perceiving is created. There are color-weak and color-strong perceivings. Thus an inevitable diversity between perceiving and perceived is set up, along with discrepancies between the relations of perceiving acts and perceived objects. By devious creative generalizations propositions are formulated concerning a possible *real* world different from anything observed. In brief, such conjoint operations are typical of all speculative theologies and metaphysical philosophies. The term *metaphysics*

[19] The science of pure geometry is generally regarded as having been evolved from the humble source of land-measuring techniques. See Nagel, Formation.

itself suggests the historical development of the coordinate operations of abstracting and generalizing. In Aristotelian times metaphysics was simply the study of the generalized aspects of events included in physics and other distinct sciences. Later, unfortunately, metaphysics became the exercise field of those who created systems without much, if any, regard to actual events.

But not only the illegitimate metaphysical domain is rich in illustrations of the conjoint operations of abstracting and generalizing behavior. The same situation prevails in every complex system-building situation. It is therefore to our advantage to consider the specific characteristic of each operation separately.

Specific Characteristics of Abstracting Operations

Abstracting means formalizing. In calculating we must abstract from the specific characteristics of things. In mensuration the units must be taken as qualitatively indifferent; numbers are viewed as ordered points without regard to what they specifically represent. However, abstracting itself is a concrete operation, and the abstractions are products of such operations. While at any moment we may say it is indifferent what particular things we are calculating or measuring, there could be no operations without materials to work upon. That these materials are abstruse and relational enforces rather than weakens the point. In *all* such abstract situations we merely interbehave with relations between events, rather than with events; or we might say we operate upon relational events instead of upon objects.

The fact that most behavior is really abstractional proves that abstractions are concrete. In everyday speech when we refer to things we already are selecting certain features out of a comprehensive continuum. Similarly, every act of perceptual discrimination involves not only one but several such abstractional procedures. First, we select a certain object from its background and related objects; then we interbehave with the object in a specific manner determined by the immediate reference frame or field of action.

Because we are unduly impressed by the product of our abstracting behavior (p. 1), once we develop a symbolism to represent the results of our operations we are apt to consider our symbols simply as records of actions, irrespective of the objects manipulated. Words or symbols, however, are products of interbehavior with things, not the results of a creational process independent of those things.

To a great extent, abstractional behavior involves isolating operations. In many cases, to observe what is going on we separate things or events from the matrix or field in which they are inevitably imbedded. Frequently the isolated datum is itself a system interrelated with other systems. How different is the isolating procedure when we are interested in a particle moving in a straight line without acceleration and when we study a particle in accelerated motion in a circular path.

Physicists[20] raise the question whether, in view of the impossibility of isolating a system in nature, we should not refer to the process as focusing attention upon a body or a system. Despite the utterly metaphorical character of this alternative suggestion the interbehavioral feature of the situation is stressed.

Typical Abstracting Interbehavior

Abstracting operations vary as the performances of individuals and according to the specific character of the things with which they interbehave. Illustrative classes called *Divisive* and *Multiplicative* may be described as follows.

Divisive Abstractions. Because of our general cultural circumstances the divisive or analytic type of abstraction is probably the more familiar. With our tendency toward simplification as a means of carrying out various activities we look upon abstractions as factors analyzed out of larger complexes. In physics, for example, it seems natural to reduce mechanical events to space, time, and mass. As a matter of fact, the notion is exceedingly common that space and time are inevitable features of all happenings. While we know that this attitude is merely a sign of our cultural circumstances, and, that with other propensities developed, we could just as well make other factors fundamental, this is still an excellent illustration of the divisive or reductive type of abstracting behavior. As we proceed from one situation and one scientific field to another the instances multiply.

[20] Dadourian, Force.

The hierarchical arrangement in the conventional classification of the sciences is a good example. It is often asserted that psychological science reduces to biology, biology in turn to chemistry and physics. But these two sciences are not always regarded as end points in this reductive procedure. Physics is made basic to chemistry; this discipline, in turn, is shaken down to mathematical relations. Nor does this terminate the process, since mathematics is often cut down to logic. Current conventions limit the fecundity necessary to reduce logic to something else.

Multiplicative Abstractions. The operations we call multiplicative abstraction occur when we not merely analyze given material but immediately add interpretative components. The operations, in other words, are constructive. We are reminded here of those continuity physicists (Mach, Ostwald) who fifty years ago denied that physical events could properly be analyzed into atoms. For them the basic and fundamental data of physics consisted of *energy*, and energy was regarded as continuous. The atomists, of course, *constructed* their analyzed factors, and, though physicists could not have foreseen recent developments in quantum theory, we might trace an unbroken line between atoms and energy quanta as abstracted units endowed with more elaborate characteristics.

Every scientific field offers numerous illustrations of constructive abstractions. Consider the multiplicative character of the abstracting operations that produced "sensations" in traditional psychology. Sensations were not only the atoms of the mind, but differed from other kinds of atoms depending upon how many types there were in the system. For Wundt sensations contrasted only with feelings. Other psychologists multiplied sensation properties to contrast with images and with will elements also. These imaginary sensations were even endowed with spatial attributes! The entire process of abstractive behavior is neatly revealed in the story of how elements of "consciousness" can be provided with spatial properties. But even these extravagantly multiplicative creations count as nothing beside the creativity of physicists who make sensations into the *fons et origo* of the *material* cosmos.

The multiplicative character of abstraction products is excellently shown by observing how they evolve in the first place. Take the abstraction *stimulus* as it developed in psychology. Originally, the term was taken over from biology to refer to some condition—for example, light rays—which incited the action of a receptor (retina), and finally resulted in the appearance of the sensation in consciousness. Then the property of inciting an organism to act, as in performing a motor response, was added to the sensation. When psychologists became interested in the behavior and adjustments of organisms to their surroundings, the properties of stimuli were again increased to include objects. Still later, the stimulus abstraction became modified in order to take on properties of field factors.

Another good example of the multiplication of abstractive products centers around the changes in such products as matter and form. Matter, as abstracted from an art object, is sometimes presumed to have no properties until impressed with form by the artist. But it is asked: "Had the block of marble no form at all when it came out of the quarry?"[21] Mill has pointed out that the word *form* should refer only to bodily figure. Beyond that every usage became vague and arbitrary.

Specific Characteristics of Generalizing Operations

Whether or not generalizing operates as a correlated process with abstracting, it is always a specific interbehavioral procedure within a particular reference frame or coordinate system. The frame of reference marks off a field of activity conditioned by certain purposes and problems. A typical illustration is that in which objects, relations, or events are constructively magnified into something more important or pervasive. Let us choose examples from everyday life, as well as from science and mathematics.

One takes a particular act performed by a person and generalizes it into a typical trait. This procedure is consonant with the process of creating abstract matter from specific qualities of things observed, or generalizing observed microscopic events as typical of microscopic happenings. Similar illustrations abound in every department of intellectual life. Through the controlled observations of repeated events scientific laws are created by generalizing processes. Consider that interesting type of generalization which begins with the specification that a thing is either A or not A; that is, it has or has not certain qualities, properties, dimensions or rela-

[21] Mill, Examination, vol. 2, p. 139.

tions. This fact is generalized into a so-called law, that of excluded middle (chap. 20). As a statement of the factual condition that a certain description or classification is satisfactory this law
is unobjectionable. Next, the law is generalized, as in Aristotle's
sea-fight example.[22] The necessity that something should or should
not take place is, of course, a verbally constructed necessity.

From interbehavior with spatial events we abstract shapes or
line structures, or we regard space as merely an order of triplets
or point representatives. In these cases the emphasis is upon certain results, but these results are always derived from very
definite interbehavioral operations. Generalized algebra may be
said to consist of the manipulation of a set of derived symbols in
order to achieve a greater degree of abstractness for certain purposes. But the history of all generalizing operations proves that
the most abstruse results can only be reached through step-by-step
operations. Indeed it would be fatal to overlook the small interbehavioral steps.

Generalization is an inevitable and indispensable feature of all
human operations. Without it there could be no prediction, no
commerce with the future, no expectation. While interbehavioral
psychology cannot tolerate faculties or powers, in a definitely
practical sense there is a generalizing propensity. In other words,
generalization is the basis for all organization of objects and
events.

In science a generalizing form of interbehavior results in the
production of laws which not only yield consistency and certainty,
but allow for the interrelationships of interbehavior over ranges
of time and place. Yet unless we regard generalization as a definite
interbehavioral process, dealing with specific stimulus objects, we
run into all sorts of metaphysical and other insalubrious predica-
ments. Our formalizations and various generalizing processes,
such as induction, deduction, etc., must be performed with strict
regard to available stimulus objects.

But how far can we go in our generalization? What are the
limits? Undoubtedly, a strict line can be drawn between autistic
constructions and serviceable principles which imply respect for
observable facts. The question is: How far can we extrapolate from
actual contacts with events? To be sure, we have a completely

[22] Cf. vol. I, p. 160.

valid test of our extrapolations when we employ the criterion of specific interbehavior. It is no great task to differentiate between extrapolation which generates and furthers our contacts with specific existential things, and extrapolation consisting of autistic constructions which implement the creation of ultimates and absolutes. In connection with the latter type, logicians have built up a formalistic cult. By abstracting from subject matter they come to the point where they emphasize form. Form, then, becomes material for erecting all sorts of structures. In itself this sort of extrapolation is a legitimate kind of system building. When regarded as significant for events, however, it results in futile attempts at application.

TYPICAL GENERALIZING INTERBEHAVIOR

Since generalizing interbehavior is continuous with the abstractional processes of all human enterprise it is impossible to indicate all its different types. We can only illustrate, therefore, some prominent instances.

Analogizing. Numerous generalizations are constructed by pointing out or establishing similarities, correspondences or analogies between one type of object, relation or event, and another. Note that in the constructional procedure the analogizing reactions share equal prominence with the characteristics of the stimulus object. If comparisons are stressed, it is done on the basis of the leads provided by the things compared. The essential creative performance consists of carrying over or generalizing similarities or congruences.

The typical analogizing processes of mathematics illustrate such operations. Temporal succession, taken to be undimensional and continuous, is analogized by the interminable succession of integer series. Thus algebra becomes the science of time. Three dimensional space, with its symmetries, is constructed into geometrical science. Similarities and correspondences in groups of things become the raw materials for the creation of classes.

Scientific models (chap. 16) of various sorts constitute similar illustrations. It is said that a scientific model constitutes a substitute or replacement of part of the universe by a simpler and similar thing.[23] At any rate, the Rutherford-Bohr model of the atom

[23] Rosenblueth and Wiener, Role, p. 316.

is merely the adaptation of the solar-system analogy to the relationship between protons and electrons in an atom. Other prominent analogical generalizations are the development of electrodynamics on the basis of classical mechanics, and Ehrenfest's Adiabatic Hypothesis for explaining the alteration in a state of motion in an isolated mechanical system. This last hypothesis is directly borrowed from thermodynamics.[24]

The following schema effectively suggests the analogical basis for generalizing constructions:

Correspondence		*Noncorrespondence*	
Identity	Similarity	Difference	Contrariety
(complete	(partial	(partial	(complete
analogy)	analogy)	polarity)	polarity)

Magnification. When the generations of classical theologians built up their theistic conception of omnipresence and omnipotence they were simply enlarging and modifying what they regarded as the most desirable personal qualities and properties. The Islamic construct of the universally merciful and compassionate Being represents an expansion and glorification of man's superior virtues. Generalizing by magnification is to stress stimulus objects, though the response factors can not be minimized or slighted. From scientific domains we may gather such examples as "mathematics is the queen of the sciences and arithmetic the queen of mathematics," also that physics is the basis and foundation of the other sciences.

A more specific instance is the glorification of mechanics in physics, or of the conductive and coordinative processes of the nervous system in neurological and psychological circles, to such an extent, in fact, that these processes become generalized as the central points in the biological and psychological economy.

Reiteration. Such abstractive constructs as the mathematical infinite and infinitesimal (p. 23) display a prominence of responsiveness rather than stimulus objects. The infinite is developed by recursive acts of addition, whereas the infinitesimal is abstracted by subtractive action.

Reiterative or recursive responses are illustrated by starting

[24] Sommerfeld, Atomic, p. 341f.

with zero and indefinitely repeating an additive act to reach the mathematical infinite. Going in the opposite direction by repetitive subtractional steps leads from minus one to the infinitesimal. Probably a still better illustration is the Archimedian exhaustion procedure. The steps taken to reduce a polygon to a circle indicate the process of repeating an action to reach a definite limit.

Repetitive behavior is a decided source of abstractional and generalizing products. For example, instants of time are reached by dividing a continuum, or an infinite duration, and continuously enumerating the items to a named but nonexistent stopping place.

Interpolation. The grand-scale form of interpolative operation is found in the generalizing creation of a mathematical continuum by interpolating a point between any two given points. Interpolatting construction constitutes an elaborate manipulation of stimulus objects in two directions. In the first place, the selection and specification of interpolated items suggest a separative instead of a generalizing procedure. On the other hand, the continuing process of placing items between given items enlarges the interpolative series to form an expanding system. The progressive filling in of parts to expand the whole surely works toward extensive abstractive generalization.

Smaller-scale interpolative operations take the form of working out all sorts of proportions and fitting in logarithmic values. Keeping actual procedures before us, we will not be too greatly influenced by the fixity and prior determination of end points, and shall thus avoid minimizing the creating and expanding operations.

Extrapolation. The astronomical domain provides great scope for the exercise of extrapolative processes. Begin with the earth or other planet of the solar system, and continue to enlarge the system to include all the nine planets and intervening spaces. The whole solar system, however, is continuous with the galactic system in which there are many other members. Galactic systems, as members of larger systems of star groups in space, afford the means of generalizing a definite and somewhat limited astronomical universe. Those who do not fill out their systems beyond fairly definite data refrain from transcending scientifically legitimate bonds. Others, more speculatively inclined, continue to extrapolate beyond any possibly observable or calculable system, and thereby attain systems of universes which can only be verbally proposed and managed.

Extrapolative generalization, therefore, is not limited to data or things, but involves a preponderant emphasis of acts and operations. As such it is a more versatile and facile type of generalization behavior. Statistical tables offer a telling example. Consider, for instance, the responsible and irresponsible creation of things, references, and propositions way beyond original data.[25]

Combined Generalizing Operations. Convenient though it be to treat generalizing operations as separate and independent procedures, in all complex situations a number of them are combined to bring about the final result. Consider such a procedure as Whitehead's[26] method of extensive abstraction. To employ the principle of convergence to simplicity requires more than abstraction and creative generalization; the transformation of observable areas into unobservable points involves magnification, interpolation, extrapolation, and other generalizing procedures.

Outside the field of mathematics this combination of operations is well illustrated by the causal theory of perception.[27] The fact of seeing the sun is analyzed into an object, the *sun*, which is then considered as the first link in the causal chain. It is assumed that the sun exists prior to seeing it; then radiation requires eight minutes to reach the eye. This radiation is set up as an independent item. Also, as parts of the causal chain, there are physiological effects when the radiation impinges on the eye. Finally, the effect is described as "seeing the sun."

Linguistic and Symbolic Techniques in A. and G. Operations

It is a commonplace that all complicated intellectual enterprises necessarily involve linguistic and symbolic techniques. But, as we have seen,[28] the precise manner in which linguistic and symbolic things and acts operate in logical situations is not so clearly recognized. This condition undoubtedly may be traced back to a lack of adequate views concerning the nature of language and symbolism.

[25] Cf. Ginsburg, Finite.
[26] Concept.
[27] Russell, Reply, p. 703.
[28] Vol. I, chap. 8.

These linguistic events are only very slowly being appreciated as essentially interbehavioral in character. Even those writers alive to the behavioral and interoperational nature of language fail to differentiate between language operations and the products of those operations. Thus, to work out the place of language and symbols in abstracting and generalizing we must separate referring from denoting action, and these in turn from selecting and enlarging behavior, as well as from any products of the conjoint operations of all.

INTERRELATION OF LINGUISTIC AND NONLINGUISTIC BEHAVIOR IN A. AND G. SITUATIONS

Simple abstracting and generalizing behavior, and the early stages of its complex forms, may be accurately described as nonlinguistic or, certainly, nonsymbolic. It is nonlinguistic in the sense of forming or building up intellectual attitudes or bringing to bear such previously developed attitudes upon present problems.[29] These attitudes may be simple cognitive orientations based upon observed locations and comparisons, as between qualities, properties, shapes, and relations. Hume furnishes an example. Despite his 18th century ideas of mind, he describes effectively the abstracting of color and figure from successively observed white and black globes and cubes.[30]

Among the simplest linguistic responses in abstracting and generalizing situations are those acts of referring to the fact that white and black, and sphere and cube, are variously distributed and interchangeable things, shapes, and qualities. Following the abstractive separation of factors there may be referential responses concerning the independence of qualities and things and of their generalized existence.

The acts of stabilizing and establishing names, and treating shapes and signs, are productive of symbolic types of language things. Various processes and stages may be noted here. In one case vocal referential acts, because they result in sound patterns, constitute potential creative acts when references become word names or symbols standing for things and qualities. In other instances substitute things, in the form of marks, signs or sentences,

[29] Cf. Kantor, Principles, vol. II, chap. 20.
[30] Treatise, Bk. I, sec. 7.

are deliberately created for abstracting and generalizing operations. At this level Recorde's creation of the equality sign "bicause noe. 2. thynges can be moare equalle" is instructive.[31]

THE ROLE OF LANGUAGE
IN A. AND G. SITUATIONS

Without all sorts of linguistic acts and products it is impossible to deal effectively with attenuated and distant things. Hence all complex abstracting and generalizing situations involve many linguistic factors. The role of language is primarily to substitute for absent and created things. Such substitutive roles differ according to whether they: (1) represent other things, as happens when we separate ourselves more and more from the objects and relations with which we have been in contact, or (2) constitute newly created things. Extrapolative operations, for example, may simply extend a bit some definite manipulative process or carry it out beyond any possible manipulation.

CRITERIA AND LIMITS FOR
A. AND G. OPERATIONS

The principle that abstracting and generalizing operations involve the manipulation of things in specific situations suggests both criteria and limits for such activity.

Criteria. First and foremost is the criterion of *specificity.* What is desirable or permissible in one situation is not so in another. Furthermore, within any given situation the amount and character of abstracting and generalizing depend upon the material and the significance attached to the procedure. In other words, the specificity of criteria for all operations curbs the freedom to abstract and generalize.

Consider Russell's assertion that $(x+y)^2 = x^2+2xy+y^2$, even if for x and y we substitute Socrates and Plato.[32] Invoking a criterion of significance we ask: what intellectual value does such an analogy have? In what way does this illustration illuminate the problems of mathematical abstraction, generalization, and systemization of relations? Instead of emphasizing that in mathematics

---

[31] Mitchell, in Young, *Lectures,* p. 236.
[32] Principles, p. 7.

the symbols must be very precise in themselves and also most meticulously structured into equations, the impression is given that mathematics is arbitrary and capricious. Let us remember what rigid limits are set for mathematical operations; for example, no division by zero, a zero product of two nonzero factors, but no zero product of two nonzero factors.

Russell is really implying that logic is a force governing all other types of intellectual activity. Hence his view:

. . . in every proposition of pure mathematics, when fully stated, the variables have an absolutely unrestricted field: any conceivable entity may be substituted for any one of our variables without impairing the truth of our proposition.[33]

Compare this with Hardy's declaration:

It is impossible to prove, by mathematical reasoning, any proposition whatsoever concerning the physical world, and only a mathematical crank would be likely now to imagine it his function to do so.[34]

Limits. How limited abstracting and generalizing operations are and how restricted by criteria is readily observed when considering such an equation model as a + b = c. It is significant to ask if c gives us something new, whether or not it is a combination of a and b, or nothing at all. Further questions are: Is b different from a? Or is b a factor which negates a? Finally, do we have a simple conjoining of a symbolic representation of an equation, with the assumption that the terms symbolize some things from which significant relations can be abstracted?

Moreover, we face the question of the limits of partition and exclusion. How far can we divide a subject matter or a series of stimulus objects? Illicit abstraction is the result of striving toward some kind of absolute and final product, such as metaphysical certainty, irrefragable law or ultimate truth. Any analysis which yields cosmically transcendent values involves the injection of arbitrariness and caprice into our operations, as illustrated by abstracting from concrete events in order to reach absolute space or time. For instance, how significant is the extrapolation indicated in the following quotation?

[33] Ibid. p. 7.
[34] Theory, p. 402. Cf. Russell's own strictures upon the Formalists; Principles, Introduction.

For it seems certain to me that the extent of hidden organization in our universe is infinite, outside as well as inside of space and time; such a conviction is very natural to a mathematician, since the three ordinary spatial dimensions and the single temporal dimension are for him only particular instances of infinitely many other conceivable dimensions![35]

This is unrestricted and uncritical generalizing *par excellence*. Concrete space, as the place or relation of objects, is generalized into tridimensional abstractions; then, of course, the procedure can be further continued to any number of dimensions. In the second step one retreats from original interbehavior with concrete events to move on to operations with dimensions substituted for by numbers or letters. A third step takes one away from space and time altogether. Henceforth no limits are set to mystic flights.

Since generalization is essentially more substitutive than is abstraction, the necessity to check the procedure is even more urgent. Particularly, one needs to place distinct limits upon the creation of universes. A good remedy is to keep projection within bounds and to remember that whatever universes one creates must be derived from interbehavior.

If any argument is needed to strengthen the principle of controlled abstracting and generalizing, we find it within the operations of formalistic logic itself. Logicians have perforce been sharply checked in their work by such problems as the completeness and consistency of deductive systems. The theory of types also symbolizes a fundamental problem of generalization limits. Whatever one may think of the Cretan liar as a problem in logic, it reinforces the need to specify precisely what situation accommodates any particular assertion or proposition. We miss the point of these problems, however, if we overlook their basic behavioral core—namely, the life conditions of logicians.

ILLICIT A. AND G. PRODUCTS

Abstracting and generalizing operations are appropriate and useful in the precise measure in which they correspond to the things interacted with in specific situations. Once they surpass such restraining bounds they result in illicit products.

The leap from counting and enumerating operations to the

---

[35] Birkhoff, Intuition, p. 608.

creation of infinites and transfinites (p. 7) supplies us with a vivid example. From concrete computational processes to assertions concerning mystic entities is, after all, a very short path. Calculators and mathematicians constantly find themselves constrained to expand their operations either toward the large or the small. But instead of keeping their own activity in the foreground, and observing themselves in particular frames of action, they move on toward entities which they fail to recognize as created in the image of their own behavior.[36] Summing integers and fractions leads to sums to infinity.

Similar illicit creation yields such products as infinitesimals. The mathematician begins with a small abstractive system, for example, a convergent series. Multiplying his fractions by definite interbehavior with integers—namely, fractionating them—he then jumps to the conclusion that an infinite number of fractions exist. Naturally, by continuing his fractionalizing operation he can go on indefinitely. Limits, obviously, would be placed upon him by his own continued vigor and life span, but he can be sure that others can carry on the process over long periods of time.

Observe, nevertheless, that the infinitesimal is really only a name for a process. When dealing with concrete events this process is very soon ended. Even if we multiply the factors in an atom to obtain protons, electrons, neutrons, neutrinos and mesotrons, the process soon stops. The boundary between actual procedures and mystical creations is very sharp, which is not the case when we operate with abstract relations.

Because mathematicians have long rejected the spurious construct of an infinite number it is strange they do not ponder more the techniques which engender such counterfeit products. That is, they do not observe that such operations as matching, coordinating, and synthesizing constitute genuine creative acts. To do so would effectively avoid the interpretation of the infinite as any sort of ontological essence or pure form of thought. Only one conclusion is available; the infinite is the name for an iterative, long-continued action, or a name for the name of that action.

---

[36] Such behavior includes linguistic performances. We should not, however, fail to distinguish between references to, and symbols for, operations and the basic operations themselves. Unrestrained operations are not just faulty uses of language, but maladjustments.

Among the notorious illicit nonmathematical products stands brazenly the universe, which, in Hegelian-Bradleyan logic, every proposition implies. This item furnishes an excellent example of uncontrolled reiterative processes (p. 16). The actual operations are primarily verbal, of course, though the illicit products are reputed to be independent existences which, for the constructor, afford venerated stimulus objects.

Aside from disregard of constructional limits, illicit products stem, too, from a neglect of the specificity principle. How else account for the unqualified proposition that the whole is greater than any one of its parts, or that the whole is greater than all of its parts? What is meant by greater is of fundamental importance and can not be neglected. In other words, the operator can not justifiably abstract from the unique frame of reference in which he works.

As comparable examples of improper generalization we may cite the basic theorems of material implication. While these theorems may be satisfactory from the standpoint of the arbitrarily defined situation of symbolic logic, the general principles involved are valid merely by express agreement. In other words, they hold only in a system constructed and accepted by symbolic logicians.

Deceptive abstractions in scientific and other more concrete domains than formal logic and mathematics can be traced in large measure to unrestrained extrapolation. Consider those wild speculations concerning the cosmos, based on far-flung extrapolations of data derived within the narrow confines of the laboratory. Numerous writers[37] have protested against extrapolating from the second law of thermodynamics that the universe is heading toward its "heat death." Such extrapolatory behavior we must characterize as inept and misleading; it indicates moreover, that the worker is motivated by sentiment and mystic inclination, and not by an objective estimation of events.

On a general philosophical level writers have frequently noted the obvious fact that much of our information is second hand and not derived from direct contact with things. James distinguishes *knowledge of acquaintance* and *knowledge about*,[38]

---

[37] Dingle, Through; Bridgman, Nature, Cosmical Inquiries, Statistical; Lotka, Probability-Increase.

[38] Principles, vol. I, p. 221.

while Russell separates knowledge of things by description from knowledge by acquaintance or actual experience.[39] With the aid of numerological constructions, such as classes having the same number without reference to any particular number[40] and pairs of unknowable integers whose product is known to be greater than 100, the mystic urge can amply assert itself. It is this urge which directs all questing for *a priori* principles, for undiscovered knowledge, and the Absolute, without which many thinkers find the intellectual way uncharted and perilous.[41]

Also to be numbered among the techniques resulting in undesirable constructional products is improper analogy. The starting point may well be authenticated facts. Take the case of malformations which comprise the one significant and general organic difference between persons behaving normally and abnormally. By means of uncritical analogy such malformations are used to jump to the conclusion that behavior differences in normal persons are likewise to be accounted for by essential structure variations. And this regardless of the fact that such structural variations are both entirely unknown and psychologically irrelevant.[42]

The examination of illegitimate intellectual products indicates that they can not always be associated with separate techniques. Many arise from combined processes. To illustrate this point we list a sample series of such products, classified as primarily abstractional or generalizational.

Primarily Abstractive Products. Prominent here are those qualities, essences, and relations abstracted from objects such as:

Numbers, as autonomous invariant relations.

Sensations, sensa, or sense data, abstractionally created from colors, sounds, etc.

Square circles, griffins, combined from unrelated things.

Average man, economic man.

Speech or reason as basic properties of man.

Abstractions equated with object source or other concrete totality from which they are derived.

Primarily Generalization Products. Such logical fallacies as *non sequiturs* and other improper conclusions should at least be mentioned here, if not placed at the head of the list. Less formal ex-

---

[39] Problems, pp. 92, 169 et passim.

[40] Eaton, General, p. 466.

[41] Cohen, Reason, p. 146.

[42] See Kantor, Problems.

amples comprise the magnification of a small experiment and its data into a huge theory. The following roll illustrates the entire series:

Color and sound can be correlated with frequency, hence color and sound are frequencies.

Color is measured with difficulty, hence color is mental.

Personal or private knowledge is subjective, hence mental.

Because some psychological activities constitute conditioning, this is true of all psychological events.

Because statistics is a necessary procedure in treating data, it constitutes the scientific method.

Logic deals with deductive systems, hence all systems are deductive.

Because mathematical things (relations) are more abstract than other things, mathematics is reducible to logic.

Because one theory is faulty its opposite is correct.

Because act or action, power to act (instincts, forces).

Begin with characteristics or properties and end with principles or powers.

Concluding our discussion of spurious abstracting and generalizing operations, we mention that such unrestricted behavior does not always lead to illicit products. There are striking instances in which apparently autonomous and inapplicable abstractions turn out to be not only useful but important in particular situations. We have referred to the development of negative, irrational, and imaginary numbers which followed the sheer formalization of mathematical operations (p. 8). These products of unrestrained generalization were finally put to essential mathematical uses. The stock example of assimilating the square root of minus one into the mathematical theory of electromagnetism not only indicates the close integration of formal and nonformal situations, but also the regulation and justification of abstractive behavior by concrete and specific adjustmental circumstances.

A. and G. Operations in System Building

So far we have not stressed the place of abstracting and generalizing operations as factors in logic or system building. On the contrary, we have been discussing these operations merely as complex forms of intellectual interbehavior. Their location in system building is a simple matter, however.

In the first place, abstracting and generalizing operations are such widespread activities that they can hardly be excluded from the building of even modestly complex systematic structures.

Secondly and conversely, system building, from the simplest to the most complex, always involves such selection and analysis of units and groups as to demand abstracting and generalizing processes.

Their systemological aspects, therefore, present no special problem. Let us briefly point up some of the details. An outstanding question in organizing specific items into structures concerns the relative concreteness of any item. When concrete things are manipulated there occurs elementary behavior of discrimination, selection, and separation, with some generalization when units are fitted into groups, series, or orders. Abstract things require more remote handling, and hence substitution by linguistic acts and things, since abstract things have been produced by prior handlings of a direct and elementary sort. Then there are such extreme abstracting processes as the complete exclusion of original properties and the construction of a new verbally supported unit. All these operations, we have seen, result in definite products.

Among these products are numbered many simple and complex objects usable in system-building enterprises. On the simpler levels are concepts, general ideas, universals, simple categories of many varieties, all of which are conjoined to produce simple and complex systems. On the level of more complex structures we include hypotheses, propositions, and many fictional component systems of still more comprehensive systems.[43] Examples are such fictions as frictionless surface, perfectly straight line, dimensionless point, perfectly rigid body, as well as the figure constructions used in building up geometric demonstrations and mathematical systems.

[43] Many examples are offered by Vaihinger, Philosophie.

CHAPTER XIV

DEFINING AND CLASSIFYING OPERATIONS

Definition and Classification in Logic

UNLIKE the classical syllogistic province, the logical sub-domains of definition and classification do not force upon the student some dazzling model which, once produced, prevents him from observing the operations which fashioned it. Quite the contrary, defining and classifying behavior attracts attention to objects manipulated, to techniques of operation, and to the worker's motivation. The essential nature and role of such behavior, therefore, are easily observed in everyday life and science, as well as in the formal logical domain.

Unfortunately, this very freedom to study defining and classifying operations engenders a plethora of conflicting views. With respect to definition especially, the logical scene is asserted to be not only confused but chaotic.[1] This claim is made because of the many disagreements among those who attempt to define the term *definition*. A much more serious problem concerns the effective description of the operations involved.

Much of the difficulty may be attributed to the philosophical assumptions of logical workers. Moved to achieve transcendent reality, most logicians harness defining and classifying activities to universal and preclusive systems. Whether or not they begin with actual events, or propositions about events, their goal is to make *one* comprehend at least *many*, and possibly *all*; to make *once*, or an instant, include *forever*; and to enlarge a minute self-constructed system to cosmic dimensions.

Even those methodological logicians who do not stress universality and cosmology seek to develop autistic specifications, and consequently misconstrue classifying and defining behavior. Bound by fixed prescription, the actual operations of scientific and logical work vanish completely. What and how to define and classify are not determined by the tasks at hand but by authoritative rules.

[1] Cf. Dubislav, Definition; Robinson, Definition; Dewey and Bentley, "Definition"; also Knowing, chap. 7.

One of the most misleading assumptions made by both onto-logic and methodistic logicians is that defining operations are exclusively concerned with words. No doubt the durability of the verbal formulae representing definition and classification (p. 35) is an influencing factor. Linguistic entanglements, however, result in confusing our own act of defining definition with the defining operations we want to describe.

In contrast to such totalitarian views we shall approach defining and classifying processes as operations. We assume that these terms represent procedures of locating stimulus objects in particular situations and for particular ends. In the logical field they con-stitute specific and heuristic operations for system building.

THE DEFINITIONAL ONE AND MANY

The opposition between the traditional and behavioral views furnishes an exemplary illustration of the famous problem of the One and the Many. Though the universalists insist upon a single definition of definition and classification they agree neither upon what is defined or classified nor upon the processes involved.[2] In consequence a large number of treatments have accumulated, meriting the adverse characterizations mentioned above. On the other hand, those who take definition and classification to be spe-cific operations suitable for particular situations precipitate the question whether these operations can be commonly delineated. Is it possible, in other words, adequately to describe what persons do when they define and classify? Our answer is affirmative.

In the present chapter we summarize the common traits of both defining and classifying operations, allowing for variations accord-ing to the situations in which they occur. Both historical and cur-rent materials will be considered. Because defining operations are more complex and more varied than classificatory ones we shall treat the former far more elaborately.

I. DEFINITION

Essences and Forms

Traditionally the treatment of definition has resulted in two sorts of absolutism: one, formalistic, the other, methodistic. The

[2] Cf. Dubislav, Definition; Robinson (Definition) lists 18 names for sorts of definition.

target of methodistic study was the discovery and organization of the ultimate essences of things; the aim of formalistic investigation was the organization of systems of equivalent terms. Both these approaches contrast with the study of concrete defining operations in which, even when words or signs are concerned, they are not endowed with absolute properties called meaning or significance.

A. *Definition as Pursuit of Essences*

Definition, defined as the discovery or presentation of the essence of that which is defined, has carried different weights in various cultural periods. In the earliest formal discussion, as in Plato's Socratic dialogues, the purpose was merely to achieve a comfortable resting place for satisfactory argument. At that time the complexity of situations and the clash of personal interests made it necessary to clarify descriptions, distinctions, and even general references to things. Moreover, such definitions of statement were helpful in isolating similarities in difference.

The emphasis on conversation and argument soon gave way to the belief that one should attain the basic character of things. Forthwith definitional history progressed from an interest in stabilized attitudes toward things, to the specification of the essential properties and relations of the things themselves.

Though Aristotle made definition the search for abiding essences, he nevertheless, on the one hand, regarded things as actual items in a naturalistic framework and, on the other, thought of definition as references or descriptions. In other words, the linguistic factors remained as media for contacts with things.

With the development of medieval cultural conditions the entire picture changes. Along with the rise of transcendental constructions, spiritual realms, domains of infinity, etc., logicians hoped that the quest for absolute essences could be furthered by definitional processes. In consequence, definition was transformed into a single absolute and all-inclusive procedure, a specialized and technical enterprise quite in line with Scholastic metaphysical logic. Naturally, linguistic techniques were invoked to achieve what was not available to persons confined within natural bounds.

The medieval period established a double fetter for logic. Not only did it crystallize the construction of essence—an absolute set of traits—but it connected essence with another construction, the universal.[3]

In modern times the search for essences gave rise to the problem whether they could be located in universals or only in particulars. Hence logicians divided themselves into nominalists, who made definition consist of the manipulation of words or terms, and realists, whose terms reached out toward the essence of things.

Nominal Definition. As a typical example of nominalistic definition consider Locke's statement that definition is "nothing but making another understand by words what idea the term defined stands for."[4] The ideas, of course, constitute psychic states presumed to be the essence of known reality. Though no less psychic than Locke, Reid builds his definition of definition with greater emphasis on words.

A definition is nothing else but an explication of the meaning of a word, by words whose meaning is already known. Hence it is evident, that every word cannot be defined; for the definition must consist of words; and there could be no definition, if there were not words previously understood without definition.[5]

By the use of such nominalistic procedures many writers have hoped permanently to grasp fixed entities. Especially the British sensationists entertained the notion that the reality of an object or an event could be seized by regarding it as a name. Definition, therefore, becomes the manipulation of verbal entities.[6] According to this plan, satisfactory definition is nothing more than the organization of words to the point of satisfying the organizer. It is unnecessary to reiterate the objections both to the fundamental sensationistic philosophy and to the concrete usage which nominalistic definition implies. On the other hand, taken in a relativistic framework, nominalistic definition is a useful and important procedure, its basic virtue being that it is not equated with the events defined. The definer, that is, remains aware that definitions constitute constructions. On this basis definition can render service in

---

[3] To be discussed in chap. 18.

[4] Essay, Bk. III, chap. 3, sec. 10.

[5] Essays, p. 10.

[6] Compare Mill's statement with the above. "The simplest and most correct notion of a Definition is a proposition declaratory of the meaning of a word" (System, Bk. I, chap. 8, sec. 1).

organizing various items of practical or scientific pursuits. A set of
verbal definitions may prove very convenient in arranging chemical elements, for instance, or differentiating between various objects of discourse. In every case, however, the defining procedure
and the final definitions are no more than particular items in specific classificatory situations.

Further, the process of organizing word equivalences helps to
clarify one's notion concerning the relationship of particular
events. But never can the adequate naming of things give the
namer a grasp on the nature of those things.

Real Definition. For those who espouse *real* definitions, words
or terms stand for the ultimate essences of things, universes existing beyond the minds or psychic states of persons. In real, as well
as in nominal, definition, words or terms are made to do heavy
duty because in such instances logicians are dealing with abstractional products somewhat remote from concrete problems. However, to define things instead of arranging word equivalents offers
a more immediate connection with actual interbehavior than does
nominal definition, which obviously is a secondary procedure.
Still, one can not regard either operation as a technique for achieving the ultimate reality of anything. Real definition merely
approximates the practical process of identifying and isolating
types of events. The advantage of such identification is excellently
illustrated by the mathematical symbolization of variables or relations, a process not essentially different from one in which different sorts of objects and relations are interacted with.

Concept Definition. A modern version of medieval conceptualism is the current doctrine that what are defined are concepts. The
essence of things is regarded as located in the knower's mind. The
import of the conceptual doctrine may be clarified by associating
it with one of its outspoken adherents, Rickert, who vigorously
rejects both nominalistic and realistic doctrines: "Definiert wird
nicht der Name und nicht die Sache, sondern allein der Begriff."[7]
Keeping before us the writer's philosophical background, his es-
pousal of such spiritistic constructs as transcendental consciousness
and absolute values, we see at once how far this doctrine strays
from the problems and behavior of science. Even when placed in

[7] Lehre, p. 85.

a natural setting this conceptualistic theory—building on the current psychological doctrine that mental processes produce concepts as psychic products—runs to nonnaturalistic essences. It therefore bypasses such legitimate objects for definitional reactions as the attitudes and opinions of persons.

B. *Definition as Pursuit of Form*

With the rise of logistic or formal symbolic logic and mathematical logic a new viewpoint has developed concerning terms and their larger structures called propositions. These elements, in their various roles as symbols, variables, and logical constants, are increasingly looked upon as sundered from content of any sort. Among the symbolic or mathematical logicians the abstractionistic ideals of pure relation, order, and coherent system fulfill all logical ambitions, and serve moreover as sufficient criteria for all system-making processes. Such logicians are guided by the purely grammatical features of language. Referential linguistic functions are relinquished in favor of the structuralistic processes of syntax and the interpretative features of semantics.

Syntactical Definition. Mathematical logicians have attempted to create a special type of nominal or verbal definition, presumed to be a purely formal system of equivalent symbols designed for convenience. The best example is the famous assertion of Whitehead and Russell, in their *Principia Mathematica*,[8] that a definition is simply a declaration that a newly introduced symbol is to be entirely equivalent to others already familiar. The new symbol they call the *definiendum*, the old one the *definiens*. To carry out the notion of pureness in the structural organization of the system the authors declare:

We express a definition by putting the *definiendum* to the left and the *definiens* to the right, with the sign "=" between, and the letters "Df" to the right of the *definiens*. It is to be understood that the sign "=" and the letters "Df" are to be regarded as together forming one symbol . . .

An example of a definition is:

$$P \supset Q. = . \sim P \vee Q \text{ Df.}$$

[8] Vol. I, p. 11.

The abstractness of syntactic definitions is indicated by the fact that they are dissociated from truth or falseness—in other words, are presumed not to assert anything, and in general to be superfluous. They can not be used as premises for deductive or other purposes.

In characteristic fashion, however, the authors of the *Principia Mathematica* do not really abide by their formalistic description of syntactic definitions. They go on to declare that definitions do yield important information beyond the original statements or terms, and serve especially as means of analogizing the ideas conveyed by them. This contradiction simply signalizes that the pretense of dealing with items possessing meaning, without dependence upon a constructor, breaks down. As long as terms, and what they stand for, are factors in interbehavioral situations, problems and purposes abound in definition making.

Semantic Definition. In a special sense, the semantic type of formalistic definition corresponds to the concept type of essence definition. Instead of at once making words or terms stand for mental states, the linguistic factors are regarded as immediately containing or representing signified elements. Semantic definition is thus presumed to stress not simply equivalences, but adequate and effective symbolism as well. Proponents of this definitional doctrine wish to avoid confusions in language by substituting terms for things or events. However, they are only indirectly concerned with ultimate essences, and opposed chiefly to mathematical or logistic essences. In this way, semantic and syntactic definition can be employed by logicians who incline toward at least a linguistic withdrawal from traditional metaphysical entanglements.

The proponents of both syntactic and semantic definition, even when they turn to one as a refuge from the other, fail to see that all definition constitutes descriptions of things for given purposes. There is no one definition of definition; as many definitions are necessary as there are particular definitory situations.

Definition as Interbehavioral Operation

From an interbehavioral standpoint the term *definition* stands for constructive intellectual operations by which one orients and relates objects for specific purposes. On the basis of various interests or motives the definer localizes or places objects by according them identifying marks. Defining operations are similar to describing actions when the latter are differentiating performances and not references to things or their qualities. Depending upon the defining situation, the identifying actions are simple or elaborate. In complex situations they may involve an abstractive analysis of the properties and significance of stimulus objects. When the stimulus objects consist of word things, the identifying background in which they are localized we call literary contexts instead of situations.

To treat defining operations interbehaviorally is to stress actions—ways of operating upon things—not things. Defining acts are in principle similar to the selective or differential performances of individuals in perceptual contact with things. Because of the obvious need to refer to definitional operations, logicians have confused such action with things—namely, words or signs. This substitution of words and signs for defining acts is undoubtedly the basis for most of the confusion we have mentioned as existing in the definitional province of logic (p. 29).

A characteristic feature of defining operations in the logical domain is that they issue in a product. This fact warrants our defining them as constructive behavior. Unfortunately, however, the term *definition* often stands for the product rather than for the underlying defining performance. Moreover, cultural need has caused this product to be fixated in a set of verbal substitutes for the achieved identifying marks or characters. Thus, as we have indicated, the embodying words and signs are frequently confused with actual defining behavior.

Range of Defining Operations. Because defining operations occur both in system-making and nonsystem-making situations, each with its own particular frame of reference, they cover a wide range, from practical-life situations to the most abstract circumstances of the symbolic logics. Rigid defining operations of formal logical systems are no different in principle, however, from those occurring in scientific and everyday-life situations. Though the variations in detail are not unimportant, they are nevertheless all bounded by criteria localized in the definitional situation.

Definitional Criteria. Compare definitions developed for formal systems and for more casual and imprecise situations. In the former the system itself constitutes the basis for treating its elements, whereas in nonformal situations the criteria are less definite and circumscribed. Whether definitions are formal, rigid, and constant, or informal, loose, and temporary, depends upon the following criteria: (1) the definer's purpose, or the character of the problem at hand; (2) the types of stimulus objects defined (things, qualities such as color, brilliance, etc., words, symbols, actions); (3) a criterion compounded from (1) and (2), namely, whether things are operated upon directly or through the intermediation of such an action as a concept or an idea; and, finally, criterion (4), the question whether definition is designed to stress form or vehicle—i.e. the words or signs, or the product of the intrinsic definitional operation. Around the fourth criterion are centered problems of vagueness and ambiguity which we treat in a later section.

Analysis of Definitional Situations. We list four outstanding factors of definitional situations:

    A. Stimulus objects, things defined.
    B. Defining acts.
    C. Defining product, i.e. definition.
    D. Linguistic aspects (statement of, reference to, or substitute for, C).

A. *Stimulus Objects.* Although the disagreements of traditional nominalists, conceptualists, and realists turn precisely about the question of what things are defined, the accepted formal and ontological dogmas remove logicians from actual things. As we have implied, the vehicular terms are generally regarded as the definitional objects. Most logicians frankly declare that what one defines are words or terms. From an interbehavioral standpoint, however, every conceivable kind of act, relation, quality, object or organism may be a stimulus object in a definitional interbehavioral field. Among acts we include concepts, of course, though construed entirely in objective terms. The striking difference in viewpoint here epitomizes the sharp variation between absolutistic logics and behavioral system building. Our view concerns the actual work of persons in whatever situations they find themselves.

B. *Defining Acts.* Preoccupied as writers on definition are with terms and what they stand for, they still can not escape the fact that definition involves action. Aside from the everyday appreciation that definition requires defining acts, logical writers have recognized both definition by use or convention,[9] and ostensive definition[10] in which the action consists of pointing to, or manipulating, things by way of showing their similarities and differences.

Acts and Materials. Unfortunately, even writers who insist most strongly upon action center their discussion around words. Definitions are thought of as constructed from words, symbols, and propositions—in short, linguistic materials. At once the whole definitional process is reduced to manipulation of signs and symbols. Such reduction shifts the description of definition, from what definers do, to the materials used in expressing and referring to definitions.

Why should defining acts be set aside in favor of signs or words? In the demand for a fixed verbal formula there is more than a reminiscence of the age-old quest to fixate the many and the fluid by singleness of verbal sign. Definitional operations, on the other hand, are many and complex, and must not be forced into a straight jacket of verbal symbolization. They can be described, therefore, only on the basis of observing the elaborate constructive procedures carried out whenever definitional activities occur.

C. *Definitional Products.* Students of logic, we have indicated, are much more interested in definitional products than in the defining operations which produce them. To logicians the products doubtless appear more adaptable for system building, and apparently more palpable altogether.

For effectively examining definitional products we present some typical examples:

Physics is a fundamental science dealing with matter.[11]
Physics is the science of energy and energy transformations.[12]
Physics is essentially a system of explanations—answers to the question "Why?"—on the behavior of inanimate things.[13]

---

[9] See Couturat, for example, Principles, p. 182; Church, Definition, in Runes, *Dictionary.*
[10] Burks, Empiricism.
[11] Semat, Fundamentals, p. 3.
[12] Spinney, Textbook, p. 1.
[13] Webster, Farwell, and Drew, General, p. 6.

Notice that the definitions embodied in these statements constitute the results of evaluating and estimating the general physical domain, reviewing the objects dealt with, and then constructing a definitional system corresponding to the essential factors.

Definitions and Propositions. Definitions as interbehavioral products, it is interesting to note, have much in common with propositions.[14] Since the latter are better known than the former we can obtain information concerning definitions by comparing and contrasting them with propositions.

As to similarities, both are subtle objects which, during gestation, have no independent existence. To begin with, they are acts of considering, evaluating, comparing, and contrasting things and subject matter. Because of the importance of the objects interacted with, the nascent definitions and propositions are as dependent on the objects as on the individual's acts. Independence as objects is achieved only when they become definitely fixated— that is, set into linguistic matrices.

But if definitions and propositions are alike in being interbehavioral products, they differ widely in use and function. Consider situations in which they stand sharpest in opposition—namely, in science. In that domain, because definitions function for simple orientation, they have a lesser import and are, on the whole, simpler products. They may be likened to first approximations, premises, even coordination points. The superficial and auxiliary character of definitions in science can not be mistaken for the profound and essential nature of propositions resulting from judgments and conclusions. Outside the scientific domain definitions and propositions are, of course, not so sharply polarized. In some nonscientific situations their functions are indistinguishable. Reacting individuals orient themselves with respect to stimulus objects by means of either product with equal facility. In such cases the scope and structure of the products are equivalent.

D. *Linguistic Aspects of Definition.* Since definitory behavior is in itself subtle and intimate, and involves a large amount of interpersonal relations, it is inseverably connected with linguistic factors. Both definitional behavior and the resulting products can be best observed when represented by diagrams, words, numerical

---

[14] See Kantor, Interbehavioral.

signs, or other visible evidences. Our task at this point, then, is not to caution against confusing definitions and their representatives, but also to outline the various linguistic factors found in defining situations.

Diagrams, words, and verbal formulae can, with practice, be kept distinct from things defined, as well as from the definition or description of them. Because words or symbols are requisite tools for making and handling definitions we tend to confuse the definitional products themselves with the names or descriptions of those products. This dilemma is avoided by keeping the definitional product as a description distinct from our secondary description of it.[15]

Defining a triangle as a triangular or trilateral figure suggests the difference between the definiens and the definiendum. The latter must be distinguished from the act of referring to it and from the symbols which stand for it. The two sentences written above and the signs $\mathbf{A}$, Δ are equivalent representations of the single definition. Consider another example, the definition of the law of the inclined plane. In algebraic form the definition is represented as: $L_1/L_2/ = W_1/W_2$. In words, however, we have:

The weight which can be moved up an inclined plane is to the weight which would balance it in a vertical direction as the length of the inclined plane is to the vertical height between its ends.

To indicate the proper place of linguistic factors in definitional situations we break them down according to their nature and function.

(a) *Language in Definition Construction.* Since defining behavior is implicit, and not grossly manipulative, the action must perforce be linguistic. The definer makes his comparisons and handlings, his trials and errors, as subvocal and sometimes vocal references. These references to the things defined comprise the materials out of which definitions are made, and are numbered among the subtle objects referred to in our discussion of definitions and propositions (p. 38).

(b) *Language for Handling Definition.* Acts and things used for symbolizing and otherwise substituting for the definition

---

[15] The problem here is similar to that involved in the hierarchical language situation and, in general, that situation in which the theory of types plays a part.

product may be regarded as language vehicles. Such are the diagrams, elaborate formulae, and other instruments to embody, exhibit, and represent definitional products.

(c) *References to Defining Actions and Products.* Distinctive language factors are the acts of referring to definitional products by way of mentioning, explaining, discoursing upon, and otherwise interbehaving with them. Reference to the acts of producing the products are very similar in character. These language factors are misinterpreted when it is thought that words, and not things or acts, are defined. The result is that idiomatic and inclusive formulae are set in the foreground of definitional situations.

Signs and Symbols for Definition. Language things, as signs and symbols, are special linguistic factors which are counters and representatives of definition products.

Defining Operations and System Building

Definitions relate to system building in two distinctive, but not altogether different, ways. In the first place, the definitional continuum includes simple designative or descriptive activities, as well as those productive of small comprehensive definitional systems. Frequently, to define something is to organize a small local system of factors and to take into account various relationships newly discovered or previously known. To set up formal definitions as discrete units and parts of a larger system displays a maximum of system building. On the other hand, defining operations have a distinctive place in general system-building situations. Here the definer's operations eventuate in the exclusion of some given stimulus object from a system or its inclusion therein. Euclidean definitions, for example, indicate what the system is to handle, what elements it comprises, etc. But defining operations are also useful in the work of classifying, relating, and articulating items in the systemizing process. It must be added at once that different kinds of defining operations are serviceable in different system-building situations.

Definition and Description

Logicians have noticed that defining operations are essentially related to acts of designation or description. Mill[16] declares, how-

---

[16] System, chap. 8, sec. 4.

ever, that all logicians reject description from the rank of genuine definition, on the ground that in description the name of a class is defined by accidents—namely, attributes not included in its connotation. Lotze,[17] on the other hand, though an absolutistic writer, accepts methodological descriptions as definition, but thinks they require checking by traditional classificatory procedures and definition rules in order to control arbitrariness. Basically, Lotze is, of course, attempting to safeguard his metaphysical interests.

Empirical writers are more favorably inclined toward description. For example, Pepper[18] has recently offered a vigorous plea for descriptive definition. Adopting a modern and improved interpretation of description, he assumes a position *vis a vis* the symbolic logicians who, because of their exclusive interest in linguistic formulations, wish to separate definition completely from propositions. Pepper objects to the idea that definitions, by contrast with propositions, are entirely dissociated from truth reference. To limit definition to the nominal form which is not responsible to facts, he holds, prevents attaining the clarity and tolerance that logic should foster.

Nominal definition, which Pepper contrasts with descriptive definition, has two species called equational and ostensive forms. Equational definition is described as a dyadic relation in which S, the symbol, is equated with, defined by, or substituted for MN, a combination of other symbols. Here we have a simple organization of linguistic things.

Ostensive definition is likewise a dyadic relation, but in this instance the symbol S indicates, or is ostensibly defined by, O, some empirical object. The ostensive feature is a pointing or other type of operation.

By contrast with these two species of nominal definition Pepper calls his descriptive definition a triadic relation. S, the symbol, tentatively indicates, or is ostensibly defined by, O; the S is tentatively equated with, or descriptively defined by, D, a description; and finally, D hypothetically describes, or is verified by, O, which now becomes a field instead of a single object. Despite the fact that the triadic relation seems to comprise the other two plus a

[17] Logik, II, chap. 1.
[18] Descriptive; Definition.

third, Pepper strictly denies it. From our standpoint it is significant that his denial is made on the basis that the act or intention is altogether different. Descriptive definitions are formulated through acts embodied in empirical enquiries.

It is no small merit to enlarge the range of definitions to include the descriptive type. But we still face the question whether nominal definitions are not also descriptive, though descriptive of symbols and words, not of things. However, we are in sympathy with Pepper as against his critics[19] who want to make the word *definition* cover only one kind of thing. What seems plainly indicated is that only a genuinely interbehavioral position can take care of this diversity of detailed actions which still have a common adjustmental base.

Highly significant, therefore, is Pepper's multiplication of definition types on the basis of acts and intentions. His opponents, nevertheless, have a wedge when he falls back on actions for diffuse and not for full whole-hearted working material. Admittedly, Pepper's theory needs revision to make it entirely defensible.

First, definitions are not to be described as relations, but as operations resulting in products. Accordingly the contrast between nominal and several other kinds of definitions will be immediately achieved.

Then, too, definition must not be confined exclusively to reactions to symbols, even if some are indicative of things while others are not. As we have seen, the definition of symbols is undoubtedly only one kind of defining behavior.

Definition and Meaning

Definitional doctrines center closely around the topic of meaning. This is most obvious in the case of the nominalistic definitions of definition. The lexicological definitions of Reid and Mill, already quoted (p. 31), also imply that definitional problems are problems of meaning. No less closely is meaning connected with definition when concepts are the things defined. In such instances concepts are often equated with names or terms, or at least concepts are closely linked with them.[20]

[19] See Pepper, Definition; also Dewey and Bentley, Definition.
[20] See, for example, Dubs, Definition; Rational, chap. 6.

Especially in nominal definition meaning is taken to be either a commonly accepted usage or the way the user intends the term to be employed by others. Meaning, in this sense of orienting a term for one or many persons, or locating a term in a system, is unobjectionable. Such treatment of meaning, however, is quite different from the usual notion that it is some sort of mental process.

Two elucidating tasks confront us: one, to show the nature of meaning as an objective psychological fact, the other, to relate meaning to definition.

From an objective or naturalistic standpoint meaning is not a "state of mind,"[21] nor even an objective status of personal satisfaction; rather, it is an elicited structure, or organization of a situation or field, which an individual discovers through his interaction with such fields. For example, when one observes that x-rays emanate from the fluorescent spot on the glass wall of a discharge tube, one assumes that there must be a close connection between x-rays and fluorescence. Indeed, Becquerel observed that a piece of uranium compound (potassium uranyl sulphate) wrapped in black paper, that had been exposed to cathode rays, blackened a photographic plate upon which it was placed. This observation led him to interpret uranium radiation as a consequence of exposure to cathode rays. For uranium to radiate meant, at that period, not radioactivity, but a fluorescent effect. Later, of course, it was discovered that uranium and its compounds radiate without being subjected to bombardment by cathode rays or any kind of electrical treatment. What it means for uranium to radiate, therefore, is an objective situation elicited by definite operations.

So much, then, for the definition of natural things. In defining verbal or symbolic things the ascertainment or specification of meaning follows a similar process. The one great difference between the two situations is accidental. Namely, in verbal or symbol meaning the various characterizing relations are established through human agency, sometimes through an elaborate series of operations.

Meaning, we repeat, when connected with definition, constitutes particular developments brought about through an indi-

[21] Vol. I, p. 206.

vidual's operations with specific field factors. If what a thing means, or how it should be defined, depends upon a specific frame of reference, obviously the meanings elicited are specific, not general and universal.

Within the conventional framework that definition is concerned with meaning, the question is sometimes raised whether definition is capable of achieving meaning. The alternative is offered that definition is only a special instance of processes designed to specify meaning.[22] It is proposed that meanings may be specified by providing a set of descriptions, called indicators, concerning the applicability of a term in various situations. The term *species*, it is said, can not be defined, but merely indicated with certain weights.

Apparently, definition is assumed to be a rigid placing of one term as equivalent to another, but with the fortunate realization that such equating is useless for situations in which things termed are taken into account. In other words, isolated terms are different from referential terms. We are constrained to ask, however, whether it is only terms or concepts that are defined. Furthermore, when things are taken into consideration, meanings clearly constitute properties and relations in specified fields. Whether or not we equate *specification of meaning* with definition, interbehavior with concrete things comes to the surface. Frequently, meaning is nothing but a momentary property of an event which is itself momentary and nonrecurrent.

The Indefinable

Because most writings on definition are environed by the logical doctrine of universality and necessity, it is not a far-fetched suggestion that the problem of indefinables has much in common with, if it does not issue from, negative theology. From what other source could logic derive the notion of inexpressible being, whose qualities are indescribable and whose identity is ineluctable! All attempts to localize this problem within the confines of simple qualities fail. Of interest here is Johnson's[23] suggestion that if the indefinable is taken to be that which is not understood, a correc-

---

[22] Kaplan, Definition.
[23] Logic, part I, chap. 7.

tion is necessary. Indefinable terms, on the contrary, are so well understood that they need not be defined. Johnson's point is also cogent with respect to the indefinability of simple qualities of things. Realistic philosophers take the view that colors are simple unanalyzable qualities.[24] Russell does not even allow that the word *yellow* as a symbol can be applied to the color *yellow*, but only the propositional function 'x is yellow.'[25] Within the framework of the writers quoted, colors are too simple to require defining. Johnson asserts, however, that while an adjective name, such as red, can not be analytically defined, it can be ostensively defined.[26] When definition is taken as defining operations there is nothing that can not be defined. In other words, everything can be localized in its setting, or the definer can orient himself to any stimulus object, including colors, odors, etc.[27]

The indefinable is not always regarded as the simple, but also as the too complex. Consider the following:

I shall not start with any definition of religion. Religion, like poetry and most other living things, can not be defined. But one may perhaps give some description of it, or at least some characteristic marks.[28]

Since there is really nothing that can permanently escape brief intelligible description, suitable for particular purposes, definition then appears to be a formal substitute for the essence of things, a sort of idol.

Applying our interbehavioral notion of definition to the term *indefinable*, we can orient and explicate it by observing where and how it operates. As an example consider Reid's definition of definition quoted earlier (p. 31). The indefinable is merely those undefined elements which constitute the beginnings of a classificatory or system-building procedure, and in no sense indicates objects resisting definition. Instructive here are Russell's "minimum vocabularies"—in other words, systems of words in which none can be defined in terms of the others.[29]

[24] Moore, Principia, p. 7ff.
[25] Logical, p. 375ff.
[26] Logic, part I, p. 94.
[27] Cf. Williams, Definition.
[28] Murray, Stages, p. 19.
[29] Mental, p. 14f.; Knowledge, p. 79f.

Operationally, the term indefinable marks a scale of definitory products on the basis of varying criteria. There are questions concerning how far one wishes to go, or how far it is necessary and profitable to go. Obviously there are no absolute criteria, and thus no final and absolute demarcations of things. It is only the urge to absolutism which leads to the view:

No truly fundamental element can be defined, since the definition would have to be in terms of still more fundamental elements, and thus the element in question would not really be fundamental.[30]

Such a view, of course, has no standing when we are concerned with actual defining problems. Defining operations, on one level of interbehavior, are activities with things. This level marks the identification-qualification level between a lower direct differential and discriminative response to things and a higher less direct one of referential and other verbal linguistic performances.

Definition, Vagueness, and Ambiguity

It is a paradox of the logic of definition that the more rigorous, binding, and exclusive the formulae, the more empty and abstract they become. Hence, definition is hardly a treatment of terms making for progress in the identification and orientation of things. Definitional operations, of course, may play a part in clarifying both things and terms, but these two fields must be kept rigorously distinct. An excellent example of how things are confused is provided by a popular elementary textbook.[31] Beginning a discussion of the purpose and nature of definition, the authors declare that everyday language is notoriously vague and the language of technical treatises not always much better. To illustrate, they assert that everyone is familiar with the difficulty of deciding whether certain organisms are plants or animals.[32] Is the difficulty here, however, one of language, of not knowing how to apply a name properly, or inadequate orientation of things? The same writers regard the ambiguity of words as a serious danger for accurate thinking. Granting the truth of this observation, we still are obliged to differentiate between the ambiguity of words and the

---

[30] Jones, Kant, p. 140.
[31] Cohen and Nagel, Introduction.
[32] Ibid., p. 274.

danger to thought arising from improper behavior with respect to things.

Ambiguity and vagueness are essentially interbehavioral terms, and, in consequence, relative to a number of coordinates. Since these coordinates are localized in all sorts of reference frames, there are no absolute criteria for ambiguity and vagueness. What counts is the availability of things, and one's competency in handling them. Sheer definitional operation can never overcome the ills of ambiguity and vagueness. This is true for language as well as for things.[33]

So far as language is concerned, the criterion of agreement, if it could be secured, would apply only to specific situations. Basically this would be a matter of word usage. Actually, the lack of commonness is no more serious than it is inevitable. Costello points out:

. . . "constants" are what may be arbitrarily changed, but "variables" are not arbitrary, being what is really constant in a system.[34]

The language of "exact science," this writer asserts, may be curiously inexact and misleading. Obviously this is true only when someone is attempting to organize an absolutely verbally coherent and homogeneous system; perhaps the adjectives *ambiguity* and *vagueness* would have no cogency in describing its elements.

In science it is things and events which are basically clarified. This fact in itself guarantees thing as well as word definitions. Accordingly, the modifications of terms and their usage indicate changes in total situations. To follow through the efforts of scientists to modify the definitions of force, energy, mass, inertia, heat, cause, atom, species, action, electron, both as terms and as things or events, is tantamount to traversing the history of science. The same observation may be made for all the specific sciences and mathematics. In the latter the process of reducing ambiguity and vagueness involves, of course, operational definitions of acts, both constructional and purely manipulative, in addition to things and terms. The definition of imaginary numbers, infinity, and infinitesimals as operations exemplifies this point.

[33] In a recent paper entitled "Empiricism and Vagueness," Burks has argued that the doctrine of the empirical origin of concepts implies inevitable vagueness.

[34] Naturalism, p. 313.

How the current bias toward language influences writers to minimize manipulative operations in science is demonstrated by a recent paper of Nagel's on the place of language in the natural sciences.[35] He offers an attractive discussion, with good examples of linguistic changes, but indicates a grudging concession to inter-behavior,[36] as the italicized words in the following quotation indicate:

. . . a critique (of scientific abstractions) must aim to prevent the hypostatization or reification of instrumental functions into mysterious, inaccessible agents, and to show how scientific language, *in conjunction with overt experimental procedure,* can render, but without illusion, the pervasive interrelations of natural processes.

If it is true, as is so often asserted, that philosophy is the realm of the vague and indefinite,[37] especially by contrast with science, then definitional problems are more acute in the former. Again, if it is true that philosophy is primarily a domain of language, particularly bad language, the type of definition useful to it is verbal definition.[38]

The neutral student of definition should notice that definitional operations may consist of word or term clarification when a particular situation demands. The study of definition implies no rule concerning what should be defined, only that no improper limitations should be set. It may well be that the sole valid definitional criterion is the organization of a coherent verbal system, as would be the case when the system is purely constructional. In general, formal or mathematical situations require mostly verbal or symbolic definition. But in other situations, such as science and everyday life, the emphasis must be on concrete objects.

Up to this point we have not attempted to distinguish between ambiguity and vagueness. Indeed, there are no standard and technical criteria for doing so. A practical differentiation is that ambiguous things require both radical investigation and definition to fit them into a system. Vagueness may be relatively cleared up by simple definition.

[35] Reflections.

[36] Ibid., p. 624.

[37] Burks, Empiricism.

[38] Weitz (Philosophy) offers an interesting summary of the abuse of language in philosophy.

Samples of Defining Procedures

To accept the operational interpretation of the definitional situation makes room at once for a vast number of defining operations. Aside from their common orientational function these operations vary on the basis of things defined, definitional products constructed, and the behavioral reference frames in which they occur. In order to exhibit the specificity of definition and its many variations, we isolate the following series of definitional classes.

Defining by Naming. The simplest type of definitional operation is obviously that which attains some measure of orientation by nominal characterization. Though the definition product is simply a name word, some of the traits of the definiendum are isolated for identification.

Examples of naming definition are best observed in mathematical writings. The following is typical:

Definition: The integral part of a logarithm is called the *characteristic* and the decimal part, when it is written as a positive number, is called the *mantissa*.[39]

This particular definition product implies a great many activities when logarithmic things are differentiated from the linguistic factors.

How can naming definition be set apart from ordinary naming operations? The answer lies in the criterion of arbitrariness. In ordinary naming there is no necessary connection between the characteristics of the object named and the name.

Defining by Delimitation. A superficial form of describing or characterizing things is simply to isolate or abstract them from other things. In the definitions of physics quoted above (p. 37), the interest is to mark off a field in which one plans to work. Such are the introductory definitions in text books and treatises, which amount to a simple means of orientation; the descriptive materials are reduced to elementary boundary marks.

Defining by Classification. When things are somewhat more closely approached than by delimiting the bounds in which they are located, we achieve classifying definitions. The most obvious form is to locate an object according to its genus and species. For example, both a diameter and radius of a circle in Euclid are

[39] Davis and Nelson, Elements, p. 349.

straight lines, the former passing through the center to the circumference at both ends, while the latter has one end in the center.

On the whole, classification definitions do not imply any thorough penetration into the properties of things defined; however, the defining operations become modified in the face of the problems the definer sets himself. Genus-species specifications from ancient Aristotelian logic penetrated to metaphysical ultimates. Classificatory definitions also cover any sort of predicative designation desirable for logical and nonlogical enterprises.

Defining by Postulation. Again, defining procedures may be differentiated on the basis of whether the objects defined or the needs and desires of the definer are stressed. When objects are not stressed the operations and products are naturally somewhat freer of the objects' characteristics as ascertained by various contacts with them. Procedures emphasizing objects involve, for instance, the construction of a map or schedule indicating their essential properties. Postulational definition, on the other hand, implies that the constructional activity is directed or influenced by assumptions brought to bear on the procedure.[40]

Consider Johnson's definition of logic:

Logic is most comprehensively and least controversially defined as the analysis and criticism of thought.[41]

This definition is so heavily charged with confidence in its appropriateness that it is recommended as departing in the least possible way from the common understanding of the term *logic*. And yet it is the opposite of other definitions, for example, that of Royce:

Logic is the general science of order, the theory of the forms of any orderly Realm of objects, real or ideal.[42]

The wide differences in postulation are apparent not only when defining such complex enterprises as logic, but also when dealing with things.

Analyzing and Synthesizing Definition. When objects to be defined are complex, and the descriptive orientation warrants, the

[40] Cf. Campbell, Physics, p. 122.
[41] Logic, part I, p. xiii.
[42] Principles, p. 69.

operations include the ascertainment of the elements of things and the organization in which they are synthesized. This procedure involves a more intimate contact with things than occurs in naming definitions, or in simply delimiting their boundaries.

Either analyzing or synthesizing operations may be stressed in some defining situations, or both may be equally represented as in the following example.

Protoplasm constitutes a colloidal complex of water, inorganic salts, and four organic substances, proteins, fats, carbohydrates, and extractives.

How elaborate or compact, how simple or complex a defining operation should be depends upon the orientative circumstances. As a rule, however, the products of analogy and synthesizing operations are more elaborate than those of naming or delimiting situations.

Defining by Relating and Analogizing. Though probably no defining operations can dispense with relating acts, some definitions are more decidedly relational than others. Mathematical definitions are, on the whole, fine examples of this type. To define a one-member class the following structure is set up:

If x is a member of a and if y is also a member of a, then y is identical with x.

The form of this definition, which belongs to a particular system, emphasizes the identity relation, but this is in no sense the only kind of relation. When we say the relation a:b is equal to the relation c:d, we may do so on the basis that when we multiply a, b, c, d by the numbers m, n, we find that whenever:

$$ma > nb, \ ma = nb, \ ma < nb$$

the same holds for:

$$mc > nd, \ mc = nd, \ mc < nd$$

This is essentially a definitional ordering by analogy—namely, eliciting similar properties.

Among analogical definitions may be cited the inclusion of fractions, irrationals, and imaginaries in the field of numbers. Thus when confronting such processes as $x \cdot 3 = 9$, or $x + 3 = 0$, the factors involved must be defined as numbers because the underlying operations are similar.

Defining by Measuring. A unique form of identifying and orienting is achieved through measuring operations. The description of things, either ordinary objects or mathematical figures, follows the elicitation of specifying marks by comparisons with given units or standards. Though measuring operations are close to ordering procedures, we can not limit our notion of measurement to the conventional correlation of nonnumerical entities with numbers. As we shall point out (chap. 23), this correlation idea does not emphasize sufficiently the operational basis of correlation.

As an example of the measuring type of defining procedure we suggest the definition of the geometric similarities of figures.

Figure A is similar to figure B when there is a constant ratio between any two points on figure A and the corresponding points on figure B.

Definitional equations, as for example, the work equation $W = PS$, illustrate arithmetic forms of measuring definitions. The relationship of work done against resistance, and over a given distance, has been discovered by measurement. The following verbal form of definition demonstrates the operation:

The work W, performed by a force P in overcoming a resistance without acceleration through a distance s, is measured by the product of the force P and the distance s.[43]

To define points by rectangular coordinates, or by determining the modulus and amplitude as in polar coordinates, is another good illustration of the measurement procedure. Notice that it displays a legitimate carrying over of the operational term *definition* to a rather abstract situation. It also shows a proper form of the ostensive or denotative type. We might compare the coordinate definition with that of a function in which the relationship is not established by measurement but by attribution, as in prescriptive procedures.

Defining by Prescription. Logicians who adopt an exclusive and manipulative notion of definition, at variance with formal or abstract symbolism, as a rule minimize and even reject the claims of prescriptive or fiat definition. Their ground is the arbitrary and inessential nature of such definitions. From an operational standpoint, however, it is impossible to deny the orienting function of

[43] Grimsehl, Textbook, vol. I, p. 82.

fiat operations. Certainly there is as much validity in prescriptive definition as in naming operations, if, indeed, the former are not merely extensions and elaborations of the latter. For convenience we differentiate between several subtypes of fiat procedures.

(a) *Temporal Operation.* Mathematical expressions beginning "Let x = y" are clear-cut examples of the fiat type of definition. Here is a procedure which lays down what a literal number *will do* in a given situation, or what the operator can do by thus delimiting the value of a number. This form of prescriptive definition symbolizes the mathematician's freedom in his manipulation of fixed relations.

Verbal counterparts of fiat procedures are constantly being pointed out in philosophical writings. Universality is equated with indestructibility.[44] Matter is a tautological equivalent of impenetrability.[45]

(b) *Formal Equating.* Probably the best example of the formal equating procedure is the substitution of one sign or symbol for another. The present operation finds its best scope and application in the domain of purely formal sign manipulation, as in symbolic logic. An example of such definition we have quoted above from *Principia Mathematica.* As Whitehead and Russell say: "A definition is concerned wholly with the symbols, not with what they symbolise."[46] For this reason they regard definition as an unnecessary process which contrasts with descriptive explanation and is no part of the subject in which it occurs. Note how sharply this view diverges from that of Dewey and Bentley[47] who look upon definition as the "throbbing heart—both as pump and as circulation—of the whole knowledge system."

Formal equating may be profitably compared with the more or less prescriptive definition of $\sqrt{-1}$ as i by Gauss and others, when those mathematicians analogized the referent of the symbol as a rotational operation through 180° in a counterclock direction. Though in this case there is considerable discretion exercised, the emphasis is on the thing defined and not on the marking substitute.

Defining by Specific Operations. Since Bridgman popularized

[44] Pepper, Categories, p. 548.
[45] Russell, Analysis, p. 385.
[46] Principia, vol. I, p. 11.
[47] "Definition," p. 287.

the contrast between concepts defined (a) by properties and (b) by operations,[48] many writers have discussed the subject of operational definition. But, as Bridgman has indicated,[49] the term *operational* as applied to definitions is superfluous, since all definition must be operational. It is indeed tautological to say that all defining operations are operations, but the important fact is that particular defining behavior involves particular operations, as we have amply demonstrated in our exposition of various defining procedures.

To elaborate this point is essentially to summarize the entire subject. This we need not do, since we have sufficiently differentiated between the operations required to define different objects in varying situations. But we might profitably distinguish between (1) operations for engendering and defining concepts, (2) operations for genuine and spurious definitions, (3) implicit and explicit definitional operations, and (4) various forms of ostensive definition.

(1) *Operations for engendering and describing concepts.* To isolate and describe specific operations is automatically to differentiate between the activity of engendering ideas or concepts and that of describing them. To the characteristics of defining operations already mentioned we might now add that of brevity, limited scope, and possibly also, auxiliary function. Defining operations are ancillary to broad and comprehensive orientation processes, as well as to those for ascertaining the properties of things.

Definitional products may in no sense be regarded as items in final and definitive systems of knowledge. At most they are tentative materials waiting to be worked over and established. All this applies only to definitions of things. The definitions of terms occupy still humbler positions in the province of investigation and knowledge.

(2) *Pseudodefinitional Operations.* Activities of simple designation or proper-name application constitute pseudodefinitional operations. But we must hasten to add that the criterion is the interbehavioral one of describing, identifying or orienting something. It is not difficult to differentiate between casual naming and naming for elementary comparing or distinguishing. "A rose is a

[48] Logic.
[49] Some, p. 246.

rose" is no trivial illustration of the difference between purely verbal play and the statement that an instance of a rose flower is a rose in the full organization of rose properties.

Metaphorical references usually are pseudodefinitions, though here again the criterion is what sort of interaction between an organism and objects is going on. To describe words or things is certainly a different act from listing them. A picture or a narrative may or may not be descriptive, but blue prints, on the whole, must be regarded as descriptive of a building as a whole and as parts. The words of a foreign dictionary may be intermediate descriptions or simply word substitutes. In a similar way we can distinguish between operations in which words are descriptive and circularly tautological.

(3) *Implicit and Explicit Operations.* Formalistic writers distinguish implicit from so-called explicit definitions on the basis that the former lack organized formulation. Those who know what "triangle" and "quadrilateral" mean will also know what "diagonal" means, if told that each of the two diagonals of a quadrilateral divide it into two triangles.[50] It is questionable whether logicians are concerned with such trivial definitions. Nevertheless, the above is an illuminating example, since it indicates that a geometric object or relation is the thing defined, not just a term. Were simply a term to be defined, we should not need to locate it in a geometric situation.

Those logicians who regard definition as important value the explicit type more highly. But if we attend to the details of particular situations the differences hardly allow for a scale of merit. Where can we find adequate criteria for preferring Euclid's explicit definitions of points, lines, angles, etc., to the modern geometer's practice of merely implicitly defining these elements through the axioms?

Still, from an operational standpoint, it is possible to distinguish between two very different kinds of operations which produce the definitional product—namely, manipulative and linguistic. In the former case the actual drawing of the diagonals constitutes the implicit definition. The clarification of the nature of a diagonal lies in the performance itself, rather than in the fact that a product is being constructed. Linguistic operations are more definitely di-

[50] Enriques, Historical, p. 119.

rected toward products, in addition to their function as references and symbolic representations of things.

Consider another illustration revealing the basic continuity in implicit and explicit defining operations. To draw an actual circle is to be alive to the constancy of the circumferential line. This, as in the case of the diagonal, may be regarded as the implicit or essentially manipulative definition. Explicit definition stresses the formula which is written as follows:

A circle is the locus of a point moving at a constant distance from a fixed point.

As always, the word structure must be kept distinct from the definition product, and notice further that the lack of a completeness or time factor simulates the absence of coordinates in the symbolic formula $r^2 = x^2 + y^2$.

In this connection it is interesting to note Heath's observation that the construction of figures in geometry marks the transition to objective definition of things from the subjective definition of names.[51] Acts of all sorts, whether they consist of vocal or graphic naming, are, of course, objective, but as far as objects are concerned it is justifiable to characterize naming acts as less descriptive of objects and more personal. As Strong points out, however, Euclid certainly did not begin his geometry with entities in his mind which subsequently became justified.[52]

Implicit definition may be further distinguished on the basis that the defining operations are more self-centered than are those involved in explicit definitions. To define for other individuals involves more formal linguistic interbehavior with the properties and relations of things.

(4) *Varieties of Ostensive Definition.* Pointing operations and casual demonstrative acts have been rightly excluded from the definitional domain.[53] For the most part, however, the ground for doing so has not been of the firmest. Most frequently, perhaps, ostensive definition has been condemned because of deviating from the use of words and symbols; or, when words are used, only right-word usage is considered proper.[54]

---

[51] Thirteen, p. 146.

[52] Procedures, p. 224.

[53] Mill, System, Bk. I, chap. 8; Dewey, Logic, pp. 53f, 120, 241f.

[54] Feigl, Operationism, p. 252.

From a strictly operational standpoint the problem of ostensive definition is easily settled since we possess a definite criterion of identifying or describing things for orientational purposes. Hence, the factors in a situation may be analyzed and assessed despite their variations. The kinds of actions involved depend not only upon the thing to be defined but also upon the general surrounding circumstances.

When words are to be defined, genuine ostensive operations include the correlation of the words with, or their application to, things or to other words in context. Those who do not limit definition to logic, or make logic something else than system building, are not disturbed by the simplicity of ostensive situations. No significant basis exists for overlooking the continuity of all definitional events.

Ostensive pointing or similar manipulative performances constitute the operations for defining things. To demonstrate to oneself or to some one else how a thing operates by provoking it to action in order to describe it—namely, identifying or locating its properties—comprises genuine definitional operations.[55]

Rules for Definition

Considered in their conventional framework the traditional rules of definition are correct and pertinent. Yet they are remote from any significant logical work. For the most part definition rules are linguistic in character and conform to grammatical principles. The way most writers expound the rules of adequate or commensurate definition—circularity, negativity, obscurity, and figurativeness— is to make them into rules of literary exposition. There is no serious reaching down to system organization or even a general handling of things. How to deal with verbal or symbolic formulations is a special logical problem, if any at all.

Probably the most significant point about conventional treatments of rules of definition is that most writers in one way or another shift their ground from words, and even concepts, to things as the objects of definition. Notice the usual insistence that the essence of the definiendum must be stated. Paradoxically, the *genus-et-differentiam* rule comes closest to a rule of thing

[55] Of considerable interest here is Aristotle's account of inductive definition; Analytica Posteriora, II, 13, 97b.

definition, but not all writers offer it, probably on the ground that it is concerned more with division than definition.

The rule of noncircularity of definition in particular marks the path from words to things. It is frequently noticed that the repetition of words is either unimportant or unnecessary, when the words are employed to refer to, or substitute for, things.[56]

For authentic system-building procedures a different set of rules is required. At the peak stands proper regard for specific problems and particular reference frames. For effective systemizing, defining behavior must be articulated with the conditions under which it is performed. In this way one avoids adopting an alternative but less adequate procedure.

Likewise important is the rule that no particular kind of definition can serve as a model for all other types. For example, though mathematical definition is exact and effective for mathematical relations, it can not be employed as a general model for material which can not be so rigidly defined (vol. I).

From the standpoint of concrete interbehavioral enterprises the conventional objection to definition by use is not acceptable. The question is: Are there specific situations in which such definition is conducive to the organization of a system? The objection to using description stems from the neglect of the psychological aspects of logic, and the prejudice against concrete behavioral, as over against abstract formal, procedures.

II. CLASSIFICATION

Classes are essentially systems. Classifying operations, therefore, constitute logical or systemizing behavior. They are even more essentially logical in nature than syllogistic construction operations. Traditional logic, however, has only been concerned with the most formal and simple types of classification.

Here is another instance of the ill effects brought about by the intrusion of linguistic factors into logical situations. For one thing, although classification lends itself to the effective arrangements and organization of actual things, it has been confined to terms and statements. Nothing has had a greater effect in trivializing logic. Consider how the processes of classification have been mishandled

---

[59] Johnson, Logic, part I, p. 104; Eaton, General, chap. 7; Lewis, Mind. p. 82.

by contamination with division, especially dichotomous division! Even the classical logician in his practical contacts with actual things[57] has had to take account of the great discrepancy between division and classification.

As system building, classifying work consists of the construction of classes as products. These products, like all logical products, may be constructed linguistically or developed on the basis of handling or describing actual things. In all cases a product class is not to be taken as an eternally existing autonomous entity. Platonic classes are, of course, simply reification of terms; as such they illustrate the substitution of a constructed description for things described. When actual things are organized, the criteria may be selected from their similar properties. Differences in identity are arranged to form a coherent system. Thus a class *men* is achieved. On the other hand, purely constructed classes are set up by means of constructed properties. Pure and preferred races, for instance, are constructed out of the autistically created properties of manufactured peoples.

Tradition has it that definition is preliminary to classification. As we have seen, however, classification may precede definition. This apparent circularity of operation is not objectionable unless one adopts an absolutistic notion. When system building concerns concrete interbehavior we can go even further and point out that instead of a circle we have here a spiral of procedures. In other words, there is a continuous ascent from one level to another. On one level definition precedes classification; on another the opposite takes place. The fundamental question is whether the systemizing operations are progressing.

Classification procedures for system building must be differentiated from similar procedures carried on for nonlogical purposes. Involved are variations in criteria, refinement of procedure, and intensity or amount of detail. Truth tables of formal logic illustrate small systems which include at the same time definition, division, and classification. By prescriptive definition such systems are limited to truth and false categories or statements. Further, they are defined as P false, and Q true is impossible or excluded. Then the systems are divided and organized into a conventional pattern.

---

[57] Joseph, Introduction, p. 133.

CHAPTER XV

SYSTEMS AS CONSTRUCTION PRODUCTS

SELECTION AND ANALYSIS OF SYSTEM PRODUCTS

IN THE two preceding chapters we have discussed outstanding system-building processes. We now turn to the products of such constructional interbehavior. The best method, naturally, of studying products is the point-by-point investigation of the system builder at work. When this direct method is not available, a good substitute is a critical analysis of sample systems.

Because of the immense number of systems and classes of systems we are immediately confronted by a problem of selection. Even the conventional logics constitute complex organizations of smaller systems. For example, inferences and the syllogism are more or less independent subsystems of classical deduction. Fortunately, the very abundance of materials helps to suggest a technique, one derived from our field-organization principle. This technique we regard simply as an investigative schema.

INVESTIGATIVE SCHEMA FOR SYSTEM PRODUCTS

Rejecting the assumption of a single universalistic system pattern, we take system products as unique outcomes of given enterprises. Thus we proceed to study the product according to the materials structured and the kinds of operations utilized in manipulating them. In addition, the plan and use of the system constitute important features of the total situation.

The field hypothesis enables us (1) to counteract the conventional view that beyond actual system building itself there are unique logical processes such as induction, deduction, and implication, and (2) to bring into prominence the concrete details of system construction. Frequently it is such details that are of the utmost importance for logical theory, since logicians, like scientists, present only successfully finished products. But even if we are denied access to the vacillating, and sometimes inept, operational trials and errors leading to the final result, we are not obliged to regard logical systems as absolute entities which are simply discovered and not contingently produced. Taking account of the great variety of systems, and the enormous number of processes required to create them, reveals the product character of all logic.

FOUR TYPES OF SYSTEM PRODUCTS

By emphasizing certain system-building factors—namely, (1) materials, (2) operations or techniques, and (3) use and function —we can arrange system products into four types:

A. Material or Content Systems.
B. Linguistic Systems.
C. Formal Systems.
D. Operational Systems.

A. *Material or Content Systems*

In material or content systems the things dealt with are emphasized, rather than the design or constructional work. Of the extensive range of material systems we shall consider only structures of things, events, relations, classes, acts, and sentences.

(1) *Things.* Systems of things fall between wide limits. They include any simple or complex arrangement of simple or complex objects, as well as such intricate structures as Mendeleeff's periodic table or an organization of atomic constituents. Notice that among such systems actual things are not distinguished from knowledge and theories about them. Moreover, both authentic things and things merely alleged to exist are included in one and the same series. In every instance the historical background and technical details of the structure suggest the facts entering into the system's construction. Frequently also, the sufficiency and insufficiency of systems at different time periods reveal their nature and the operations employed in building them.

(a) *Titius-Bode Planetary System.* The organization of the relative distances between the sun and the planets constitutes an elementary but interesting scientific system. The basic materials operated on were the known planetary distances. For Titius (1729-1796) these distances concerned Mercury, Venus, the Earth, Mars, Jupiter, and Saturn. Bode also (1747-1826) knew Uranus, which was discovered by Herschel in 1781.

Now it was easily suggested to Titius that, except for Jupiter whose distance from the sun is 3.5 times that of Mars, each succeeding planet is roughly twice the distance of its predecessor. Accordingly, the following system was set up. The last row in the table indicates the approximate distances.

Mercury	Venus	Earth	Mars	?	Jupiter	Saturn	Uranus
4 o	4 3	4 6	4 12	4 24	4 48	4 96	4 192
4	7	10	16	28	52	100	196
3.9	7.2	10	15		52	95	191

It is interesting to note that the discovery of Uranus, between the dates of Titius and Bode, fitted into the scheme. This is all the more remarkable because the original figure for Mercury should have been 1½, since o is not ½ of 3. But even more exceptional was the incident of the missing planet or empty space. Here was an astonishing feat of prediction whereby the planetoid or asteroid Ceres was discovered on the basis of a crude and unworkable system. Just how baseless the system was came into full view when it broke down with the discovery of Neptune and Pluto, as the continuation of the above scheme indicates. In the case of Neptune, however, both Adams and Leverrier assigned distances to the planet on the basis of the erroneous system which thus played a part in its discovery.

Neptune	Pluto
4 374	4 768
388	772
300	396

(b) *Balmer's Spectral Line System.* Among the early striking observations in the spectral analysis of hydrogen was the constancy and regularity of the four lines in the visible region. How to account for the relation between them became an exciting problem. Thus J. J. Balmer (1825-1898), a Swiss mathematics teacher, constructed a system which he published in 1885[1] consisting of these line things. He began with Ångstrom's careful measurements of the first four spectral lines, which yielded the following values in Ångstrom units: 6562, 4860, 4340, and 4101. Dividing the Ångstrom numbers by an arbitrary constant 3645.6, which he denoted by h, he obtained the following fractions:

$$9/5, \ 4/3, \ 25/21, \ 9/8.$$

These he put into the forms:

$$9/5, \ 16/12, \ 25/21, \ 36/32.$$

obtaining:

$$\frac{3^2}{3^2 - 2^2}, \quad \frac{4^2}{4^2 - 2^2}, \quad \frac{5^2}{5^2 - 2^2}, \quad \frac{6^2}{6^2 - 2^2}.$$

The completed system consists of the generalized formula:

$$\frac{hm^2}{m^2 - 2^2}$$

which can be written as follows:

$$\lambda = 3645.6 \times \frac{m^2}{m^2 - 4}$$

Balmer, calculating the following series, assigned different values to m as below:

m	Calculated	Observed
3	6562.08	6562.1
4	4860.8	4860.74
5	4340	4340.1
6	4101.3	4101.2
7	3969	3968.1
8	3888	3887.5
9	3834.3	3834
10	3796.9	3795
11	3769.6	3767.5
12	3749.1	3745.5
13	3733.3	3730
14	3720.9	3717.5
15	3711	3707.5
16	3702.9	3699

[1] Annalen.

The significance of the system lies in the fair agreement of the calculated with the observed values of spectral lines, which, of course, Balmer could not know since they were only later discovered.

A further important feature of Balmer's work lay in his realization that the 2^2 denominator in his formula restricts its application to waves shorter than 6562Å, if m is an integer. He therefore modified the formula to give:

$$\frac{hm^2}{m^2 - n^2}$$

When $n = 3$, the formula becomes applicable to the Paschen infrared series, while $n = 1$ corresponds to the Lyman ultraviolet series.

(c) *The Bohr Quantum System of Atoms.* The Bohr quantum-mechanical interpretation of atomic structure excellently illustrates scientific system products and their construction. Essentially the system consists of organizing into a single structure: (1) the Rutherford planetary atom, (2) the Balmer series of wave lengths, (3) the Rydberg constant of wave frequencies, and (4) the Planck-Einstein quanta.

Consonant with the general principle that all construction is reconstruction, the building of this system begins with Bohr's improvement of Rutherford's atomic model. Retaining the general planetary idea of an atom, a frequently suggested construction,[2] Bohr altered it to conform to accumulated information following the development of classical electromagnetic theory, especially the data obtained from spectroscopic observation concerning radiation emission and absorption.

Proceeding from simpler to more complex atoms, Bohr accepted the view that the hydrogen atom constituted a simple system with a single positive proton as a nucleus and a single negative electron revolving about it. At first the orbit was assumed to be circular, but later, in conformity with Coulomb's law of electrostatics, the electronic orbit was described as elliptical; the electron thus moved about the proton with a force inversely as the square of the distance between them.

[2] Perrin, 1901; Nagaoka, 1904; cf. Tucker, in Taylor, Physics, p. 820; also Poincaré; Foundations, p. 317.

At this point, further reconstruction of the Rutherford atom was necessary. The problem was to show how electrons could maintain themselves in the outer atom. According to classic electromagnetic theory the circulating electron must continuously radiate energy and describe a spiral path until it collides with the proton. Since the observed facts of the hydrogen spectrum did not accord with the collapse of atoms, Bohr had to construct a bold postulate.

It was no less than the creation of a stationary motion or state. This consisted of the circulation of an electron in its orbit with a constant energy. Unless the electron jumps from one orbit to another there is neither radiation nor loss of energy, nor absorption or increase of energy. But when the electron shifts from one of the many possible orbits to another, it gains or loses energy and emits or absorbs radiation. Energy is lost and waves emitted, when the electron jumps from an outer to an inner orbit. The instantaneous change from an inner to an outer orbit marks the absorption of energy, in which case the atom is said to be excited and to show an absorption line in the spectrum.

With respect to radiation, the spectral series of hydrogen can be envisaged as follows: When the electron jumps to the second orbit from the third, H α is emitted; from the fourth, H β; from the fifth H γ, etc. This is the Balmer series. Shifts from outer to lower-energy levels up to $n = 3$ give the Paschen infrared series, up to $n = 1$ the Lyman ultraviolet series, and to $n = 4$ the far infrared series of Brackett.

Doubtless the most important item of the system is the importation into it of the quantum theory. Whenever an electron jumps from one orbit to another it either gains or loses energy in discrete quanta. For example, in moving into an orbit of higher energy, as the electron might do by colliding with another electron, by absorption of radiation or by high temperature collisions, the change would answer to the formula $h\nu = E_2 - E_1$. Similarly the loss of energy by radiation of light is described by the same equation. It is observed that the frequency ν of the radiation is measured in terms of Planck's constant h.

So far the Bohr system combines the constructs of classical mechanics with Planck's quantum theory. We have next to see how the system assimilates the Balmer and Rydberg items. This assimilation may be regarded as predictable, since the quantum theory itself is a radiation theory, and because of the close association of the Balmer and Rydberg constants. As early as 1900 Haas had shown the probability of expressing the Rydberg-Ritz constant in terms of h and electronic data.[3] Certainly, evidence was already available that the particular structure of an atom or molecule determines its spectrum. What was needed, then, was to interrelate the known facts of the hydrogen spectrum with the relations obtaining between the hydrogen electron and proton. Now, the quantum atom made possible a theoretical basis for the Balmer and Rydberg work.

We have seen (p. 5) that the Balmer formula for the hydrogen series:

$$\lambda = 3645.6 \times \frac{m^2}{m^2 - 4}$$

was arbitrary and purely empirical. Yet it was sufficiently descriptive of the order and regularity of spectral lines to be predictive. Rydberg (1854-1919), interacting with the same datum—namely, the hydrogen spectrum—proceeded from the wave length and the known velocity of light to the calculation of the number of waves that pass a given point in a second of time. λ became expressed in cms., through the following developments.[4] First, Balmer's formula was written:

$$\frac{1}{\lambda} = \frac{1}{3645.6}\left(\frac{m^2 - 4}{m^2}\right),$$

Then, by multiplying the numerator and denominator on the right side by 4, the following expression was obtained:

$$\frac{1}{\lambda} = \frac{4}{3645.6}\left(\frac{1}{2^2} - \frac{1}{m^2}\right).$$

When this formula is expressed in cms., it reads:

$$\frac{1}{\lambda} = 109,720\left(\frac{1}{2^2} - \frac{1}{m^2}\right).[5]$$

[3] Sommerfeld, Atomic, p. 89.

[4] The present system illustration is derived in large part from Tucker (Taylor, Physics, (p. 820f).

[5] The factor 109,720 is, of course, the spectroscopic constant or number of Rydberg. Later determinations of this number gave the more accurate figure of 109,677.8 cms⁻¹.

Taking into account the Lyman and Paschen hydrogen-spectral series, as well as those of Balmer, we obtain the two following formulae. For the Lyman series:

$$\frac{1}{\lambda} = R\left(\frac{1}{1^2} - \frac{1}{m^2}\right)$$

where m = 2, 3, 4 . . . and for the Paschen series:

$$\frac{1}{\lambda} = R\left(\frac{1}{3^2} - \frac{1}{m^2}\right)$$

with m = 4, 5, 6. . . .

Generally, for all spectral lines of hydrogen we have:

$$\frac{1}{\lambda} = R\left(\frac{1}{n^2} - \frac{1}{m^2}\right)$$

which, when written as follows:

$$\frac{1}{\lambda} = \frac{R}{n^2} - \frac{R}{m^2}$$

fits in with the Bohr differences in energy levels.

Considering:

$$R = \frac{2\pi^2 e^4 m}{ch^3}$$

we have an equation:

$$\frac{1}{\lambda} = \frac{\nu}{c} = \frac{2\pi^2 e^4 m}{ch^3}\left(\frac{1}{n_1^2} - \frac{1}{n_2^2}\right)$$

which is equivalent to Rydberg's expression for Balmer's hydrogen series. The remarkable thing about this is that such an approximation is obtained with an equation whose constants e, m, c, h have been obtained independently of the spectrum of hydrogen.[6]

Widely acclaimed as a superlative product of imaginative genius, the Bohr quantum system was found to be applicable to more complex atoms than hydrogen, as well as to the light conditions of molecular substances. For our study of system products it is significant that the Bohr atom system was successful insofar as it integrated and organized the kinds of data with which it was

[6] Tucker, in Taylor, Physics, p. 824.

intimately concerned. It is of cardinal importance to keep before us the enormously detailed operations of Bohr, Sommerfeld, and numerous others, as they attempted to combine the data obtained from spectroscopy and chemical behavior in order to construct the various arrangements of electrons in the atoms of different elements.

No less important is it to consider the inherent weakness of the system occasioned by combining classical mechanics with quantum ideas. In a letter to Bohr, written in 1913, Rutherford speaks of a grave difficulty in the hypothesis:

". . . namely, how does an electron decide what frequency it is going to vibrate at when it passes from one stationary state to the other? It seems to me that you would have to assume that the electron knows beforehand where it is going to stop."[7]

It is part of our illustration to suggest that with the discovery of the Compton effect and the discrepancies of the photoelectric process physicists had to begin the construction of a wave instead of a particle system of quantum mechanics.

(d) *The System of Chemical Elements.* The proposition:

The properties of the elements, and therefore, the properties of the simple, and of the compound bodies formed from them, are in periodic dependence on their atomic weights

marks the construction of a scientific thing system of major logical importance. The apparent difficulties in organizing the atoms of all substances, and the exceptions that the arrangement disclosed, brought to light the work and conditions making for a system product. Even to Newlands (1838-1898) the correlation of chemical properties and atomic weights was apparent. To Lothar Meyer (1830-1895) and Mendeleeff (1834-1907) the greater knowledge of both atomic weights and chemical properties offered materials for setting up a system. Its success in enabling gallium (1875), scandium (1879), and germanium (1886) to be predicted testified to the acumen of the systemizers in choosing a criterion and collecting information.

Though the Meyer-Mendeleeff periodic table is rightly regarded as an enormous scientific triumph, it is also characterized as

[7] Eve, Rutherford, p. 221.

an empirical construction and a comparatively simple taxonomic structure. The value of the system, with its important role in the prediction and discovery of new elements, obviously stems from its connection with actual, though imperfectly known, things. The faults of the system—for example, incoordination of periodic chemical properties and atomic weights, variance of position and property resemblance, fitting elements into groups despite the contraindication of their major valences, etc.,—are traceable to the relative insufficiency of knowledge and the need of increased and modified operations.

Assuming a continuity in the system of elements, we find a distinct evolution from the periodic phase, based upon atomic weights, to Mosley's (1887-1915) establishment of the criterion of amount of positive nuclear charge. A more significant and fertile system was achieved by arranging the elements on the basis of the number of unit charges of the atom's inner structure. All the elements, without exception, fit into their group formulae and relative table positions. In a sense, too, the table becomes self validated; between hydrogen and uranium there can be only 92 elements.

The evolution of the chemical-element system presents a lucid picture of the operations in thing system making. Following an increased acquaintance with things come modification, enlargement, and general reconstruction. The development of radiation science, the discovery of isotopes, and, in general, the prevalence of electrical events in the existence and changes in things all have their influence. These developments are pointed up in Mosley's (1913) observation that spectral lines are displaced toward the shorter wave lengths as the atomic number of elements increases.

The achievement of a more significant arrangement of chemical elements yielded its reward in prediction and discovery. Soon masurium with atomic number 43, illinium with number 61, hafnium with number 72, and rhenium with atomic number 75 were announced.

(e) *Aesthetic Thing Systems.* Interesting examples of thing systems are found in the various ways writers have constructed the factors or elements of aesthetic objects. To reduce or analyze an aesthetic object to form, content or subject matter, and meaning or significance illustrates an abstractive type of generalized system product. Compare different systems of factors alleged to make up aesthetic products—for instance pure form by itself (one-factor system), form and content (two-factor system), and form, content, and meaning (three-factor system). Each of the factors, of course, as well as the different combinations, represents a special creation.

(f) *Petrie's System of Sequence Dating.*[8] Two major problems in archaeology are the recognition of different stages in the development of a culture, and the correlation of these stages within a chronological framework. In many regions of the Near East the remains of various cultural phases were deposited, one on top of another, in mounds; hence, it is possible to solve the problem of chronological sequence by the excavation of ancient settlements. Very little such stratigraphic evidence is available for predynastic Egypt. Nearly all the material remains of that time were recovered from graves, which in all periods were dug from the surface of the desert. When Sir Flinders Petrie found, for the first time, a large number of prehistoric graves, he faced the problem of establishing the time relationship between the various individual burials, each of which was a separate unit physically unrelated to the others. To solve this problem Petrie developed his ingenious sequence dating system.

He noticed that one general type of pottery vessel—the wavy-handled class—occurred in many graves, but in different forms. Some had well-made handles and ovoid bodies; others had rudimentary handles and roughly cylindrical bodies. Certain graves contained intermediate forms. Petrie correctly assumed that these various types represent different stages in the development of the wavy-handled jars. He assumed further that the functional handles did not evolve from the rudimentary ones, but that the reverse was true. This view was confirmed by the occurrence of the cylindrical types in graves with pottery of the First Dynasty, and the complete subsequent disappearance of this type. On the basis of this evidence Petrie arranged all graves containing wavy-handled jars in an approximate chronological order.

But not all prehistoric graves contain wavy-handled pots. In order to incorporate such graves in his chronological system

---

[8] For this material I am indebted to Dr. Helene J. Kantor.

Petrie assumed that all objects found in a single undisturbed grave must be contemporaneous. This means that other types of pottery (black-topped, polished red, etc.), found in the graves containing wavy-handled vessels, could also be relatively dated. Through them, many burials without the wavy-handled class of pottery could be fitted into the sequence. This method was, of course, extended, to other classes of objects (palettes, stone vessels, etc.).

Petrie observed also that the wavy-handled pots never occur in the same graves with white cross-lined vessels, and concluded that these were earlier than the earliest wavy-handled jars. In this manner the relative data of still another group of graves was established.

Accordingly, Petrie was able to arrange a large number of graves in a relative chronological order. He then arbitrarily divided this series into fifty groups, each of which represents a particular stage of change. To allow for possible finds of earlier date he numbered these groups from 30 to 80 and referred to them as *sequence dates*.

When an object is assigned to a sequence date, it is placed within a particular phase in the development of predynastic culture, but is not dated in terms of years. A sequence date may represent either a long or short period. However, there is no evidence as to which sequence date was relatively long or short. By means of the sequence dating system Petrie was able to distinguish clearly two successive predynastic cultures, Amratian and Gerzean.

(2) *Event Systems.* Everyone sensitive to the specificity of systems and to the necessity of keeping in view the building materials is alert to the many ways in which events of all sorts are structured. The following examples are chosen to emphasize the variety of materials or content.

(a) *Chemical Events.* Tables of chemical reactions and constants, and handbooks of such tables, certainly illustrate system building, if only of an elementary and casual sort. The great number of such events, and the corresponding need to organize them for effective use, require classifying and ordering operations (chap. 2). Chemical work demands systems of solubilities, densities, boiling and freezing constants, and so on.

(b) *Biological Events.* Workers concerned with biological

events can not be limited to systems of constants or fixed units, as
in the case of chemists, but must deal also with variabilities of all
sorts. Accordingly, systems need to be devised for handling ranges
and limits. Classes are more or less arbitrarily chosen as established; frequencies are selected in order that comparisons and
other relations can be set up. On the whole, statistical techniques
must be invoked.

(c) *Historical Events.* As our third illustration we choose the
enormous mass of events conventionally regarded as outside the
pale of the rigorous and settled domain of logic. Still, all those
interested in intricate political and social events, and in human
happenings in general, strive to order and relate them for purposes of control and understanding. It is an invalid argument to
deny the systematic character of philosophies of history because one
can not accept the criteria (working out of spirit, right, etc.) and
the products resulting from such system-building activities. Such
denials simply bespeak a preference for the certainty, simplicity,
and compactness of systems, with abstractive sentences as building
materials.

(3) *Relations as System Materials.* From the operational point
of view, relations constitute things to be ordered and integrated in
logical work (chap. 15). Operational procedures upon relations
imply the manipulation of related things, or records of, and substitutes for, the relations. For example, in material-implication
systems the symbol T stands for the relations FF, TT, FT, but
not for TF. Relations importable into logical situations are already
small-scale system products. For instance, basic and crude natural
relations may be manipulated as a preparation for logical operations. As manipulable materials, relations are things both for the
local systems into which they are set and the larger systems into
which they are ordered.

(4) *Classes as System Materials.* More definitely than relations, classes constitute constructed things, inasmuch as they already consist of minor or small-scale systems previously developed. The possibility is not excluded that the term *class* may
refer to genuine independent events, such as similarities in things,
which make them potentially classifiable when the investigator
operates upon them.

In system-building situations, however, the important task is organizing similar things by isolating them from others on the basis of one or more criteria. The very existence of classes shows that a significant system-building enterprise has occurred. Again, on an operational basis classes may exist simply by casual assertional activities. Asserted or alleged classes are also the raw materials of systems. The procedural and localized character of all logical situations is something not to be ignored.

And finally, classes may be arbitrarily brought into existence irrespective of any natural or independent properties. In this sense classes are more autistic than in the assertional situation, since in the latter instance the references may have an existential basis.

(5) *Acts as System Materials.* Acts or behavior, no less than any other material, can be structured. The only requirement is that the operator be able to interbehave with actions as stimulus objects. This is no difficult matter as long as the acting thing— particle, organism or person—is in observable range. The simplest system of acts, as in the case with other materials, consists of various classifications. Examples are found in every science; for instance, voluntary and involuntary action in physiology and psychology, reversible and irreversible action in chemistry. Through series of organizing operations the logician or system maker can interrelate behavior to form all sorts of systematic arrangements. These behaviors can themselves be organized into a hierarchical structure with a base in definition and classification.

(6) *Linguistic Things as System Materials.* A literate universe is a fertile field for every possible type of language thing system. An obvious and inescapable system is represented by the hierarchy of letter, syllable, word, phrase, and sentence. A better example indicating the essence and scope of linguistic thing systems is available in classic grammar. The departments of accidence, lexicology, and syntax comprise innumerable systems of parts and wholes. Words are constructed from roots, affixes, suffixes, and infixes in a rich array; then the words themselves are syntactically interrelated in series from one-one, through one-many, to many-many structures of illimitable variety.

B. *Linguistic Systems*

Linguistic systems constitute unique systemological products. Essentially, they are organizations of responses which can be described as references or designations. When building such systems, the system builder works with referential actions intimately and inseverably interrelated with the things referred to.

That linguistic systems consist of actions and not things can scarcely be overstressed. Although the products represent an emphasis on language factors, they must not be confused with linguistic content systems of which language things are the ingredients.[9]

The constituents of language systems are describable as assertions of every sort and for every purpose. Such assertions may be magnified to refer to things of cosmic import, or constructed to designate simple and petty details of events. It is not a reflection on logic to indicate that organizing a complex court plea is building a logical system. To distinguish such logical acts from others we might characterize them as mediate, remote, or nonexecutive responses. The system builder is handling things assertionally.

At this point we must again call attention to the factors of the system-building field. In referential acts the system builder's work takes precedence over what he interacts with. In this sense linguistic systems are first-degree language systems. Such acts, when referred to, recorded, or fixated in transcription, become descriptively transformed into second-degree or thing-language systems (p. 73). Second-degree language systems take their place among the content structures.

(1) *General Reference Systems.* The primary distinguishing feature of these systems is the intimacy of the references. Even if the referents are regarded as important, there is a personal factor in the system.

(a) *Operational References.* Instructions to perform operations with respect to given things form genuine, and sometimes extremely important, systems. Their range (p. 84) is enormous when we take into account references to actions, such as preparing a prescription, following a recipe, and carrying out complex mathematical operations.

(b) *Systems of Argument.* The organization of a series of assertions to form arguments is a good illustration of a type of linguistic system. Consider a lawyer's series of references to alleged events

---

[9] For a discussion of language behavior and language things see Kantor, Objective, chap. 2, and Principles, chap. 23.

in order to establish a particular belief or conviction. Perhaps a more formal, and hence more tightly knit, aggregation of assertions is exemplified by the classic paradoxes of Zeno.

1. Motion is impossible because a body cannot arrive at another place without passing through infinitely many and infinitely small separate parts.

2. Achilles cannot overtake the tortoise, since he must first reach the point simultaneously left by the latter. The tortoise will thus always be in advance, if only by an interval which constantly decreases to a minimum.

3. The flying arrow is really at rest since at every instant it occupies a discrete point of its path. Of such zero movements no genuine magnitude can be summed.

(2) *Method Systems.* Important examples of linguistic systems are found in various reference organizations for the conduct of reason and scientific work. Here we may cite such classic systems as those of Descartes, Newton, and Mill.[10] These systems, as organizations of references to operations, differ from simpler operational reference systems in their generality and specialization for achieving important results in comprehensive situations.

(a) Descartes' precepts for rightly conducting the reason and seeking for truth in the sciences.[11]

The first of these was to accept nothing as true which I did not clearly recognize to be so; that is to say, carefully to avoid precipitation and prejudice in judgments, and to accept in them nothing more than what was presented to my mind so clearly and distinctly that I could have no occasion to doubt it.

The second was to divide up each of the difficulties which I examined into as many parts as possible, and as seemed requisite in order that it might be resolved in the best manner possible.

The third was to carry on my reflections in due order, commencing with objects that were the most simple and easy to understand, in order to rise little by little, or by degrees, to knowledge of the most complex, assuming an order, even if a fictitious one, among those which do not follow a natural sequence relatively to one another.

The last was in all cases to make enumerations so complete and reviews so general that I should be certain of having omitted nothing.

[10] Mill's system is treated in chap. 19.
[11] Haldane and Ross, Philosophical, vol. I, p. 92.

(b) Newton's rules of reasoning in philosophy.[12]

Rule I. We are to admit no more causes of natural things than such as are both true and sufficient to explain their appearances.

Rule II. Therefore to the same natural effects we must, as far as possible, assign the same causes.

Rule III. The qualities of bodies, which admit neither intensification nor remission of degrees, and which are found to belong to all bodies within the reach of our experiments, are to be esteemed the universal qualities of all bodies whatsoever.

Rule IV. In experimental philosophy we are to look upon propositions inferred by general induction from phenomena as accurately or very nearly true, notwithstanding any contrary hypotheses that may be imagined, till such time as other phenomena occur, by which they may either be made more accurate, or liable to exceptions.

(3) *Metalogical Systems.* Metamathematics and metalogics constitute unique forms of recently developed linguistic systems. Essentially, these are systems of reference to the rules for, or operation boundaries of, complex system building and their components.

(4) *Autological Cosmic Systems.* Autological cosmic structures in science and philosophy provide excellent illustrations of large-scale assertional systems. Most of the absolute philosophical systems (Hegel's dialectic absolutism, Schopenhauer's will projection) are determined by traditions and doctrines wittingly and unwittingly adopted by the system builder. Such assertional structures are quite remote from things. Contrast such arbitrary structures with those that are genuinely referential and descriptive, and which form integral parts of concrete enterprises. For example, in the mathematical domain, systems of description and explanation refer to the operations and things involved in the mathematical task. Similarly, descriptions and recordings in scientific work make up the linguistic structure which is an essential feature of the operations.

C. *Formal Systems*

The factor stressed in the formal system product is the structure or organization, rather than its material or use. The basic specifications for formalistic structures center about such items as sym-

---

[12] Principia, p. 398.

metry, balance, regularity, order, and completeness. By contrast
with material systems, formal structures depend greatly upon the
system builder's attitudes and motivation. Thus he and his work
stand out in the system-building situation. Observe how the logician in choosing the domain in which to localize his system favors
the one offering least resistance to shape or structure.

Two primary considerations govern the construction of formal
systems: First, the achievement of certainty, and secondly, the
satisfaction derived from closed and finished products. Seldom
do logical writers indicate that the achieved certainty and finality
constitute functions of the constructed systems. Obviously, the
intimate and direct path from premises to conclusions is a product
of the logician's work. His constructions, of course, may be influenced or determined by the material structured, but in that instance the formal features of the system are secondary in the
enterprise. Also, in such "empirical" situations the structures are
not so rigid and stable as when actual characteristics of things are
abstracted or canceled out. We offer four examples of formal
system products.

(1) *Implicatory Systems.* Traditional logicians, greatly concerned with valid reasoning, have constructed numerous two-item
subsystems. Frequently these items have been chosen to show
invariable reciprocal relations. Such implicatory systems may be
illustrated by immediate inference and opposition squares.

(a) *So-called Immediate Inference.* Demonstrations of valid
and stable inference naturally can best be made by setting up, or
isolating, situations involving closed mutual connections, such that
if A sustains a certain relation to B, then B must sustain a similar
relation to A. For example, if Chicago is west of New York, it is
at once inferable that New York is east of Chicago. If 7 > than
5, then 5 < than 7. The term inference in this situation con-
notes a sort of game-playing activity. For the most part, it is
merely turning things about verbally. But this process is not to
be condemned as trivial or remote from reasoning. Consider the
place of such activities in building formal system products, and
observe, moreover, the interrelation between this type of inference and other activities referred to by the same term.

(b) *Square of Opposition.* The traditional square of opposition
illustrates a more complicated version of the immediate inference

type of system product. The materials are verbal: alleged sentences or propositions which are so interrelated that any one may be inferred from the other. Including the diagonals, there are six pairs of relationships.

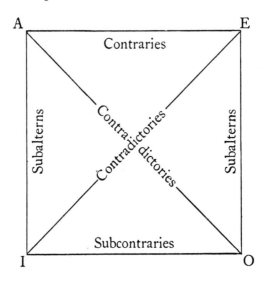

The square is constructed to display the following points:

a. Contradictory statements can not both be true or false.

b. Contraries can not both be true, but both can be false.

c. Subcontraries can both be true, but both can not be false.

d. Subalterns are so related that if the universals are true the particulars are true, but true particulars do not imply true universals. On the other hand, if particulars are false the universals are false.

(2) *Truth-function (Matrix) Systems.* Consider as a typical achievement of symbolic logic the truth-function table or matrix, which effectively exemplifies formal system products. Beginning with the criterion of material implication, formal system makers have organized statements and their interrelationships to satisfy the criteria of simplicity, completeness, and "playability."

P	Q	P · Q	P + Q	P → Q	P = Q
T	T	T	T	T	T
F	T	F	T	T	F
T	F	F	T	F	F
F	F	F	F	T	T

Systems involving more than two values require more elaborate structures. Suggested modifications become necessary when systems of simple dichotomy are opposed to those involving some content material. On the whole, the two-valued systems can be kept free from content and so-called meaning.

(3) *Complete Induction.* Of all formal situations that of complete induction provides the best illustration of the nature of system products, chiefly because such systems involve an equal stress of material and form factors.

The materials consist of relations organized into a stable structure. No doubt, emphasis on material has given rise to the historical term *induction.* The interbehavioral process involved here is primarily the selection of type of relation to be organized. Complete induction products, more than ordinary deductive systems, stress structurization activity.

Turning to form, complete-induction products consist of systems in all aspects comparable to the circular structure of deductive systems. This is well illustrated by the following classic example. For all integral values of n:

$$1 + 3 + 5 + 7 \cdots \cdot (2n - 1) = n^2.$$

Whoever first developed this system observed the relations involved, and then set up a formula indicating them. The formalization procedure consists for the most part of constructing the formula, a procedure which belongs to the symbolic phase of system making.

(4) *Mathematical Systems.* The acme of formal systems is presumably attained by constructing a pure mathematical system or aggregation of axioms—that is, assumptions or postulates—as in the following example.[13]

1. If A and B are distinct elements of S, there is at least one *m-class* containing both A and B.
2. If A and B are distinct elements of S, there is not more than one *m-class* containing both A and B.
3. Any two *m-classes* have at least one element of S in common.
4. There exists at least one *m-class.*
5. Every *m-class* contains at least three elements of S.
6. All the elements of S do not belong to the same *m-class.*
7. No *m-class* contains more than three elements of S.

[13] Veblen and Young. Projective, p. 2f.

Now, although the synonyms *axiom, assumption,* and *postulate* imply that mathematicians and logicians no longer accept absolute and self-evident propositions, it is still true that the formality of postulate systems leads to notions of pure reason and ultimate systems of objective relations. Many individuals concerned with formal systems overlook the fact that systems can only be constructed by operating upon building materials. Frequently it is asserted that logical processes may be performed without any knowledge of concrete objects to which the primitive propositions or postulates refer,[14] or that mathematical deduction can be made without knowing what one is reasoning about.[15] More careful writers, however, go only so far as to say that a pure mathematical system can be constructed without explicit reference to specific subject matter.[16] Such writers acknowledge, then, that a mathematical system merely intensifies the work of any system which consists of abbreviating and abstracting specific complex materials. Whether or not in presenting the final product any explicit reference is made to specific subject matter, that reference is definitely indicated in the operations performed.

Compare the above abstract system with the following more concrete point-line system. Is it not obvious that the former was derived from the latter, which, aside from the last item, is essentially Veblen and Young's set of assumptions for a plane projective geometry?

1. If A and B are distinct points, there is at least one line on both A and B.
2. If A and B are distinct points, there is not more than one line on both A and B.
3. Any two lines have at least one point in common.
4. There exists at least one line.
5. Every line contains at least three points of the plane.
6. All points are not on the same line.
7. No line contains more than three points of the plane.

In the present situation it is impossible to overlook the abstractor's work (chap. 13, p. 3), and how that work constitutes system building. Notice his labor in moving from geometry to the

[14] Carmichael, Logic, p. 110.
[15] Veblen, Problems.
[16] Cohen and Nagel, Introduction, p. 135.

logical system. That such work with definite materials is indispensable in all system building is amply enough demonstrated throughout the evolution of all abstruse geometries, which are based upon the observed relations of concrete things in practical situations.

How can we fail, then, to emphasize the factors governing the choice and arrangement of axioms? This, we ask, despite the tremendous force of opinion that we should disregard all influences on the constructor, and focus only on the product.[17] Does not the entire modern theory of postulation demonstrate the necessity to take into account the constructor's work and circumstances? Is not the whole history of non-Euclidean geometry a sharp reminder that the belief in Euclid's infallibility long obstructed the evolution of geometry?[18]

As to the particular influences on system makers in setting up their geometric axioms, why does Hilbert choose his five basic items, whereas Pieri and Veblen each makes use of only two differing ones?[19] There is no question that all these mathematicians, no matter how they vary in their results, are influenced by specific features of the geometric universe of discourse. True, they have freedom to choose what aspects to stress, but since they are builders in specific situations they are constrained by the subject matter with which they work.

Mathematics as Postulation. As we have indicated (Vol. I), the employment of postulational methods in mathematics emphasizes system making and the role of the system maker. But we must stress further the specific interbehavioral details of mathematical work. The whole point to glorifying Pythagoreans, Eudoxus, and Euclid[20] as the first explicit employers of the postulational method calls attention to the systemizing operations in arithmetic and geometry. To a certain extent this postulational method consists of analyzing and stating the processes necessary for organizing a system of things or numbers. Incidentally, the mathematician's motivations are indicated here—namely, the felt need for order

---

[17] It is especially those who work with abstract or formal systems who stress the genetic fallacy, which they interpret as an undue interference with the study of finished products by concerning oneself with irrelevances of origin.

[18] Young, Lectures, p. 28f; Bell, Development, p. 302.

[19] Vol. I, p. 231.

[20] Bell, Development, 66ff.

and completeness to give rigor and certainty to the demonstrations.

The recent identification of mathematics and logic (vol. I) through the postulational method of systemization may be interpreted as a realization of the system-making operations more or less common to both disciplines.

Intuition in Mathematics. The present conflict between intuitionists and formalists in mathematics sharply points up the need to consider field factors in mathematics. In the first place, from an interbehavioral standpoint we observe here two types of workers, each stressing different assumptions and attitudes. The two basic views represent variant methods of handling the factors in the mathematical field. The formalists stress the results of achieved system, whereas the intuitionists are unable to abstract completely from the scene of work.

Both the intuitionist and the formalist are describing actual interbehavior with relations as stimulus objects. It is fatal to assume that the intuitionist is concerned with the sensuous materials which he injects into his descriptions. On the other hand, one need not assume that the formalist implies any rational mentality which exists above or beside his work, and which conditions or determines that work.

Formal Systems as Logically Typical. Doubtless because logicians have historically been concerned with universality and absolutism, with certainty and necessity, they have regarded mathematical and formal systems as typically and essentially logical. But if logic is an enterprise of system building, a wide gulf exists between the work of man and the omniscient and omnipotent powers implied by the absolutely necessary and certain.

Why have modern logicians turned to mathematics, to abstract and formal systems, in order to satisfy their craving for the absolute and the certain? The reverberating answer is that turning away from particulars, from details of events, allows for stability and fixity. To evacuate events, to leave the skeleton of things, has always appeared as a step toward solidity and perpetuity.

Illumination on this point is provided by the classic condemnation of Mill's allegation that the propositions of mathematics constitute generalizations from experience. The basic issue is clear in the controversy with Whewell.[21] The latter, a Kantian, emphasized the permanence and validity of mathematical principles and propositions. Hence he argued for *a priori* factors, for the necessity and givenness of axioms. As Mill[22] put it, for those who hold to Whewell's view the truth of axioms is perceived *a priori* by the "constitution of the mind itself."

Mill, on the other hand, rejected the proposition of fixed mathematical principles or axioms not empirically derived. In the extreme, then, even $2 + 2 = 4$ may not be true on another planet. The lesson here is that the opponents in the Mill-Whewell controversy simply build on two improbable notions of mind. For Whewell mind was a unified entity basic to all proposition making, while for Mill mind consisted simply of a series of associated states. The latter type of mind did not allow for any *a priori* principles—that is, permanent and primary propositions beyond experience.

What is often overlooked is that Mill's logic is just as absolutistic as that of the rationalist or *a priorist*. The difference lies simply in the constructs employed. Since Mill, no more than his opponents, is concerned with concrete propositional products derived from contacts with actual things, there is no merit in his denying preexperiential principles or axioms as tools for organizing systems of propositions. On the other hand, we must recognize the humanistic source of the most abstruse and solidly established mathematico-deductive system.

The *a priori*-experience controversy is neatly solved by considering actual system-building procedures. When we look upon system products as the outcome of personal and cultural evolutions, we see how systems can be set up with a very tight connection between premise and conclusion, such that the latter follows directly from the former. But this is not incompatible with the activity of constructing the system in the first place. Moreover, this view allows for the construction of such systems as imply objective relations between events, relations which force the construction of tightly knit systems. It would not, however, permit any absolute or nonpostulational construction for mathematics.

[21] Mill, System; Whewell, History.

[22] System, I, p. 262.

D. *Operational Systems*

Operational systems emphasize executive action. They consist of structures or organizations of techniques, methods, and work plans. Although operational systems are conditioned by the things operated upon, the factor stressed is the interbehavioral feature of the structured situation.

Logicians willing to renounce the exalted character of abstract systems need not hesitate to number among operational products every sort of prescription or recipe, whether the ordering operations are performed in the kitchen or pharmaceutical laboratory. To be sure, such structuring of prescriptive operations may be very differently rated or evaluated from other systems; nevertheless, as a system it differs only in detail from the most abstruse mathematical or logical systemizing.

(1) *Chemical Analysis.* The immediate problem here is to differentiate five cation groups and then to isolate the three members of the first group—namely, lead, mercury, and silver.[23]

Step 1. Adjust acidity of original solution and precipitate with HCl.
    The following cations will precipitate as chlorides:
    Cations Pb^{++}, Hg_2^{++}, Ag^+.
    Chlorides $PbCl_2$, Hg_2, $AgCl$.
Step 2. Acidify solution and precipitate with H_2S.
    The following cations will precipitate as sulfides:
    Cations Pb^{++}, Bi^{+++}, Cu^{++}, Cd^{++}, Hg^{++}, As^{+++}, As^{++++}, Sb^{+++}, Sn^{++}, Sn^{++++}.
    Sulfides PbS, Bi_2S_3, CuS, CdS, HgS, As_2S_3, SnS, SnS_2, etc.
Step 3. Add the proper amount of ammonia and H_2S to the solution.
    The following cations will precipitate as sulfides:
    Cations Zn^{++}, Ni^{++}, Co^{++}, Mn^{++}, Fe^{++}.
    Sulfides ZnS, NiS, CoS, MnS, FeS.
    The following cations will precipiate as hydroxides:
    Cations Cr^{+++}, Al^{+++}.
    Hydroxides $Cr(OH)_3$, $Al(OH)_3$.
Step 4. Adjust alkalinity and add NH_4Cl and $(NH_4)_2CO_3$.
    The following cations will precipitate as carbonates:
    Cations Ba^{++}, Sr^{++}, Ca^{++}.
    Carbonates $BaCO_3$, $SrCo_3$, $CaCO_3$.
    The solution will contain the following cations:
    Na^+, K^+, Mg^{++}.
Step 5. To precipitate of Step 1, containing $PbCl_2$, Hg_2Cl_2, and $AgCl$, add boiling H_2O.
Step 6. To confirm Pb^{++} add K_2CrO_4 to solution and precipitate $PbCrO_4$.

[23] The materials for this illustration have been drawn primarily from Meldrum and Daggett, Textbook.

Step 7. To residue from solution in Step 5, containing Hg_2Cl_2 and AgCl, add NH_3 and precipitate black Hg and $HgNH_2Cl$; this confirms Hg_2^{++}.

Step 8. Acidify solution from Step 7 with HNO_3; the presence of white precipitate AgCl confirms presence of Ag^+.

This system is, of course, simply a skeleton of the elaborate set of directions which imply many other operations that the analyst may be expected to carry out. It is assumed, for example, that he is working on a level beyond the point where the system of operations includes the elementary directions to keep the utensils clean, to boil and pour chemicals a certain way, etc., etc.

(2) *Solution of a mathematical problem.*

To differentiate $3x^2 + 5$ the procedure may be structured in the five following steps.

Step 1.

$$\text{Arrange } y = 3x^2 + 5$$

The operation here is simply preparing the situation for the necessary future operations.

Step 2.

$$y + \Delta y = 3(x + \Delta x)^2 + 5$$
$$= 3x^2 + 6x \cdot \Delta x + 3(\Delta x)^2 + 5$$

This step involves another preparatory operation, that of replacing x by $x + \Delta x$ and then a calculative determination of the value of the function $y + \Delta y$.

Step 3.

$$y + \Delta y = 3x^2 + 6 \cdot \Delta x + 3(\Delta x)^2 + 5$$
$$\underline{y = 3x^2 \qquad\qquad\qquad\qquad + 5}$$
$$y = \qquad\qquad 6x \cdot \Delta x + 3(\Delta x)^2$$

Here the given value of the function is subtracted from the new value to determine the value of y, the increment of the function.

Step 4.

$$\frac{\Delta y}{\Delta x} = 6x + 3 \cdot \Delta x.$$

This operation divides the increment of the function by the increment of the independent variable.

Step 5.

$$\frac{dy}{dx} = 6x$$

The derivative is obtained by finding the limit of the quotient of step 4, when the increment of the independent variable (Δx) varies and approaches zero as a limit.

SCIENTIFIC STRUCTURE AND DEDUCTIVE SYSTEMS

To consider the place of deduction in science aids greatly in elucidating the nature of system products. Fundamentally, this problem concerns the efficacy of science in the control and prediction of events. Writers who incline toward a rationalistic, and even moderately absolutistic, view[24] attribute the rigor and completeness of scientific structures to a basic deductive core. This view is generalized into the claim that science is, at bottom, deductive, and that the tradition of inductive science is false.

It is argued that prediction, as an important scientific principle, constitutes the drawing of a conclusion from rigorously established premises. Undoubtedly, the ideal of invariable relations and necessary connections, or abstract implication, is overstressed, whereas actual interactions with complex recondite events are minimized.

Instead of arguing for a deductive faculty or power—some autonomous reasoning technique—why not observe that proof and rigor are achieved by setting up a symmetric or circular structure of propositions? Such constructed systems we may properly call deductive. When scientific workers erect a fairly complete and well articulated system it may be viewed in two ways. First, knowing one part of the system, we can deduce the others. On the other hand, prediction may be described as anticipating that the particular elements (items) will be found at their particular points of articulation in the system. To concern oneself with system construction and system products keeps one's speculations within the domain of natural action, instead of allowing them to fall into the abyss of transcendentalism.

INTERRELATION OF SYSTEMIZING OPERATIONS AND MATERIALS

If logical work consists of system building then the processes or operations must be appropriate to the things worked upon. In

---

[24] For example, Cohen, Reason.

every other field this point is a commonplace; in logic it has been obscured by several traditional but false views.

Foremost among the latter is the formalistic fallacy, responsible for the view that formalized structures exist independently of things and of the auspices under which they are generated. In other words, the actual work of system building is completely disregarded. The formalization of acts, processes, and descriptions is undoubtedly a necessary and valid technique for organizing the elements of a system. The importance and use of this technique, however, is derived precisely from the fact that the elements are located in a definite set of coordinates. In other words, to formalize events, or our operations upon them, does not allow any retreat from specific conditions. On the contrary, effective formalization carries with it an index to the circumstances under which the formalization occurs (p. 77). Hence it is alogical to regard formal propositions as holding for a genuine and transcendent universe of discourse, or to erect general logic as the organization and transformation of "language."

What constitutes a logical system in one frame of reference is illogical in another. In some logical systems, for instance, it is eminently proper to stress formality on the basis of, say, noncontradiction, but even here one must shun any arbitrary acceptance of a criterion. Non-Euclidean geometry contradicts Euclidean. Surely this only means that we must take account of the specific conditions of our systems, even if they are abstract mathematical organizations of elements.

To treat the materials of a mechanical object as though they were sentence things obviously violates the first principle of system construction. Nothing can be more detrimental, unless it be summarily to declare that logic is an abstractionistic enterprise which organizes sentences.

Another fallacy concerns projection. Once a system has been formulated, it is overlooked that the product has been projected. The difficulty is that one identifies the projected system with some form of autonomous entity, without regard to the particular things which have occupied the system builder.

A variant fallacy is confusing cultural customs—that is, structures built up through successions of time—with nature. Abstract logics are the historical projections of cultural groups.

And finally, the universalistic trend in logic favors overlooking the materials worked upon, since the assumption is made that there are generalized rules for organizing systems and that the manipulations are more important than the materials structured.

From the viewpoint of the present treatise, that logic is an enterprise of constructing organized wholes out of relevant or selected items in a specific situation or in a given field, certain conclusions follow.

In the first place, since we are always concerned with a particular job, we can never place *a priori* limits to the factors and processes involved. Otherwise logic soon turns into illogic. Whatever processes we isolate as logical operations are only random samples taken for convenience from the records embodied in logical treatises. To these must be added other processes, both formal and informal. Some of the latter may be regarded as auxiliary; that is, they are manipulating and experimenting activities which lead to an acquaintance with ideas, techniques, and relevant methods of system construction.

In the second place, we need to be alert to the great hiatus existing between the generalized and fixed descriptions of what we do, the methods by which we do it, and the actual work. Recall the frequently mentioned fact that while we can throw our reasoning into a syllogistic form of description our reasoning behavior may actually be casual, uncertain, and hesitant. From our standpoint, to ignore the simple and casual details of our materials, and our approach to them, staticizes system building.

Characteristic Variations of System Products

System products vary on the basis of many factors, such as the motives of the system creator, his methods of work, and the elements with which he operates. Out of these variations arise the following system types.

Tight and Loose Systems. Tight systems are typified by the absolutistic structures designed to be impenetrable and without exit. Their builders are motivated by the ideals of rigid and nonexceptionable rules. Obviously, such tautological systems require arbitrary techniques of construction, and are usually formal, as well as circular. They are built out of self-fashioned words.

In some cases, however, tightly knit systems may be constructed out of concrete things, but in such instances the materials are carefully selected and arranged on a preconceived plan. Tight content systems may be illustrated by an organization of selected properties of things, as in the classification tree of Porphyry.

Systems which stress content are relatively loose and tentative. But loose systems may be so characterized because the builders allow for contingence, for factors dependent on local needs and conditions.

Complete and Expanding Systems. When building systems which stress the form or product aspect, one may adopt such rules and criteria as to produce finished and permanent structures. Contrariwise, to stress primarily the materials or building operations allows for expansion, correction, and development of the finished products. What stage of completion is attained depends upon the particular building blocks, as well as upon the persistence and curiosity of the system builder.

Discovered and Constructed Systems. While every system is constructed, specific systems vary in the freedom of organization and according to the resistance of the systemized materials. Thing or content systems allow great scope for selection and invention. Still, the various manipulations are conditioned by the type of materials organized. Descriptive and formal systems afford greater scope for the production of system products.

At bottom the issue of discovery and construction comes down to the ratio of c/d. When working with geometries one is restricted to three ranges, with similar basic starting points in the relations with which one works. Only relatively different types of system can be constructed by beginning with circular or rectilinear relations. When occupied with generalized features of physiological and anatomical events, one may choose between (1) a continuum of one-dimensional time, plus a three dimensional space, and (2) a four dimensional time-space continuum. Among other choices we may mention (1) discontinuous vs. continuous items, and (2) individual vs. mass events.

Witting and Unwitting Systems. No matter how analytic and searching a systematist may be, there are always influencing factors of which he may be completely or partially unaware. The formalistic system builder seeking or assuming absolute knowledge asserts that "we know the correctness of the syllogism in its abstract form (i.e., when it is stated in terms of variables) without needing any appeal to experience."[25] All that really happens is that he either does not know, or ignores, the fact that he is talking about a system product.

To be oblivious to the history and surrounding circumstances of syllogistic or other formalistic systems is to risk confusing a system or assertion product with some sort of Platonic existence, and ignorance with *a priori* knowledge.

Whether or not a system builder knows the origin and nature of a system or its components depends upon the possibility of tracing the system's cultural evolution. What evolves as a cultural product—a set of syllogistic triplets, for instance—should not be taken as some absolute set of relations. Very few logicians stress the fact that the angle sum of triangles is an evolved system, not a Platonic Real capable of being known *a priori*.

Absolutistic logicians unwittingly foster the cult of ignorance. Writers realistically or Platonically inclined argue against the pertinence of history, and for the potency of analysis, in determining truth or establishing fact. What this view amounts to is a plea for ignorance concerning the work of system construction. Validity or truth established through a cultural process is accepted, along with the implication that the cultural factors may well remain in oblivion.

[25] Russell, Introduction, p. 204.

CHAPTER XVI

INSTRUMENTS FOR SYSTEM CONSTRUCTION

Models, Schemata, and Formulae as Logical Instruments

SYSTEM building requires tools. The investigation of logical situations uncovers a formidable array of instruments and apparatus aids. These tools, so effectively enabling us to carry out our system-building operations, vary extensively in form, specific use, and technical efficiency. They are all similar, however, in reflecting the fact that an individual is engaged in fashioning a product.

The very tools we find it necessary to forge in the present chapter are a good illustration. These instruments, which we construct in order to systematize our knowledge concerning logical tools, are really valid for all kinds of systemological situations. We name our tools: (1) *models*, (2) *schemata*, and (3) *formulae*. Every system-making enterprise requires one or two of these types; often all three are used in complex situations.

Models stress primarily the materials and products of the system-building situation. They pertain to the properties and operations of things and events. Functionally, models are analogically descriptive. For example, mechanical models duplicate on a small and manageable scale the machines that at the time are only designed and projected.

Schemata emphasize the constructive work involved in system building. Such tools are either employed as scaffolding or as the essentially operative means of carrying out some project. As such they facilitate the development of new systems, as well as the enlargement of those already set up.

Formulae operate primarily by way of fixing and symbolizing items used and systems attained. Bracketing propositions with formulae suggests the enormous number and importance of referential and calculated procedures in system building.

Logical and Scientific Instruments

Proportional to the importance of logical instruments is the difficulty of analyzing and describing them. To adopt the threefold classification mentioned above, we admit, constitutes only a very elementary step in handling them. An item in our favor, however, is the fact that owing to similarities in logical and scientific behavior[1] we may profit from our familiarity with scientific models to illustrate system-building tools. Formulae and schemata such as propositions, algorithms and theories are employed as aids both in science and logic. Carnot's heat cycle, for instance, and Maxwell's demon-operated sluice gates were constructed in the interest of particular heat theory and general scientific system building. They are in all respects similar to the instruments created for primarily logical purposes.

LOGICAL INSTRUMENTS AS PRODUCTS

The production of logical instruments may be legitimately compared with tool making of any sort. In each case the basic event is the system builders' constructive activity, which, when properly emphasized, restrains us from overstressing the product. Neither the system product nor the description of it must be allowed to conceal the definite enterprise. To adhere tenaciously to the crude data of system production finally brings us back to the constructive act, no matter what approach we first make.

What is true for logical systems in general is true for the instruments by means of which they are constructed. Excluded, then, are all self-sustaining and self-evident assumptions, formulae, and propositions—in brief, all conventional *a priori* principles. The Pythagorean theorem can not be false: but only because it is a part of a system so constructed as to make it true.

All such system-building tools as *logical necessity*, the distinction between *matter of fact* and *relation of ideas*, and various *implications* must be evaluated on the basis of the constructor and the situation in which they are created. To keep the constructional process in view—that is, to take seriously the product character of logical tools—is to clarify the entire logical enterprise. Likewise, the effect of school and general cultural influences on logical instruments will assume the prominence it deserves.

INTERBEHAVIORAL SOURCES OF LOGICAL INSTRUMENTS

Although tools are constructed for the particular task at hand,

---

[1] We might add everyday behavior, too, in its system-building aspects.

it is frequently possible to borrow or adapt them, instead of inventing them. Among the striking instances of tool borrowing is the adaptation of conic sections in astronomical science, complex numbers in electrical engineering,[2] matrix algebra in building up quantum mechanics,[3] and tensor calculus in constructing relativity theory.[4] Creative instruments are illustrated by the definitory fiats which result in the existence of dimensionless points and one-dimension lines.

Whether the system builder exerts himself much or little is the criterion of his originality. Adaptation and creation actions are points on a continuum, each representing interbehavior with certain things within the bounds of a logical situation. Whatever tools are used constitute constructs for a given purpose.

Any given instance of tool making is illuminated by the ratio of adaptive to initiative action required for its production. The simplest type of model or schema is, of course, the reproduction of some object on a given scale. Here the construction is based primarily on variations in appearance and magnitude. In this case the a in the a/i (adaptive-initiative) ratio is the smaller magnitude. At the other extreme is the tool in which the i is at a maximum, and where one can detect no resemblance between the original stimulus object initiating the model or schema, and the apparatus itself. In popular language the tool is asserted to be entirely imaginary, as, for instance, when the construction is arbitrary and represents no existing event. From the standpoint of interbehavioral psychology, however, there is no dearth of contact with original stimulus objects, even though the tool is extremely analogical, or, as traditional language has it, logical. The most elaborate instances of this sort of construction are not regarded as frivolous or impossible. For example, need we recoil from the fact that Vassar graduates reproduce 2.6 children?

Ratios with large i denominators fall into a range of autistic behavior, and bespeak the assertiveness of system builders. On the whole, such autistic construction is more in evidence when abstract materials are being organized.

[2] Dantzig, Number, p. 232.
[3] Born, Restless, p. 132.
[4] Bell, Development, p. 194.

THE SPECIFICITY OF LOGICAL INSTRUMENTS

Logical tools must fit the situation's requirements. Models, schemata, and formulae vary according to the type of system built. Furthermore, models, on the whole, are better adapted to practical situations. By comparison, formulae and schemata fit more closely abstruse and abstractive system building. In general, logical tools are more efficacious when they are analogical, representational, or symbolic according to the problem at hand.

LOGICAL INSTRUMENTS IN OPERATION

Logical instruments, we have said, are constructs (products) designed for interbehaving with events in order to achieve practical and intellectual orientation. We can not regard them, therefore, simply as *forms* in the traditional sense. Recall that in conventional logic a distinction is made between the formal and the material, or the formal and the contentful.[5] In other words, models for the traditional logician are logical or formal as over against the existential or the ontological.

Another way in which this distinction is made is to differentiate between concepts, on the one hand, and things, on the other. A telling illustration is Dewey's view that the law of excluded middle, for example, applies only to the formal realm, not to the ontological. Dewey does not allow for things being exclusively of one sort or another; he argues that the transition stages partake of both extremes. This is certainly reminiscent of Hegelian dialectics, which reduces ultimacy to some form of spiritualism or verbalism. According to such logic, universals are formal elements or models which are not in whole or part the things handled. Such views are rooted in the theory that logic deals with sentences and/or propositions, not with ordinary interbehavior with things. Universals are thus regarded as having merely formal, not existential being or existence.

In contrast, our interbehavioral view that logical instruments are constructs immediately introduces a new factor. The original situation may be simply some natural object, such as a stone, tree, or an organism's action. Next in the series, this original datum is reacted to by some observer. When the result of this observation

[5] Cf. vol. I, pp. 28f., 102f., 159f., 294.

is referred to or described, we have some sort of construction, whether or not regarded as a model. A genuine model is an elaborate construction for some particular purpose—personal orientation, or communication. But the most abstract construction is always continuous with the crudest contacts of individuals with things.

Envisaged as orientational tools, logical instruments are removed from any contact with metaphysical problems. On the one hand, we are free from a logic dealing with verbal abstractions remote from actual things. On the other, we avoid the implications of Platonic reals, according to which propositions or mathematical formulae are presumed to constitute realities. Logic on our basis does not therefore consist of propositions or forms which constitute an autonomous and unique realm, nor is it concerned with fundamental tautologies—with language, as the logical positivists have it. Rather, all models, no matter how elaborate, are specific interbehavioral procedures fitting a particular logician's purpose.

Because of this specificity, it is inevitable that certain elements of the construction are not derived from the crude data. Everyone, depending upon individual experience both professional and private, has various predilections for certain models. For instance, one person chooses verbal instruments as over against mathematical. Another powerful factor is the worker's cultural background. A scientist bred in a religious culture sees no incongruity in using creative and spiritual ingredients to account for a certain event, whereas another person finds such elements extremely objectionable. In each case there is a thorough mixture of personal experience with cultural conditions.

Logical and Nonlogical Instruments Compared

Although there is no fundamental difference between the instruments of science and logic, such that we can expound the latter by referring to the former, variations do exist which are neither unimportant nor negligible. To summarize these differences adds to our understanding of both.

The basic variation, of course, is simply that scientific instruments are forged for immediate investigative purposes. On the whole, it is informing to regard such instruments as *Hilfsbegriffe*,

Gedanken-Krücken, und Rechenpfennige, as German writers say.[6] Logical instruments, on the other hand, are more intimately involved with system building as such. Naturally these distinctions are relative, since scientific work may well stress systemization, while logical work may emphasize precise investigation.

In a brief but informing discussion by Rosenblueth and Wiener on the role of models in science,[7] scientific and logical instruments are identified. These writers regard models as central necessities of scientific procedure and divide them into (a) intellectual or formal and (b) material types. Pitching their discussion on a definitely operational basis, they consider a series of tools ranging from commonsense models to scientific theories. Formal models are not kept within the bounds of work with things and the problems they evoke. In the limit:

> The ideal formal model would be one which would cover the entire universe, which would agree with it in complexity, and which would have a one to one correspondence with it.[8]

Theoretical models thus move out to comprehensive system making, unrestricted by actual contacts with events.

The limits and character of intellectual tools have been well demonstrated by the distinction which Rankine[9] made between abstractive and hypothetical procedures in science. The former are assumed to start with concrete data; the latter to be more autistic in constructional technique. Recently, Dingle[10] has identified the extreme hypothetical procedure with quantum mechanics, and the extreme abstractive method with relativity theory.

LOGICAL INSTRUMENTS AS MINIATURE SYSTEMS

We have already indicated that in some cases system-making instruments are really themselves miniature systems. In conventional logic a truth table may be regarded either as a schema for building a large logical system or looked upon as a small but finished structural system. Similarly, a graph from one vantage point may be an autonomous system, whereas from another it is

---

[6] Winderlich, Ding, p. 29.
[7] Role.
[8] Ibid., p. 320.
[9] Miscellaneous, p. 245.
[10] Science, chaps. 4, 5.

only an item in a larger system. Moreover, a theory concerning certain specific events or some general structurization of data may be merely an aid in building an extensive thing or theory system.

Thus we achieve a genuine relativity of systems and tools. Models and schemata which in one situation comprise mediational factors in system-building enterprises, in another are end results or products. The primary differentiating criterion of model and schema instruments is independence or autonomy. When we adopt the interbehavioral viewpoint, there is no difficulty in distinguishing between those situations in which models are smaller and more immediate units, and those in which they become more comprehensive, and, in general, systematic.

Logical Instruments as System Items

When system building is treated as strictly operational, it is not surprising that instrument products may serve as items in a system. For example, the classical points, lines, and surfaces of geometry were invented as instruments for organizing the facts of space. Once these instruments were constructed it became very difficult to distinguish them sharply from the items in a space system. In physics, too, we often find that models or formulae, originally designed to aid in systemizing events, come to be entities making up the system in question.

Materials of Systemological Instruments

The materials with which system-building instruments are forged naturally vary with the tool types. We plan to discuss only the general kinds of available material, irrespective of final product.

Fixated behavior of various sorts, traditionally called concepts and ideas, provides extremely important materials. To begin with, concepts and ideas constitute forms of responses to things and situations. But along with attitudes, beliefs, and conjectures, they become fixated and transcribed as tools in systemizing things. To such fixated behavior we owe the conventional assertion that imagination is a tremendously important feature of science and logic.

Words and signs, as constituents of propositions, of symbols, and of mathematical patterns, also serve as materials. Mathematical patterns are exemplified by various types of curves and their equations. Frequently, such curves, instead of being regarded as analogical or descriptive constructs, are mistaken for the originals they are presumed to represent.

The materials so far considered—namely, fixated acts, signs, and words—are simple and uncompounded. But as we have already indicated, they soon become integrated into all sorts of amalgams and mixtures, and can therefore be hierarchically ordered. Thus it is possible to arrange in different series a profuse variation of curves, icons, diagrams, symbols, schemata (nomographs, abacs), tables (of functions, relations), scales, algorithms, etc.

The Orientational Function of Logical Instruments

Logical tools, we have seen, vary according to the type of inter-behavioral situation for which they are developed. A clear-cut difference between them is whether they are used for general or special systems.[11] A more intimate differentiation depends upon whether the system builder is engaged in intellectual or nonintellectual interbehavior. For intellectual operations four general types of tools may be indicated: (1) representational, (2) analogically descriptive, (3) explanatory, and (4) speculative fictional. The amount of autonomous construction involved is a pivotal criterion of differentiation, and depends upon whether the model makers are interacting with natural or constructed events.

Representational Tools. Consider those situations in which there is the least addition of an autonomous sort. As the name *representational* suggests, the operator faces a situation in which he merely wants to indicate or represent some object, as in the case of graphing the figures of a table or producing a model of a building in order to indicate its general form. Interaction at this level does not depart very far from the first stage of contact with things, or beyond what we may call the zero point—namely, the simplest contact with an object.

Take another example. An individual has just observed for the first time the rising tide on a beach. Now in order to fixate his impression, or to tell someone about it, he develops a drawing which in some form represents the original change in the sand. In the

[11] Hempel and Oppenheim, **Studies.**

same way, a map constitutes a model construction of this type. So far as systems go, we need postulate only that a set of these models is put together for some purpose. Undoubtedly, such a system may be regarded as the simplest in the logical domain.

Analogically Descriptive Tools. When the original objects are too complicated to be represented simply, they must be referred to in a more constructive manner. That is, one adds more or less to them. Samples of such tools are verbal descriptions, which always involve some metaphorical elements. Mathematical formulae of all sorts, built on the definite analysis or measurements of the properties of things, are excellent illustrations of analogically descriptive tools.

Explanatory Tools. On this level of interaction the general orientation is one of understanding the events handled. In the case of natural happenings, instruments are designed to relate observed objects to other objects. Or, when in contact with artifacts, scaffolds are erected in order to reach the events in question. Fundamental illustrations are the graphic representations of numbers, and, in general, the geometrizing of numerical relations. The differentiation between positive and negative numbers as points in lines either to the right or left of a zero point constitutes such a tool, as does the construction of the statement that negative numbers are the addition of what one owes as over against the enumeration of what one actually possesses.

Speculative Fictional Tools. As implied, such tools are constructed for interbehaving with imaginary things. The constructional factor, therefore, completely outweighs the direct-contact factor, since the whole process is substitutional. Whatever the purpose—whether it is an attempt to account for something, or to control people and situations—one verbally or graphically creates objects, processes, forces, etc., without much connection with actual things. Such are systems of demons, universes, and deities. At best, a constructional procedure of this fashion is guided at long range by assuming similarities between observed things.

In no sense is it necessary to exclude from our domain of system building or instrument construction the most elaborately abstract systems. Perfectly arbitrary starting points and materials find their places in the continuity of system construction. Even such tenuous and diaphanous materials as spiritual entities may be the building blocks. It would be fatal, indeed, to any kind of logical theory to exclude systems constructed by poets and metaphysicians. In such cases, of course, it is necessary to indicate the extrapolatory lengths to which constructors have gone. The expert observer never fails to trace step by step the system builder's starting point, no matter how far the final construction transcends natural events. In this sense an objective or naturalistic psychology becomes an essential factor in all logical theory.

Instruments in Various Orientational Situations

The following examples of instrument making and their use in different fields of study throw into relief a number of fundamental problems.

Logic. Among outstanding logical instruments we must count the general and comprehensive syllogism. Historically, of course, the syllogism has been considered as a process of correct reasoning, but modern logicians admit that it is simply a sort of construction into which reasoning, when made into a specialized form of procedure, can be placed. Perhaps the basic character of logical instruments is even better revealed by the specialized syllogistic figures—for example, Barbara and Celarent. Incidentally, the inspection of syllogisms indicates precisely how instrument constructions are projected into the world of reasoning, and then made into the stimulus objects interacted with, instead of being used merely for certain orientational purposes.

The universe of discourse is another familiar logical instrument. Whether regarded as a classificatory mechanism or as a set of boundary stones to delimit a domain, it is a product constructed for actual system-building enterprises.

Of considerable interest are the recently developed so-called logical languages, such as those of logical positivism. Syntactic and semantic characteristics of ordinary speech are employed as a basis to develop language structures for transforming such systems. In this case, as well as in that of the historical syllogism, the scaffold is confused with the building for the construction of which the scaffold is merely a tool.

Additional technical logical instruments are represented by the various coherent and symmetrical word or symbol structures designed to orient workers in formal thinking or reasoning situations. An example is:

If every .... is .... and .... is a .... then .... is ....[12]

Mathematics. As the domain of relations, mathematics is preeminently the field where representational instruments are copiously employed. Innumerable models, schemata, and formulae have been constructed, beginning with geometric figures and number ratios, as in the relation of strings in Pythagorean theory.

An interesting type of mathematical instrument is found in Klein's description of the *a, b,* and *c* plans of mathematical development.[13] In his *a* plan the development begins with the formal theory of equations—that is, operating with rational integral functions and handling cases in which algebraic equations can be solved by radicals. Next, is the treatment of the idea of power and its inverses, which is basic to logarithms. Then follows the handling of transcendental or trigonometric functions, and, finally, algebraic analysis. Plan *b* is dominated by the ideas of analytic geometry; it centers around the graphic representation of various functions and the geometric treatment of curves. Plan *c* is algorithmic; it concerns systems of calculation, in the sense of calculating with letters, and, in general, using calculative models for mathematical development.

Such mathematical constructs as classes, constituting numbers, or classes, types, and hierarchies of numbers, excellently exemplify products of the tool-making enterprise. Other samples are signs and symbols, algorithms, formulae and schemata of many varieties.

Deserving special mention are such instruments as the diagrams and schemata representing systemizing operations and results. A comparative gnomon diagram, which clarifies the principle that the sum of any group of consecutive odd numbers, beginning with one, equals the square of the number of terms in the group, is shown in the accompanying figure (Fig. 1).

No less effective mathematical instruments are the variant constructions for demonstrating geometric propositions. A glance at two (Figs. 2 and 3) of the 35 or more figures constructed to prove the Pythagorean theorem[14] is instructive here.

[12] See vol. I, p. 314.
[13] Elementary, p. 77f.
[14] Hoffman, Pythagorische.

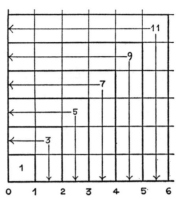

Figure 1

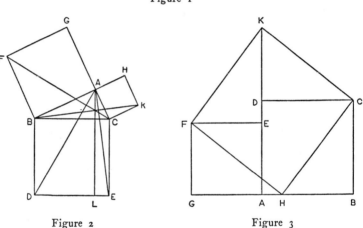

Figure 2　　　　　　　　　Figure 3

Physics. In its range from practical technology to all-embracing theoretical systemization, physics has assiduously fostered every variety of logical instrument.

For the technological department of physics the important type of instrument is, of course, the mechanical model. Even today, with the increasing ascendence of field theory, Kelvin's assertion is still valid—namely, that unless one can produce a mechanical model one does not really understand the processes to be studied.

On the all-or-none principle that "not all physical events are mechanical" the view developed that mechanical models should be extruded from physics. Hence, the model of the electromagnetic field which stresses not bodies in interbehavior but something between them. Problems connected with the deflection of the magnetic needle, and with the ether medium for wave transmission, suggested the invention of new descriptive and explanatory instruments.

Such inventions as tubes and lines of force carried the descriptive constructs of electrical science from things to the more abstractive domain of energies and processes not directly visible. To construct systems concerning such events called for tools of a schematic and operational sort. Directions and specifications were included to provide orientation with respect to particular types of physical events.

More subtle, naturally, are the various symbolic instruments developed on the basis of mathematical techniques. A striking illustration is the use of the calculus to describe and explain motion, with the result that mathematical models are employed to staticize motion as a means of controlling dynamic events, as in D'Alembert's principle.

Another type of physics instrument is the reduction of such natural events as colors and sounds to wave frequencies. In this instance the instrumental character of models is strikingly evident, since events like color, sound, and radiation lack any similarity to the numerical symbols which represent them.

Biology. The consideration of biologically oriented instruments for system building at once brings to the fore the distinction between large- and small-scale systems. Among the former stands preeminently the construct of the organic character of the cosmos, a conception already present in Greek thought when the cosmos was regarded as alive and breathing. In more recent times the construct of the cosmos as an organism has been presumed to help greatly in elucidating ontological problems.[15]

Not far from such cosmic systems is the building of a series of mechanisms for comprehending biological things and events. To make organisms and their parts into bits or portions of machines is to construct a wholly gratuitous and excessive analogy as a substitute for more or less elaborate system making. We call such analogical constructions cosmic because they depart from specific structure and operation. These models may be of considerable interest and value, but they do not enlighten us concerning characteristics of the originals.

[15] Whitehead, Science; Needham, Biologist's.

The tools for building fairly small systems, close to biological events, we designate as intermediate biological instruments. Here we may cite such constructs as natural selection, adaptation, species, and functions. Whether or not definitely recognized as such by biologists, a potent form of instrument construction has been the various classifications of organisms basic not only to taxonomic but also to genetic biological investigation. The classification of Linnaeus provides us our best example of an explanatory form of schema.

The verbal construction of biological evolution is likewise an excellent illustration of a schema for the relationship and development of all organisms. As one might expect, most biological models and schemata are unique to the organic field. Prominent among biological tools is the oil-drop model, which, by its properties of viscosity and sensitivity to temperature changes, simulates activities and properties of organisms. The iron wire of neural conduction,[16] though sometimes severely criticized,[17] has played a large part in physiological circles. Not to be ignored either are the many models and schemata concerning brain seats and centers. Recall the hierarchical model of neural operations as a telephone or telegraph system in which the nervous system is made into a large complex of centers controlling the remainder of the organism. The scope of such instruments can be measured by the enormous substitution of alleged brain and neural control for events involving complex factorial fields.

Immunological literature offers especially interesting biological instruments. The lock-and-key model of the operation and effectiveness of toxins, antitoxins, and other antibodies is a paragon of instrumental construction for system building.

Psychology. The instruments of psychological system making have been modified again and again to bring the constructions into some connection with events. This history starts with the development of a purely fictitious soul, or mind, to set in place of the person's behavior as the psychological crude datum. Psychology, of course, did not begin as a science on a proper objective basis, such as the Aristotelian treatises made possible. Instead, it was completely dominated by theological presuppositions.

---

[16] Lillie, Transmission of activation; Physical; Transmission of physiological.

[17] Rosenblueth and Wiener, Role, p. 318.

Through the contacts which psychology gradually developed with actual events there began the century-old attempts to construct brain mechanisms with which to describe the workings of the psyche, and thus to account for the existence and effectiveness of these tenuous processes in complex behavioral situations. Hence the contrasting models, cooperatively constructed by psychologists and biologists, which are designed to differentiate between voluntary and conscious action operating on the basis of cerebral functions and involuntary, or unconscious action, working on the basis of reflex arcs.

Neural models in psychological situations are employed to effect a transformation of crude data. The procedure is to assume that neural mechanisms are somehow related to psychic processes. Accordingly, the confidence which system builders derive from their preoccupation with the palpable nervous system leads to the continuation of the view that psychological events are actually implicated with psychic processes.[18]

An historically interesting model constructed for building a scientific psychological system is the "threshold of consciousness." This model is a subfeature of a larger system developed by analogy with various mechanical models of particles crossing from one region to another. Its character is obvious when one considers the original event being described—namely, the availability or nonavailability of things for reaction. In other words, an object must be of a certain size in order to be seen—in order, that is, to cross the "threshold of consciousness."

A construction related to the threshold mechanism is sense distance, which vacillates between a model and a schema. Essentially, it fixes intervals between things available for reaction.

Other distinctive psychological models consist of apparatuses, such as a chemical analogy for conditioning. In principle, this type of instrument resembles the oil-drop model for biological behavior.

The history of psychology affords us a series of schema created for the purpose of making plausible the inexistent, yet effective, powers of mind. Interesting examples are (1) the Wundtian chemical analogy, and (2) the Jamesian functional analogy from biology.

[18] Kantor, Problems.

Social Sciences. An impressive illustration of system-building tools in this field is the Spencerian invention of the organismic character of the state or society. That political or other human-group entities constitute organisms is a construction which plays an extensive role in descriptive and explanatory systems of political science. Other examples from the same domain include economic man, the average man, living wage, and standard of living.

Techniques in Instrument Production

How well the techniques of instrument making help to achieve organization and pattern is a measure of their effectiveness. Of the many sources of variation in tool making the operators may stress either the system product or the work of constructing it. Again, the system may be more an organization of materials than a carrying out of systemizing specifications. In every case the techniques employed reflect the behavior of an isolated system maker, or a plurality of such workers integrated in schools, logical traditions or general cultural groups.

Naturally, the particular technique chosen coincides with the system maker's interest, as well as with the cultural backgrounds influencing his work. Certain cultural milieux, for example, provide a system maker with a relatively large measure of freedom, whereas another individual is seriously limited by political or religious controls.

Nor can we overlook the original motivation of the system maker, as, for instance, his attempt to achieve simplicity or symmetry, or, in general, some sort of connectedness. In other cases his motivation may be the desire to control events or their factors in systems, or merely to obtain the satisfaction of understanding or becoming familiar with the materials handled.

Sampling the behavioral techniques we find the following uniquely representative:

Iconography. In simple cases, and in those involving immediately manipulative objects, tool making consists to a great extent of producing an icon or a picture of a thing. A similar process is that of symbolizing objects in order to manipulate them, as in drawing curves which rise and fall with the rise and fall, increase or decrease of the original objects represented.

Abstraction. We have already noticed that system builders constantly resort to abstractive processes; for example, in dealing with periodicities we omit differences and slight variations; or in certain mathematical operations we select our populations or attribute certain class marks to the variables we use.

De Novo Construction. While there is no absolute difference between what we might call free creation and pictorial representation, there are variations which can be measured in terms of the distance one retreats from actual contact with the things with which one interbehaves. Thus the creational process in constructing logical tools must be regarded as highly distinctive and variant.

CHAPTER XVII

CATEGORIES AND SYSTEM BUILDING

CATEGORIES AND LOGIC

A SUPERFICIAL examination of logical works seems to indicate that categorial problems are no longer treated in an explicit manner. Actually there can be no diminution of interest in categories, for they are inevitably involved with all logical processes and products. The fashion of neglecting categorial issues simply reflects the fact that logic is not regarded as system building. As a result the following historical misinterpretations have predominated: Categories are (1) ontologically abstract characteristics of being, (2) ultimate elements of thought, or (3) linguistic or grammatical elements.

Every systemizing operation, either casual and practical classification of things or construction of elaborate technical systems of science or mathematics, reveals the importance and prevalence of categories. As the enormous range of system building suggests, categories constitute such widely differing items as quality, quantity, event, and relation, used by scientific and ontological system builders, as well as the defined and undefined terms, variables, and constants of the formalistic or symbolistic logicians. When categories are operationally described, all the different varieties can be interrelated, both as items and as criteria and limits for system building.

NATURE AND OPERATION OF CATEGORIES

Though categories as system-building instruments are not exclusively related to conventional logic or philosophy, it is convenient to illustrate their nature and operation by means of historical category systems. Indeed, traditional category systems exemplify the entire process of system building, as well as the characteristics of logical products. No matter what criterion a system builder adopts, his logical products reflect such typical categories as completeness, universality, indispensability, and ultimacy.

What, then, are some of the characteristic properties of categories? From the traditional standpoint at least, they constitute basic descriptive or evaluative factors for system construction. In order to build ontological, cosmic, or epistemological systems, philosophers have had to invent intellectual tools for identifying, characterizing, relating, and organizing the items comprising their particular type of system. Logicians such as the mathematical or symbolic system builders, who are interested not in substances but in formal operations, still search for such abiding systemic factors as indefinables and the *a priori*. Though they do not use the term *category* and regard themselves as somewhat independent of the general categorial tradition, they nevertheless *operate* with categories. Think merely of the various symbols and operators of symbolic logic.

Categories, then, are basic materials of all conventional logics, whether Aristotelian, Kantian, or Hegelian. In Aristotelian logic categories assume the form of raw-material terms—namely, symbols and substitutes for classes. In Kantian logic, categories constitute the basic constructs underlying all analytical processes, and, taken together with the aesthetic forms and dialectical ideas, they make up the building materials of all intellectual systems. A similar role is played by the categories of Hegelian logic. Since considerable information concerning categories may be gathered from their cultural evolution, we glance briefly at the history of category systems.

EVOLUTION OF CATEGORIAL SYSTEMS

Pre-Aristotelian Categorization. Philosophical or, better perhaps, technical categories were first constructed by the pre-Aristotelian cosmologists of the Greek tradition (vol. I, chap. 3). Striving toward a universal and simple summing up of nature's essence, early Greek thinkers constructed such categories as water, fire, air, and the unbounded. That these categories were implicit constructions for achieving large-scale results in man's orientation to reality was not, of course, recognized by the thinkers of the period. Their procedure, however primitive, was essentially objective. They pushed toward the primary stuff or action of all things, without the elaborate and sophisticated analysis represented in Aristotle's organized logical corpus.

Aristotelian Categorization. In Aristotle's time, with the evolution of a definite appreciation of expository problems, categories were set up in a simple linguistic way as an attempt to summarize all the verbal elements necessary to describe specific things. On the basis of current grammatical knowledge Aristotle presented ten categories,[1] which subsequently became the paradigms for all categorization attempts. Categorization for Aristotle was explicit and sophisticated, although from the standpoint of later periods the whole procedure appeared remarkably simple. It is traditionally recognized that Aristotle merely set down words to represent the various characteristics of things. Another not less felicitous interpretation is that he simply attempted to describe things in their diverse appearances and relations.

The Ten Aristotelian Categories

1. substance	6. time
2. quantity	7. situation
3. quality	8. status
4. relation	9. action
5. place	10. passion (being acted on)

Obviously, the categories listed above are elementary objective descriptive terms which would scarcely be different, no matter what language was spoken by their constructor.

Post-Aristotelian Categorization. Not until the development of science in modern times were new categorization principles introduced. This does not mean, however, that the interpretation of *given* categories has remained the same.[2] On the contrary, from the earliest medieval reintroduction of Greek learning into Europe the distinction between existence and thought, and the superiority of the latter, have made categories more and more into symbols for subjectivistic, or thought, qualities.

Kantian Categorization. Not only did Kant adopt the personalistic character of categories, but he modified them to accord with the Newtonian physics current in his day. One of his most fundamental alterations was to differentiate between the actual, the possible, and the necessary. Kant conceived of categories as the most essential thought forms under which, or by means of which, elabo-

---

[1] According to von Hartmann (Kategorienlehre, p. ix) Aristotle took over his categories from the Platonic school.

[2] See vol. 1, p. 48f., for discussion of Scholastic transformation of Aristotelian logic.

rately abstracted things could be organized or synthesized, rather than as a straightforward set of predications of existing things. This is indicated in the accompanying categorial schema:

The Kantian Categories

I *Quantity*	II *Quality*	III *Relation*	IV *Modality*
unity	reality	inherence + substance	possible — impossible
plurality	negation	causality + dependence	existence — nonexistence
totality	limitation	community (reciprocity between active and passive)	necessity — contingency

The Categorial System of von Hartmann. Modern categorial systems reflect the various metaphysical or philosophic viewpoints of their constructors. Hegel, for example, criticized the Kantian organization because it was too abstract and formal. For Hegel categories must be ultimately constitutive of things. Von Hartmann, who has treated the category problem most elaborately, attempts to organize a categorial system by adopting the results of the Hegelian formalistic criticism, adding the correction that categories, in addition to being logical, must include the nonlogical, and even unconscious, characteristics of a world system. His results are indicated in the accompanying tabular scheme. For the most part, the represented items are treated as they are presumed to operate in the subjective-ideal, objective-real, and metaphysical spheres.

Von Hartmann's Categories

A. *Sense Categories*
  I. Sensation categories
    1. Sense quality
    2. Sense quantity
      a. Intensive quantity
      b. Extensive quantity or temporality
  II. Perception categories
    Extensive quantity or spatiality
B. *Thought Categories*
  I. Primitive category of relation
  II. Categories of reflective thought
    1. Categories of comparative thinking
    2. Categories of separating and combining thought
    3. Categories of measuring thought

4. Categories of inferring thought
5. Categories of modal thought
III. Categories of speculative thought
1. Causality (etiology)
2. Finality (teleology)
3. Substantiality (ontology)

Current Attitudes toward Categories. Contemporary philosophers, inclining more toward the unification of science, or the
criticism of language and concepts, than toward elaborate total
systems of the universe, content themselves with small numbers
of categories. A recent writer[3] proposes only three basic categories
for a naturalistic philosophy—namely, event, quality, and relation. Embedded in this proposal is a shift from the substantive
matter and motion categories of older philosophical systems
toward the currently more favored functional categories.[4] A critic
of the three-category system argues that the event category is
not as basic as those of quality and relation, and apparently assumes that the latter are sufficient for all purposes.[5]

The rejection of a single exclusive metaphysical system radically changes one's attitude toward the category problem. For one
thing, there is no longer a need for a unique and inclusive set of
basic categories. In fact, for various nonmetaphysical purposes
many categorial systems are required. Pepper[6] has recently proposed that each different world hypothesis demands its own type
of category system. World hypotheses, however, are simply selected metaphysical systems. Aside from asking why we need world
hypotheses as metaphysical systems at all, we object to the implied
limitation of the number of categorial systems. Such limitation
sets up a faulty presupposition concerning the nature of categories.

CATEGORIAL SOURCES

Writers of contrasting cultural backgrounds locate the basis of
the universal and necessary thought elements in somewhat different sources. We have just referred to the Kantian notion that
categories represent *a priori* forms under which things must be or-

[3] Dennes, Categories.
[4] Cassirer, Substance.
[5] Aiken, Notes.
[6] Categories.

ganized in knowledge. Essentially, this source of origin derives categories from the ultimate character of mind. Mind is thus regarded as some sort of cognitive power, which, even if it does not supply the laws of knowing, does provide the forms in which knowledge of things is organized. Actually, of course, mind is made to do more than synthesize objects for experience; by the categorization technique it "produces" phenomena. The source of categories, according to this view, lies in the individual—specifically, in his cognitive power.

In contrast stands the view that the mind derives categories secondarily from cultural sources. In Spencer's type of evolutionism the basic categories for the individual mind are evolved through hereditarily transmitted racial habits. Such a theory as Spencer's is often taken to constitute an empirical doctrine. For the members of the French school of social anthropologists, such as Durkheim and Lévy-Bruhl, categories are forms of knowledge, ways in which things and conditions must be cognized; and these ways are derived from the characteristics of particular social organizations. The emphasis here shifts from individuals to groups, from individual to collective mentality. It is part of the French sociological doctrine that individual mentality reflects the group's general mentality. Aside from the difficulties involved in a conception of social mentality, we confront the fallacious idea of essential and fixed forms without flexibility and without the local functional character which actual categorization entails.

Even though writers on categories depart considerably from the traditional emphasis of the synthesizing power of the mind, as represented, for example, by such a study as Windelband's[7] they do not escape the notion of ultimate and totalitarian analyses of things. Turning toward the analysis of terminal properties only partially modifies the interest in an underlying mentality capable of reaching out to ulterior categorization processes.

To eschew both the direct and indirect connection of categories with mental powers makes room for the operational enterprises which persons foster either in furtherance of personal achievements or as part of large-scale undertakings in which many individuals participate. At once the sources of category making are extended indefinitely.

[7] System.

CATEGORIES AND CONCEPTS

Since the development of subjectivism and dualism, and their application to logic, categories have been equated with concepts.[8] In other words, categories have been regarded as mental or psychic entities which play a part in the operations of judging and reasoning. This identification, we have seen, attained its full flowering in the Kantian theory of categories.

Nothing is more certain than that this identification is based upon the confusion of our reactions to things with those things themselves. Notice the sharp transition from the Aristotelian categories as descriptive elements of things—or the referential elements of such descriptions—to the Kantian assumption that categories are the mental processes by which the creative mind organizes objects and events (vol. I, p. 59). The Kantian doctrine is essentially a rounding out of the spiritualistic principles developed by Patristic and Medieval thinkers.

Even when concepts are not regarded as psychic states but as forms of interbehavior, they are not to be identified with categories. In operational situations categories are definite constructions—that is, products developed for system-building purposes. As such they constitute manipulable objects. The range of their character and use varies as the systems which they help to form vary from simple classification and description of particular events to large generalized ontological or epistemological structures.

CATEGORIES, CLASSES, AND UNIVERSALS

How are categories related to classes and universals? Not a far-fetched interpretation is required to number classes and universals among the categories. At the very least, we must stress their great similarity to the latter. Traditionally, classes and universals (chap. 18) constitute structural elements built up for particular purposes by means of verbal or symbolic fixation, whereas categories have been regarded as more general and pervasive. Historically, classes and universals have always been connected with large-scale ultimate systems. From an interbehavioral standpoint such large-scale systems are merely special cases; and system building, which constitutes concrete activities in all orientational situations, is common to all intellectual work.

[8] Cf. Child, Categories; also Wolff, Unique.

Classes and universals, therefore, are merely limiting factors in various descriptive and explanatory enterprises. Since no sharp line exists between formal and informal system construction, it is a mistake to restrict classes and universals to formal structures.

CATEGORIES, LANGUAGE, AND SYMBOLS

Both the importance and fixity of categories are owing to their interrelationship with words and symbols. Categories are the fundamental points of contact between logic and language. Recall that all constructions, whether based upon actual contacts with things or built out of cultural traditions, must be linguistically referred to or recorded. Categories, then, are the abstracts and brief chronicles representing the results obtained by system builders who point out the essential characteristics of things and the processes by which they are known.

The technique of categorial creation is extremely simple. It involves two stages. First, categories are developed as descriptive elements derived from reacting to things and are therefore dependent upon the circumstances of such reaction. Secondly, the descriptions become encased in words and symbols. Thereafter, their apparent durability suggests that they are ultimate entities. This fixation conceals the contingent situations out of which categories arise, endows them with an importance superior to that of the original events quite beyond their descriptive function.

CATEGORIES AS INTERBEHAVIORAL PRODUCTS

From a logical standpoint categories constitute system-building materials created for some specified enterprise. They become the end products of interbehavioral processes in particular reference fields. On such a basis they are never far removed from the operational situations out of which they arise. Not that categories are capricious or arbitrary. Their interbehavioral origin permits us to evaluate them on the basis of how the category constructor has worked. Fundamentally the criterion is whether categories are derived from contacts with events or simply imposed upon the latter. Notice that whenever sets of categories are established as exclusive or most basic, in the sense of the ultimate and complete Kantian forms, the category systems are empty and unproductive. Probably in no case is it possible to achieve more than a relatively satisfying practical set of categories for any particular intellectual situation. It is highly doubtful whether in any instance alternative products are unavailable. Witness the various geometric systems which mathematicians are constantly setting up. What are the fundamental categories? Point, line, and plane, point and motion, or line and plane? Again, how many fundamental categories are necessary?

CATEGORIAL CONTINUITY

Interbehaviorally understood, categories are functional factors in system building. And since system building covers every type of human activity, a definite continuity runs through the categories of the most abstruse formal logic, the elements of scientific systemization, on down to the most elementary descriptive terms of our everyday contacts. Even the most abstract categories—for example, n-space or relative time—are evolved from everyday life conditions.

Consider for a moment the hierarchical development of interbehavior resulting in products for system construction. Space, for instance, as a category of formal mathematical relations, represents a refinement of operation beginning with the basic descriptions of simple place location. The S of a mathematical equation is an abstracted and refined product developed from the *place* or *location* constructs engendered in everyday contacts with things. Similarly, T is derived from the most elementary changes of time. The obvious fact is, however, that the accidents of our culture have not furnished us with a beginning category for time, such as the *place* category for space, unless we take *when* as the missing end point for time. We believe that our continuity hypothesis gains, rather than loses, from the need to take account of such cultural variations in category origin and development.

Note, too, that categorization continuity may appear to be completely broken when categories are artifacts developed in experimental situations. Such experiments may engender questions concerning the reversibility or irreversibility of time, and time's continuity or discontinuity, as in the development of a time quantum or chronon.[9] It is our point, however, that, no matter how remote the experimental situation or how far the constructed categories

---

[9] See Lindsay and Margenau, Foundations, chap. 2.

are extrapolated from everyday events, there is no break in the interbehavioral continuum.

CATEGORIAL SPECIFICITY

Not only do categories differentiate themselves according to kind of work—logical, scientific, etc.—but within any one type the investigations call for particular sets of categories. A classic scientific illustration is the derivation of *work* by the Cartesians, in contrast to the Leibnizian *force*. Accordingly, for Newton and others following Descartes mass, force, and momentum are the original categories, while for Huygens, following the Leibnizian view, they are work, mass, and *vis viva* (energy).

Categorial specificity bears directly upon the hierarchy or reduction principle in science. It is frequently, though improperly, held that the sciences are hierarchical (chap. 13, p. 12), with mathematics as the most fundamental. A variant of the hierarchical view discriminates against mathematics as a science, but makes physics basic and its categories the primary ones. Biological, psychological, and anthropological events are regarded as reducible to physical and chemical happenings; thus the physical categories, such as protons, neutrons, and electrons, are made basic to those of all sciences.

From the specificity standpoint, however, each set of categories, when found sufficient for the needs of a science, is irreducible. The criteria, therefore, for setting up any set of categories are localized in the investigative problems of the particular discipline. Two distinctive enterprises are involved: (a) setting up verbally unifying systems and (b) constructing categories for systemizing events and their observation.

SPECIAL CATEGORIAL FUNCTIONS

Aside from their general instrumentality in system building, categories subserve specific functions in particular situations. The following four are illustrative of many others.

Differentiating Functions. Certain categories mark off items or elements. Though they may aid in naming and recording the materials dealt with, their primary function is to separate and fixate items. Excellent examples, on an elaborate scientific level, are the cognate categories of kinetic and potential energy, centrifugal and centripetal forces, and organism and environment.

Classifying Functions. Since classification is essentially system making, classifying functions are naturally very prominent. Taxonomic categories, for instance, loom large in logical situations. Hierarchical categories in biology illustrate such classifying functions as exemplified in the series *phylum, family, genus,* and *species.* These categories differentiate general and particular characteristics in an organic continuum.

Descriptive Functions. Categories like *ampere, volt, coulomb,* and *gauss,* employed in the electrical branch of physics, demonstrate quantitative descriptive categories. Similar ones are produced for all science departments on the basis of both mensurational and nonquantitative operations.[10]

Explanatory Functions. Categories subserving elaborate descriptive or relating functions may be regarded as explanatory. The biological, medical, and psychological sciences afford such outstanding category examples as the organic, the functional, the structural, and the ecological. Similar explanatory categories are the theoretical constructs *watt* and *ohm,* and the practical *power* and *energy* categories of electricity.

Range of Categorial Systems

As an indication of the range of categorial systems we consider a few class types. In a later section categorial family members are enumerated.

Scientific Departments. While in no department of science is the ideal of total and inclusive systemization ever achieved, there is always an attempt to organize data and principles. It is possible, therefore, to differentiate a set of typical categories for biology, physics, psychology, sociology, and other disciplines. Within these various departments, of course, there is further categorial specialization. Physics, for example, requires different category systems in mechanics, optics, and electricity. The same may be said for biology (p. 127), in which the exigencies of specialization introduce subsystem categories for anatomy, histology, genetics, and ecology.

---

[10] See an elaborate category system developed for the social sciences by Goldenweiser, History.

Obviously, a vast number of categories are derived from such multiplicative processes.

Specific Researches. Within any one department of scientific activity specialized researches entail the organization of categorial systems which bear directly, and to a certain extent exclusively, upon the particular work in progress. Following the development of atomic physics unique categories evolved pertaining to these particular researches. For instance, the study of emitted particles in nuclear bombardment gave rise to the scattering and nonscattering categories and the subcategories of large-angle, small-angle deflection. The specializations go deeper and deeper as individual researches demand.

Property and Dimension Systems. Categorial systems may also be organized on the basis of a particular property or dimension. Consider such a category as length. The choice is ours either to adopt the conventional attitude that length is a unique and integral property or that it constitutes a dimensional system. On the latter basis length is a construction symbolizing not only a certain dimension or continuum, but a dimension which varies with different investigations and scientific departments. The fundamental point is that the unique properties of length-scales depend upon the particular interbehavioral situation. The centimetre or any other length unit on a measurement stick is different from the corresponding length on a thermometer scale. Again, in various equational transformations the length taken in terms of time is a still different member of this length class.

Illustrative Categorial Operations

The nature and development of categories, their multiplicity, constant change, and specialization for particular systems may all be summarized by sampling categorial situations and systems.

1. *Mechanics*

If we are looking for variation in the fundamental categories employed to develop a scientific system we find it in the history of mechanics. Originally the basic categories of inertia, velocity, force, acceleration, energy, and the implied categories of space, time, and mass were regarded as powers, properties, and existences. Only recently have they come to be considered as constructions derived from, and tested by, operations upon actual events. A typical example is the category *force*, which at one time was presumed to represent a power inherent in things to bring about certain effects, but which today is regarded as an index to the character and result of the impact of one body on another.

2. *Electricity*

The electrical branch of physics provides many striking instances of the origin and increase of categories. First, there were the simplest categories of positive and negative electricity; later the systemization of electrical knowledge engendered such categories as inductance and electrical field. At still later stages the categories of capacitance, conductance, and resistance elaborated the system. With the evolution of electrical science, categories cross the mechanical borders and culminate in such products as electrical mass and velocity.

3. *Geometry*

In this most stable and deductive field there is a perennial shift and reevaluation of categories as knowledge progresses. Only when the geometrician is preoccupied with particular data—that is, the solution of specific problems—can he overlook the evolution and multiplication of such basic categories as *point, line, surface,* and *solid*. Such obvious geometrical transformations as in the development of non-Euclidean systems is proof enough of categorial modification. For example, the solid or space of older Euclidean geometry is certainly a different sort of space from that evolved in the investigations of Grassman, Riemann, and others. Nothing is more striking than the transformation of the categories *point, position, line,* and *extension* into operational space categories. In other words, simple absolute position evolves into a relation, defined by triplets of numbers in a system of coordinates.

The following statement of Brewster concerning Newton effectively indicates geometric shifting:

In imitation of Cavalieri, he called the momentary increment of a line a point, though it is not a geometrical point, but an infinitely short line, and the momentary increment of an area or surface he called a line, though it is not a geometrical line, but an infinitely narrow surface.[11]

[11] Brewster, Memoirs, p. 17.

4. *Everyday Categories*

The categorizing series constructed by a political candidate demonstrates in the best possible manner the nature of categories. Notice how he builds up a system of "my performance." To be sure, the candidate may sincerely believe in the political and social improvements supposed to follow his election. Actually, however, he is not referring to existing events. What happens is that by means of substitute stimulation he is able to operate with a set of categories which are products of his interaction with nonexistent situations—namely, those situations he promises to bring about. The fundamental import of such categories is that they represent modifications in present conditions regarded as unsatisfactory and capable of improvement.

A similar set of categories may systemize a particular individual's attitudes concerning actually existing conditions. As such they are simply products of immediate interbehavior. In other words, they do not represent any necessary analysis of things or conditions, but stem from an individual's views, reactions, or beliefs. While the above is not an essential description of everyday categories, inasmuch as such categories may be precisely like those so well established in logical and scientific domains, an appreciation of the nebulous and unstandardized processes of engendering categories indicates that category products are not always formal or ultimate.

5. *Religious Categories*

Valuable ideas concerning categorization processes may be gleaned from the theological problem of positive and neutral categories centered in the negative theology developed from Philo, through the Gnostics and Christian apologists, to Plotinus and beyond. These writers struggled with the question: What categories can be applied to the deity? Negative theology implies the recognition that all categories are constructs and thus finite in character. How, then, can categories, which are simply fixations of qualities or characteristics observed from concrete interactions with things, apply to deities?

Even early theologians observed that the glorification of a deity is not achieved by ascribing to him qualities which, in so far as they also apply to mundane things, are clearly not sufficiently exalted. To their credit they discovered that God could not be omnipotent and omniscient, since these categories simply extrapolate from the characteristics and actions of men. Incidentally, the linguistic habit of masculinizing or feminizing deities bespeaks the powerful influence of cultural institutions upon categorization. Even the negative theologians of Western Europe could not escape the influence of their cultural traditions in speaking of God as He or Him.

What better evidence is required for the interbehavioral process than the entire enterprise of deity creations? The description of this procedure has not been improved upon since Xenophanes of Colophon (570-480 B.C.):

But if cattle or lions had hands, so as to paint with their hands and produce works of art as men do, they would paint their gods and give them bodies in form like their own—horses like horses, cattle like cattle.[12]

6. *Dimensional Analysis*

Dimensional analysis, as a domain of measurement, exemplifies not only the construction and use of categories but also their integration into systems. Dimension categories serve as units for deriving interrelations as functional systems. Velocity is a structure deriving from L and T as fundamental dimensions:

$$[V] = \frac{[L]}{[T]}$$

L is constructed to serve in whatever capacity is required to deal with length as distance, interval, etc. V, as a derived unit, is a local system capable of functioning as an item in more comprehensive systemization. For example, velocity is only a subunit in acceleration systems. When F symbolizes acceleration, its relation to V, L, and T is clear from the following:

$$[F] = \frac{[V]}{[T]} = \frac{[L]}{[T^2]}$$

Assuming that dimensional analyses concern specific types of mensuration systems, we may ask whether the C.G.S. units or dimensions are ultimate or basic, either as ontologic, phenomenologic, or epistemic categories. The phenomenologic units are im-

---

[12] Fairbanks, Philosophers, p. 67.

mediately derived as a matter of course, since such units are elements of intolerable spiritistic systems. But, though with proper interpretation, the ontologic and epistemic systems may be acceptable, we still face the question whether they are unqualifiedly basic and indispensable.

Although such a writer as Campbell believes that all fundamental measurements belong to physics (267),[13] and that the basic characteristic of physics is its propensity for measurement (33f.), he does not regard length, mass, and time as basic magnitudes, even when to these three are added temperature, dielectric constant, and permeability. This does not mean, however, that he does not consider some magnitudes as basic (393), since he realizes that of such are mensuration systems made. Which are fundamental depends upon the mensurational task at hand. Campbell plainly asserts that measurement is a means toward an end; consequently, the tools and procedures are dependent upon the operational systems in which they are found.

Dimensional analyses as systemological factors were appreciated by the earliest students of the subject. As Larmor[14] points out, Newton originated the essentials of dimensional doctrine as a means of comparing the properties of correlated systems; for example, (a) particles of different systems, (b) particles and bodies, and (c) resting and moving parts of systems.[15] As is well known, Fourier more explicitly worked out the theory of dimensions and their exponents in his development of mathematical systems, or equations, in which the homogeneity of terms must be maintained. The correlation of heat conductivity with other measurements involved equations expressing necessary relations between common units of length, time, and weight, to which are added temperature and heat quantity.[16]

So far we have accepted the view that dimensions are quantitative. But we must go further. If we begin with the operational basis of categories, instead of with conventional notions of ontological or epistemic postulates, we may allow for other sorts of dimensions. Such dimensions imply nonadditive orders and ar-

[13] The numbers in parentheses refer to pages in *Physics*.
[14] Dimensions.
[15] Principia, Bk. 2, prop. 32.
[16] Analytical, chap. 2, sec. 9.

rangements, basic comparisons, and, in general, systems differing from those of conventional mensurational theory. Further consideration of these problems we postpone to our chapters on Measurement.

7. Axiological Categories

The comparatively recent development of axiology as a distinctive field also illustrates the fundamental principles of categorization, and its place in system building. Because of a deepening interest in the basic problems of ethics, aesthetics, and normative logic, the category of value has been constructed as a fundamental core in the fields mentioned. Around this core a systematic set of categories has been arrayed.

Fundamental among secondary axiological categories are the *objective* and *subjective,* a differentiation based on whether values are taken as characteristics or properties of things and events, or simply as evaluations of individuals interested in ethical or aesthetic situations.

Relation, too, constitutes a distinctive type of axiological category. Even scholars who are fairly sympathetic to the idea that values might be objective are unwilling to admit the objectivity of relation. Axiological constants they consider as relational, and as depending in part upon the observer or evaluator. The fundamental basis for their hesitancy is that evaluative categories are difficult to establish. But many natural-science categories are also equally difficult to establish. As for the categories of the medical sciences, how shaky are such constructs as influenza and inflammation![17] To what system of natural happenings are they related? Moreover, it is overlooked that all categories are operational products; thus, even in physical constants there is a selective and cognitive factor.

A unique feature of axiological categories is that values are regarded as problematic primarily because they are considered as exclusively human factors, and thus as categorically different from materials of the natural sciences. Even those scholars who assent to the proposition that physical constants, or natural-science values, are derived from the characteristics of things hesitate to regard human-science values as objective and likewise derived

[17] See Crookshank, Importance; also Harding, Science.

from things. Obviously, there is a lingering prejudice that human-istic happenings involve psychic, or nonnatural, elements. Thus it is overlooked that in both humanistic and natural determinations all categorization evolves from interaction with things.

Axiological category study provides an important lesson con-cerning the relativity of logical systems. It is conventional to assume that wherever we have difficulty in our observations, when-ever events are recalcitrant, the final categorial products are not stable, basic, or satisfactory. Actually, this situation simply puts the different categorial products upon a relative scale. The single conclusion is that we can have various types of systems; that is, the materials and results of our logical processes are different, and hence the logics themselves are diverse.

The value, then, of considering axiological categories lies in the contrast they afford between the notions (1) that logic is a universal and inclusive form of action—in other words, that there are certain absolute logical constants—and (2) that logic con-stitutes innumerable specific enterprises of system building.

8. *Thermodynamics*

The evolution of thermodynamics as an area in physics provides the systemologist with a splendid instance of novel system con-struction. As a domain of rapidly changing events, thermodynamics has had to forsake the all-embracing mechanics of well established categories. Thermodynamic events could not be put into the frame-work of enduring particles, which, even in dynamics, moved so slowly as to be assimilable to selected static systems founded on geometric constructs localized within definitely closed and boundary-fixed limits.

By contrast with particle mechanics the study of rapid molecular changes required a new system of categories. Attempts to throw these happenings into the old mechanical framework at once brought to the fore the probability category. Mechanics conse-quently became statistical mechanics. The events dealt with were so complex and variable as to make it seem impossible to trace out paths of single molecules. In a sense, therefore, the categories of this area had their sources in operational procedures, rather than exclusively in ontologic analysis.

Perhaps equally as fundamental as probability is the category of conservation, formulated in the first thermodynamic law. The associated proposition is that, unless bounds are placed on rapidly occurring events, no system can be achieved. Here is a vital system-building situation characteristic of all scientific enterprises. The physicist facing a set of difficult, but unquestionable, happenings made his first attack, history relates, by constructing a model such as the Carnot cycle. This model indicated what might happen if the system were regarded as closed, in line with the conservation principle.

Next came the development of the entropy category, an invention to account for happenings within the system. In any actual thermodynamic system—that is, one which can not be thrown into the ideal form of the Carnot cycle—energy must be regarded as dissipated. Entropy is thus a polar category to conservation.

Other fundamental categories in thermodynamics are *transformation* and what may seem to be subcategories: *reversibility*, and *irreversibility*. Thus, all sorts of systems are possible in which the processes usually take one direction and at other times the reverse. To these categories must be added many others necessary for describing the events—namely, *state, degree of freedom*, etc., —all of which reveal the qualitative and quantitative changes taking place.

It should be noted that, in consonance with all scientific work, categories are interrelated. In a thermodynamic system, for example, such categories as *molecule, pressure,* and *temperature* are also elements of other systems. Even so-called common categories like space, time, and energy, despite linguistic fixation, are really operationally unique in different situations. Moreover, in such an area as thermodynamics the more particularized categories may comprise units of subsystems within the same general system.

9. *Biology*

In no scientific domain are categorization principles better illustrated than in the descriptive and interpretative systems constructed in the biological sciences. In addition to the importation of categories from other investigative fields, some are constructed with unique application to biological events. Biological categories are differentiable on the basis of observational derivation or free construction.

Biologists are undecided whether their categories should incline more toward (1) structure, (2) function, or (3) both. On the one hand, the organism is emphasized as distinctive and self-maintaining. Here the fundamental categories are morphological in type, such as cell, tissue, and organ. On the other hand, since biological systems are always active and changing units, the actional or physiological categories, such as metabolism, may be stressed. Ecological events lend themselves best to interrelations of structure-function categories.

Change and action categories divide themselves into two series, one of which has to do more with particular organisms, their growth and coincident anabolic and catabolic processes, and the other with such general processes as evolution, which is concerned with the development of types, or individual forms.

Characteristic of the problematic, and perhaps speculative, biological categories are those which began historically with the category of vital force, and which, especially in the modern embryological branch of biology, come under the heading of organizers, determiners, etc. A unique form of this type of category is the gene, which, on the one hand, is deductively constructed from observations of happenings during reproductive cycles, and, on the other, may be regarded as a freely constructed category for the purpose of interpreting changes not easily observed but necessary in accounting for observed happenings.

10. *Ethical Categories*

The number and type of ethical categories are dependent upon the views of writers concerning the nature of ethics. A very general category of this field is that of the *summum bonum*. There has always been an implicit recognition that the field of ethics has to do with some sort of norm or value. The innumerable interpretations of what the *summum bonum* should be depend upon various cultural situations with their foci in particular intellectual formulations.

Obviously, ethical categories as constructs are primarily autistic. This fact perhaps explains why ethicists have differed so radically in their ideas concerning the *summum bonum*. Ethical categories are most freely constructed when the supreme norm is asserted to be given, and to regulate the inclination of man toward the will of God. It is a paradox that the most absolutistic and transcendent writers are the most arbitrary in their constructional procedure.

Conventional ethical categories may be grossly distinguished on the basis of whether they concern (1) essences of various sorts; that is, are names for ultimate qualities of goodness, or (2) goals and types of action. When the highest good is regarded as happiness, or self-realization, ethical categories imply goals of action; though self-realization, like the pursuit of the ideal, to some extent may be the name of a certain desirable quality. Other ethical categories are intimately connected with actions themselves, such as *the good*, in the sense of good action, the proper, the worthwhile, and so on.

11. *Logical Categories*

Logical categories constitute items regarded as necessary for building a technical logical theory or system. Since there are many types of technical logics, despite the prevailing belief in a single cosmorational system, we choose but a few typical categorial illustrations.

In classical Formal Logic the three primary categories are term, proposition, and syllogism. Correlated with these three are the equally conventional concept, judgment, and inference or reasoning.

In symbolic logic similar technical categories are the indefinable, propositional function (propositional form), primitive proposition, class, relation, etc. Out of such abstract elements symbolic logicians build up symbolic systems.

12. *Grammatical Categories*

The categories of formal grammar are widely regarded as connecting links between language and thought, or logic. We need not commit ourselves to such a view in order to see that grammatical categories admirably show the process of categorization. Grammarians convert actual speech into textual materials—not deliberately, of course, because this procedure has a very definite cultural history—and we may say that grammar arises from an investigation of forms or symbols. At the present time, however, grammars constitute just such transformations.

An examination of conventional grammatical categories, especially parts of speech, indicates the formalization both of language events and references to them.[18] The resulting products consist of a series of categories, usually eight—namely, the familiar noun, verb, adjective, adverb, preposition, etc. In this connection we may refer again to the widespread notion that the Aristotelian categories have been derived from the analysis of parts of speech, or different ways in which things are spoken of.

13. *Philosophical Categories*

Throughout its historical development philosophy has centered about categorization, since philosophers traditionally have attempted to systemize the universe. Accordingly, they have constructed such fundamental products as being, essence, substance, function, and cause. These categories are taken to be ontological —that is, concerned with the contents of the universe. When epistemological, or knowledge, problems came to the front, other categories, such as ego, knowledge, and mind became prominent. Categories involving creative powers have extended the list, though the latter have converged with the religious categories (p. 121) already examined.

14. *Aesthetic Categories*

Aesthetic categories are frequently connected with general axiological (p. 124f) or more comprehensive philosophical systems. The question here is whether the aesthetician adopts a general philosophical standpoint, or whether he undertakes to analyze aesthetic events in a more limited frame of reference. Aesthetic categories are variously called form, content, significant form, beauty, ugliness, etc. That many of the essentially aesthetic categories have names similar to those of other systems is only to be expected. The category *form*, for instance, is not only a special type of systemization factor, but is also qualified as *significant*.

[18] Kantor, Objective.

15. *Mathematical Analysis*

Even a casual inspection of the constantly developing field of mathematical analysis requires an elaborate dictionary merely to list the categories. Because of the abstract relational nature of mathematics, its general terminology comprises a unique set of categories. As is true elsewhere, mathematical categories are derived from operations performed upon crude data, and are thus specific kinds of constructions. Important mathematical categories are operation, continuity, field, function, rational, inductive, variable, limit, parameter, constant, infinitesimal, infinite, operator, magnitude, convergence, divergence, etc.

These categories, which have always impressed thinkers as ultimates and as independent of particular enterprises, are definitely functional; they vary with the problems, types of field, and mathematical interest of the worker. The many interpretations put upon such categories as the infinite and the infinitesimal are sufficient to remind us of their operational and constructional character.

CHAPTER XVIII

UNIVERSALS: SYSTEMOLOGICAL COMPONENTS AND PRODUCTS

THE LOGIC OF UNIVERSALS

UNIVERSALS occupy an ambiguous position in conventional logics. When mind and reasoning are regarded as transcendent powers or ontological essences, disturbing problems inevitably arise. Are universals concrete or abstract? Granted that they are abstract, may they be contaminated with qualitative and content residues, or must they be pure forms? Again, when logic is deeply concerned with problems of class membership and class inclusion, must classes be dispensed with as merely linguistic conveniences because they are "not as genuine objects as their members are if they are individuals?"[1]

No ambiguity attaches to universals in interbehavioral logic. Universals are products of system-building operations, but they are something more than end points in the operational procedure; in addition they constitute the raw materials of further system-building operations. This characteristic, it should be noted, universals share with relations, classes, kinds or species, mathematical functions, and other constructional forms.

HISTORICAL TREATMENT OF UNIVERSALS

A definite cultural continuity relates the current universals problem to that of earliest antiquity. The natural history of universals constitutes a fascinating and informing story when considered as the behavior of persons called logicians who occupy themselves with the universals issue.

Universals among the Greeks. Greek interest in universals may be justly stated to have arisen out of a systemological problem. The development of forms, ideas, definitions, and genera is surely localized in the work of setting up systems of knowledge (science) or logic.

Since the Greeks did not work with nonspatial, or mental, con-

---

[1] Whitehead and Russell, Principia, p. 72; Russell, Principles, p. x.

structs,[2] universals for them constituted definite products of abstracting and generalizing operations. In other words, they abstracted and generalized forms or universals from things in order to establish science and system—that is, stabilized operations. These forms the Greeks regarded as patterns or laws for fixing and organizing the fleeting events of everyday life. They were harried by no problem concerning the existence or subsistence of generals or universals as over against particulars. In fact, Aristotle criticized Plato primarily for separating the *Ideas* or *Forms* from occurring things. What later took the name of Realism was inevitable for the objective Greek way of thinking.

The Medieval Concern with Universals. Modern problems of universals sharply reflect their close articulation with post-Greek or medieval origins. Psychic realms of existence and process now take the lead. By contrast with the Greeks, medieval writers were no longer interested in systems of things or knowledge; they were obsessed by the intimate problem of personal salvation, by the establishment of the continuous existence and value of soul or intrinsic human nature. Universals at this time consisted of soul in that sense. Supported by their special cultural backgrounds, the Scholastics divided themselves into distinctive schools.

(1) *The Realists.* Seeking as the most real that which is least subject to change and time, the Realists argued that the universal maintains an independent existence. In this wise they sided more with Plato than Aristotle. But this doctrine yielded too little to individuals, and was far from satisfactory to those who stressed the basic value of individuality.

(2) *The Nominalists.* Unsatisfied with Platonic doctrine, many resorted to Aristotle. The greatest value and significance, they declared, was attached to individual souls, to particular persons; and that which is common to all of them, or universal, is the *name*. Only individual things are substance, hence real. Thus names are used to comprehend a multiplicity of individuals, and to analyze them for thought and communication.

(3) *The Conceptualists.* For the conceptualists psychic processes and existence comprise, besides soul and all essential things, the mental acts of dealing with them. Universals, then, became interpreted as concepts in the mind. Concepts, it was thought, could

[2] See vol. I, pp. 46ff.

mediate between spaceless existents and their names or designations.

CURRENT TREATMENT OF UNIVERSALS

Present-day discussions of universals, as we have indicated, are based on a three-point support. The first is post-Greek psychism. Arguments are bandied back and forth whether universals are real or whether they exist only in the mind. Secondly, the doctrines of universalism and necessitarianism influence writers to transform universals into words or terms. And, finally, writers on universals do not differentiate materials, work, and products from each other. All three points can be taken into account by organizing current treatments under the following headings: (1) spatiotemporality, (2) character value, and (3) the participation problem.

(1) *Spatiotemporality.* Two phases of spatiotemporality are employed to differentiate between universals and particulars. The first has to do with plurality of spatial location. A universal *red* can be simultaneously localized in two objects when each object can only be in one place at any given time.[3]

There are several objections to this phase of universal description. For one thing, it is asserted that despite its importance[4] this is not the essence of the matter. So-called physical distinction is set below logical distinction. Even more significant is the denial that universals are no more pluralistic than particularistic. For example, Ramsey begins his discussion of universals by asserting:

The purpose of this paper is to consider whether there is a fundamental division of objects into two classes, particulars and universals.

His answer is negative, but later he reconsiders the matter.[5] Though he departs somewhat from the spatiotemporal problem to work more with linguistic materials, he is obliged to reject this distinction because of the complete lack of differences in things.

The more crucial phase of spatiotemporal argument interprets universals as real but not spatially confined, as in the following: Of course, wisdom and triangularity exist nowhere, but they are as real as triangles and blackboards.[6] On this basis one embraces

---

[3] Cf. Ramsey, Foundations, p. 112ff.
[4] Ibid., p. 113.
[5] Ibid., p. 135f.
[6] Moore, Why, p. 686.

the absurdity that round squares, triangular circles, griffens, and the paupers' millions exist. Of course, those who adopt realism as a fundamental philosophy argue that serious logic must have a metaphysics, and that they really are interested in the relationship between triangles and triangularity, wisdom and wise acts, blueness and blue things. Any doctrine, however, that makes these relationships precisely identical with the relationship between *assertions* concerning unicorns and *real* nonspatiotemporal unicorns is self condemnatory. Spatial location is, however, not a fundamental distinction, because writers on universals immediately jump to terms—that is, linguistic or verbal items. The problem of universals is made into a problem of substantive versus adjective, substantives being singular and adjectives universal.

(2) *Character Value.* Present-day realists who are willing to accept eternal forms or ideas as universals are not troubled by the problem of their character value. This problem, however, is a poignant one for those who believe that "whatever is, is particular." The latter writers deny the existence of so-called Platonic universals, but, on the other hand, face the issue of associating blueness or triangularity as general characters with blue or triangle as particular instances. If the universal is an existence in the domain of particulars, must it not be described as a character like other abstracted traits of things?

One negative answer is given in terms of classes. For example, McGilvary[7] asserts that the universal *blue* is the entire class of blues. Universals comprise classes of properties abstracted within synthetic wholes.[8] McGilvary thus regards universals or generals as analyzed, but inseparable, constituents of complexes or wholes. By comparison, the common or similar components are made to stand out. Universals, then, are real existences different from the character which they comprise in series or classes, and yet are far from being timeless or spaceless essences. Incidentally, the view of objectively existing classes implied in McGilvary's theory of universals is not agreeable to other writers.

(3) *Participation.* This section heading reminds us of the ancient ontological proposal that particulars participate in universals. Since that era the descriptions of the relationship, regarded as

[7] *Relations,* p. 30f.
[8] Ibid., p. 36.

either logical or ontological, have centered around words. Such is the case which Goethe describes:

> Denn eben wo Begriffe fehlen
> da stellt ein Wort zur rechten Zeit sich ein.

Thus words, in the form of assertions and statements, are employed to mediate and interrelate universals and particulars. Russell[9] and Johnson[10] divide off and interrelate universal and particular terms by making the former into adjectives or predicates of propositions (sentences), and the latter into substantives. How little this subject-predicate solution satisfies the participation question becomes apparent when considering Johnson's contention that, while a substantive can only serve as the subject of a sentence, adjectives can function either as predicates or as subjects. For example, in the sentence: "Punctuality is a fault," "fault" may be taken to be a secondary adjective. Russell objects, and asserts that the proper handling of these words must be as follows: "For all x, if x is unpunctual, x is reprehensible."[11] A "particular" or an "individual" can be defined as "anything that can be the subject of an atomic proposition." This is not true for "universals"— that is, a predicable character or relation.

This treatment of participation is a modern linguistic form of realism. Nominalism, too, mediates verbally between singulars and generals. Current nominalists declare that universals are names for properties abstracted from actual objects, events, or behavior—*triangularity* from triangles, *wisdom* from wise behavior, *blueness* from blue hat, etc. In other words, universals are abstractional products embodied in words or terms. There is justification for this notion in the sense that the referents for the autonomous terms *triangularity*, *wisdom*, and *blueness* are different from the referents of the terms *wisdom* (wise action); *triangularity* (three-sided figure); *blueness* (a blue hat).

The question now arises: What is the relation between the subsistential references for universal terms (words) and concepts? Notice that the latter, too, are regarded as nonexistents, represented by words. It is plainly indicated, therefore, that we should

---

[9] *Problems*, chaps. 5, 9.
[10] *Logic*, part I, p. 11.
[11] Whitehead, Russell, *Principia*, p. xix.

not look upon universals as names for names, or words, but as references to, or symbols of, constructive action with respect to existential objects and events, such as wisdom, triangularity, and blue things.

LOGICAL FORMS AS THINGS, TERMS, OR THOUGHTS

Given the traditional ideas of things, language, and mind, we can locate the universals problem, as well as the conflict in solving it.

The proponents of each of the three views that forms are things, terms, and thoughts, use the same general argument to support their beliefs. A paradoxical situation! The realists, who are unwilling to relegate universals to the ephemerality of mind, create a new realm of existence—namely, subsistence; yet they assert that the basis must be something in the "real world."[12] They are unwilling, it seems, to relegate universals to mind or to names. In their favor it may be said that universals are definitely stimulus objects, in the sense, of course, of constructions formed by abstraction from concrete things, thus allowing for the obvious differentiation between greenness and the green hat. This theory, however, is fundamentally inept in building up a reality independent of any specifiable space-time.

The nominalists, believing that universals are verbal terms, argue that the ordinary events of experience and science show common characteristics. Russell,[13] for example, declares that words are necessary because of things, that words correspond to things, and thus the necessity to say certain words is determined by the existence of corresponding things. Without the word *similar* one can not get on, because there just simply are similar things. In this view that universals are terms we observe the confusion between words as things, and language as action or assertion. Universals are regarded as autonomous words, but the justification for this view is that by means of words one refers to common characteristics of things. To be sure, references to common characteristics may be important aspects of symbological forms, but can forms, as universals, be made identical with the terms or words?

Do the difficulties of the first two views lend plausibility to the

---

[12] Moore, Why, p. 685.
[13] Inquiry.

conceptualist's idea that logical forms in the final analysis are thoughts or concepts?[14] Those who believe so stand on good ground in their denial both of the name doctrine and the theory that there are real "things" called universals. However, as we have already seen (p. 132), conceptualism is invalid because based on traditional mentalism which introduces a new kind of existence—that is, concepts which are neither names nor things.

INTERBEHAVIORAL CHARACTER OF UNIVERSALS

Historical and current quarrels about universals stem from the general dualistic treatment of thought. An objective psychology might well be substituted for the logistic principle which closely interrelates, and even identifies, linguistic products and things. Our proposal, then, to treat logical forms in general, and universals and relations in particular, as products of interbehavior, as well as items in the development of all sorts of systems, means we reject the theory that terms constitute common denominators of forms. As interbehavioral items, terms are features in an individual's concrete operations with stimulus objects. These objects may be of an immediate or direct sort, or they may require substitute stimulation.

To illustrate the essential features of our presentation, compare the interbehavioral with a classical mentalistic-psychological description. For this purpose consider Sellars' projection description.[15] With regard to universals he indicates that the mind, working with concepts as instruments, projects "the recurrence of the same meanings in the mind" into the things thought of. In this way, logical identity—that is, identity of a concept—is transformed into universals and things.

This description requires complete translation and transformation to make it accord with what actually goes on. To begin with, "the recurrence of the same meaning in the mind" refers to a similar reaction to a similar stimulus object. There is, therefore, a correspondence between actual objects and responses to them. Instead of projecting psychic meanings into things in order to create universals, on an interbehavioral basis we describe the construction of a form represented by a term.

[11] In the scholastic sense of *verbum mentis*.
[15] Philosophy.

The entire process is exemplified by the situations which give rise to the successive creation of the universals *blueness, color, similarity*, etc. By simple reference to the color similarity of different objects such quality universals as blueness and redness are abstracted and fixated. Then a universal color, or colority, is engendered. Finally, the abstracting and generalizing behavior produces the apical universal *similarity*. Such creative processes also manufacture the order of the universals. Actually, we can not know what was the precise succession in the cultural history of system making, or whether there was such a succession altogether. These speculations, however, serve the purpose of bringing to the front the concrete interbehavioral conditions under which the creation of universals occurs.

Light is also thrown upon the problem of the reality of forms as urged by realists of all sorts. For example, Cohen,[16] maintaining a notion of psychic mind, has argued that universals as abstractions must have some existence aside from the mind that makes them. Such a question of the reality, existence, and validity of forms never arises when we observe how they are derived from actual problems, solved by persons dealing with objective things.

Specificity of Forms

Universals are the specific products of abstracting and generalizing behavior such as we have described in Chapter 13. These procedures take place in definite interbehavioral fields. It is encouraging to find the specificity principle not only recognized, but appreciated, in logical writings. For example, McGilvary[17] asserts that relations, even though generalized to a high degree, are specific. This view follows from his general realistic philosophic standpoint. Indeed, pragmatic realism has much in common with an interbehavioral view; certainly there is considerable appeal in the idea that universals are really always particulars. The fact that one generalizes or constructs a universal does not detract from the specificity of the situation in which the process takes place.

Specificity has to do with the particulars of the relations themselves. In other words, we have a check on the conception that there is a generality or universality of forms which gives them a

[16] Reason, p. 204.
[17] Relations.

unique status different from particular things. In every case such generalized or universalized relations constitute simple constructions which are mere generalized referents of verbal propositions.

Forms as Products

In carrying out all sorts of operations upon things it is necessary to develop or create instruments for performing large-scale operations in order to summarize, organize, and refer to things (chap. 16). In calculating we require a form which will span a class of values; thus we create a variable. In comparing things we need an instrument for carrying over from one relation to another. Hence the construction of a relational form. This is a genuine constructional process derived from contacts with things.

Three sources of raw materials from which to construct forms or generals are: (a) things and events interacted with, (b) acts themselves, and (c) the products which result from such acts. Let us characterize each in turn.

(a) *Thing or Event Sources*

Recall that it was philosophical convention to classify all forms as universals and relations. But when we start from actual contacts with things we find that they result in the construction of many types of forms. The following list, while not exhaustive, illustrates a series of forms constructed from thing and event sources.

1. *Qualities.* Quality forms, traditionally known as universals, are definitely derived from things, and for the most part are abstracted from structural characteristics such as color and hardness.

2. *Properties.* Conditions of things and their changes provide the basis for abstracting forms or generals such as lastingness, continuity, and irregularity.

3. *Relations.* These forms are abstracted either from parts or aspects of stimulus objects, or from some situation or complex involving several objects. In the former case the complex consists of the discernible features of a single thing—for example, front or back, up or down. Out of a configuration involving several things such relational forms as "between," "higher," and "lower" are derived.

Notice that relations are features likewise of the connections between objects. For example, we interbehave with the relation or geographic placing of two cities quite as much as with the individual cities. Their relationship, in other words, is as much a natural fact as their existence. The eastness or westness of New York with respect to Chicago comprises a definite fact of land, mountain, etc. It matters not what frames of reference we adopt; nor is this principle interfered with even when we find New York to be west of Chicago, in the sense that one may start from Chicago, and by traveling constantly westward reach New York on the east.

From an interbehavioral standpoint the relations between more abstract things, such as mathematical objects, constitute similar definite stimulus objects from which relational forms are produced. When we develop such forms as transitivity, intransitivity, symmetry, asymmetry, and connexity as parts of logical or mathematical systems, we are interbehaving with relationships between things, even though we have previously constructed those things and the relations between them. What we need to distinguish, therefore, are merely abstract stimulus objects from concrete ones, the former being derived from the latter by a long psychological and cultural history (chap. 13).

4. *Classes.* It is a well-known observation that classes are constructed from similarities and differences between things. Certainly there is no objection to the view that the qualities of some things resemble each other more than the qualities of other things. It is only unique philosophical postulates which make classes into autistic constructions, developments of "the mind itself." The fact that logicians have drawn their ideas concerning classes chiefly from mathematics probably accounts for the autistic view. Biologists, geologists, and astronomers, definitely concerned with things, are most sympathetic to the derivation of class forms from the actual characteristics of natural objects.

5. *Behavior.* The behavior of things as interrelated with similar or dissimilar things is a fertile source for the production of universals or forms. Historically, of course, the waxing and waning of things, and the influence of one thing on another, have given rise to the constructs of functions, powers, forces, etc. From such behavior the mathematical construct of *function* has undoubtedly arisen, an elaborate evolution transforming action into detached relation.

6. *Number.* The natural-history observer has no difficulty in

seeing how all the number forms or universals, such as unity, singularity, particularity, plurality, and manifoldness, are by longer or shorter procedures derived from contacts with concrete objects. Natural things exist as singles, couples, triples, and higher multiples. Also, through various conditions they become divided and thus multiplied. It is only the Platonic bias which excludes the derivation of numbers from such processes as counting or otherwise manipulating things.

(b) *Action Sources*

Traditionally, writers on universals divided themselves primarily into ontologists and epistemologists. The latter—the conceptualists who projected universals into things—proceeded on the basis of knowledge, rather than of things. To signalize their differences from ontologists they worked mostly with terms.

On the whole, epistemologists or logisticians operate on the basis of a relationship between utterances (references) and denotational terms and things. They stress relations which are, as Dewey[18] asserts: "expressed by such words as "is, is-not, if-then, only (none but) and, or some-all." Many logicians turn to problems of subject-predicate, substantive-adjective, and similar grammatical items for instances of universals.[19]

(c) *Product Sources*

Many logical forms are higher-order abstractions and generalizations. For example, qualities and properties of things are abstracted and generalized to produce such products as sensations (chap. 13, p. 12). These products serve in turn as the raw materials for further abstracting and generalizing processes, with the resulting product *sense data*. Higher-order products are also illustrated by propositional or sentential forms. Abstracting from "the man is tall" one reaches such consecutive products as "x is tall," "x is y," "x = y."

Higher-order product development may be part of a short or long series. In view of the evolution of all psychological events (vol. I, chap. 6) it is probably safe to generalize that all abstracting and generalizing involves a number of successive develop-

[18] Logic, p. 1.
[19] See p. 6.

ments. In any instance, however, we need only distinguish between prior interbehavior, in which we originally construct generals or universals, and the posterior interbehavior of further abstracting and generalizing.

No doubt the highest orders of forms are describable as imaginary relations between imaginary terms (things). Responses to such higher-order relations may be illustrated by comparing the relationship between $Xisx$ and $Xezl$ with that between $Xuxl$ and $Tyxl$. All four terms in the preceding sentence refer to planets, each one larger than the whole of the known galaxies. In this case, instead of interbehaving with a dyadic relation of concrete or abstract things, we have a triadic relation because we must consider the constructive powers of the interbehaving individual. Keeping alive the interbehavioral principle, we have definite referents for our propositions concerning the existence, reality, and significance of the terms and their two aspects.

FORMS AS SYSTEM COMPONENTS

So far we have studied forms as products by departing from all historical views of mental faculties and mental objects. Also, we have not stressed the logical or system-building character of forms, except to deny, by implication at least, that forms are logical in the conventional sense of being nonexistential. We turn now to their system-building aspect.

A preliminary step is to compare forms with things as system-building components. Forms are products developed for particular systems, whereas things are any kind of stimulus objects found ready at hand. Systems can be built of many sorts of blocks. The following table may help to clarify this distinction.

System Components	
Forms	*Things*
Thing constructs	Objects (natural and artificial)
Relation constructs	Relations (discovered and contrived)
Property constructs	Properties (observed or attributed)
Number constructs	Quantity (singularity and plurality)
Magnitude	Dimensional extent
Terms	Words, reference acts

Conventional logics are built from forms, though the builders may not be aware that their materials are constructs produced from specific manipulations of things. Conventional logical building is carried on in two steps: (1) compounding forms into propositions and (2) organizing propositions into complexes and sets of propositions.

Propositions as Form Compounds. As constructs propositions are compounds developed by elaborate abstractions from events. The proposition P(Iron is a metal) compounds certain qualities and certain substances for classificatory or manipulative purposes. No one probably would object to such a description of the formulation procedure, nor to the implication that the products constitute formulae. The question is: Can one accept the total set of implications?

Basically, we are occupied with persons operating upon things in a remote way. No dualistic version of concepts or ideas is admissible. We have already excluded all notions of mental states as over against actual things. Nor are we concerned with a number of individuals (class aggregate) as against the individuals as members. We are dealing, rather, with products of prior interbehavior with things.[20] In short, any logical view harboring universals, forms, symbols, or propositions which are identical with things we regard as logistic and derived from historic identification of thoughts, things, and words.

Propositional Complexes. Propositions organized into complexes or minor systems are illustrated by syllogisms, implications, sorites, etc. We must, however, differentiate sharply between the sentences which refer to, or stand for, the propositional chains and the propositional complexes referred to or denoted. All such formalistic systems take their place among those other systems built on the basis of actual things, relations, acts, etc. A genuine operational theory, by keeping clear the situations in which persons are interoperating with their stimulus objects, avoids the pitfall of distinguishing between generic and universal propositions as absolute and inclusive types. Instead we handle interbehavior with all sorts of things, abstractions, constructs, and so on.

ABSTRACT FORMS AS TOTAL SYSTEMS

To describe total systems as products built out of prior form products would be tantamount to expanding the classical univer-

---

[20] Our view probably has much in common with Dewey's emphasis of forms accruing to subject matter by inquiry, but we object to things arising from inquiry out of a vague matrix called "subject matter."

salistic and exclusive logics. This is not our intention; we merely want to indicate the trend followed by typical formal logical systems: the dialectical, analytical, symbolic, and methodological logics.

Dialectical Logics. By dialectical logic we mean the traditional ontological systems of Hegel, Bradley, Bosanquet, and others who identify thoughts and things. Such logic is built mostly of universals or quality forms. Relations are regarded as internal—that is, continuous with terms related. As such, relations are presumed to be qualitative essences. Also, for such logics quantities merge with qualities.

Whatever representation of fact one can find in such systems is vitiated by the universalistic and necessitarian character given them. Precisely because these systems are articulated with commonsense events, rather than with scientific or mathematical materials, the fall is all the greater when the system maker climbs above the reaches of concrete data.

Analytical Logics. Logical systems derived from Aristotelian sources are built with classes or aggregates as building blocks. The primary problems concern the interrelation of members of classes. The subsumptionistic features of such logics really concern class inclusion or exclusion.

But what of the great emphasis upon sentences or propositions? The answer: Verbal or sentential materials are representational, and are employed only to interrelate class members and classes.

Symbolic Logics. Symbolic or mathematical logics are constructed of relations. The fact that mathematics is the ideal and prototype of symbolic logic in itself substantiates this point. In the symbolic domain propositional logic deals only with propositions as terms in relation. Various truth functions serve to relate sentences or propositions.

Methodological Logics. Operations, actions, and methods abstracted from various manipulations are the building materials of those logics claiming to be methodologies of science. We have discussed such systemological products in Chapter 15.

CHAPTER XIX

INTERBEHAVIORAL LOGIC AND CAUSATION

CAUSATION AS APPLIED LOGIC

THE study of causal problems brings us to the essentially applied division of our treatise. This division includes, besides causation, the consideration of probability, laws of thought, measurement, and scientific method. These are topics not treated by all logicians, nor, indeed, even regarded as necessary subject matter of logical investigation. For us, however, their examination is extremely important, as it enables us to observe the results we obtain from applying interbehavioral principles to such materials. The procedure we follow in this work of application is illustrated by the following questions:

(1) Do such problems as causation, probability, measurement, and the nature of scientific method belong to the logical domain? If so, on what basis? And do they belong to logic exclusively?

(2) To what extent do answers to the above questions depend upon cultural presuppositions, as well as upon prior assumptions concerning psychology, epistemology, and logical theory?

(3) Are there single and unique descriptions of the above topics, or are there many?

(4) Do any or all of these topics pertain exclusively or primarily to the event, language, or system-construction domains?

In the present chapter we ask: What light can specificity logic throw upon the causation problem?

IS CAUSATION A LOGICAL PROBLEM?

Historically, causal problems were not apportioned to the logical, but rather to the ontological field. Some logicians still declare: "Cause and effect are not logical categories."[1] They may add that cause and effect are "recalcitrant metaphysical ideas."[2] In a similar mood it is asserted that the analysis of the meaning of causality is not the logician's task.[3] It is not uncommon, however, to find

---

[1] Eaton, General, p. 508.
[2] Ibid.
[3] Cohen and Nagel, Introduction, p. 245.

logicians firmly insisting that cause is not an ontological but a logical category concerned with the organization of means and ends.[4] Some logicians even declare that inquiry into cause is an inevitable feature of logic.

The question whether causal problems are at home in logic obviously involves more than a simple adjudication of the boundaries set to inquiry. It is a question of the nature of cause itself. Moreover, any answer implies a distinctive logical theory. Whether a logician treats causation, and in what manner, depends also upon his psychological views—his notions of the way individuals operate in causal situations. Those who hold that logic is essentially system building find that causal situations provide scope in a unique way for logical work.

EMERGENCE OF CAUSALITY IN METHODISTIC LOGIC

To Kant's Copernican revolution and to Mill's renovation of Inductive Logic we may trace the entrance of causal problems into the logical domain.[5] The synthesis of ontological and logical investigation was initiated when Kant forced objects to conform to the knower's modes of cognition, which, of course, comprise causal as well as other categories.

But if Kant originated this tradition, Mill established it by welding logic to the methodology of science. Mill thoroughly incorporated causal problems into logic when he attempted to convert logic, in whole or part, into a science of scientific method.[6] There is hardly a doubt that Kant and Mill emphasized cause as a logical problem in order to build up an empirical world system. In line with their architectonic interests their logics were designed to show how reason operated in ordering actual facts, rather than to demonstrate the interrelation of inferential propositions, as in traditional Formal Logic.

The formalistic tradition, however, has never really been supplanted. Certainly the tremendous development of mathematics as a rigid constructional or hypothetico-deductive enterprise has only served to support and vitalize it. The encouragement which

---

[4] Cf. Dewey, Logic, pp. 455ff.

[5] We pass over any claims made for the Hegelian system of concrete universals.

[6] The procedure is to incorporate ampliative induction into logic, and to equate induction with the search for causes. Cf. Kneale, Probability, Part 2.

deductive mathematics gave logicians resulted in the evolution of logical systems featuring symbol structures, organizations of relations, types of order, and similar abstractional organizations. Thus logicians have increasingly inclined toward formulating and transforming propositions (sentences) and away from observations concerned with particular existential occurrences. The latter are even spurned as experiental and intuitive.

Cause, therefore, treated other than as an abstract formal category, is not welcome in conventional logic. Certainly, cause envisaged as an interrelationship of particular happenings has a very precarious place in logical treatises. Methodologians are formalists even when they are interested in setting up large general method systems for scientific work; thus they make cause into a category belonging to the logical domain. In such a methodological treatise as Dewey's *Logic*, the adjective *logical*, employed to qualify the cause category, removes cause from the domain of existence and actual things and places it among the constructs.

Conventional logicians apparently can only assimilate causal problems as long as the latter remain detached from concrete events, although sometimes cause is regarded as a leading principle which directs contact with existing things. This middle course is adopted because, like species, essence, purpose, end, and simplicity, ontological cause has been interpreted as an objectionable property of nature.[7] We suggest that the fault of contemporary theories of causation lies not in their inclination toward ontology or epistemology, but in their departure from objective happenings and their attachment to some culturally influenced attitude. At the basis of illegitimate interpretations of causation is the absolutistic logical tradition. It is this same tradition which accounts for unsatisfactory ontologies and epistemologies.

In order to clarify the causal problem and its relation to logic we examine briefly the development of ideas concerning causation.

CULTURAL BACKGROUND OF CAUSALITY

It is an appealing convention that the technical notion of cause originated among the Greek scientists who developed it as a replacement for ideas of indetermination and chaos. In order here is the declaration of Leucippus:

[7] Dewey, Logic, p. 462.

No thing arises without a cause, but everything through determined grounds and under the stress of necessity.[8]

The widely held view that when thinkers adopted the causal notion to account for things they discarded mystic processes and became exclusively occupied with events as caused by other events is, however, scarcely true. The evolution of the causality construct did not once and for all establish a mode of thinking concerned only with laws derived from observed things and events. Actually, the interest in cause in no sense excluded the mystical from the explanations of natural happenings. Worse, from time to time cause itself was made into a mystical process, for under this rubric were placed innumerable magical forces which were presumed to bring things about in some unknown, and sometimes impossible, manner.

Under simple cultural conditions causes have been regarded as elementary agencies for producing various objects and events; not infrequently the term *cause* refers to acts of personal creation. Again, causes are powers exerted by an agent in carrying out some purpose. As is well known, even thinkers of the 17th and early 18th centuries were not emancipated from such views. Hence the controversy between Leibnizians, who believed the supreme power so created the universe that it was everlastingly self-operating, and Newtonians, who held that the cosmic mechanism required occasional divine intervention to run smoothly.

It is clear, then, that the causal construct has had an uneven career in the history of thought. What lends credence to the belief that among the Greeks cause became a definitely naturalistic idea is the simple but straightforward presentation of Aristotle. He begins with the problem of knowing a thing and asserts that knowledge depends upon cause or primary conditions.[9]

Thus he enumerates four causes: (1) material, that from which a thing comes into being—the silver of the bowl, the bronze of a statue, (2) the formal, in the sense of shape, pattern or formula —for example, the ratio 2:1, in the case of the octave, (3) the primary source of the change, "what makes of what is made," an

[8] Diels, Vorsokratiker, vol. II, p. 10.
[9] Analytica Posteriora, 71b, 9; Physica, 184a, 12.

agent, as an adviser, parent, etc., (4) the end or "that for the sake of which" a thing is done—health is the end of walking.[10]

Under more sophisticated conditions cause became an all-embracing impersonal principle or law employed to account for everything that happened, and to order events within a single system, or set of systems. The scientific problem was construed as the search for the powers or conditions which gave rise to certain events. Such ideas were reinforced by the quest for certainty and incontestable knowledge.

On a somewhat higher level of cultural evolution cause became transformed into a series of conditions requisite for explaining observed events. Causes were accordingly regarded as rules of order and regularity, or as laws describing, or referring to, events. This type of construction had its peak development when cause was finally conjoined with problems of predicting and controlling future happenings.[11]

CLASSICAL CAUSAL THEORY

Causal theory originates directly from a cultural matrix. Logicians and other writers who espouse a single and universal causal construct therefore have a large range of items from which to choose. They may variously characterize cause as some kind of entity—a category, a power, a relation, or an action.

To facilitate the inspection of classical causal constructs we differentiate three types of theory: (a) formal, (b) epistemological, and (c) ontological. Each type represents a special mode of interbehavior with causal situations. The basis for accepting a particular theory is one's adherence to a certain philosophical school and proximity to scientific research. Such factors influence the kind of problems formulated, the descriptions of cause, and the way the causal situation is handled.

(a) *Formal Cause Theory*. The formal theory consists of assertions concerning symbolized relations. Causal events are interacted with as abstruse entities. Even when particular happenings are alleged to be the sources of constructed theories, the ideas are pitched on the abstract plane of formal and verbal systems.

The following questions represent typical formal issues:

[10] Physica, 194b, 16; Metaphysica, 1013a, 24.
[11] Cf. Burtt, Value.

Is an exception possible to the law or to the fact of causal necessity?

Are cause and effect absolutely distinct, or can one contain the other?

Must cause inevitably precede effect, or can cause and effect be simultaneous?

Can cause continue after the cessation of effect?

Can effect continue after the cessation of cause?

Can causes produce their effects at a distance, or must they operate through a contiguous medium?

Are causes different from, or identical with, conditions?

On the whole, interbehaving formally with cause results in systems of compatible sentences (p. 147). Ample scope is therefore available for the autistic creation of cause-and-effect things and relations.

(b) *Epistemological Cause Theory*. Epistemological causal theory concerns processes of knowing the connections existing or alleged to exist between things. Kant's categorial theory to the effect that cause is an *a priori* determiner of invariable and irreversible succession is an excellent illustration.

The epistemological handling of causal happenings is well demonstrated by the discussions concerning causal necessity. It is asked: Is causal necessity an objective necessity of things, or a logical necessity of thought or assertion? Again, do assertions of causal necessity refer to hypothetical and existential things or only to absolute and mathematical connections?[12] Still other questions concern the exclusive applicability of cause to past events or predictions of the future.

(c) *Ontological Cause Theory*. Theoretical constructs of the ontological type stress relations between things and events. They are effectively demonstrated by the following classic examples.

Thing Causes. Though Hume finally settled down to the belief that cause basically consists of relations between things, he vacillated between this view and the notion that causes are themselves things, as the following passages indicate:

The idea, then, of causation must be derived from some *relation* among objects.[13]

---

[12] Cf. Pap, Meaning.
[13] Treatise, p. 75.

Whatever objects are considered as causes are *contiguous*.[14]
A cause is an object precedent and contiguous to another.[15]

Hume's choice is influenced, of course, by his doctrine that all things are reducible to sensation; and cause is not a sensation or a quality of an object.[16]

For the more stable prototype of the view that causes are objects we must go back to Hobbes' attempt to establish a natural philosophy. He opens his discussion of cause and effect with the statement:

A body is said to work upon or *act*, that is to say, *do* something to another body, when it either generates or destroys some accident in it.[17]

Concerning the cause of motion, Hobbes is clear:

There can be no cause of motion, except in a body contiguous and moved.[18]

Though statistics are lacking, there is no doubt that a tremendous number of thinkers regard causes as things, as in the case of chemicals or drugs causing death. The entire traditional formulation of agents and patients, of doers and sufferers, is supported by the pillar of cause as object, or property and accident of an object.

Relation Causes. Abstractive and universalistic habits of thought automatically result in the notion of cause as relation. There are Hume's constant conjunction, Kant's irreversible succession, and Mill's uniform and unconditional sequence. Also there are variations as to constancy of conjunction,[19] or absence of recurrence with a residue of relations between particular concrete events.[20] Again, writers differ as to the terms that are related; some lean toward objects instead of events; still others define the causal relation as connecting factors in a single event.[21]

[14] Ibid., p. 75.
[15] Ibid., p. 170.
[16] Ibid., p. 75.
[17] Works, vol. I, p. 120.
[18] Ibid., p. 124.
[19] Hume, Treatise.
[20] Ducasse, Nature.
[21] Winn, Nature.

Event Causes. Change, Wundt declares, is the primary condition of causality. Cause accordingly concerns not things but events.[22] Obviously, however, even the doctors who agree differ as to the nature of events. For example, it is asserted that causation always involves transmission of energy from place to place.[23] This formulation is opposed to such characterizations of cause as that it is motion[24] or change,[25] or, finally, action.[26]

CAUSALITY: UNIVERSAL AND SPECIFIC

Everyone who approaches causality from the angle of events must be impressed by the variety of causal situations. Still there is no repressing the great urge to set up a single comprehensive theory. Conventional doctrine projects the general presupposition that causality constitutes a basic law of nature or of science. The assumption is made either that the universe is constructed on a plan of necessary connection or that scientific explanation demands a universal causal principle.

Once more we see exhibited the enormous hold of abstractionism and generality on logical thought, as well as on the analysis of science. The result for causal study is such a vaporization of events as to allow anything to be said about them. In such a vacuous causal universe it may be asserted that "Whatever is, may not be," "Not everything that could happen does happen," "The contrary of every matter of fact is still possible."

The universalistic claim that the world is a system of necessary connections—namely, "every effect must have a cause"—is not condemned by us merely because it is a vain apothegm. Not at all. The gravamen lies in assuming that such an assertion is factually significant. Even more serious is the fact that it serves to cover up the inevitable specificity of causal situations. No general formula can ever satisfactorily symbolize the complicated concourses of events comprising causality.

The assumption that the goal of science is to discover universal absolute causes is to equate science with metaphysics. Insofar as

[22] Logik, vol. I, p. 586.
[23] Winn, Nature, p. 202.
[24] Carus, Problem.
[25] Schopenhauer, Fourfold, p. 20; Gotschalk, Nature.
[26] Mercier, Causation.

Hume and his followers intended to prohibit this kind of equation they were on the right path. The search for absolute causes obviously goes counter to any procedure actually practiced in a scientific laboratory. It is doubtless this type of abstract and remote cause to which Newton referred in connection with gravitation:

Hitherto we have explained the phenomena of the heavens and of our sea by the power of gravity, but have not yet assigned the cause of this power.[27] . . . Hitherto I have not been able to discover the cause of those properties of gravity from phenomena, and I frame no hypotheses; for whatever is not deduced from the phenomena is to be called an hypothesis; and hypotheses, whether metaphysical or physical, whether of occult qualities or mechanical, have no place in experimental philosophy. In this philosophy particular propositions are inferred from the phenomena, and afterwards rendered general by induction.[28]

One might argue that the very number and variety of causal situations are so great as to accommodate the two grand generalizations that the universe is a set of necessary connections and that science demands a universal causal principle. Even if this result could conceivably be brought about by judicious deflation and translation of the original assertions, their relevancy at once becomes severely limited. Similarly, by proper treatment the more specific formulations that we have called formal, epistemological, and ontological may be adapted to certain phases of causal situations. In all cases in which generalized formulae are adapted to specific instances it is the detailed variation of the events under consideration which becomes emphasized. Causal principles are the more cogent the closer they approach concrete events.

Keeping close to events makes irrelevant any large-scale formal assertion. Important only are analyses and formulations that serve to connect one event with others in a class. Specific causal formulations exclusively enable us to make predictions[29] and in general achieve some experimental control over certain situations.

---

[27] Principia, General Scholium, p. 546.
[28] Ibid., p. 547.
[29] Cf. Schlick, Causality.

Logical Necessity and Factual Cause

Formalistic logicians separate themselves into two camps. The strictly mathematical logicians remain completely within the bounds of mathematical forms. The philosophical formalists incline toward the more contentful systems which articulate with scientific materials. It is the latter who are confronted with challenging causal problems. On the one hand, they are concerned with propositions or sentences implying absolute and universal necessity. On the other, causality implies events and their relations—in short, probabilities, specificities, and, in general, inductive as over against deductive processes.

The way out of this discrepancy is found, of course, in the very fact of formalism itself—that is, sententiality. Thus arises the construct of logical necessity. For the most part, this sort of necessity consists simply of assertions—"Every event must have a cause," "Order is the essence of nature." Formal logic comprises, in fact, a stock of sentences containing the word *cause*—sentences which have no connection with the interrelations of things, their properties, and relations in concrete event systems.

Logical necessity and causation are close to classical metaphysics despite the fact that formal logic is presumed to be concerned exclusively with abstruse sentences. Certainly logical necessity is remote from any causal system of concrete happenings. It has nothing to do with such factual necessity as providing oxygen for stratospheric flying or an adequate diet to maintain growth. The domain of formal logic allows for such mystic ideas as a deterministic or indeterministic universe, a causal or an acausal cosmos.

The gulf which linguistic logic creates between logical and factual necessity is thrown into relief by a comparison recently made between causal and formal implication.[30] Hofstadter asks his readers to suppose that the formula "All men are mortal" represents a formal implication, and at the same time a causal law. Now, he says, the real possibility of an immortal man is compatible with the truth of the formal implication. But the very supposition that under certain conditions a man might live forever signifies the possibility of violating a causal principle. And this goes counter to the idea of a causal law.[31]

[30] Hofstadter, Causality.
[31] Ibid., p. 259.

The attempt to differentiate logical (analytic) necessity from causal (real) necessity succeeds only in revealing the irrelation of formal logic and concrete events. The formal interrelation of sentences can not be connected with descriptions of specific happenings. Concrete linguistic events can be handled only by non-formalistic sentence systems.

Causal events are clearly different from the constructional systems connected with them. Of the latter there are many different types. Logicians, accordingly, must choose among these systems. Every logician sensitive to things, events, and conditions inclines as far as possible toward sentence systems describing actual interrelations of pattern components. But few logicians accept the view that they are operating with objective happenings; thus they are inevitably limited to systems of abstruse sentences. It is significant, however, that logicians attempt to get at least so close to events as to consider the relationship between formal and causal implication.

From an event standpoint the logically possible consists of a set of incomplete actualities (factors). The chemicals are present but not the catalyzer. No relevance or significance is attached to any factor or combination except as it is known from observation and experimentation—that is, through prior interbehavior.

Unfortunately linguistic logic and its occupation with logical necessity can only lead to argument and verbal systemology, which does justice neither to logic nor to causal events. Linguistic logicians, for example, may entertain the metaphysical assumption that the world is such that not everything that could happen does happen.[32] What "could happen" is regarded as a product of a selective or restrictive action.

What is meant by the logically possible may be illustrated by considering the number of possible combinations of S and P. A may be both S and P, S but not P, P but not S, and neither. Now the assumption is made that one of these combinations does not occur. This is interpreted as a causal necessity limiting logical necessity or possibility.[33]

Connected with such a view is the belief that when we seek the

[32] Hofstadter, Ibid., Oliver, Logic.

[33] The term *possibility* is used to avoid saying *certainty*. Cf. Oliver, Logic; also Hofstadter, Causality.

cause of an event we seek the reason "why" this event, and not some other logically possible one, is occurring. It is chiefly the linguistic influence which fortifies the belief that a causal investigation involves anything but the problem "how" an event occurs[34] —namely, how the constituent factors of things, their properties and conditions, are organized in an event situation.

Causality, Functionality, and Correlation

Sophisticated views of causality as a feature of nature have developed under a number of influences. Outstanding has been the effect of detailed facts such as the sciences uncover. The ideas of powers and potencies appear unserviceable and even repugnant to the scientific worker. For this reason causality in the traditional sense of potency or productivity has been replaced by the notion of functionality. $x = f(m)$, or more elaborately dy/dx^2, symbolizes the kind of relationship of variables envisaged by the scientist. It may well be that such symbolized relations are constructs that can not be properly descriptive of events, but they nevertheless help to avoid occult powers. We are willing to sponsor such formulae if they are descriptive, since no description can be more than a referential construct.

Statisticians, too, concerned with concrete data make a sharp distinction between correlation and cause. Sometimes they go so far as to declare that statistics is fundamentally the investigation of events which, because they can not be causally interrelated, must therefore be statistically correlated. On the other hand, many students admit no cause relation except Hume's constant temporal sequence. They believe, then, that cause and effect amount to no more than a covariance of presence and absence.

Cause and causal relations, therefore, may simply be regarded as the interrelations of field components. Certainly, causation can be formulated as correlation. At first, correlationists were primarily interested in organizing two-factor systems. Later, the development of partial and multiple correlation techniques amplified the original view. The above paradox is easily resolved by indicating that cause is, after all, only a type of correlation.

Always there remains, however, dissatisfaction with the simple association of factors lacking any efficacy with respect to each

[34] Cf. Hempel and Oppenheim, Studies.

other. Causation, it has been thought, must be an essentially effective sort of factorial copresence. On this basis it is argued that causal factors consist of actions of things or persons, which, in combination with each other, constitute new fields as compared with other correlations. In other words, causal correlations are regarded as a special sort of factorial combination, a coming together of causal factors which, when together, constitute a different event system.

To avoid an unwitting return to previously rejected ways of thinking we must differentiate between effective combinations resulting from a conjunction of "potencies" and effective combinations resulting from changes in event fields. We exclude here all forms of causal antecedents. No object, or action of an object, may be regarded as a causal factor prior to its presence or occurrence in a specified field. These antecedent potencies are rejected when they are presumed to have inhered in any copresent object, as in the classical single causal antecedent. Causal changes or fields are functions of mutual and reciprocal changes in every aspect of a factorial system.

Causal changes in any field constitute a rearrangement in the simultaneous coexistence of factors in a unique pattern. When we say that an inflammable substance is caused to ignite by a spark which happens to fall upon it, we utter a misleading statement. No such change of field or event actually occurs without the copresence of both the spark and the inflammable substance in a particular spatiotemporal reference frame. The emphasis here is on the things, properties, and conditions making up the particular event field. In some fields the factors constitute a pattern which may not be intense nor even discernible. Frequently an explosion is required to stimulate causal investigation, but other event changes consisting of less noticeable factorial arrangements are not different in principle.

The fact that many changes and transformations of events are neglected or regarded as inconsequential suggests a differentiation between three features of causal situations. First, there are the combinations and recombinations of factors under specific conditions. Here we must point to events occurring without human intervention—for example, complex reversible chemical reactions. Next, we have descriptions of such reactions in the form of functional equations. Here the observations influenced by the observer's problems and interests stand out. And finally, there is the more remote descriptive interrelating of certain events with other similar and analogous events. In such instances constructional operations are emphasized which are only partially stressed in describing and recording events.

Operational Causal Theory

Classical cause theories are metaphysical—at least, cosmic. Their proponents interbehave with causal problems in a grand manner. By contrast we propose an operational mode of causal interbehavior, based on the assumption that causal problems arise directly from the scientist's contact with objects, events, and relations. His operation with causal problems is best examined in a particular type of situation—a fact which is true, of course, of anything he investigates. Operational cause can only be studied in connection with problems localizable in a certain domain—chemistry, biology, physics, and so on. The operations consist of assessing events, or interbehaving with their varying factors on the basis of developed techniques and available materials in order to arrive at some specific answer to a particular question. As a rule, the answers are stated in the form of propositions indicating the interrelationship of event factors. Whether or not general causes exist, and why, are questions falling outside the scientist's field of interest.

According to our hypothesis that causal processes and relations constitute factors in event fields, causal elements consist of objects, their combinations and relations in particular systems. All things existing as parts or features of a certain pattern of happenings may be said to *participate* as factors in that particular causal field. In some causal events there are few factors, in others many. In case there are many we find great variations in the proportion of those factors that appear more prominent than the remainder. Again, in some events there may be no outstanding factors at all. Whether there are many or few, the factors may be either sequential or coordinate in time. Causal situations must further be differentiated on the basis of the relative availability of the factors for observation and experimental manipulation. In some instances the factors can only be hypothetically named and enumerated.

Correspondingly, causal description consists of enumerating the factors comprising the causal situation. This analysis is initiated by some problem of immediate achievement or prediction. Since causation basically amounts to the copresence of a given number of components, every vestige of ultimacy and absoluteness is barred. Furthermore, the only element of universality lies in the identifying and specifying formula. Beyond that there is no resemblance to any view that reduces cause to a single exclusive type of event or construction. Faced with the multiplicity of specific causal systems one can scarcely remain convinced that there is but one adequate interpretation of cause.

Classical Psychology and Causal Theory

Causal theories, we have indicated (p. 149), always originate and maintain themselves as part of a comprehensive cultural complex. This means that among the many intellectual counterparts to cause we find a psychological theory. Outstanding variants of causal theory are associated with their corresponding psychological doctrines of either monistic or monadic mind. For instance, a rationalistic and *a priori* causal theory correlates with a doctrine of unitary mind, while an empirical and *a posteriori* notion fits into a monadistic or atomistic mind theory. To consider some historical examples, such an adherent of unified mind as Kant naturally entertained a causal theory according to which necessity was a determining condition for the existence of events, while Hume's psychic atomism had no room for necessity among existing things and their relations. In general, it is psychistic psychology which provides comfort to those who must differentiate between the abstraction of necessity and the contingency of existence.

Much recent writing on the causal problem centers around the associationistic psychology of Hume and Mill. Scholars are influenced by atomistic psychology when they (1) adopt the Hume-Mill pronouncements on cause, (2) modify them in detail or (3) oppose them entirely. Discussions of causation, centering around the possibility of immediate spatial contiguity of antecedent and consequent or necessary connection, as well as inevitable conjunction, definitely reflect the Hume-Mill reduction of psychological events to the appearance and reappearance of psychic states as discrete elements tied together by habit and custom, or by the gentle forces of association. As we have already intimated, the British empiricists, for whom both knowledge and the world consisted of sensations and their interrelations, could not make cause a substantive quality such as sensations were presumed to be, and therefore had to turn to cause as a relation. It followed that for them causation was a necessary sequence of sensations or their combinations.

From an historical standpoint no one can deny that Hume's notion of causation has been of great value in upsetting the inept rationalism rampant in his time. But it is questionable whether his own type of sensationism, which, of course, is not altogether different from rationalism though of another order, should be allowed to confound the study of causal problems.

Certainly, cause is no quality, as Hume's "impressions" are presumed to be. Nor are objects reducible to psychic processes, so that notions of precarious existence or interrelation are warranted. No less objectionable are the mentalistic constructions which differentiate between experiencing on the basis of impression or sensation as immediate psychic states, and reasoning, which is more or less independent of such immediately given states.

Rationalistic causal doctrines which, generally speaking, imply that cause is a necessity of existence, correspond to monistic psychology involving a continuously existing unitary mind. In formulating causal principles this version of monistic psychology is no more helpful than the monadistic one. No connection can be postulated between natural events and creative powers, regarded either as mirrored in a unified mind or as independent of such a mind. Rationalistic causation may be characterized as *why* causation. It certainly harks back to impersonal or personal creative powers, and, in the latter case, to the projection of human desires and interests into events. When such a procedure is fortified by some sort of psychic psychology its weakness is doubled. No traditional spiritistic psychology can do justice to any occurrence or interpretation of natural events.

Such ways of thinking are, of course, completely superseded by objective psychology. When dealing with concrete situations the causal agency may be a thing or an event. By thing we may refer to a chemical compound, which, when brought into combination with other compounds, results in an explosion. But since in all cases causation has to do with events, causal or agentive things are themselves events (p. 157). Admittedly, there is a definite interrelationship of objects in the sense of crude things, such as the interrelationship of chemical elements or compounds, or when water is thrown upon a burning house. The reduction of causation to relationship in the British empirical tradition is, of course, completely set aside.

On the other hand, interbehavioral logic allows for the specification and emphasis of the relational factor as primary in description. This is to be expected, since according to interbehavioral psychology the term *relation* refers to the combination of concrete factors in a causal situation. In no case, however, are we dealing with relations remote from actual things, for, obviously, from an objective point of view, relations are only features abstracted from the relationships of objects or events.

PATTERN OF CAUSAL INVESTIGATION

Conclusions concerning the logic of causation must be drawn from two sources. First we analyze the causal situation and secondly we observe the logician interacting with that situation. This double requirement we can carry out by examining the pattern of causal investigation.

Following our general paradigm of interbehavioral study we differentiate between three large classes of factors: (A) data of various sorts (crude = prior to analysis, or refined = analyzed); (B) investigative operations (experimental, mensurative); and (C) constructions (hypotheses, theories, laws).

A. *Data*

There are two sorts of causal data: (1) constructs and (2) events.

(1) *Causal Constructs.* Constructs as data consist of reactions or products of reactions. "Arsenic caused Smith's death" as descriptive of Jones' reaction to the event involving the death of Smith is different from the death event. Smith's actual death as part of a system involving arsenic is an event independent of any reaction to it, though without such a reaction it would be unknown. Causal stimulus objects as reactions consist of beliefs, utterances, or writing acts performed with respect to organizations of systemic factors

which we refer to as Smith's death by arsenic. As products the data, or stimulus objects, comprise propositions, allegations, or theories concerning events or alleged events.

Because such data are secondary—that is, come to the observer by means of a person's (Jones') intermediating action it may well happen that no arsenic death has actually transpired. Jones' belief may be delusory, his assertion mistaken or false. In such cases we assume that he is responding to substitute stimulation, not to the direct Smith-arsenic-death event. Substitute stimuli, of course, can stand for mystic and magical apparitions as well as for actual events. Because of this latter possibility we may regard Jones' interaction with the substitute stimulus object as an authentic—though nevertheless fictitious—causal datum.

On the whole, construct data play a larger role in the causal investigations conducted by logicians and philosophers than in those carried on by scientists. The latter are definitely more interested in causal situations in which the data consist of events. We must not, however, lose sight of the fact that scientists may regard all causal data not as natural-event data but as construct data.

This point is illustrated by Russell's assertion that there is no such things as cause and that the classical law of causality is unscientific and false.[35] Scientists are never interested, Russell asserts, in necessary succession, but in functional relations among variables. The causal data of philosophers, or what they interbehave with, according to him consist of sentences—in our terms, substitute stimulus objects. Pepper, who regards causality as a characteristic of natural events, asserts that Russell is not talking about causality at all, but about physicists' expressions of natural law.[36] These expressions refer to observations of correlations.

That Pepper is probably correct is indicated by the following:

The essential business of physics is the discovery of "causal laws" by which I mean any principles which, if true, enable us to infer something about a certain region of space-time from something about some other region or regions.[37]

Substitute stimulus objects may correspond to authentic causa-

[35] Notion.
[36] How.
[37] Russell, Reply, p. 701.

tion if one grants the occurrence of such events. Assuming the correctness of the hypothesis that causation consists of a pattern of subevents or event factors we find a continuous series of inter-behaviors with such events. The simplest level is that of every-day or "commonsense" situations. Here simple questions are asked: the goal of the inquiry is a practical outcome of the inter-action of events. On the scientific level more significant questions are posed, with a correspondingly greater capacity on the part of the investigator to analyze the interacting factors; hence, a more sophisticated procedure of interrelating events. The scientist, too, works out elaborate experimental techniques for the dissociation and technical reassociation of factors in order to discover their variants and invariants.

In more formal (logical) situations causal interbehavior proceeds on the basis of contacts with substitutes for highly analytic data. The direct stimulus objects are kept at a remote distance for the sake of achieving precise descriptions and interpretations of causal factors and their interrelationships.

(2) *Causal Events.* Causal events as data consist of particular interrelationships of observed happenings. The essentially causal feature comprises the copresence of the event components. Events can be observed to occur through the addition and subtraction, the separation and contiguation of the factors. Certain chemical components are present together, and only a temperature or pressure change is necessary for a new chemical state to ensue. Again, a slow chemical reaction may be speeded up by adding another compound or varying temperature or pressure. If, while describing our investigation of an event we refer to our observation, this has nothing to do with the event itself; its factorial combinations constitute things independent of our observation or description. In psychological terms, these combinations and recombinations of factors and events are independent stimulus objects with which the observer interacts.

Now in some cases it may be legitimate to describe one factor as agentive, causal, or key, since it may be the factor required to complete the combination—for example, when a person facilitates or hastens the occurrence of an event by switching on the current necessary for an explosion. His behavior must be regarded as a natural component of the causal system. It operates like any other factor necessary to complete a particular kind of event combination, and thus constitutes a part of the causal data.

Interbehavioral data of both the construct and event type must be sharply distinguished from everything pertaining to psychophysical philosophy. This admonition is necessary because of a similarity in the use of terms. The terms *construct* and *construction* have frequently been employed since Russell formulated "the supreme maxim in scientific philosophising"[38]—namely, "wherever possible, substitute constructions out of known entities for inferences to unknown entities."[39]

Russell and all the many writers who deal with the contrast between constructions and inferred entities[40] are concerned with relations between mythical *sensations* and *sensibilia* of externally caused mental states and the products of purely psychic operations of the mind. This is the case even when writers do not accept Russell's view that objects of everyday circumstances and of technical physics consist of logical constructions made up of the crude data of sense.

Such problems and solutions belong to a philosophical system which entertains questions concerning the construction of an external world (p. 206) and its relation to private and individual mentality. No contrast could be greater than that marking off such a philosophy from investigations which exclude "mind," "sensations," and "immediate experiences," either as building material or as constructing powers. Constructs as products, from our standpoint, are always (a) recombinations of things, as the synthesis of water from hydrogen and oxygen, (b) measurements achieved by definite operations, (c) descriptions and recordings of events and of our operations in securing them, and (d) indirect interrelations of things by means of manual (drawings) and vocal behavior. In each case the constructing activities consist of concrete interactions of the individual with his stimulus objects on the basis of problem presented, motivation, expertness, and other concrete factors.

Central to the constructional problem is the nature of linguistic

---

[38] Mysticism, p. 155.

[39] Logical, p. 363.

[40] See, for example, Feigl, Existential; and Beck, Constructions, and the writers to whom they refer.

acts and the use of linguistic products. As in so many other situations, commerce with mythical subject matter is possible by means of linguistic factors. It is possible to construct real existence, systemic existence, possibilities, and determiners of all sorts without adequately analyzing acts and stimulus objects. We suggest that the elimination of traditional mind constructions clarifies the general constructional and inferential situation and enables us to make a direct approach to events as data.[41]

B. *Investigative Operations*

A study of the pattern of causal investigation demands that we differentiate between the two orders of observer and investigator. The behavior of the operator mentioned in the agentive illustration above constitutes a first-order operation. His activity belongs within the pattern of a causal system.

The second-order observer analyzes the work of the first operator as part of the causal data before him. He is especially interested in the interaction of the experimenter as he unravels the interrelated threads he finds among the materials with which he works.

Investigative causal operations can be demonstrated by considering the work of an experimenter as he arranges and rearranges the factors in his event situations. We select for this purpose an experiment by Hopkins.[42]

Beginning with the hypothesis that young animals grow normally on a diet of protein, fat, carbohydrates, mineral salts, and water, the investigator discovers that when these substances are purified and fed to animals they do not produce the assumed results. To groups of six rats each he fed purified milk casein (protein), lard (fat), sugar (carbohydrates), and salts obtained from oat and dog-biscuit ash. In addition, he fed one group 2 c.c. of milk per day. The milk-fed rats increased in weight normally, while the control group without milk feeding began to lose weight after 10 to 15 days.

Assuming that the operations are well controlled and the results valid, the next step in the causal investigative pattern is to

---

[41] For a comprehensive study of construction in logical situations see Kantor, Interbehavior.

[42] George, Scientist, p. 291f.

construct propositions concerning them. Convenient terms for such constructions are descriptions and interpretations.

C. *Constructions*

Descriptions and interpretations of causal occurrences naturally differ on the basis of the type of crude datum upon which they are constructed. Causal theories based on construct data are very different from those based on independent event data. Even in the case of independent event data, theory constructions may show divergences. One may set up descriptions and laws of causal events which are altogether independent of human agency, such as the tidal relationships between the moon and earth. Other constructions of causal factors involve the activities of the agent or investigator who deliberately produces certain changes in the crude data.

Cause and Effect. Faithful to the traditional relation conception, writers on cause have maintained in their descriptions two related factors, *cause* and *effect*. Critics of such a notion as necessary or inevitable relation have pointed out that it is impossible to keep these two factors distinct. Since we are dealing with event patterns, the terms *cause* and *effect* must serve specific descriptive purposes. Accordingly, when they refer to stimulus objects, these terms refer to prior and subsequent combinations of factors. Cause and effect as constructive terms serve only to isolate particular stages of observed events.

Causes and Conditions. As we have seen (p. 152), writers on causation regard the term *cause* as standing for a single and unique process or agency. From the standpoint of field theory, instead of singularity, we meet with all sorts of combinations of factors. Some writers[43] insist upon the distinction between cause and condition on the ground that cause implies a sufficient factor, and condition a necessary one. This is good as far as it goes, but in actual investigations a much larger number of differentiations must be made. When we deal with concrete situations we perforce discover innumerable degrees of availability or participation of causal factors.

Causes and Causal Interpretation. Both in the event and in its interpretation we may specify all sorts of causal conditions and

[43] Ducasse, Nature, p. 58.

relations, depending upon the investigator's interest. From the standpoint of specificity logic the investigator's purpose is a definite objective fact to consider when causes are to be determined. For instance, there is a vast difference between an investigator's interbehavior with particular causal conditions—as in his attempt to understand a certain disease or how X-rays are diffracted—and that of an individual attempting to set up a generalized definition for all possible causes. The latter procedure can not yield any significant result, and the acceptance or rejection of such a formal schema depends upon the formulator's caprice.

Here is a convenient place to point out again that interacting with concrete events is vastly different from interacting with verbal or propositional substitutes for such events. The construction of formal propositions achieves a certain degree of significance only if the formulator takes account of concrete situations.

Cause and System Building

Causal events as natural occurrences are completely independent of any person's activity. Accordingly such events may be far removed from logical or system-building behavior. Despite this fact cause and system building may be brought very close together. In the first place, causation is essentially systematic. Causal situations, as we have seen, comprise interrelations of factors, and this in itself is system. Again, human behavior occupies an exceedingly large place as an integer in causal systems, as all scientific experimentation testifies. Those who regard logic as system building are therefore in a favorable position to conjoin logic and causation. On a systemological basis logic can be closely connected with causal situations in two ways: (A) as a general structurization enterprise and (B) as a local instrumental procedure.

A. *General Causal Structurization*

Here we observe the behavior of the system builder as he erects a universalistic causal edifice.

The first thing he does is to develop or borrow comprehensive assumptions or postulates as the criteria of his projected system. We do not imply that he deliberately seizes upon these assumptions. On the contrary, he is most likely in full possession of them through the subtle influence of his general cultural milieu.

Whatever specific materials he builds upon he is forthwith prepared with a ground plan.

From a number of universalistic systemization enterprises we abstract the following series of assumptions. "Everything is arranged or governed by necessity or law," "nature is uniform and recurrent," "invariant relations exist," "every event has a cause."

A prominent feature of general structurization behavior consists in applying these principles to things. This procedure may be described as defining and interpreting operations. Certain things are asserted to cause or produce other things as effects or results. Causes are invariably antecedent to effects. Events which occur under precisely the same circumstances must cause or produce the same effect.

From this sort of activity issues a product which may consist of systems of actual things and events or systems of arguments, symbols, sentences or propositions, or a combination of these. The following examples from event, language, and formalistic levels illustrate the processes employed in the structurization of causal materials.

(a) *Event Level*. Things, conditions, and combinations of things may be conjoined for many different purposes. Naturally, system builders are motivated in diverse ways, and thus employ all sorts of criteria. Concomitantly, the system products assume every possible grade of quality.

Generally speaking, causal situations are systemized on either an analytic or a synthetic plan. In the former case, a situation is chosen which is regarded as causational, and an organization of the factors is then made. Synthetic systemization, on the other hand, stresses the organization of factors for some purpose. The features of a situation not immediately apprehended as causal are creatively connected in order to demonstrate causal relationships. The aim may be description, explanation, or prediction. Features of events are ordered as sequential or coexistent, more or less proximate or overlapping. Favoring such logical or system-building procedures is our hypothesis that causation consists of interrelationships of field factors.

(b) *Linguistic Level*. Systemization of this type is more or less autistic—namely, independent of events. The emphasis is on system as asserted and alleged, rather than on events and their intra-

and inter-relations. Here we have organizations of references to, or symbols of, causal events, such as the structures of nonontological propositions. While one can hardly put high value on a logical system so remote from actual events as to exclude singular and existential happenings, it is quite possible to organize such systems.

The most famous illustration of linguistic systemization is Mill's set of four or five causal methods which he regards as the only possible modes of experimental inquiry. Because this system so admirably exemplifies linguistic causal systemization we present in full the items which he names *methods* and *canons*.

1. Method of Agreement

   First Canon. If two or more instances of the phenomenon under investigation have only one circumstance in common, the circumstance in which alone all the instances agree, is the cause (or effect) of the given phenomenon.

2. Method of Difference

   Second Canon. If an instance in which the phenomenon under investigation occurs, and an instance in which it does not occur, have every circumstance in common save one, that one occurring only in the former; the circumstance in which alone the two instances differ, is the effect, or the cause, or an indispensable part of the cause, of the phenomenon.

0. Joint Method of Agreement and Difference

   Third Canon. If two or more instances in which the phenomenon occurs have only one circumstance in common, while two or more instances in which it does not occur have nothing in common save the absence of that circumstance; the circumstance in which alone the two sets of instances differ, is the effect, or the cause, or an indispensable part of the cause, of the phenomenon.

3. Method of Residues

   Fourth Canon. Subduct from any phenomenon such part as is known by previous inductions to be the effect of certain antecedents, and the residue of the phenomenon is the effect of the remaining antecedents.

4. Method of Concomitant Variations

   Fifth Canon. Whatever phenomenon varies in any manner whenever another phenomenon varies in some particular manner, is either a cause or an effect of that phenomenon, or is connected with it through some fact of causation.

Mill's four (5) experimental methods stand out starkly in their linguistic nudity. All the more so perhaps because he intended them to be descriptive of actual situations. To begin with, the whole system is based upon a verbal and general atomistic universe in which the determination of causes consists merely of interrelating what are said to be antecedents and consequences. But even the succession of differentiable factors becomes reduced to the simple abstractive common absence and presence of formalized circumstances.

Mill, and hosts of logicians after him, have clearly recognized the many difficulties and insufficiencies of the system of experimental methods. This fact is illustrated by the following points.

(1) Mill was troubled by the problem of plurality of causes which negated considerably his simplicity of approach. For this reason the method of agreement, originally regarded as coordinate with the method of difference, had to be devalued. (2) Again, Mill realized that his system was not as elaborate as it appeared, since the methods of agreement and difference were basic to the others. Later writers have charged that treating the formulations as so many separate methods seriously darkened the subject of induction.[44] Furthermore, it has been pointed out that the methods are essentially negative. Their function is to eliminate combinations of factors which do not meet the causal conjunction criterion.

Conventional criticisms, however, do not really focus on the fundamental objection that these formulae and systems are essentially incongruous with actual events. To describe methods of discovering causal relations implies taking some account of the vast number of contacts an investigator must have with things. So far as Mill's methods went, his idea that they were inductive syllogisms or, at least, similar sorts of schema indicates that he dimly realized he was concerned with an enormous job of linguistic constructionism.

(c) *Formal Level.* Generalized causal systems on the formal, like those on the linguistic, level are built primarily out of words. The former may be distinguished from the latter, however, on the basis of linguistic function. Because linguistic systems are reference systems they still are indexes to something beyond themselves. Not so formal systems, which in some cases are completely removed from things. Since word or symbol systems have no referents, the systems themselves constitute the only things in the situation. When concrete things are forcibly dragged in to illustrate the systems, they are clearly only descriptive analogies to actual objects and events.

Formal causal systems are exemplified by the classical maxims:

44 Joseph, Introduction, p. 430.

"post hoc propter hoc" or its opposite, "Every effect has a cause," "Same cause same effect" and its reciprocal. As we have indicated, the assumption is made that these maxims are related to data, but the enormous differences between specific events and generalized formulae are sufficient to nullify the assumption.

Another excellent example is the causal principle alleged to exist in identical structures.[45] The causal system here is characterized by the presence of the least possible content. An assertion is made about basic interrelations of things and events on the abstract ground of sameness of structure. Causal connection is asserted both on the ground that structural identity in different things implies a common causal ancestry and that earlier items in successive identical structures cause or produce the later ones.

B. *Systems as Specific Causal Instruments*

On the whole, the locale of systems to be used as instruments in studying causal problems is the field of scientific investigation. When the goal of causal study is the discovery or explanation of specific events, local systems are constructed as definite instruments of research. Aside from the fact that instrumental causal systems are constructed for the solution of specific problems, they are kept close to, and influenced by, the events they are designed to elucidate. They can not therefore assume the proportions of abstract grand-scale systems.

In one sense we may say that every specific scientific research is an example of the construction of a specific causal system. Every such research involves at some point or other the organization of event factors. Even when analytic processes prevail over synthetic, there is no less a demonstration of concrete causal system. The work of dealing with systemic components and combinations marks the characteristic causal construction.

It might be argued that the lack of a specified causal interest in a routine research minimizes somewhat the prominence of a definite causal element. This point, however, loses validity as soon as an attempt is made to explain one's results. Such an explanation is always made in terms of building a system stressing interrelations of component factors in an event situation.

Although instrumental and noninstrumental system-building

[45] Russell, Knowledge, p. 46off.

behavior is in general associated with scientific and nonscientific situations respectively, the correspondence is not at all complete. It may well be the scientist who attempts to construct universalistic causal systems, while nonscientists may be keenly interested in specific causal patterns. Recall, for instance, those rationalistic scientists who are ambitious to construct a single universalistic system. Working with mathematical tools they may be interested in developing systems of equations, all of which are interrelated, and when taken together may constitute a single system. Even here, of course, certain criteria may be preferred, but the singleness of system remains the ideal of achievement. An excellent example is Laplace's classic statement of essential causality:

> An intelligence knowing, at a given instant of time, all forces acting in nature, as well as the momentary positions of all things of which the universe consists, would be able to comprehend the motions of the largest bodies of the world and those of the smallest atoms in one single formula, provided it were sufficiently powerful to subject all data to analysis; to it, nothing would be uncertain, both future and past would be present before its eyes.[46]

On the other hand, scientists may employ specific causal principles for developing unit systems in any particular scientific field, such as in chemistry, physics, biology; or within these fields units may be developed on the basis of the interaction of field factors. It is also possible to construct instrumental systems outside scientific domains.

So large is the scope for employing specific systems in authentic causal situations that any one of the many system instruments discussed in Chapter 16 may be pointed to as an example of a logical tool for causal interpretation.

CAUSATION AND INDETERMINISM

The causal paradoxes which have turned up in connection with quantum mechanics vividly remind us of the curious part which causality has always played in scientific methodology. The rumor that quantum-mechanical investigations have led to the astounding discovery that the universe is bereft of causal principles, of determining relations, of systems of order and regularity, is only a

---

[46] Théorie, Introduction.

routine episode in causal history. The recent allegation that the findings of quantum mechanics afford no stable basis for prediction, but only for imprecisely fixating random movements by statistical coefficients, is not the most startling of causal ineptitudes.

The belief that causal law is suspended in the case of microscopic events reveals, above all, the incongruous views concerning both facts and laws—in short, events and constructs. No greater contrast can be imagined than exists between (a) the search for an organizational pattern tying together a series of things as factors and (b) the metaphysical approaches to causal problems provided by the various philosophies.[47] Obviously, such problems as the determinism or indeterminism of events are unmitigatedly metaphysical. If we agree that metaphysics, unlike science, deals with spurious problems, then the determinism-indeterminism issue is only a pseudo-problem. Be this as it may, this issue certainly misconstrues (a) relations between events or partial events, (b) knowledge and event patterns, and (c) descriptions of such knowledge.

Indeterminacy notions in the domain of quantum mechanics merely add another item to the repetitions of intellectual history. Recall Hume's enormous paradox of locating the constancies of causation, which did not really exist for him, in the customs or habits of an insubstantial mind, which does not exist for anybody. Such confusions between events, alleged events, and the way both are treated (explained) suggest the wildest flights of sentence making.

Since the problem of quantum indeterminacy arises from a concrete scientific situation in which all sorts of interrelated objects are under consideration, we can only conclude that the problem is simply a matter of metaphysical interpretation. In other words, indetermination is a free construction not from quantum-mechanical facts but from metaphysical sentences.

Even if it were the case that the simultaneous locus and state of an electron eluded observation or measurement, there would be no doubt about the existence of electronic events which are described in terms of behavioral properties.

Here, as in so many other philosophical situations, the existence of a thing and its properties are confused with knowing and recording them. There are many operationalists and phenom-

---

[47] Cf. for example Feigl's survey of nine viewpoints in Existential.

enologists who identify observational acts with the things observed. Since most writers who take this position are mentalistic in their psychological views they reduce the observational formula to Berkeley's *esse est percipi*.

What may well be lacking in a specific causal situation is knowledge of the pattern of events—that is, causal knowledge. If we differentiate explanation and reason from ground we may correlate the former with knowledge, the latter with the combination of factors. These factors are given and are the basis for inquiry and subsequent knowledge. True, such factors may be missing, but never the ground about which knowledge is sought.

The essentially metaphysical interpretation of scientific situations is strikingly exemplified in the assumption that properties of things are constituted of the process or result of measurement.[48] The analogy is the metaphysical one that since things seen are created in the act of seeing, things measured are created by acts of measuring. This analogy is made plausible by the presence of numbers. Numbers, in such instances, are taken to be either symbols of properties or the properties themselves. Once we take account, however, of that with which we are interbehaving, we find no warrant to confuse things with the acts or results of measuring them, nor constructions with the numbers which represent the dimensions of things.

[48] Cf. Lenzen, Indeterminism.

CHAPTER XX

THE LAWS OF THOUGHT AND THINGS

LOGIC AND LAW

LIKE all human enterprises, logic is a domain of rules, laws, and norms. Logical laws, however, envisaged as the conventional Laws of Thought, or as principles expressing the absolute and necessary structure of things, are not properly interpreted. Because the trinity of logical laws—namely, identity, noncontradiction, and excluded middle or third—have suffered misconstruction, they have been perennially employed to implement the dogmas of universality and necessity.

The basic flaw in the conventional notion of logical laws is that although few in number they are regarded as universal regulators of thoughts and things. To make logical laws into fundamental normative principles reflects the creed of logical omnicompetence. To reject such an interpretation means in no sense to disparage principles, rules, and norms, nor to deny them an important place in the logical field; it means merely to evaluate more effectively the rules required for understanding things, acts, and even for comprehending rules themselves. What, then, are rules and normative principles?

Above all, they constitute guides to the operations and procedures comprising the work performed in logic, science, and organized occupations. At once we must distinguish *a priori* and absolute norms from operational principles. The former are well illustrated by Kant's definition of logic:

Diese Wissenschaft von den notwendigen Gesetzen des Verstandes und der Vernunft überhaupt, oder, welches einerlei ist, von der blossen Form des Denken überhaupt, nennen wir nun *Logik*.[1]

In contrast, scientific and logical laws are definitely constructed principles based upon observed events; any normative suggestions are prompted only by the conditions of the enterprise. Principles or laws so construed constitute a definitive concern of logic. They are not only to be distinguished from the three classical principles,

---

[1] Jäsche, Kant's Logik, p. 14; see also vol. I, this treatise, p. 59.

so long presumed to be the sole and exclusive laws of logic, but also from any finalistic set of prescriptive formulae.

Normative principles on an interbehavioral basis comprise the theory or significant description of an enterprise. Any enterprise, logical or otherwise, can go on, however, without a definite and overt statement of principles. The particular behavior contains within it its own procedure and justification. In this sense we may distinguish between logicizing and abiding by formal logical laws. It is an admirable practice, therefore, to set up clear and forthright statements concerning our procedures, and especially to derive our principles from ongoing enterprises.

It follows, then, that logical norms must be closely integrated with the behavior which they describe or regulate. And because these norms can be generalized and formalized, criteria for organization can be set up and met, such as consistency, noncontradiction, and precise alternatives. There is a limit, however, to generality, for in each case the criteria are applicable only to particular systems, or classes of unique systems. Put otherwise, the generality is specific, and in no sense attains universality. Criteria, therefore, are not indifferent and absolute regulators of thoughts or things, but particular reference frames set up for specific systems.

On the ground that people think wrongly or illogically[2] a number of logicians have, tacitly at least, objected to deriving the principles of logic from actual thinking. Thereupon they inflate the normative character of logical laws to an absolutistic and unmeasurable magnitude transcending behavior.

Normative principles must, of course, be separated from legal prescriptions which are extraneous to the behavior regulated. Laws of social organization stem from a source and criterion different from, and often broader than, the immediate conditions of the prescribed behavior. Civil and criminal laws may have their origin in theological beliefs, in social organization and theory, in personal fiats of dominant rulers, economic conditions, etc.[3]

And, finally, logical principles, either as laws, postulates, norms or criteria, need not be exclusively concerned with abstruse intellectual operations, nor necessarily involved with knowledge, reas-

[2] Jevons, Principles, p. 7; Bain, Logic, p. 223; Keynes, Studies, p. 457; Cohen and Nagel, Introduction, p. 182.
[3] Cf. Robson, Civilization.

oning, or scientific activity, since logic is merely system building. These considerations may sometimes make logical laws appear to be trivial rules for games or other simple activities. There is an advantage in this if we are thereby helped to combat the view that logical laws are universal regulators of cosmically important activities, or organizers of such fundamental things as scientific events.

Varying Formulations of Logical Laws

Although the classical principles of identity, noncontradiction, and excluded middle or third are generally called laws of thought, logicians have not agreed that they are exclusively concerned with thinking. As the following statements from authoritative treatises indicate, even though logicians vary considerably in their detailed views concerning the laws, they adhere to the notion that they are all-inclusive and compelling:

Every A is A.
Every object of thought is conceived as itself.

Nothing can be A and not-A.
No object can be thought under contradictory attributes.

Every possible object is either A or not-A[4]

Whatever is true in one form of words, is true in every other form of words which conveys the same meaning.

Contradictory propositions can not both be true.

Of two directly contradictory propositions, one or the other must be true.[5]

Whatever is, is.
Nothing can both be and not be.
Everything must either be or not be.

Everything is identical with itself.
Nothing can have at the same time and at the same place contradictory and inconsistent qualities.

[4] Mansel, Prolegomena, chap. 6.
[5] Mill, Examination, vol. II, chap. 21.

It is impossible to mention any *thing* and any *quality* or circumstance, without allowing that the quality or circumstance either belongs to the thing or does not belong.[6]

If anything is A it is A.
Nothing can be both A and not A.
Anything must be either A or not A.

If any proposition is true, it is true.
No proposition can be both true and false.
Any proposition must be either true or false.[7]

Symbolistic formulation yields further variations. For example, the principle of identity gives:

$$A = A, \text{ or } X^2 = X \text{ (Boole)}.$$

Noncontradiction is represented by:

$$A \neq \sim A, \text{ or } A = \sim \sim A, \text{ or } x(1 - x) = 0 \text{ (Boole)}.$$

Excluded middle is written:

$$X = A \sim A.$$

The many differences in name[8] and formulation of the classic laws are exceeded by variety of interpretation: Are they: (1) applicable to things only, to thoughts only, or to both? (2) injunctive or not? (3) positive, or simply negative, aids in thinking? (4) applicable to terms only, to judgments only, or to both? and (5) do they involve truth or falsity, or not?

Despite all these diversities the tradition surprisingly maintains itself that these universal laws regulate inferential acts and determine implication and other relations of things. This is all the more remarkable since actual logical work demonstrates the specific interbehavioral and constructive character of what passes for *a priori* and invariant logical laws.

Not that logical laws have been without their critics. Hegel vigorously attacked them insofar as they were interpreted as abstract principles of understanding.[9] From his dialectical standpoint, however, he declared that "contradiction is the very moving prin-

---

[6] Jevons, Elementary, lesson 14.
[7] Cohen and Nagel, Introduction, chap. 9.
[8] Boole called the law of contradiction the law of duality, while Jevons applied this name to the law of excluded middle.
[9] Wallace, Logic, p. 213ff; see also Bogoslovsky, Technique.

ciple of the world."[10] In more recent times logical laws have been regarded as tautologies,[11] while the constructional mathematicians, such as Brouwer,[12] stage a powerful attack on the law of excluded middle. In the latter case the laws are presumed to concern invariant objective relations rather than statements or propositions.

A study of historical and current variations in logical laws really constitutes a survey of the whole of logic. From this survey one may hope for answers to such questions as: whether and when logic is normative, regulatory, or descriptive; whether it deals with things, thoughts or sentences; whether it is a specific process of system building or a set of absolute principles governing ultimate reason or necessary existence.

LOGICAL LAWS AS PRODUCTS OF CULTURAL DEVELOPMENT

That logic is the study of thought and that the classical laws are the most pervasive and general features of logic are derivative notions. A brief glance at the historical origins of these principles leaves no doubt that the trinity (p. 175) of logical laws was not always regarded as a universal regulator of the rational or ontological domains.

Within the framework of the finite and objective Greek culture, laws of thought were merely generalized commonsense principles. For Aristotle, as the first systemologist, logical laws were axioms or the most common principles of demonstration.[13] It is significant that Aristotle discussed the laws not in his logical books, but in the *Metaphysics*, where we find six chapters (3-8) explicitly dealing with what later came to be known as the Laws of Thought. In the *Analytica Priora*, on the other hand, there occurs only a fleeting passage (I, 32, 47a, 8). Undoubtedly, Aristotle is interested in things—their organization and arrangement—though, of course, he puts the matter in the form of being as being. Unless we read Aristotle through the spectacles of a later age we learn that Metaphysics is the study of the most general aspects of things. It is the function of the philosopher or metaphysician, as over against the special scientist, to investigate all things.[14] But such

[10] Wallace, Logic, p. 223.
[11] Wittgenstein, Tractatus.
[12] Hedrick, Tendencies.
[13] Metaphysics, Gamma, chap. 3.
[14] Ibid., chaps. 1, 2.

investigation, in its widest and most abstract form, is dialectical in the sense of abstract reference and description.

In consequence, Aristotle makes no sharp distinction between investigating things and linguistically organizing them. From our standpoint this is indeed a naive and commonsense view, but it is nevertheless objective in keeping close to actual things. There is no sophisticated reduction of things to ideas or symbols, as in later times. When Aristotle discusses the laws as principles of being he sees no necessity to distinguish them from principles of thought. On the contrary, for him axioms or principles are at once, in different aspects, principles of existence and of reflection, as well as of demonstration or argument.

The practical and commonsense—we may even say the operational—character of the Aristotelian principles is demonstrated by Aristotle's variance in emphasizing them. The principle of contradiction he regards as the most certain:

The same attribute cannot at the same time belong and not belong to the same subject in the same respect.[15]

Somewhat subordinate is the principle of middle exclusion, formulated at the beginning of Chapter 7.

There cannot be an intermediate between contradictories, but of one subject we must either affirm or deny any one predicate.[16]

The identity principle is subordinated to both of these.[17] Identity Aristotle treats as the problem of the meaning, and singleness of meaning, of words, especially the words *being* and *not being*.

First then this at least is obviously true, that the word "be" or "not be" has a definite meaning.[18]

For not to have one meaning is to have no meaning.[19] There is no question that he is concerned with references to actual properties or attributes of specific things.

Though Aristotle is, no doubt, primarily interested in commonsense objects, with ordinary discourse and practical demonstration, as a philosopher he naturally attempts to attain generality, even

[15] Ibid., 1005b, 18ff.
[16] Ibid., 1011b, 24.
[17] Ibid., 1006a, 29ff; and 1011b, 26ff.
[18] Ibid., 1006a, 31.
[19] Ibid., 1006b, 9; 1006b, 13.

absoluteness of formulation. Still, his formulation of abstract and general principles has to do with concrete things in specific situations. Aristotle's thought was always thought about things, not a reaching out to transcendent and sophisticated ideas and entities beyond the borders of spatiotemporal happenings (vol. I, chap. 3).

Not until the post-Aristotelian (psychistic) era of logic were the practical principles made into regulatory laws for the conduct of Reason. Only when logic became thoroughly formalized could the principles of identity, contradiction, and excluded middle become universal and absolute laws of Reason which not only legislated for things, but also subordinated them to thought. This formalization involved a different type of psychology from that of Aristotle's. Psychological events were no longer regarded as functions of biological organisms, but as psychic or spiritual powers independent of the organism and the things with which it interacted. Since Plotinus, who was the essential transformer of Aristotelian objective psychology, mind as Reason or Logos has been considered not only as self-creative, but also as the source of all things.

Because many of the Plotinian doctrines revolve around the reinterpretation of Logos doctrine, neo-Platonism becomes greatly preoccupied with words and symbols. The stage is thus set for the commentating and interpreting Church Fathers—in short, for the general precipitation of a gigantic verbological industry. Verbal symbols rather than actual things become the materials for all sorts of theories concerning events. Thought and logic are so far removed from things as to attain a self-enclosed domain. Logic not only becomes primarily concerned with names, but the laws of logic are confined to rules for their manipulation. Here is the basis for the doctrine of first and second intensions. Logic deals not with notions of things, but with notions of things as thought, or with names of the classes of things.

To trace out the thorough formalization—that is, the verbalization—of the laws of thought is to encounter the abstruse theological arguments of the Middle Ages. The laws of identity are emphasized to the point of establishing the permanence and unchangeability of an eternal ground for all things.

The growth of science and technology in the Renaissance period soon called for a logical reformation. As far as our present problem is concerned, logic was no longer confined exclusively to purely formal principles; and, happily, the question of the application of laws began once more to concern things in a substantial way. From this point on we have a genuine differentiation between types of logic; for example, the logical concern with mathematics, the new methodology of science, and also the continuation of formal logic in the sense of propositional and classical logic.

Significant for this period is the formulation of the so-called fourth law of logic—the principle of Sufficient Reason. Though this law in its various formulations by Spinoza[20] and Leibniz[21] is rooted in theological and general cosmomonistic ground, in Leibniz especially it at least indicates that logic is concerned with contingency and fact as over against pure *a priority* and formality of Reason. Further, its very presence in the speculations of Galileo[22] marks it as a link between the pure and remote propositions of the Scholastics and the scientific occupations of the scientists and technologists of the early period of our own era.

Since the medieval logicians took over and transformed the rules of argument and demonstration formulated by the Greeks, these rules have been universalized and instituted as canons or regulators of thought, despite many disagreements concerning their number, nature, and origin. During the 19th century the notion developed that logical laws are more or less closely connected with things. This view was increasingly fostered when logic was overtly related to mathematical processes. The incomparable illustration is Boole's notion that logic is a mathematical procedure (p. 187), and further that the basic purpose of logic in mathematics is to indicate the fundamental laws of the mind's operation when reasoning is performed.[23] Were it not for the obsession that thought is a psychic process or an exercise of mind, it might have been clear that the laws of thought are really criteria of principles designed for organizing systems. In the case of Boole, and those who agreed with him, the type of systems capable of regulation by the laws of thought were the abstract systems of mathematics. For organizing systems of things other

[20] Ethics, I, 11, proof 2.
[21] Monadology, secs. 31, 32, 33, 36, and in other works.
[22] Enriques, Historic, p. 55.
[23] Vol. I, p. 113.

than mathematical abstractions more resort must be had to the type of objects dealt with. Laws of logic in the latter case are not so much concerned with abstract organizations of formal sentences and symbols as with specific things.

Current treatments of logical laws correspond more or less to the historical divisions of philosophy—namely, Nominalism, Realism, and Conceptualism (chap. 18, p. 132f.; vol. I, p. 37f.). Accordingly, while all logicians associate logical laws with linguistic materials on the ground that logic must be formalized, they may stress (1) linguistic structure, (2) relations, or (3) classes.

(1) Those who emphasize linguistic forms may be identified with the nominalistic tradition. For them logic ultimately reduces to organizations of symbols, or to systems of tautologies. Such logicians, when concerned with mathematical or symbolical materials, become modernized into syntacticists. Logical laws for them govern the relationship between formal sentences.

(2) Logicians emphasizing relations link themselves with the realistic tradition in philosophy. They deal with formalized statements concerning things represented by the laws. Thus, logical laws take on the character of semantic rules. The more scientific logicians of this type—the modern extreme ontologists—regard the things ordered by the laws as invariable relations of existence.

(3) Our third group, the logical epistemologists, emphasize the formal aspects of knowledge. They want logical laws to integrate statements or formulae with data or relations. Logical laws, as well as logical sentences in general, become conceptualistic. Logic on this basis is a discipline for ordering data to thought. These logicians, who may be called modern Aristotelians,[24] are, on the one hand, merely concerned with commonsense objects. On the other, because they are formalists they are occupied simply with the truth or falsity of sentences. Hence the stress on classes; for the most part, classes confined to the true and the false.

Universality and Necessity of Logical Laws

Without exception writers on logical laws take for granted that they are universal and necessary, even though they can not claim a further understanding of their nature. They accept without ques-

[24] For example, Joseph, Introduction.

tion the belief that logic is a universally normative discipline, and assume that all thinking and reasoning exemplify such laws.[25]

Naturally, the experts on logical laws have attempted to support their belief with as powerful arguments as they could muster. But the very differences in argument demonstrate the absence of any necessary principles.

As we know, the older logicians sought a basis for logical laws in the nature of mind or of things. More recently, with the impact of mathematical theories on logical thought in conjunction with changing ideas of logic and mind, the source of laws has become relatively more localized in mathematical operations. Now in view of the differences in theory concerning (1) the nature and number of logical laws, (2) their basis or origin, and (3) the range of their application, it is hardly possible to regard them as absolute, pervasive, and necessary. Let us look into the procedures employed for retaining the notion of universality.

(1) *Nature and Number of Logical Principles.* If there were universal and necessary principles of logic they would demand a single, exclusive description. We find, however, that depending on the writer's philosophical persuasion, the formula ranges from the classic proposition that logical laws are regulatory principles for all reasoning to the modern view that logical laws express conditions to be satisfied.[26] We must agree either that only one view is correct or that logical laws are really not unique pervasive principles. Indeed, writers sometimes do not limit logical principles to the usual three, but make identity, contradiction, and excluded middle coordinate with the laws of syllogism, tautology, simplification, etc.[27] Undoubtedly this universalistic theory originates in verbal creation; that is, through the development of a general formula the idea is engendered that the things referred to are general or universal, whatever the particular formula may signify.

(2) *Source of Logical Laws.* Logicians willing to surrender the notion that logical laws have their source in the nature of mind or in the character of things stress necessity more than universality. The self-evident and *a priori* are concerned with formal criteria of the genuine, normative, and valid. The criteria may be derived from a postulational procedure.

[25] Avey, Law.
[26] Dewey, Logic, p. 343ff.
[27] Cf. Cohen and Nagel, Introduction, p. 182.

As far back as Mill's attack on Hamilton's philosophy it is suggested that the classical laws of thought, although universal, are postulates of reasoning.[28] This postulational view is followed by Keynes[29] who regards the laws as indispensable for consecutive thought and coherent argument. Schiller, the arch opponent of formal logic, likewise adopts this conception with the added notion that, once adopted, such postulates are absolute.[30] Though these conceptions depart from the traditional notion that logical laws regulate the operation of a reasoning faculty, can we, even in this modified form, adopt such a notion of generalized and authoritative postulates? The same question may be asked about Mill's conception of logical laws as generalizations from experience. In all these forms thought or reasoning is reduced to generalized processes not easily related to concrete human activities. The basic assumption is that logic is concerned with abstract verbalistic or formal systems comprising terms, judgments, and objects of thought. These abstract systems are then expanded into a monopolistic universalism.

Whether logicians adhere to the three classical laws or add various modern principles the assumed necessities are founded on abstracting and formalizing procedures. By emptying sentences of actual referential and symbolic functions they are made to take on a necessary character. By reducing a situation to a pair of sheer alternatives it is easy to demand that only one be chosen. But the necessity here lies clearly in the specific situation, not in any general law.

(3) *Universality and Necessity of Application.* An implied argument for the universality and necessity of logical principles is their presumed universality of application. Whether such principles are limited to the classic laws of identity, contradiction, and excluded middle, or broadened to include the law of sufficient reason, syllogistic laws, rules of inference, etc., the argument is supported by reducing things to empty forms. By thus reducing everything to being, substance, quality, essence, to A or B, the principles are made to cover everything. One might conclude that everything is nothing. Certainly, there is a shift here from the

[28] Examination, II, p. 179.
[29] Studies, p. 450f.
[30] Formal, chap. 10.

things to which the laws apply to the forms of statements or linguistic systems.

Specificity and Contingency of Logical Laws

From the standpoint of specific logical situations it is necessary to reject every form of absolutism and universality. So far as the origin of logical laws is concerned, any principle that may be legitimately regarded as logical has arisen from some concrete situation. Hence there must be a variety of principles. The applicability of logical laws is similarly determined on the basis of the situations to which they may be adapted.

If conventional logical laws belong to the field of logic at all, they pertain to organizational or system-building enterprises. Employed in such situations they concern the organization of things, words, sentences, and relations.

As with every other item in the logical domain, the cardinal criterion with respect to laws is the behavior of logicians. Not the least important feature is their motivation. Do they seek the self-evident and *a priori?* Are logical laws for them the guarantors of some absolute necessity, the manifestation of universal mental powers or invariances in things? Or, quite otherwise, are they actually constructing a definite system, and developing particular principles on the basis of the specifications and particular materials of that system?

Logical Laws in Reasoning and Thinking

Outstanding in the history of logic is the opposition between those who favor either mind or world order. The former insist that the conventional laws of thought refer to the capacities, limitations, and necessities of mind. For such logicians the laws of thought constitute either descriptions of, or prescriptions for, the mental operations of reasoning. On the whole, it is implied that thinking and reasoning constitute generalized powers or processes subject to formal regulating principles.

Thinking and reasoning, on such a basis, become empty and trivial occupations, rather than modes of interbehavior involving particular acts and things.[31] On an interbehavioral basis the only formalized laws are those that caution us against general rules

[31] See vol. I, chap. 7; also Kantor, Principles, vol. I, chaps. 20-22.

or regulatory principles. If thinking is to be significant it has to be adapted to the situation at hand. This means that the laws of thinking are laws of the problems or conditions about which we think.

It is extremely important to differentiate between thinking, in its various forms, and reasoning. On the whole it is the latter, with its basic inferential processes, that has interested logicians. Now, inferential behavior can be performed in specific situations with actual things to be inferred, or in generalized circumstances with empty forms. It is only to the latter that conventional and formalized rules apply.

Consistency of thinking, or the application of general and permanent principles, can only be interpreted on the basis of personal habits or cultural conditions. Such descriptive generalizations as, for example, that we always think or reason by analogy clearly are imposed upon, and not derived from, situations. Whenever we follow generalized prescriptions, particular operations are robbed of their essential character as thinking or reasoning. Indeed, there is no way of escaping the essential demands of the specific situation. Our objection, therefore, to the universalistic conception is chiefly against the fundamental assumption that any prefabricated principle can be valid in general, as we proceed from one particular situation to another.

Again, the number of laws required depends upon the situation. For example, in some situations only consistency may be necessary. Of the classical laws one, two or three may be needed. When more than one general principle is used, they may or may not be intimately related.

Conventional treatments of reasoning and thinking laws really come down to formalized system making. Though Boole regarded himself as a discoverer of the fundamental laws of thought,[32] he was, of course, concerned with the construction of systems based on the procedures of algebra. As an absolutist and mystic Boole believed it possible to limit logic to the exclusive and abstract paradigms of mathematical systems. When, however, all sorts of system-building procedures are taken into account, the principles of construction can not be restricted to any variation of the classic laws of thought, nor to any fixed number and type.

[32] Laws.

At this point it is appropriate to consider the relation of logical laws to objects of thought. Is it acceptable to consider logical laws as especially concerned with the organization of thought objects? A prompt reply involves the counter-question: What is the nature of thought objects? Are they things thought about, or are they constructions about things in the form of verbal or other linguistic responses? In the latter and more correct case, we are occupied with descriptions or definitions. In no instance, however, need we regard thought objects as so related to formal thinking procedures as to require the application of classical laws of thought.

Logical Laws and Existence

Absolutistic logicians with a flair for Platonic ultimates have interpreted logical laws as laws of things or, at least, of essences. Unlike the tautologists, the realistic or ontological writers insist that in the final analysis logical laws must be inherently applicable to existence "because they are concerned with ontological traits of utmost generality."[33] We have already quoted an ontologist's profession that logical laws represent factors invariant in every subject matter.[34] In other words, they are principles of being, not merely principles of inference.

What are the ontologist's motives in constructing logical laws? In the first place, he aims to achieve wholesale rigorous formulae for events and relations—in short, to legislate for science. His basic method is to begin with scientific propositions, and then to extrapolate and formalize to the point of reaching ultimate and invariant existential relations.

The argument used to justify applying such formalized principles to actual things is that logic constitutes the study of the most general and pervasive character of whatever is and whatever may be.[35] This argument is objectionably circular. Only by reducing events to general characters can one equate them with formal logical processes and propositions.

Laudable as are the motives to bring logic into contact with science, we nevertheless ask the following questions: First, does not logic in confining itself to such extrapolations and formaliza-

---

[33] Cohen and Nagel, Introduction, p. v.
[34] Vol. I, p. 162.
[35] Cohen and Nagel, Introduction, p. 185.

tions renounce the benefits derived from its connection with science? Secondly, do not the very processes of extrapolation remove science too far from actual events?

True, science thrives on formal descriptions. The scientist's interest, however, is not in the formality, but in the scope such formulae afford for interacting with the events which are the grounds for the system constructed. Sheer abstraction in science helps not at all in analyzing problems, in formulating hypotheses, in carrying on experimentation, and in verifying theories. On the contrary, abstractionism belongs to the domain of argument, in which, for example, no thief can be proved to be a religious man, since to be a religious man is tantamount to not stealing.

There remains, then, the contention that by means of logical principles an abstractive systemization of science can be effected. But is it possible to achieve a unity of science through abstract formulae? Here we must differentiate sharply between verbal assertion and operational achievement, a difference excellently illustrated by the following incident. At the head of his treatise, *On the Equilibria of Heterogeneous Substances*, Gibbs sets the following propositions from Clausius:

Die Energie der Welt ist konstant.
Die Entropie der Welt strebt einem Maximum zu.

In the body of his work, however, Gibbs abstains from all reference to the world, and, as is inevitable and proper, works out his laws on the basis of specific isolated physiochemical systems.

Interesting in this connection is Bridgman's[36] protest against attempting to apply the second law of thermodynamics to the universe. In general, he objects to the extrapolational use of a statistical model for reaching into remote epochs of time and remote reaches of space. Would it not be even more fatal to deal with a universe if extrapolating sentences are replaced by completely self-constructed propositions?

We are now prepared to consider the general problem of universality or unity in science. It is possible, of course, to regard science as unitary, as essentially systemic, since there is a continuity in natural events, or at least in our operations upon, and our knowledge concerning, them. But this work of systemizing

[36] Statistical.

all of science at once can only proceed to the point of specifying the upper and lower boundaries of a comprehensive scientific system. The logical or systemological laws to be invoked here are exclusively concerned with these boundaries.

What may be designated as the upper boundary is determined by the rule that the scientific field of operations has a spatiotemporal frame of reference beyond which it is impossible for any scientist to go. Whenever propositions transcend these spatiotemporal limits, we may be certain that someone is indulging in fantastic verbal construction.

The corresponding rule applicable to the lower boundary of a scientific system stresses the limits of specific happenings. However well justified the insistence upon a continuum in events, and in our scientific operations upon them, valid knowledge consists of propositions concerning the specific character and mode of occurrence of objects and processes. This fact places distinct limitations upon carrying over conclusions reached in one particular scientific domain to other fields. It is simply futile to reduce one science to another, or to overlook the differences between the observed factors in the physical, biological, and psychological sciences. These scientific specificities apply not only to particular techniques, methods, and apparatus, but also to conclusions. What peculiar form of scientific uneasiness lies at the basis of our repugnance toward specificity and particularity?

Logical Laws and Data

Even the most formalistic logicians do not really wish to confine logic strictly to formal structures. No, they insist that logical forms reach out toward something more significant, if not to actual existence. It is therefore best to regard our triplicate of doctrines (p. 183) as varying in degree. If the extreme tautologists stress sentences and sentence systems it is because they tie up most closely with mathematical materials, which, if only at long remove, are related to things. The realists connect with ultimate relations linking together mathematical statements and concrete events. Our third group, the epistemologists, wishing to articulate logic still closer with actual things, relates logic to knowledge problems, at least to the extent of connecting logical laws with processes of verifiability. It is assumed, then, that the truth values of statements are interrelated with data.

In conventional logic this connection is assertional only. It results more in formalizing knowledge than concretizing statements. The general technique is to begin with a formula—say, S is P. The assumption is made that this formula has a definite referent, and the question is whether the sentence is true—in other words, whether S really has the property P or not. Apparently, this sentence connects directly with certain definite things; thus its truth or falsity can be determined—namely, verified.

Such verification, of course, is logical—that is, formalistic. There is no checking of assertion or of formal statement with actual things. Truth and falsity signify purely dichotomous classification. Thus the conventional abstract laws of contradiction and excluded middle are presumed to underlie all logical truth and falsity. An interesting illustration is to show that the logical constants or relations such as implication, disjunction, and conjunction can be defined in terms of truth and falsity, but truth and falsity are made to depend upon the logical laws.

As McGill points out:

Implication can be defined as holding for every pair of propositions, p q, except when p is true and q false, disjunction, when they are not both false, while conjunction only holds when p and q are both true. With the logical constants defined in terms of true and false possibilities, we can test the truth of all of the elementary propositions.[37]

When the truth tables are originally constructed, the laws of contradiction and excluded middle prevent sentences from having both true and false values.

Epistemological logicians do not overlook, however, the vacuous nature of logical laws, and, indeed, try to overcome this fault. The laws, they argue, are objective because we must not confuse the significance of a proposition with the means of knowing it. For example, if one knows that S is either P or not P it does not follow that S is not P. Otherwise put, to be unable to know the truth of a proposition is not the same thing as the proposition being not true. This argument about the object or datum as a basis for

[37] Concerning, p. 200.

the verification of a proposition is reduced to bare alternatives in order to support the law of excluded middle. In other words, it is argued that whether or not you can verify the proposition it is either true or false,[38] and hence the law of excluded middle is established.

That logical laws are concerned with data or events is a matter of assumption only. Epistemological logicians assume that when they assert S is P the symbols represent something definite. This, in spite of the fact that, as we have just seen, the simple-alternative argument precludes us from even attempting to discover what the original event is. The statement, therefore, remains a simple assertion; and despite the belief in its objective and referential character it is merely a sentence. Secondly, it is implied that once the sentence is formulated there must be some actual referent. This is the familiar smoke-fire fallacy, which presupposes such a tremendous faith in texts that the existence of the sentence is presumed to guarantee an existential referent.

Epistemological and semantic logicians have recently developed a general technique for supporting their faith in formal and autonomous statements by stressing the contrast between verifiability and verification. The basis of this technique is the eager acceptance of the antimetaphysical proposition that unverifiable statements are meaningless. This proposition signalizes the simple recognition that verification must deal with contents or things in order to yield genuine knowledge. In other words, the truth of a statement must involve, in addition to simple coherence of structure, some definite relationship to data.

But the logician's absolutistic and formalistic attitudes remain paramount. To begin with, logical statements are traditionally not designed to operate directly with actual events. To be formal and universal they must tend toward the simple and tautological. On the other hand, most knowledge propositions can not be absolutely verified. To be occupied with actual events means that many lacunae in the conditions necessary for verification are often present. Logicians seek a way out by enlarging the concept of verification to include indirect as well as direct, and incomplete as well as decisive, verification.[39] Thus is constructed the notion of veri-

[38] Cf. Toms, Law.
[39] See, for example, Lewis, Logical.

fiability. This notion is similar to that of probable confirmation[40] which is centered in empirical knowledge and inductive logic.

To illustrate their principle of verifiability logicians naturally turn to number. For example, it is asserted that though there is no whole number which can not be counted, the counting of whole numbers can not be completed.[41] Is this other than a case of formalizing a sentence instead of concretizing it by the verification technique? We ask: In what sense is number a thing which is not counted? In what sense do we expect to complete the counting of whole numbers? Notice that given numbers are products of a counting process, and that naturally we can set up limits to the counting procedure. Such argument is not only remote from the application of logical laws to data; it is another instance of employing an arbitrary conception of language or propositions.

Epistemological formulations of logical laws therefore aim primarily at establishing truth without evidence. A typical example is the employment of the law of excluded middle to establish:

. . . the logical theory of truth, involving the possibility of events that no one experiences and of propositions that are true although there can never be any evidence in their favour.[42]

The technique is to invoke the great power of disjunction, the abstract either-or. We are brought headlong to a forked road, forced to go either one way or the other. If we reject one way, it is declared we have accepted the other. If one is false, the other must be true; if one does not exist, then the other exists. The technique is presumed to become completely compelling when the "two forks of the road" are allegedly connected with concrete events by analogical description, as in the case of Aristotle's seafight example.[43] Even Dewey agrees that while this necessity does not apply to existence it does apply to the object of thought. He believes the disjunction is necessary. This is certainly questionable. Actually, the necessity lies simply in the form of the sentence, but patterns of sentences must be related either to events or reactions

[40] Reichenbach, Experience.
[41] Lewis, Logical.
[42] Russell, Inquiry, p. 383.
[43] Vol. I, p. 160.

to events. Where is the necessity for a sea fight to occur alto-gether? Why the question or assertion?

If, in order to point out that the disjunction is potent, this alternative is set up after an event, our comment would be that we are no longer concerned with formal sentences but with a simple statement of facts. What point is there in translating occurrences into statements of logical necessity?

Logical Laws and Language

Language plays a double part in relation to logical laws. First, of course, it serves as a means to formulate and organize logical principles by way of symbolizing the systematic features referred to; secondly, language in the form of sentences or linguistic forms constitutes a field for applying the formulae.

Language serves admirably to absolutize things (vol. I, p. 41). Because of the willingness to accept finalistic assertions there is un-limited scope for establishing what one wishes by declaration and proclamation. Who can dispute: "Whatever is, is," "No thing can both be and not be," "No thing can escape either being or not being." Language is so pliable a medium that one can do remark-able things with it, even use it to achieve universality, ultimacy, and *a priority*. The procedures vary. Logicians may make language identical with an invariant correlate of, or an absolute substitute for, things.

How language can be used to establish the *a priori* is well illus-trated by Kant's separation of dichotomy from polytomy.[44] Only the former involves primitive and *a priori* division, since the mem-bers are set over against each other such that the opposite of A is non-A. The real basis for the division is the exclusive verbal han-dling of the alleged members. Ostensibly things or their proper-ties are referred to. However, the principle of contradiction is op-erative here because no actual things aside from the words are in-volved, unless we assume that words substitute for things. The principle of noncontradiction can not apply to polytomy because that type of division involves perception of objects.[45]

The writers referred to above are the ontologists. Those who

---

[44] Jäsche, Kant's Logik, p. 161.
[45] For Kant polytomy in mathematics, as in dividing the conics, can involve *a priori* intuition.

retreat from this position, but who still hold that logic is the authority and legislator directly for thought and indirectly for things, make language the basis for necessary knowledge and truth. Such formalists hold that logic is primarily, if not exclusively, concerned with language or symbols. The final goal of logic is a series of self-contained sentences. Formalistic logicians, then, are concerned only with ultimate linguistic products of description and mathematical formulation, that is, with tautologies.

Here is an erroneous conception of the nature of language and symbols. Descriptions and formulations are abstracted from their setting in interbehavioral situations. For example, accurate descriptions are properly differentiated from inaccurate references to events; and then the former are given an autonomous place in the domain of knowledge. In this connection, a mathematical formula is substituted for, and made into a law of, events. The ultimate result is to separate the truth of statements from the reality of events in order to attain a domain of forms as against a domain of contents. It is as though one were to study scientific protocols and records in order to check the syntax of sentences, rather than the correspondence of the protocols with observed facts.

Logical laws for linguistic logicians consist of rules for regulating the abstract properties of symbol systems. Logic is thus regarded as a relatively simple and effective instrument for the easy and permanent accession of ultimate reality and absolute truth.

Since Leibniz logicians have hoped to develop a strict language for the precise ordering of all knowledge. Leibniz's ambition was to evolve a universal formal language to serve as the commodious capsule for storing all knowledge. Actually, this is a 17th century resuscitation of the Pythagorean notion that number is the essence of things, and that everything can be reduced to numerical symbols. Especially inept, however, is the assumption that we can build up linguistic structures which unify all scientific findings. Our observations and experiments convince us that we can not even sum up the nature of a single event, such as light, within the bounds of one type of equation or verbal proposition. We have done with such views as those of Jevons: "Science arises from the discovery of Identity amidst Diversity."[46] Maxims and proverbs

[46] Principles, p. 1.

may be interesting, even instructive, but often have nothing to do with the substance of science or logic.

From a study of sentential logic we may well conclude that not only can linguistic systems be organized, but that there may also be value in doing so. It is definitely implied, however, that the systems built are specific and compresent with many others. Whoever wishes to construct systems of sentences can discover system-building laws to further this work. Such laws must differentiate between referential and symbol language, as well as between language which constitutes autonomous things and language which describes and represents things.

There are logical laws or principles for the organization of sentences without any regard to existences. Similarly, there are logical laws for structuring sentences concerning things. In the latter case, further specifications may be made as to the existence and nature of things with respect to particular times, places, and conditions.

Instead of assuming that language consists of sentences, which in their elements or totals "express" thought or things, we need to establish a critique of language (p. 194) within the large matrix of actual personal behavior. Such a critique, concerned both with systems of sentences as things and as acts referring to things, can be useful in guiding scientists in the right direction. The proper use of sentential formulation or precise reference, however, does not compete with, but is only ancillary to, observation and experimentation.

Logical Laws and Mathematics

Throughout the history of logic the source of necessity and certainty lay close to numbers. But not until the 19th century did logicians conclude that logical and mathematical laws are identical, and therewith attempt to make logical laws independent of thought and thinking. The identifying process mentioned was carried on under medieval realistic auspices. Logical laws as ultimately mathematical were presumed to deal with what must absolutely be, because transhuman reality is absolute.

Mathematics, too, has undergone its evolution. It has likewise been unable to escape its human origin, its specific operations in a particular behavior domain. Let us note a few high spots in its transformation. First, there was the freeing of geometry from the absolutistic trammels of Euclidean assumptions. Out of the development of non-Euclidean geometry may be traced the germs of the postulational principles of mathematics. Then came Hamilton's and Grassmann's discovery that algebra, too, need not be eternally bound by the commutative law. Mathematics thus became reasonably free to build its own unique and specialized systems.

The emancipation of mathematics soon exerted an effect upon logic. The discovery that mathematics could renounce the numerology of Pythagoras, and that by investigating groups, point sets, and mathematical fields one could move on to the study of relation systems and their structures,[47] was exploited by the logisticians in the interest of a Platonic absolutism. Mathematics became formalistic and transhuman logic. Of the formalist and logistic mathematician no question may be asked concerning the essentiality and validity of classical logical laws. Because the mathematician is intimately concerned with abstract things—with simple and complex relations—he may regard himself as bound by a logic of simple alternatives—yes or no, true or false, existence or nonexistence—without regard to the specific details of the systems involved. Is it absolutely essential, as Russell and other logistic writers assert, that $P \vee P'$ is always the case?[48] Does x or y exclusively exist; or is it possible to have a three or multi-valued logic?

Brouwer stands out as the most vigorous recent assailant of the law of excluded middle (LEM). This attack has been made in connection with the intuitionist's assault upon the logistic and formalistic schools of mathematics. From our standpoint, however, we regard Brouwer's position as operational or constructible, as recent writers have indicated. His point is that in no mathematical situation is it proper to assert that a certain number exists, when no technique of operation is available for exhibiting this number in a finite number of steps. In point here is Brouwer's famous question: Does a number K exist expressing the number of digits in the decimal representation of π at which, for the first time, the series 0123456789 begins? Brouwer insists that in the absence of calculative operations one can neither answer yes or no exclusively.

[47] Bell, Development, p. 177.
[48] Cf. Russell, Reply, p. 682f.; Inquiry, chaps. 20, 21.

A similar problem is posed by Becker in the following form. Take the series of numbers $x = 2^n + 1$ for increasing values of n, and define another series k such that if x is prime the number 1 is assigned to k, if composite the number 2. The series k, then, has the appearance 1, 1, 2, 1, 2. Now, if we ask whether the number 1 is contained in k after the 16th place, we can neither, according to Becker, answer "yes" or "no," nor even "yes or no." The reason is that our knowledge does not extend beyond $n = 16$ for primes of this form.[49]

If the universalized LEM breaks down in so abstract a domain as mathematics we not only can draw our own conclusions concerning its place in other more concrete situations, but assess its general value as well. The whole matter revolves around the interpretation we make of logical laws. Those who insist upon their absolute character maintain that the problems we have indicated do not interfere with logical principles. For example, one writer declares:

Brouwer indeed is not denying the *tertium non datur* in the generally accepted interpretation of that logical principle, but rather emphasizing that existence in mathematics is synonymous with constructibility.[50]

Other attempts to save the law are based on the interpretation of truth. Church,[51] for instance, declares that the truth of a proposition is an indefinable, not depending upon a possible operation of proving it. He does admit, however, that such an interpretation is a matter of choice rather than necessity. Russell assumes an uncompromising position against Brouwer's view that truth should be subject to verification. Russell's view of verification is some limited personal observation such as perceiving or remembering.[52] As an adherent to an ancient psychophysical dualism he also regards personal psychological processes as psychic. His argument, on this basis, is well taken. There are unverifiable truths—that is, events unknown to particular persons as internal states of consciousness. But to go on from this point to true propositions (sen-

[49] Mathematische, p. 67.
[50] Black, Nature, p. 196.
[51] Hedrick, Tendencies, p. 339.
[52] Inquiry, chaps. 20, 21.

tences) that can never be confronted with evidence in their favor opens wide the door to obscurantism.

Truth interpretation offers an interesting item for specificity logic. It is appealing, of course, to believe that truth is independent of actual demonstration, but this belief, though rational in the world of concrete events, hardly has a place in mathematics. While analogous demonstration of relations is legitimate in mathematics, the analogical relation must be demonstrated. Not so in the case of concrete events, in which instance analogous situations are more easily observed and accepted.

It turns out that in any rigorous thinking we can not appeal to traditions, however firmly entrenched. Certainly, we can not universalize and hypostatize observed conditions into general principles as a means of avoiding further observations or demonstrations. We conclude, therefore, that truth can not be guaranteed by resorting to such a universal law as excluded middle, but must be determined upon the specific conditions dealt with. Nor can a generalized and arbitrary interpretation of truth establish the LEM. Of course, by reducing it to a single alternative it may be acceptable, but while such a logical law is one of many possible ones, it does not on this assumptional basis constitute a factor in any universal logic.

Significant here is Lewis' assertion that the LEM is not a universal law, but that it "reflects our stubborn adherence to the simplest of all possible modes of division."[53] We go even further than his negative proposition that "there are no laws of logic which can be attributed to the universe or to human reason in the traditional form."[54] We point out the specific and operational character of logical principles in all system-building enterprises.[55]

LOGICAL LAWS AS FACTORS IN SYSTEM BUILDING

A summary of the difficulties of the traditional treatments of logical laws includes the following assumptions: (a) there are universal binding principles for the conduct of thought or for the character of existence, (b) linguistic or verbal formulae substitute

[53] Alternative, p. 505.
[54] Ibid., p. 483; see also Waismann, Alternative.
[55] Vol. I, p. 211.

for both thoughts and things, (c) thinking or reasoning consists of mental acts of persons more or less remote from things, which raises the question whether it is binding or not with respect to those things, and (d) things are objects of thought either independent of, different from, or conjoint with thought.

In contrast to traditional discussions are the following points: (a) logical laws are constructions made by students of logic on the basis of observing organizational activities, (b) thinking and reasoning are specified forms of interbehavior with stimulus objects, which may be events, objects, acts of things and persons, or products of these acts—so-called imaginary things. In general discussions of logical laws the concrete human character of logical events is passed over. Writers on logic are slowly, if at all, becoming cognizant of an objective and scientific psychology.

An analysis of the formulation and employment of logical laws promptly leads to the conclusion that what are called logical laws are not especially or exclusively connected with logic. Hence, their employment in other situations is entirely legitimate. Many are the instances in which logical laws serve as regulatory guides to various kinds of intellectual work not describable as system building. To stay by the original issue (identity), to avoid confusion of one thing with another (contradiction), and to maintain a point (excluded middle) are cardinal rules for significant intellectual behavior.

Indeed, if logical laws are not treated as Platonic reals with an autonomous and remote ontological existence, they stand out as concrete functional principles, as criteria for putting things together. For example, numerically different things may be qualitatively identified; qualitatively different things, in whole or part, may be numerically classified or put into a single class.

Our aim is to place principles, whether or not rigidly formalized, in their proper interbehavioral setting. Are we concerned with ways of citing, equating, and identifying things or processes that might or might not be similar? Are we setting up a criterion for equating more or less similar things? Are we equating expressions or making x equal to y or y^2? Again, are we asking whether ptomaine poison is like some other poison? Is there a substance or chemical element in this case, as in others? Is a virus a living substance? Are vitamins capable of identification with

Bios? Such questions illustrate our operations with constructions based upon our contacts with things. We may also identify pure constructions—that is, free creations sustaining no discernible analogies with known things. In every instance the emphasis is upon particular events, not upon cosmic schemes which escape our control and depart, presumably, from the scene of specific human affairs.

In logical system building the classic laws of thought serve as definite operational tools. When necessary or convenient the laws of identity, contradiction, and excluded middle are employed as limiting principles for organizing particular kinds of systems. They may function as references to qualities of things or to the existence of events; they may concern propositions or other system-building materials.

In such enterprises the principle of identity is a scheme for ordering and relating events for a certain purpose, putting them into classes or groups which can then be manipulated. An excellent example is the development of class marks in statistics. Items are regarded as practically the same or similar. Our educational systems show the presence of so many children in each of so many grades, so many teachers, etc. For administrative purposes a university may list auditors, curators, librarians, and others among its professors.

The principle of contradiction, or consistency of organization, is used for building systems of things, as well as of propositions. In other words, if we apply a principle of action to a certain individual we do not make an exception, if we are consistent, in the case of another person. In general, the principle supplies a rule of consistent action.

What is conventionally called the LEM becomes in specific system building a principle of alternativity. If x is put into a certain class y, then it is excluded from class z. Whenever the situation calls for such alternativity the principle is fairly rigorously applied. But there are orders of alternativity, such that in some cases a dichotomy is made between those situations in which x is either y or z, or x is y and z, as compared with other systems in which a different rule operates. In some instances x is not to be connected with y or z at all, but with l and m.

Depending upon particular enterprises the rules of system

building may apply to things, manipulations, actions, judgments, and propositional arrangement. All these enterprises must be kept strictly apart in order to avoid confusion. In the case of identity we may be interested exclusively in the sheer verbal formula *a* is *a*, and more generally in the arrangement of the words *is* and *is not*, or in making things similar, as in counting, classifying, ordering or mathematically equating things. Again, we may be interested in merely asserting that there is or ought to be constancy or certainty.

Logical Laws and Systemological Behavior

The difficulties which current logicians face with respect to logical laws arise directly from an excess of knowledge and sophistication. Though dominated by the cultural heritage that logic is the discipline of principles, of the *a priori*, the basic, the necessary, the stable, and the ultimate, logicians discover, after all, that these principles do not stand up in the face of scientific and mathematical analysis. To their credit they are unwilling to cleave to necessary systems which are remote from developments in mathematics and science.

Glance at one of the many excellent examples showing the effect of the assumption that logic is prior to, and regulates, other disciplines—namely, the problem whether logic is or is not ontological. Logic is ontological, it is declared, and reveals the invariant traits and relations of things. Then, when a closer approach to scientific investigations demonstrates that the Realistic identification of a set of sentences or propositions with events in nature is untenable, it is asserted that logic is free from ontology.[56] Why such leaps from ontological to nonontological logic except for the assumption that logic regulates? The solution usually offered for the incompatibility of logical principles and the nature of things is to relegate the governing powers of logic to sentences. But to make logical laws into instructions for establishing necessary connections between statements either reduces statements to innocuous and empty things or continues the ontological procedure. All this confusion is avoided by holding firmly to the behavior of system builders. It is not sufficient to show that language does not

[56] Compare Nagel's shift of view from Can logic to Logic.

constitute things, or that words and terms should be precisely employed.

What is required is an analysis of the behavior enterprise under investigation. Above all, it is necessary to observe that rules belong to the job at hand, and that all rules have been derived from specific enterprises.

Significant here is Whitehead's remark:

In formal logic, a contradiction is the signal of a defeat: but in the evolution of real knowledge it marks the first step in progress toward a victory.[57]

To maintain and revere any set of absolute principles, to attempt to make all things and events match them is to behave reverentially, instead of logically, to be concerned with religious, instead of with logical, laws.

[57] Science, p. 267.

CHAPTER XXI

PROBABILITY AND INTERBEHAVIORAL LOGIC

PROBABILITY: GUIDE TO LOGIC

LOGICIANS as professional system builders inevitably turn to probability study. Howsoever imbued they may be with the ideal of certainty, with absolute systems, they are invariably brought sharply to the dead end of abstract and formal structures. Hence the unique place which the probability field occupies in logic. Every alert approach to probabilities—that is, to actual events—brings to the surface the necessity to organize or structure things—in brief, system making. Even if the system maker fails to appreciate that he is actually structuring problematic objects and conditions, or his reactions to them, his work can not escape a system-building description. Depending upon his behavioral circumstances he produces system products by way of (a) intellectually adjusting to elusive things, (b) calculating chances, (c) playing winning games, (d) predicting events, and (e) performing manipulations effectively.

There exists, to be sure, the *paradox* of probability. Though inevitably dealing with contingencies, with partial and changing facts, with complex and indeterminate events, logicians nevertheless like to set up univocal descriptions and fixed rules. This situation is well illustrated by Bertrand's remark in beginning his *Calcul des Probabilités:* "How dare we speak of the laws of chance? Is not chance the antithesis of all law?"[1]

This paradox plumbs the depths of logic. There is a domain of chance. It is not only the ancients, as Poincaré says, who were forced to face the uncertainties of prediction, the difficulties of establishing laws for recondite events. As he himself at once observes, his definition of chance "as only the measure of our ignorance" will not do. For so-called fortuitous events are constantly predicted and calculated. Moreover, the predictions and calculations appear plausible, since they result in the distribution of dividends.

And so the logician is obliged to enlarge his traditional domain

[1] Poincaré, Foundations, p. 395.

to assimilate, if possible, those elements which resist his urge to achieve totality and certainty. The systemological difficulties which he could pass over while confining himself to formal linguistic structures stand out sharply when actual events obtrude themselves. The logician's task, then, has become that of developing a logic of induction to complement his venerable deductive logic, a logic of errors and estimates to match his logic of truth and reality.

Nothing, however, stands in the way of thus enlarging the scope of system building except the strictures imposed by the historical philosophy of mind. It is only the unified mind of the rationalist which affiliates with rigid realities; only the diffuse subjectivism of the empiricist which devalues the continuity of concrete events. Probability logic calls into play naturalistic psychological resources. Problems of chance and fortuity as objective fact, problems of belief, expectation, and prediction among contingencies can only be solved by a logical theory based on an objective psychology.

For the interbehavioral logician the probability problem presents no difficulty. All types of situations offer occasion for system construction. His horizon is broad enough to encompass the most rigid and certain systems, as well as those remaining close to problematic facts, to events which will not bear hammering into the shape of empty abstractions.

The Domain of Probability

Upon examining source material, students of probability logic immediately discover that system makers approach probability situations with presuppositions foreshadowing the pattern of their systems. In other words, instead of producing system products on the basis of their contacts with probability materials, they impose upon the latter such binding specifications as to affect the system product. The resulting description of the probability situation is then erroneously presumed to be identical with the original situation.

Two factors influence this circumstance. In the first place, the probability domain consists of a vast and heterogeneous series of relative and unstable events. Consequently there is free play for the workers' presuppositions on the basis of their diverse backgrounds and interests. In the second place, the historical origins of probability studies are rooted in the calculation of chances and in the philosophical attempts to justify nonrational knowledge.

In order, therefore, to arrive at the fountainhead of probability situations we shall examine some of the presuppositions blocking the way. For convenience we separate them into two types: first, the philosophical, stemming from a more general cultural background than immediate probability situations; secondly, the historical presuppositions growing out of the accident that probability studies were originally concerned with calculating chances.

Philosophical Presuppositions. Logicians who so frequently quote Bishop Butler's maxim: "To us probability is the very guide of life,"[2] do not point out that Butler is making a grand concession to beings of limited capacities. For an "infinite intelligence," "nothing which is the possible object of knowledge, whether past, present or future, can be probable." In other words, probability is not the guide of life because it is characteristic of actual living conditions, but because men live only in a pale reflection of absoluteness and universality. Though logicians may regard themselves as remote from theological situations, they fail to recognize the similarity between theology and speculative cosmology. For instance, they see no disharmony between working on the basis of sound scientific method and accepting the belief that there is a problem concerning the existence of an external world.

The point is that the prevailing presuppositions of universality and absoluteness of probability systems have little to do with the situations out of which probability problems arise and upon which valid systems must be built. We have already mentioned the tendency to regard probability systems as conforming to the certainty specifications of deductive structures. By reducing probability to situations satisfied by a single univocal system, it is assumed that their respective systems are exclusive and absolute.[3] Actually, any probability formulation, even when most solidly grounded, constitutes only one example of many possible types of construction.[4] In other words, there are many kinds of probability situations, each demanding a specific sort of investigation.

[2] Analogy, p. 73.

[3] Greenwood, in Runes' *Dictionary*, describes seven interpretations of probability.

[4] This statement holds for general mathematical or calculative probability, as well as for any probability theory applied in practical statistics.

Both the neglect of the concrete situation and the formulation of unsatisfactory probability theories can be traced directly to traditional ontological and epistemological presuppositions. Historical ontologism lies at the basis of the problem whether the world is one of ultimate chance and contingency, or of irrevocable determination. Ontologies, coupled with rationalistic epistemology, foster the notion that probability is a form, or degree, of certainty, while the sensationistic subjectivist inclines toward a view of haphazardness that can only be corrected by calculating ignorance and indifference.

Calculative Presuppositions. Because the first quantitative probability studies were initiated by problems derived from calculating gambling chances, probability has become identified with simplified things and events which can be treated by a calculus with fixed and narrow limits. In earlier days probability systems centered around the symmetrical ratio $1/2$, and the definite possibility of a die's $1/6$. When probability came to be applied to vital statistics, insurance problems, and scientific data, the calculation of limits themselves became a problem.

Probability Events and Situations

Assuming that we can clear away the presuppositions blocking the path to probability events, we still face the problem of isolating them within their wide domain. We start with an interbehavioral field. An individual is interbehaving with things, events, or relations, but his intellectual orientation, his manipulatory action, and attempts at prediction can not be rounded out and completed. Either he has insufficient access to data or the data themselves are neither established nor stable. In fact, this description applies to every complex human situation. Keeping close to concrete happenings, we discover that problematic situations are not uncommon, nor are they unique; rather, they are instances of what happens when we face a situation different from one to which we habitually and automatically adjust ourselves.

Several important implications follow. In the first place, we can distinguish between (a) the scientifically useful admission that all complex situations are problematic, or that all knowledge is less than certain, and (b) the metaphysical presupposition that the existence of an external world is doubtful, problematic, or requires proof. Writers on probability set up the proposition that truth is a form of probability, not, however, on the observation of human behavior, but on the untenable ground of spiritistic epistemology and fallacious ideas of the psychology of perception, knowledge, and intellectual construction.

A second implication is that we can welcome any, and all, factors of a given situation. From the interbehavioral standpoint a probability situation involves the actions both of persons and of the various problematic objects upon which they operate. One factor can not be separated from the other. The history of probability theory is in part a record of writers who erroneously identify probability either with the stimulus events, which they sometimes reify in a Platonic manner, or with the reactions to those events. The latter instance occurs when probability is defined as the degree or quantity of knowledge, belief, or ignorance. But whenever equations or propositions are set up to symbolize something concerning the probability of events, the interbehavioral process is immediately acknowledged.

In the third place, the interbehavioral approach implies that stimulus objects within problematic situations are objective. For example, the problem may concern the adequacy of a sample, the weight of a thing, the velocity of an object—in sum, any of the manifold conditions to which persons must respond in their everyday activities or in scientific laboratories.

Probability Range and Continuity

As genuine happenings, all probability situations constitute points on a continuum ranging from ordinary life situations to the abstruse entities of mathematical and conventional logic. A similar continuity pervades probability operations. This view, however, in no sense implies that contingency always characterizes events. We must not violate the principle of specificity. Our characterization of a situation follows our contacts with it. There are stable and relatively fixed things and events whose nature and operation we need not doubt. Contingency here is at a minimum.

Of considerable importance is the enlargement of the probability range to include single events as a matter of principle. This is contrary to the opinions of mathematical writers who approach probability investigation exclusively from the standpoint of series or collections. We include in the probability range both past events and those to occur. In the latter case anticipation and prediction operations come into play. These operations imply that the task of the investigator in contact with a number of factors is to foresee the probable course of their interconnection. It goes without saying that his operations involve a complement of knowledge derived from previous observations, without which he could not arrive at a prognosis. Can one deny, for instance, the probability problem in situations complicated by extremely important conditions, such as predicting the outcome of a disease?

From the interbehavioral standpoint, it is futile to deny that probability has to do with degree of belief. Belief consists of a form of interbehavior with particular conditions; it is an objective and definite situation in which we attempt to determine whether a certain outcome will be x instead of y. Even in this type of case, probability is figured on the basis of the character of events and the knowledge and expertness of the individual interbehaving with such events. Thus, while the emphasis may be on one or another factor, probability as a degree of belief is an integral part of all probability situations.

Behaviorally speaking, there is no ultimate difference between probability as degree of belief and as frequency. In the case of frequency the difference in detail may be summed up as an accumulation of records, whereas in the case of belief there are not so many data upon which to base a prediction. A fundamental difference is the amount of possible manipulation of data on the part of the operator.

Adherence to specificity principles obviates the exclusion from probability situations of relations between propositions. But here we must differentiate between propositions taken as records of analogous events and as isolated empty sentences or word combinations. In each case we construct a different kind of probability system. In the second or word-combination case we have a system based upon prior or primary constructions, whereas in the former the constructions are founded on more direct contacts with things. Sentential records of an indirect sort are often necessary in order to operate effectively in direct probability situations, though this does not mean that the observer is not in some sense concerned with objective events.

PROBABILITY: UNIVOCAL OR MULTIVOCAL?

So powerful is the influence of universalistic logical tradition that, on the whole, probability is univocally defined. There are, to be sure, suggestions[5] that the term *probability* refers to different types of situations, but in the end writers do not go much further than a differentiation between probability occurrences and probability judgments or estimates. The following observations illustrate the point.

Reichenbach.[6] This writer adopts the uncompromising univocal position that all probability situations sum up to a pattern of an unknown infinite series of items which require precise determination or at least relative delimitation. While Reichenbach is willing to consider a distinction between (a) mathematical and (b) logical types of probability, his systematic constructions are designed on a strictly mathematical basis.

Russell.[7] Writing as though he were analyzing situations, but really building on historical constructions, Russell distinguishes between (a) mathematical probability, and (b) degree of credibility. The former, he asserts, can be numerically measured, and hence satisfy the axioms of the probability calculus. Credibility probability applies to single propositions, whether or not based on available relevant evidence. It is this sort of probability which underlies the view that all knowledge is probable. What Russell says, in effect, is that, whereas different probability interpretations are inescapable, actually the important systems of propositions are those of the probability calculus.

Nagel.[8] Many writers on probability differentiate sharply between the probability calculus and various interpretations of it. The calculus is taken as a neutral objective instrument for evaluating probability events. This fact does not, however, prevent certain writers from interpreting the calculus in a manner which helps to assimilate it to their own ways of thinking. Nagel, for example, differentiates between (a) series of recurring events capable of treatment by a frequency calculus and (b) nonquantitative happenings. In the latter subdomain fall single instances

[5] Hawkins, Existential; Kemble, Probability; Ryle, Induction.
[6] Experience; Wahrscheinlichkeitslehre.
[7] Knowledge, part 5, chap. 1.
[8] Principles.

which require us to ascertain the adequacy of whatever evidence is presented in their favor. As a supporter of a frequency theory of probability he then identifies his own interpretation of the calculus with the quantifying instrument. Probability events do not therefore ordinarily include single instances. But by making suitable verbal adjustments the frequency calculus can be made to cover single instances as well as series.

Carnap.[9] Without differentiating between single-instance situations and those involving series, and by keeping in view future action, Carnap distinguishes between two concepts of probability: (a) frequency and (b) confirmation. The former covers relations between events or series of events, whereas the latter concerns relations between events and the evidence accepted for them. Probabilities of the first type lead to propositional systems of the analytic and deductive sort; the latter involve sentential structures of the synthetic and inductive order.

Hawkins.[10] This writer proposes to set off (a) epistemic from (b) existential probability. Existential probability raises the question whether events occur or whether we may speak only of the truth of propositions about events. The propositions concern physical relations—the metrical properties and causal relations of chance mechanisms. Epistemic probability involves propositions about weight of evidence and the reliability and correctness of beliefs or inferences.

Kemble.[11] In order to make room for what he calls an operational concept of probability this author distinguishes three probability concepts. The first is the Laplacian *a priori* type based on a judgment of equal likelihood. Inductive probability is the statistically based calculation of past experiments and trials. Both of these are primary. The third is the secondary, or theoretical, concept of probability, consisting of a construct in a universe of constructs. Not completely unrelated to these is the operational concept which describes probabilities as numbers computed from data according to standardized rules. Kemble bases his conception on the Machian notion that the external world is created or invented as an interpretation of invariant patterns of sensation in the stream

---

[9] Testability; Probability; Two Concepts.
[10] Existential.
[11] Probability.

of consciousness. Since this view combines the mental and the physical, it can reconcile frequencies with expectancies.

Ryle.[12] Assuming that all probability concepts are concerned with relations between "premises" and "conclusions," Ryle differentiates from each other (1) the plausibility of abstract theories, (2) numerical odds, and (3) reliability of inductions. Only the last two he regards as normally employed in science. Numerical odds may be correlated with the Laplacian tradition, while inductive reliabilities belong to the statistical frequency area.

Polya.[13] An extremely interesting attitude is exhibited in Polya's coupling of probability and plausibility. As a mathematician this writer is wholeheartedly committed to an exclusively objective frequency interpretation. Still, he is sympathetic toward a subjective or a degree-of-belief principle, for the latter, which belongs to the domain of heuristic reasoning, possesses—like deductive reasoning—a certain pertinence in human affairs. The counterpart of probability Polya calls plausibility. Although the difference is great between plausibility and probability, a calculus can be formulated for it. But unlike probability, which is measured by a determinate number between 0 and 1, plausibility corresponds to an indeterminate number with the open interval (0, 1) as its domain.

All these examples reveal the influence of philosophic and technical theory. Of course, since we are examining systematic pronouncements, a certain amount of formalism is to be expected. What is lacking, however, is the recognition that systems are constructed within a domain of concrete events, and that because construction is different from the ground materials it should therefore be placed in perspective with reference to them.

Generality and Specificity of Probability Systems

Probability logic is hampered in its development, even more than general logic, by the totalitarian and monopolistic attitudes of logicians. System builders clash with respect to motivation, presupposition, material selection, and operational techniques.

Probability systems should be differentiated on the basis of the criteria of generality and specificity. We have already mentioned

[12] Induction.
[13] Heuristic.

(p. 206) that from the standpoint of general and exclusive systems the number has been limited to seven. Interbehavioral logic demands that we take into consideration the factors confronted in probability situations—the eventualities and conditions which are to occur or have occurred. We are therefore opposed to any view that limits the number of probability systems, or excludes certain situations from the probability domain on whatever ground.

To indicate the difference between general and exclusive systems and practical structures concerning actual life situations we consider briefly the system of von Mises.[14] This author argues that probability must be regarded as a scientific concept, and like other terms, such as *work* in mechanics, it must be separated from any popular usage. He goes on to argue that probability concerns only three types of happenings—namely, games of chance, life insurance, and the treatment of certain mechanical and physical events— for example, the movements of gas molecules or the random motion of colloidal particles. What he would exclude is the probability of one country's going to war with another, the historical existence of certain persons or events, the reliability of witnesses, the correctness of judicial verdicts, and so on.

Whether or not von Mises has the right to include games of chance and life insurance in the scientific field, he is on solid ground when he asserts that there are three fundamental purposes of science; namely, bringing order into events, predicting their development, and bringing about particular happenings in which we are interested. Is it the case, however, that these three are exclusively the interests of science? Or that science alone can accomplish such purposes? These assertions are merely arguments for limiting the definition of probability in a way acceptable to the author. The statistical study of kinetic-gas theory is certainly an important type of probability investigation, but it does not rule out other kinds of probability inquiries.

Von Mises may well ask whether the usefulness of probability in life insurance and mechanics is owing to the adoption of a single correct probability definition (frequency), or whether it happens that in these situations classifiable instances are available and allow one to set up series or isolate repetitive elements. But why must one limit one's interest to such types of situation? Certainly

[14] Probability; see also Popper, Logik.

it is hardly fair to regard von Mises' frequency theory as rational by contrasting it with all competitive views, with the implication that the latter are mystical and intuitive.

Interbehavioral theory, on the other hand, allows for the probability of theories in science and everyday life, as well as for the classical head-or-tail tosses or the appearance of a die face. It is only the adherence to a frequency theory of some form which draws the line at single events. The test of the opposing view is, of course, whether it fits problematic situations.

Von Mises' conception is susceptible to two interpretations. Insofar as it indicates that science consists of a rigid analysis of events we should indeed agree that refined intellectual operations are designed to clear away the superficialities and irrelevancies of ordinary contacts with things. All science consists of more analytic and more exact investigations than simple everyday interbehavior permits. On the other hand, if von Mises implies a generic difference between scientific and everyday interbehavior it is not acceptable, since there is no break in the continuity of our contacts with things and events. To be sure, the constructions of science can not at every point represent, nor be integrated with, actual events; nevertheless, science is bound to such events. Probably no one would disagree with this statement were it not for the influence of philosophical traditions which make us forget that our scientific constructions are in no sense arbitrary, and that no matter how complicated or abstract they become they are designed for the purpose of describing and interpreting observable events. Even though scientific work may become so channeled that much of its activity consists of the production of artifacts for purposes of rigid control, we still can not get far away from interbehavioral situations.

Relative Value of Probability Systems

Faced with large numbers of possible probability systems we must ask whether there are any evaluative scales with which to weigh or measure them. Are there criteria for allotting a higher or lower value to a system involved with drawing balls out of an urn, as compared with one based on the relative frequencies of car loadings or dice gaming?

From a strictly systemological standpoint, the only criteria are those pertaining to the effectiveness of the system products themselves. In view, then, of the fact that the urn situation can furnish rigid rules for a probability system, we may accord it high value. On the other hand, though drawing balls out of an urn provides calculative events with fixed conditions, such as the total number of balls, number of kinds, and relative number of each kind, do we want to tie ourselves to absolute relations at the sacrifice of richness and complexity of events? Wherever we can employ mathematical techniques we are in possession of invaluable calculative instruments for achieving prediction. But to value mathematics as calculative devices is one thing; to make calculation the exclusive systemological criterion is another. The latter has led to the futile conception of absolute and intuitive probability determinations, and to the idea that probability is an irreducible and indefinable property.

We conclude, then, that a place must be made for many criteria, based on all sorts of human interests and types of probability material. The acceptance of a variety of criteria argues nothing against their value. We need only justify choosing such criteria, and make sure of the evidence for the actuality of their sources.

Historical Evolution of Probability Systems

Students of logic divide themselves sharply into those who find profit in the teachings of history, and those who are sure that only by timeless analysis can one achieve significant systems. Anyone sensitive to the records of history may easily detect a progressive evolution of probability systems toward an operational goal. The evidences are of two sorts: first, changes in intellectual culture; secondly, structural transformations in probability systems.

Of the cultural shifts one of the most important is the reception by science of probability ideas and techniques. When scientists gave up the search for absolute laws and exceptionless propositions, in favor of statistical data and significance tests for observations, it became possible to interpret probability systems as sets of interbehavioral factors in contingential situations.

Operational progress in the probability field has also been furthered by the development of the postulational conception of mathematics. To move away from the absoluteness of Euclidean geometry to the relativity of premises and conclusions bespeaks a growing appreciation that even mathematics is the home of operational principles. Howsoever far mathematicians and logicians have been motivated by their zeal in searching for rigor, they have learned that accuracy and precision can only be achieved by operational procedures.

The cultural changes mentioned, along with the acceptance of the postulational principle, in the final accounting have only hastened a trend. The goal is yet to be reached. The full realization of effective probability systems must wait upon further relaxation of the powerful hand of cultural tradition. Still needed is a separation of probability logic from dualistic psychology. The lag of psychological ideas behind mathematical operations prevents logicians from seeing that operations are interbehavior, and that the analysis of probability and probability calculation must have better foundations. It is strange that what the historical evolution of probability studies shows so plainly is not yet put to work.

Pragmatic Beginnings. Laplace finds it remarkable that a science which began with the consideration of games of chance should have become the most important object of human knowledge.[15] That was because the founder of the modern phase of probability theory was most at home in the lofty study of celestial mechanics and the system of the world. Actually, the situation marking "the humble beginnings" of probability study possessed the same factors as any study more highly assessed.

That games are under consideration plainly indicates that we are observing interbehavior with things. Let them be a pair of dice which Cardan throws to meet a certain criterion[16] incidental to winning the game. Dice throwing is the basic interbehavior and may be described as the lowest-level operation. The next level is the analysis of the play situation, the ascertainment of the results given the original conditions. There is only one way in which two or twelve dots can appear. Eleven can be thrown in two ways, and ten in three ways. Whether it is Cardan, the player, who makes

---

[15] Théorie, Introduction, p. cxli.
[16] Todhunter, History.

the analyses, or Kepler or Galileo, all are operating by way of a simple ordering and counting of results bounded by the character of the devices employed under the rules of the game.

There are two important arguments for accepting the conventional view that the beginnings of probability study lie in the work of Pascal and Fermat. In the first place, by their time analytic operations had become elaborate enough to be dignified by the term *theory*. Workers responded to themselves as factors in the probability situation. The question had been raised whether the propositions of arithmetic were inconsistent. Moreover, Pascal criticized Fermat's solution of the Problem of Points. In general, probability situations had become enormously complex. In the second place, Pascal and Fermat formulated a theory that the entire probability situation can be handled by the operational techniques of permutation and combination.

Response-Centered Systems. Following a long developmental period in which the calculation of chances was assiduously cultivated by mathematicians interested not only in games but also in mortality and life insurance, there appeared a system pitched on a highly sophisticated plane. The work of combinatorial analysis and probability theory, carried on by Huygens, Leibniz, the Bernoullis, Montmort, DeMoivre, Euler, D'Alembert, Bayes, Lagrange, and Condorcet, culminated in the technical construction of Laplace.

The outstanding characteristic of Laplace's system of probability is that it is response centered. Not only is probability regarded as a determination of things by a calculating individual, but personal psychological processes are emphasized. For this reason Laplacian probability has been seriously condemned as subjective. Laplace declared:

The theory of chances consists in reducing all events of the same kind to a certain number of equipossible cases, that is to say, cases such that we are equally undecided about their existence, and determining the number of cases favourable to the event of which the probability is sought. The ratio of this number to that of all the possible cases is the measure of the probability which is no more than a fraction whose numerator is the number of favourable cases and whose denominator is the number of all possible cases.[17]

[17] Théorie, Introduction, p. iv.

This excerpt makes clear that, for Laplace, the power of intelligence is such as to penetrate the mysteries of nature, even if it has to begin with nothing but symmetrical ignorance. The difficulty which critics find in the Laplacian view is that states of mind can neither be measured nor calculated.

But ignorance and belief need not be regarded as states of mind. Such an interpretation stands in complete disregard of the newer objective psychological theory. After all, the situation must be described as one in which Laplace, a mathematician, is operating upon certain data. And there are degrees of efficiency of contact with the events of which the probability or possibility is to be calculated, or otherwise determined.

A more substantial criticism than the charge of subjectivism is that Laplace does not explicitly indicate his actual contacts with things. He is determining the ratio of favorable cases to the sum of both favorable and unfavorable cases, and that means he is observing or otherwise interbehaving with events and situations.

Event-Centered Systems. Thinkers who harbor mental states in their intellectual households finally escape from subjective probability systems by turning completely to objective things. A comprehensive system was thus built up on the pattern of a material or frequency theory. The frequency theory was proposed by Ellis[18] and Cournot,[19] and established by Venn.[20] An extreme empiricist, Venn regarded his logical interest of attaining certainty as satisfied only by turning away from subjective belief to the objectivity of series or frequencies.

The frequency theory of Ellis, Cournot, and Venn is an incomparable example of the discrepancy between a logician's operational procedures and his formal structurization, between his practice and his theory. Venn assumed that he was avoiding subjectivity, that he was dealing exclusively with external things or conditions. Actually, of course, he was concerned with system building, which offered him confidence in the data with which he was interacting. His practice, however, belied his theory that he was not dealing with belief, conditions of ignorance, etc.

Such theory-practice discrepancy stems directly from the under-

[18] Foundations.
[19] Exposition.
[20] Logic.

lying mentalistic psychology. Had not Venn, like the frequentists since his time, been dominated by mentalistic psychology, he would have realized (1) that the *a priorists* whom he was attacking were systemizing calculations and schemas having to do with objective events, as DeMorgan and other belief proponents held, and (2) that centering on objects is arbitrarily selecting only one interbehavioral factor. Accordingly, both the empirical frequentists and the opposing rationalists ignore the fact that probability situations may be of different kinds. What they could not know at their time of historical development was that since there is no mental, but only interbehavior, each type of probability system really goes back to contacts of individuals with stimulus objects.

Because the empirical frequency system is so vigorously recommended as objective, the paradox exists that objects and their frequencies become dissipated into nebulous states of mind. Some device, therefore, must be invented to keep close to the basic situations giving rise to probability problems. Venn's formulation that probability is a body of rules for drawing inferences about classes of events which combine individual irregularity with aggregate regularity is an appealing one.

Propositional Probability. A decidedly new level of probability systems emerged when probability problems became centered in propositions instead of in responses or objects. For one thing, propositional probability mirrors a more complicated set of situations. It surpasses the relatively unsophisticated inclination toward one pole or the other in what is essentially a bipolar situation. The superior sophistication of propositional probability is measurable in its greater or lesser articulation with operational processes. While it does not renounce the psychology of mind, it still constitutes a step toward an objective analysis of probability interbehavior. Such is the case when propositional relations are regarded as unique and rational, and as referring to the conditions of things.

(a) *Probability Propositions and Things.* This form of propositional system, for which we choose Peirce as an illustrative proponent, is based squarely on Venn's formula stressing the observation of recurrences of events. Peirce modified the system of emphasizing the quantitative precision which mathematical calculation supplies. Propositions are best interpreted as equations. This is exemplified by his statement:

Probability is a kind of relative number; namely it is the ratio of the number of arguments of a certain genus which carry truth with them to the total number of arguments of that genus.[21]

We may call this propositional system the truth-frequency theory; it implies that propositions must be observationally confirmed, and thus reveals its connection with scientific problems. Confirming a proposition is tantamount to contact with things. A high point is reached here. But the system stops short of a thoroughgoing interbehavioral position. To a certain extent the emphasis of propositions neutralizes the underlying philosophy and psychology of sensations. When propositions are taken to be equations they appear strongly supported. Still, the lack of a basic objective psychology, coupled with the influence of formal and monopolistic logical theory, does not allow a full-fledged operational interpretation.

Completely carried out, an interbehavioral view emphasizes the operational character of calculations. Moreover, calculations are not regarded as detached actions leading to products which are later applied to situations; instead they are treated as interactions with substituted-for relations—in other words, interactions with things handled by means of substituting symbols. On this basis the calculus is necessarily bound by the calculated things, and probability events are not shied at because they can not be measured or ordered—at least, in conventional ways.

(b) *Probability Propositions and Rationality.* Of the many forms in which this probability theory can be described we choose the one sponsored by Keynes.[22] He moves on from happenings or events to propositions in order to avoid the subjectivity of belief or knowledge doctrines. The theory's primary design, then, is to favor operations instead of things, but with a stable and calculative basis. Probability has to do with a relation of propositions.

Let our premises consist of any set of propositions h, and our conclusions consist of any set of propositions a, then, if a knowledge of h justifies a rational belief in a of degree a, we say that there is a *probability-relation* of degree a between a and h. This will be written $a/h = a.$[23]

[21] C. P. (Collected Papers) 2,657.

[22] Treatise.

[23] Ibid., p. 4.

Under the influence of mentalistic psychology and realistic philosophy the rationalistic probability view turns squarely away from an interbehavioral situation, though it connects with it at long range. To assume that premise propositions must be weighted by evidence is an excellent provision. Again, the application of the system to particular cases, instead of exclusively to frequencies, carries with it a good principle. All the advantages, however, are cut short by a rationalistic and intuitive philosophy.

To avoid subjectivism Keynes holds to a Platonic version of probability—namely, probability is indefinable. In other words, since empirical evidence or frequencies of occurrence do not lead to the determination of probability, he resorts to mystical intuition.

PROBABILITY AS STATISTICAL OPERATIONS

Statistical operations in the various scientific domains constitute the presystematic basis for a probability system in line with objective psychology. The point is that particular systems are organized as adapted to specific situations. Such systems are constructed by way of overcoming the inevitable contingencies of technological research and scientific investigation.

Even if it is true that only a negativistic approach is made to an interbehavioral type of probability, there is the advantage of not involving oneself in a disserviceable system based on philosophical rationalism or empiricism.

Such a statistical probability system as we have been suggesting is not to be confused with the conventional frequency structure. The basic idea consists of the concrete activities of individuals in making measurements and estimates in order to carry on the various operations of science and technology.

BASIC ORIENTATION OF PROBABILITY SYSTEMS

So numerous and varied are the sources for probability systems that it is advisable to make clear whether we are concerned with (1) the reliability of knowledge, (2) the existence of things, (3) the adequacy of statements, (4) the effectiveness of a method, or (5) some combination of these. Furthermore, it is of considerable importance to make sure that we properly locate probability situations preliminary to organizing probability structures. Because of epistemological and ontological influences such orientation has been lacking. In the following paragraphs we consider some of the conventional landmarks for isolating and comparing probability situations.

Probability, Certainty, and Necessity. Keeping close to specific systems means that we incline toward a critical isolation and comprehension of probability structures as over against large-scale philosophical systems. In addition, we achieve workable criteria to differentiate between the probable, the certain, and the necessary. This is no less a task than the separation from each other of linguistic, philosophical, and scientific problems. The situation can be well illustrated by a quotation from Jevons:

In nature the happening of an event has been pre-determined from the first fashioning of the universe. . . . A steam-vessel, for instance, is missing and some persons believe that she has sunk in mid-ocean; others think differently. In the event itself there can be no such uncertainty; the steam-vessel either has sunk or has not sunk, and no subsequent discussion of the probable nature of the event can alter the fact.[24]

At once we can sift out and discard the metaphysical remarks about predetermination, unless, indeed, we are interested in ontological speculations rather than actual events. Next we should clear up a terminological problem. While it is true that terms such as certainty and necessity have no standard and fixed usage, certainty really refers to response rather than to stimulus object. Jevons appears to equate certainty and necessity as matters of existence, as over against probability concerned with thought or belief. Not much can be said in favor of the term *necessity*, for it belongs to the metaphysical domain of determination and predetermination, but if it is used it belongs more to objects than to reactions to them. The criterion invoked here is altogether a practical one.

Whether or not a steamer sinks depends upon a number of factors. For example, a certain combination of meteorological circumstances, the materials out of which the vessel is built, the nature and disposition of its cargo, the lack of cargo or ballast, the number and competence of officers and men aboard, and so on. In case of war, there are the conditions of pursuit by destroyers, whether or not they are able to overtake the vessel before reaching the stipulated limits in their orders, whether they have run out of fuel,

[24] Principles, p. 198.

etc. In such cases, of course, knowledge of the event should never be confused with the conditions of the event. There are no absolutely isolated events, but combinations and interrelations of events which make room for probability. It is precisely the estimation of such probabilities which constitutes the work of probability system building.

However, once the ship has sunk there is no longer a probability in the event. All probability systems now have to be built upon the basis of knowledge factors. Concerning a repetition of the sinking one can build alternative systems based upon available data. We must weigh our evidence upon a variety of scales possessing a greater or lesser basis in combinations of factors.

Probability, as knowledge or reactional attitudes, is an approximation based upon definite contact conditions—that is, availability of data or techniques of securing data. Among objective events we also have a set of approximations, but here the conditions are matters of interrelations of natural conditions. For instance, how much reaction between chemicals takes place depends upon pressure, temperature, the nature and amount of material, and the presence or absence of catalyzers.

Probability, Truth, and Error. There is a factual basis for the conventional differentiation between truth and existence. *Truth* as a term refers to knowledge and belief—in short, to reactions to things as over against the existence of things. This statement may be extended also to the conventional view that truth as compared with existence concerns a reference to things or a statement about things. How far do sentences conform to events? Statements or propositions are true and definitive when they match things to which they refer or which they symbolize.

Complete and satisfactory agreement between statements or beliefs and things is not always attainable. We need only mention the limitations imposed by complexity of things and events and the need to meet criteria of precision and accuracy. The reactor in such situations faces the problem of relative and approximate conformity. In science we fully appreciate the approximate character of our propositions. We must be fully aware of the specific conditions under which the propositions hold. Scientific propositions always carry with them the realization that they are not absolutely true.

We conclude, then, that probability systems pertaining to knowledge and belief can be clearly separated from systems stressing things or events. But we must next insist that the distinction is a relative one when we deal with actual situations as compared with epistemological or ontological theories. Notice, therefore, that truth and falsehood depend upon many specific conditions, and not upon some general metaphysical criterion. Probability does not differ from truth or certainty (1) because all certainty is metaphysically regarded as probable, or (2) because probability has to do only with "matters of fact" different from "matters of reason."

That probability propositions are never true or false is set up on a generalized metaphysical basis that there is no truth, only probability.[25] Taken in a specific context the view that differentiates truth from probability is agreeable. Namely, there are true propositions and there are probable ones. In each case the situation must be described in terms of the things and events involved, and of what the responding individual does to them. We have already seen that the reduction of all truth and existence situations to probability situations is based upon elusive constructions concerning mental states and the creation of external worlds.

The distinction between "matters of fact" and "matters of reason" goes back to an earlier phase of the doctrine that psychic states must be taken into account. We must keep in view that this distinction was developed by Locke, Hume, and other rationalistic empiricists because they were committed to an identification of things with states of mind.

Probability, Possibility, and Impossibility. When probability problems center about a knowledge criterion, the question is asked: How reliable is knowledge? The degrees of knowledge, or probability, cover the range from the possible to the impossible. Basically, the criterion focuses on the range of conformity of propositions with corresponding facts. If the proposition refers to an impossible situation it is totally unreliable; if to a possible one, its reliability is a function of coverage, or of degree of correlation.

Systems of knowledge reliability should, of course, be confined to concrete situations, where alone they can have significance. Nevertheless, the attempt is frequently made to establish systems

[25] Reichenbach, Experience.

of absolute possibility or impossibility. In such cases the criteria are useful only in estimating the credulity of the system maker, rather than in determining any correspondence of his knowledge with evidence.

More significant systems are developed in concrete situations when reliabilities can be checked in terms of events, their measures and ranks. In scientific investigation the possibility or impossibility of either an event or a response to it can be established in terms of probable errors, of standard deviations centering around means, and by other devices. And these checks and balances are added to whatever other tests are used.

Probability, Potentiality, and Actuality. Despite the fact that logicians do not think much in terms of behavior, they can not escape it. When dealing with inductive systems they are forced to take activities into account. Whenever they consider questions of expectation, reasonableness, and belief or evidence, activities surge to the surface. Again, when logicians are confronted by problems of risk and play, by problems of making wagers and posits, developing sampling techniques and organizing predictive systems, they enter with full force into behavior situations.

Activities already performed, along with the present general status of the behavior field, constitute an actuality factor from which future potentialities may be estimated or calculated. Past or present operations become premises for inferential structures. On the stimulus-object side, sampling techniques are designed to ascertain what the potentialities are, so that the mass from which the sample is taken will measure up to a certain standard.

PROBABILITY IN SCIENCE

The hypothesis that scientific enterprises are inevitably occupied with probability situations has become established only at the cost of considerable struggle. Even now many writers accept the proposition grudgingly, at best. Though science is obviously investigation—namely, interbehavior with events that are difficult and changeable—scientists still cling to the notion that they are seeking absolute knowledge. Hence their bewilderment when relativity, discontinuity, and indeterminacy are forced upon them.[26]

[26] Cf. Darwin, Logic.

Probabilities appear strange and disconcerting. Let us glance briefly at the course of this absolutistic tendency.

To go back only to the Renaissance, the establishment of science, so extravagantly celebrated as the turning away from authority toward investigation, did not, in fact, release the scientist from the fetters of the absolute. On the contrary, faith in scientific discovery was established upon an absolutistic basis. For example, the three laws of Kepler were achieved by his ability to correlate Brahe's observations with Euclidean geometry. By splendid acts of creative imagination Kepler transformed the sun into a focal point of an ellipse, which itself was the locus of the successive points described by the earth in its motion about the sun, and thus established astronomy. Though the orbit of the earth is not actually an ellipse, this fact did not interfere with the development of a thoroughly dependable deductive principle. From this, and other expressions of loyalty to Euclidean absolutism, arose the brilliant achievements of celestial mechanics.

From this time, to beyond the middle of the nineteenth century, the reign of deduction and Euclidean geometry and the conception of a fixed universe operating according to absolute laws supported the *a priori* powers of the scientist, and stabilized faith and certainty. Investigation and experimentation only appeared to confirm the alleged certainty that facts could be subordinated to the scientist's rational powers. Hence, the overweening faith in cause as the antecedent of effect in a closed system (chap. 19), and the facetious assertion that absolute laws were only substitutes for deity.

Science, however, is, after all, investigation. And, despite the fact that the cultural conditions of the time demanded and received their due, changes inevitably took place in the general scientific structure. In biological nature, for example, it was discovered that fixity is not the law, but that changes are constantly occurring in animal forms. In physics itself, contacts with thermal and electrical happenings proved that the old closed system, with its Euclidean background, was not a universal system. Work with thermal events indicated a break, in the sense that events were not reversible. Problems of entropy revealed that the old particles, which were really Euclidean points, could not be traced in their movements as though they conformed to the lines of geometric figures.

Statistical mechanics was the result. It meant the introduction of probability into physics. At first, this probability notion diverged but slightly from the old conceptions dominated by Euclidean geometry and the power of absolute numbers. Maxwell still thought of the distribution of molecular velocities as determined by the Gaussian law of errors. Quite lacking in this sort of statistics is the derivation of variables and laws from actual observation. Facts are still fitted to *a priori* principles. For this reason statistics does not necessarily articulate with genuine probability; nevertheless, an entering wedge is available. Unfortunately, however, in the sense of statistical data, probability is still regarded as inharmonious with experimentally derived facts, although, as a method, probability techniques are safely ensconced. How long deductive science will remain the dominant form is hard to say, but nondeductive, nonexact, or statistical materials can no longer be excluded from science.

In addition to the general deductive tradition, science is often handicapped by the cost and stability of apparatus which make findings appear inevitable.

A definite impact of probability upon scientific thinking has its source in the Heisenberg Indeterminacy principle. Briefly, the simultaneous observation of the exact position and velocity of a particle can not be achieved because the use of light necessary for the observation modifies the character of the thing observed. Undoubtedly, this intractability of events, with a corresponding difficulty of mastering them, is really common in every investigative field, but it has influenced scientists tremendously, simply because it occurs in the traditionally most exact science. The law of error distribution, the obvious fact that all measurements vary, and the ample use of hypotheses in all science have not hitherto appeared very impressive.

All these factors can no longer be interpreted as obstructions to knowledge, nor can they be used to support ideas of cosmic chance or fortuity. What they confirm is the fact, so frequently emphasized throughout this volume, that all creditable laws are constructions resulting from the scientist's operative contacts with the things and events which set him his problems. In other words, to determine probabilities on the basis of frequencies of occurrence is to interbehave with probability circumstances. The tools we use, such as propositions and various calculations, are only tools. Some particular probability task may consist of sorting out and arranging certain propositions concerning the presence, absence, and frequency of various participating factors, but the probability enterprise itself is a more inclusive type of event.[27]

It is necessary to recognize that statistical or experimental studies are only designed to discover the natural properties and relations of data. This means that scientists can not reject things and events not subject to calculation or measurement. Such qualities are as genuine and as real as mathematical relations. Indeed, it is precisely the lesser availability of these measurable properties and relations that makes for probability enterprises.

PROBABILITY AND INDUCTION

The area of induction is the locus of the technical aspects of probability system building. In fact, in this area the basic issues of probability logic come to the fore. We have already mentioned that inductive logic developed as the correlate of the logic of certainty.

Logic and Events. The relation between probability and induction at once brings up the general question: How can logic be related to events? The development of science and the upsurge of investigative manipulations, including measurement and calculation, promoted a need for a system to correlate with traditional deductive logic. Influenced by the historical convention of universal systemization, logicians felt obliged to assimilate scientific facts to their cosmic structures. This they did by means of the processes of reduction and substitution. Inductive processes, which should have suggested specific content systems for particular contacts with events, became subordinated to the universalizing process of cosmic system building. The need for absolute criteria engendered the problem of how inductive logic is related to deductive logic.

Relation of Induction and Deduction. Uneasy about inductive processes, logicians pursue their futile search for ways and means

[27] Cf. Kantor, Operational.

to transform induction into deduction. Induction has been characterized as disguised deduction, a mere method of making plausible guesses.[28] This view has been severely criticized;[29] in the interest of science it is declared that much deduction is disguised induction.[30]

One thing is certain: both the opponents and defenders of inductive logic stand upon metaphysical foundations. Neither group takes the position of the actual system builder. Often those who support the inductive principle do so in the interest of a sensationistic metaphysics. Thus the inductionists attempt to approach a stable system. Induction is set up with bracing straps and made into a law for scientific work. To approach the inductive situation with an interest in system building requires no strait jacketing of science, nor of any other domain of human action. System building is a type of labor performed for its own sake, or in conjunction with some scientific, technological, or even more practical pursuit. From this standpoint there is no problem of induction, no need to justify any sort of preoccupation with metaphysical principles. Above all, there is no problem of either-or, as between deductive and inductive system making. System builders are many, and they build all sorts of systems. The problems, then, concerning their activities and products should be examined in their local habitats.

Probability and Inductive Principles. Logicians, we have indicated, inevitably feel the pressure of events which disturb totality and absoluteness. Events somehow force to the front inconstancies, irregularities, and inconsistencies. But, on the other hand, system implies structure and this, in turn, suggests stability. Consequently, in the history of culture various notions have arisen concerning the existence of principles which guarantee propositions, or systems of propositions, about contingent matters.

Principles in this sense are directly related to all the historical varieties of *a priori* constructions. In every case such principles constitute in the final analysis a verbal structure referring to some feature abstracted from contacts with stimulus objects. When stabilities and recurrences in events are noticed, a principle is set

[28] Russell, Principles, p. 360; Jeffreys (Theory, p. 5) suggests that Russell objects to being too frequently quoted on this point, but Cohen (Preface, p. 19) endorses the statement.

[29] Broad, Relation.

[30] Campbell, Physics, p. 9.

up that things sustain invariant relations. To account for the observer's ability to discover these relations, writers invent *a priori* powers in the human mind, or necessary principles abstracted from all knowing. In general, processes and operations are hypostatized by verbal description.

A very instructive *a priori* notion is located in the recently developed argument from perception. Curiously enough, this argument begins with the everyday observation that in our perceptual behavior we respond to things on the basis of past responses to them, instead of purely on the ground of immediate contacts with available properties. But at once this fact is lifted out of its native domain of interbehavior with things into the empyrean of the mind knowing something *without* experience.[31] Here is an excellent illustration of imposing traditional interpretations upon events, while erroneously assuming that the events point to such interpretations. The *a priori* is established by events which really show the complete antithesis to all *a prioris*.

Probability and Prediction. Prediction problems constitute a bridge between probability and Inductive Logic. Historically, inductive problems have been concerned with the interrelation of past, present, and future events, by way of anticipating what may occur. Now probability events can be selected for their bearing upon the future. Can we assert that any future event is probable, or will probably occur?

Future events are as yet nonexistent. How can we say anything about them? This is a sample of the purely syntactically formulated question. Notice how greatly it differs from a concrete interbehavioral question. Future events taken as actual life situations may be regarded as no different from any event not yet observed. What we call future event situations consist of a particular collocation of factors of the same general sort as those with which we have had considerable experience. Thus, we must rely upon the frequencies with which the type of anticipated event has previously occurred. In other words, our determination of probability value is made on the basis of interbehavior with similar events. Very little significance can be accorded any kind of prediction which is not so grounded. Naturally, interbehavior with future events is

[31] Kneale, Probability.

more hazardous and open to error than the determination of what factors have contributed to an observed event. Still, this circumstance presents no serious difficulty when we operate with specific situations. Only when we deal with purely verbal questions, such as what right we have to believe that conditions in the future will be similar to past ones, do we run into the philosophical and, we might add, futile problems of Hume.

CHAPTER XXII

ANALYSIS OF PROBABILITY SYSTEMS

DESIGN FOR PROBABILITY SYSTEM ANALYSIS

THE most effective method for studying probability logic is the critical examination of probability systems. To pursue this method we follow the study design already prefigured in the interbehavioral fields in which persons interact with contingent and indefinite things.

We feature five outstanding components of this investigative pattern: (1) the builder, (2) the work he performs, (3) his building materials, (4) the conditions influencing his work, and (5) the product he completes. These are most effectively structured in the following set of questions and specifications.

(1) *The System Builder.* Concerning the worker we ask:

(a) Is he building a general system—say, an inductive logic? Or is he constructing a localized system for a more particular purpose?

(b) Is he motivated by the principle of system for system's sake, or system designed for some further end?

(c) Is his guiding preconception absolutistic or relativistic, leading respectively to rigorous results or to those valid for particular situations?

(d) Is he so dominated by traditional notions of mind that he builds an epistemologically rational or empirical system, or is he erecting a nonmetaphysical system for carrying on some specific enterprise?

(2) *Methods and Procedures.*

(a) Linguistic: constructional work performed by setting up references and symbols.

(b) Mathematical: constructional work reduced to calculating and computing.

(c) Observational: what part is played in system building by recording and structuring the results of observation?

(d) Manipulative: what place have manipulations among the systemizing procedures?

(3) *Materials.*

    (a) Events (chemical, physiological, astronomical, biological or humanistic).

    (b) Propositions (sentences and relations between them).

    (c) Statistical frequencies and ratios (or similar subject matter).

    (d) Acts or processes of various sorts.

(4) *Working Auspices.*

    (a) Philosophical.

    (b) Scientific.

    (c) General systemological.

    (d) Programs of everyday activities.

(5) *Work Products.*

    (a) Theoretical (abstract systems).

    (b) Practical (statistical tables, lists of constants, other tools).

    (c) Actual processes (recipes for calculation, etc.).

This design for system analysis sets aside all conceptions of philosophy and psychology built on the traditional views of mind. The mind theory basic to both historical rationalism and empiricism is replaced by hypotheses derived directly from observations of system-building situations.

Once more we refer to one of the basic postulates of the interbehavioral-field theory pointed out in Volume I—namely, that all psychological activity, including that of the scientist, mathematician, and logician, constitutes the interaction of persons with stimulus objects, whether natural things (trees, land, water), or creations such as round squares, souls, and psychic states which can only substitutively exist through assertions or symbols.

Because the interbehavioral-field construction is based upon actual observations of persons at work under particular conditions our study design enables us to see whether things and events or traditional theories are stressed. To illustrate, how much were the constructors of electrical field theory influenced by the need to oppose action at a distance? Again, how much has theological thinking influenced the development of the infinite in mathematics?

Our study design constitutes a mirror image of probability situations. We set up interbehavioral-field postulates on the basis of interbehavioral situations in order to derive interbehavioral construction products. Interbehavioral fields are therefore based upon interbehavior. Implied, then, is a limited regress. Is this regression objectionable? Hardly; for all the levels are definitely set in human events, from which all theories are derived and beyond which none, in any significant direction, can go.

Types of Probability Systems

Despite their belief that probability systems are exclusive and authoritative, logicians build different types of systems. In this manner they unwittingly endorse the interbehavioral view that it is impossible to confine probability theory to a single type of formula or situation. By reviewing a number of typical probability formulations we shall find that the arguments for exclusivistic theories are based on overemphases of particular items. Hence the numerous conflicts in probability theory.

(1) *Probability as Rational Responses*

Laplacian Probability Theory. Historically, the earliest theory of probability was formulated under the auspices of an excessively rationalistic culture. Recall the classical formulation that probability is a fraction whose numerator is the number of favorable cases, and whose denominator is the total number of equally likely favorable and unfavorable alternatives. This was a development, surely, from the Renaissance awakening to the powers of mathematics. The source of probability studies is the same that gave rise to man's confidence in his deductive powers, and which was encouraged by the pursuits of geometry. An effective symbol of the period was Galileo's and Kepler's faith that authority could be replaced by an *a priori* reading of the numbers in which the book of nature was written.

We have seen in Chapter 21 how probability theory originated in the application of mathematics to the practical problems of chance. Recall the effects of Pascal's and Fermat's assistance to the Chevalier de Méré in his gaming problems. The rationalistic emphasis, with a recession of stimulus objects, is favored by the situation in which one desires to gamble successfully when knowledge of the eventualities are not, to be sure, completely unknown, but certainly not sufficiently known.

When the vast intelligence can not embrace in the same certain formula all the past and the future, it must, according to Laplace, fall back upon the principle of sufficient reason for help in formulating judgments concerning equally likely eventualities. In direct line with this general view an equivalent statement could be developed in the form of an equal distribution of ignorance with a fraction of one-half.

Unless one is alive to the postulational character of mathematics one may be surprised that Laplace's essentially mathematical theory of probability should result in an impotency of probability calculation and a consequent subjectivity of viewpoint. Opponents of the classical *a priori* theory find it easy to discover its faults, though they fail to produce a satisfactory substitute. The following examples indicate the mode of attack.

Equally Likely Cases do not Always Exist. Suppose the face of a die is somewhat imperfect; then it is impossible to apply the equally-possible or equally-likely criterion. Again, assume that a biased coin is estimated to turn up head with a probability of .63; it eludes the equipossible ratio.[1]

The critics go even further in the case of more complicated happenings. When mortality records show that a thirty-year-old man has a probability of .950 of living another year it seems absurd to say that, of a thousand possible events, the ratio of favorable to unfavorable cases is $950/50+950$. Similarly, should mortality tables indicate that the chance of a man of forty dying within the next year is .011, what are the equally likely alternatives? Should the ratio be $11/989+11$ or $33/2967+33$?[2]

Perhaps it is too much to expect a theory to be applicable to conditions from which it was not derived and which it was not the author's intention to handle. Of course, what the critics point out is entirely valid—namely, the classical theory is not a universal one. Nevertheless, they are mistaken in assuming that the classical theory alone lacks universality; all theories do. By all means, of course, when frequencies are involved, a frequency theory has to be resorted to, but will all probability problems involve numbers of cases? Frequency theorists naturally contend that they can always construct series or collectives. Must they not, however, consider that at least sometimes the frequencies are not essentially

---

[1] Nagel, *Principles*, p. 45.
[2] von Mises, *Probability*, p. 102.

numerical, but are really based upon the abstraction of specific qualities or characters?

Unimportance of Equally Likely Cases. The classical theory is also attacked because in the final analysis it consists only of a mathematical calculation of permutations and combinations— that is, the interrelationship of numbers. In simple cases of penny tossing the probability ½ does not indicate whether the head or tail actually will fall up. Or, in a more complex situation, knowing that a geometrically symmetrical cube is also kinetically symmetrical—that is, possesses equal statical moments and moments of inertia, yielding a probability of $1/6$ of falling on any side— does not enable one to know that it will actually fall on any one particular side.

Again, equally likely cases are said to be insignificant as against the type of probability concerned with averages, dispersions, average error, probability function, and the law of error. The greater importance of the latter is taken for granted because of its application to scientific work in physics (kinetic theory, thermodynamics), astronomy (star origin and distribution), and biology (genetics).

Equiprobability Involves Trivialities and Contradictions. As a mathematically originated theory the classical formulation of probability is presumed to be *a priori* because of its independence of, and potency concerning, actual events. Its fundamental ratio with respect to, say, the tossing of coins is ½. From whence is this fraction derived? The answer: Equiprobability means one can not say beforehand what will happen except in terms of the alternatives. In other words, the only basis is the presence of two factors, each of which is equally likely. Despite the circularity in the definition classical writers have, of course, persisted in applying this type of calculus.

In support of this issue Bernoulli invoked the *Principle of Insufficient Reason,* which Keynes has renamed *The Principle of Indifference;* it is also called *The Principle of Equal Distribution of Ignorance.* According to this principle two events are equiprobable if there is no reason for supposing either one or the other will occur.

Keynes,[3] on the basis of some suggestions of von Kries, indicates

[3] Treatise, p. 43.

the inherent contradiction. For example, knowing nothing concerning the color of a book we could say that the proposition "This book is red" has a probability ½, but the same thing could be said of any other color. Accordingly, we would have the impossible case of 3, 4 or more equally likely exclusive cases. In other words, the sum of probabilities would be greater than 1.

It is questionable whether the criticism is justified, since according to the proponents of this theory the emphasis is upon the ratio and not upon the concrete events involved. On the other hand, one may argue that there is always something known—namely, there are two sides to a coin.

To correct the classical theory, and to confine it to its proper domain, we need only consider that it was proposed for problems involving dice throwing and for the selection of hands in card games. Though we may regard such situations as trifling, there is good reason for defending the work done upon them. In the first place, aside from the fact that such intellectual heroes as Cardan, Galileo, Fermat, Pascal, Leibniz, Huygens, the Bernoullis, Laplace, and Poisson were concerned with such situations, they stimulated the development of a probability calculus—one of the most significant mathematical building stones. Indeed, it would be cultural myopia on our part to be insensitive to the origins and ramifications of cultural factors. In addition, there is considerable intellectual profit in observing the specificity of situations and keeping our formulae thoroughly articulated within their framework.

Despite the almost universal condemnation of the classical or rational theory—and the impetus given to this condemnation by the absorption into probability situations of scientific problems, such as those of statistical mechanics—one may still find justification for it. For one thing, the condemnation is ameliorated by the fact that the critics themselves are merely using a certain kind of situation for the basis of their criticism, one which, moreover, favors acceptance of their own formulations. Howsoever correct they may be in cleaving to more important sorts of probability events, they are still universalizing a principle. The result: They exclude all other kinds of probability situations.

(2) Probability as Knowledge Responses

Probability as Quantity of Knowledge. British writers on probability, in contrast to those on the Continent, are concerned with individualistic rather than with general cosmic happenings. Even when they accept probability as an *a priori* factor, as Jevons does when he declares:

The Laws of Probability rest upon the fundamental principles of reasoning, and cannot be really negatived by any possible experience,[4]

they prefer to put it in the form of belief or knowledge, rather than of reasoning. For Jevons, probability theory:

defines rational expectation by measuring the comparative amounts of knowledge and ignorance.[5]

The value of probability is its efficacy in regulating action with regard to future events, in a manner leading to least disappointment in the long run.

Jevons develops his specific formula on the basis of a criticism of DeMorgan's description of probability as degree of belief and Donkin's interpretation of probability as quantity of belief. Jevons finds the conception of belief too difficult. He rejects Donkin's emendation of DeMorgan on the ground that probability is not a quantity of an entertained belief, but rather what one ought to believe. Probability for Jevons, then, is the quantity of knowledge.

The line of British writers, including DeMorgan, Donkin, Jevons, and others, is referred to as subjective. Certainly they stress reactions instead of things. Jevons specifically asserts that "Probability belongs wholly to the mind."[6] Chance, he believes with Laplace, is only an expression for ignorance. Since he accepts a complete determinism there is no such thing for him as chance in nature.

Subjectivistic theories like those of the writers quoted are almost universally condemned, even by the British writers of the time. Certainly, as universal theory they are unacceptable. The question remains: Do they represent any facts whatever? By way of answering let us relate them to underlying interbehavioral principles.

It is a significant fact that Jevons is the man who endorses Herschel's dictum that "Numerical precision is the soul of science," and who was certain that "Every science as it progresses will be-

---

[4] Principles, p. 206.
[5] Ibid., p. 200.
[6] Ibid., p. 198.

come gradually more and more quantitative."⁷ Again, Jevons is counted among the forerunners of those who applied mathematics even to economic data. Penetrating below the surface of his doctrine, we find it is concerned with much more than psychic or subjective phenomena in the historical sense. In short, we should not dismiss a probability doctrine simply because it resembles an unacceptable theory, or is itself unacceptable in some form.

We can not reject this type of probability interpretation on the ground that it is impossible to measure belief as a subjective event, although, as we have indicated, the stress here is upon the response phase. The assumption is that events are not probable but certain, and that our reactions to events, in the sense of knowledge or belief alone, are probable. Since there can be no probability reaction without reference to an event, and since degree-of-knowledge situations are not only authentic but occur frequently, we must regard them as a genuine type of probability situation. Moreover, it would be very difficult to support the idea that such probability situations do not occasion various system-building operations.

From the interbehavioral or field standpoint there is nothing mysterious about the connection of "subjective states" or beliefs with calculation. The earliest probability studies have been interrelated with calculation, especially the processes of combination and permutation. We need but recall that all probability theory consists of constructions derived in some sense from crude data. True, such constructions do not always adhere closely to the data, in the sense that the final theory adequately represents the original events. This is scarcely surprising, since probability data themselves are problematic or inadequate. For the most part, then, the theories represent considerable autistic construction based upon the manipulation of mathematical processes. The result is a tendency to abstract from event factors, which nevertheless may still be available despite their general problematic character.

One more point. All mathematical or calculative processes are interbehavioral and in the final analysis go back to contacts with events. The fact that these events may be relations—and therefore permit a formal treatment irrespective of objects upon which to act—makes possible the traditional purely formal manipulations

⁷ Ibid., p. 273.

or the recent tautological and purely syntactic processes. Precisely because scholars have historically regarded believing and knowing as subjective states these psychological processes have inevitably been condemned as a basis for probability determination. Hence arose the powerful tradition that probability must be reduced to statistical frequency. On the other hand, it is difficult to displace the proposition that probability situations are limited to events which occur frequently, or in general that probability is exclusively concerned with collectives or series. This being the case, it is no anomaly that such competent logicians and mathematicians as De Finetti and Ramsey, clinging to a so-called subjective theory, still contend that probability has to do with belief, and that we are obliged to measure such belief.

Important for the view of these writers is the connection of beliefs with readiness to act; that is, belief is regarded as measured by the readiness with which those entertaining beliefs act upon them. Ramsey also proposes the wager conception, according to which the willingness to wager serves as an index to the strength of a belief or the intensity with which it is held. A favorable aspect of this subjective view is that it does attempt to bring probability down to actual human situations, an attempt substantiated by Ramsey's rejection of the convergence principle.

The convergence principle may be described as a statement of possible results in throwing coins. Thus, for example, it would have to be established that "In n consecutive throws the number of heads lies between $n/2 \pm \varepsilon(n)$."[8] Ramsey, however, argues that aside from the fact that no such proposition has been established, it would be broken if enough instances were tested. He goes on to say:

Nor is there any fact established empirically about infinite series of throws; this formulation is only adopted to avoid contradiction by experience; and what no experience can contradict, none can confirm, let alone establish.

Unfortunately, Ramsey's argument against abstract logical relations in favor of concrete events remains only an argument. Howsoever valid the strictures of Ramsey and other proponents of the subjective theory may be with respect to an opponent's theory,

[8] Ramsey, Foundations, p. 206.

they fail to support their own argument because they are not really interested in actual occurrences—namely, beliefs as concrete inter-behavior with specific objects. Adherence to a single probability formula is sufficient evidence. Moreover, even on mentalistic ground there is a powerful objection to limiting probability exclusively to inferential reactions, whether belief, judgment or any sort of expertness.

(3) *Probability as Laws of Things*

Probability as Frequency of Occurrence. Frequency theorists insist upon stressing the stimulus-object phases of probability events. This fact is evident from the essential frequency formula—namely, probability is the limiting value of the relative frequency with which an event occurs in a class or series. Especially the early frequency theorists—for example, Ellis,[9] Cournot,[10] and Venn[11]—emphasized the necessity of keeping in contact with actual events. Subjective theories were rejected; the restriction of probability calculation to permutations and combinations was opposed. Authentic probability problems were claimed to concern actual things observed to happen in established series. Similarly, probability calculations were based upon the observed recurrences of events.

Because of its emphasis on things the frequency form of theory is by far the most important and the most widely held. In fact, it fits eminently into the culture of the present century, and symptomizes the developments and achievements of modern science. With the transition of science from the mechanical and historical to the statistical phase, as Maxwell put it, this has indeed become the century of statistics,[12] and hence of probability. Still, we must not overlook the differences between frequency theorists; for they are animated by different attitudes concerning probability problems. Accordingly, we now consider three types of frequency theory, leaving for later examination a fourth distinct form called by the same name.

(a) *Probability as Empirical Frequency.* One of the earliest frequency formulations, that associated with Venn, was developed as

[9] Foundations.
[10] Exposition.
[11] Logic.
[12] Merz, History, vol. II.

a criticism of the intuitive or rational mathematical theory. Emphasis was to be placed upon experience or empirical records. The theory is definitely an expression of the British Empirical philosophy in opposition to Continental Rationalism. Instead of reactions objects are stressed, and all probabilities are presumed to be calculated on the basis of actual observations with similar materials.

Although this theory presumes to discover *how* things really *are*, it attempts to avoid subjectivism. In this connection Venn asserts:

Probability is not so extensive as that over which variation of belief might be observed. Probability only considers the cases in which this variation is brought about in a certain definite statistical way.[13]

As a generalized theory the frequencies involved are not specific and limited, such as those having to do with particular enterprises of individuals. Though the theory ostensibly takes its departure from actual statistical frequencies it does not feature specifically determined data, but rather a general explanation of uniformities and divergences. In other words, it is an empirical philosophical, rather than a scientific statistical, formulation.

Central to this theory is the conception of series. Probabilities as over against certainties have to do with attributes, or classes of attributes, the causes of which are numerous but not evident. Probability series are defined as a combination of individual irregularities and aggregate regularities. From an indefinitely large number of terms representing an attribute *a*, one can differentiate a smaller class of which the members possess a more restricted attribute *b*. Now, choosing *m* members, in all of which *l* belong to the less class, the probability of *b* assuming *a* consists of the limit *l/m*, when *m* becomes indefinitely large.

General Series are Certain. Critics have objected that this is not a probability, but a certainty, theory. Indeed, since the essential background of Venn's theory is the uniformity of nature, it misses actual probability. The latter has to do not with ascertained uniformity or certainty, but merely with samples.

Neglect of Unique Occurrences. Another equally valid objection to Venn's formulation is that it does not allow for specific occur-

---

[13] *Logic*, p. 143; see also Edgeworth, *Probability*.

rences, which are certainly among the most characteristically probable events. It is in connection with such events that the notion of probability is most valuable. Frequency theories which deal with classes or repetitions of events are defectively exclusive when nonrepetitive happenings are in question; as, for example:

... when we speak of the probability that the solar system is formed by the disruptive approach of two suns, or that the stellar universe is symmetrical.[14]

Others[15] who oppose Venn on the same ground admit that he realizes the restriction.

The Paradox of Measurement. Aside from avoiding subjectivity, Venn argues that his theory allows for exact measurement. But critics[16] point out that on Venn's basis even a judgment concerning the tossing of a penny can not be made until it has been tossed an infinite number of times. Accordingly, there is no case where the value of a probability is known.

(b) *Probability as Statistical Frequency.* This theory is an outgrowth of the original empirical frequency formulation. Essentially, however, it has developed out of the application of a probability calculus to the fields of life expectancy and to various scientific problems such as thermodynamics, biological relations, and, more recently, quantum mechanics. According to this view probability is defined as the limiting value of the relative frequency of a given attribute within a given collective.[17] Furthermore:

The purpose of the theory of probability is exclusively the calculation of probability distributions in collectives derived by means of given distributions in the initial collective.[18]

This type of theory frankly makes probability synonymous with statistics. The bridge, of course, is the theory of error. As Sheppard puts it, the theory of error is the main link between the theory of probability and the theory of statistical frequency:

It forms a large part of the former, and is a particular case of the latter.[19]

[14] Jeffreys, Scientific, p. 219.
[15] Keynes, Treatise, p. 96.
[16] Jeffreys, Scientific, p. 219.
[17] Cf. von Mises, Probability, p. 38 et passim.
[18] Ibid., p. 308.
[19] Probability.

In contrast to the empirical theory the present version is based upon the actual manipulation of data for specific scientific purposes. Accordingly, the frequency limits are not known prior to handling the data, nor are they rigidly set. Frequencies are presumably observed or arranged on the basis of the recurrence of events.

Intellectual Probability a Form of Certainty. Like general empirical probability this theory is subject to the criticism of aiming at certainty—though a different certainty, to be sure. Here the series or collective is derived from actual calculations. But even so, the development of series or frequencies is accomplished by invoking the normal law. If such a limit is really placed upon them the charge of translating probability into certainty appears supported. Again, if the proponents of this view believe that probability can never be given a true value, but only an approximate one based upon actual past findings—in other words, that probability is always inverse probability—then the pragmatic certainty charge is indeed substantiated.[20]

Statistical Probability Restrictive. It is perhaps valid criticism of this theory that by hypothesis it is restricted in scope, and therefore not a theory of probability but only a type of probability confined to particular situations. Howsoever powerful this criticism may be, it only holds against the proponents of the statistical frequency theory, because they, like their opponents, regard probability as a general theory, and not as one applicable to specific operational fields.

Statistical Probability Only a Technique. Connected with the above is the criticism that this theory is really only a technique for the manipulation of certain events. In other words, it is no more than a generalized principle of calculative processes—of great importance, indeed, in science—but not a general theory.

Statistical Probability Points Backward. Another argument is that such a theory deals too much with recorded past events and has slight, if any, bearing upon future actions or knowledge. The counter to this criticism is that there is no other way of predicting or applying knowledge than on a frequency basis. But the question remains whether the frequency theory does not set aside experimental and other investigations which may be much more effica-

[20] See Sheppard, Probability.

cious for any or all scientific purposes, and which require neither numbers large or small nor series of any sort.

(c) *Probability as Mathematical Frequency*. When at the outset fixed limits are assigned to frequencies (whether or not such frequencies are regarded as concerned with concrete occurrences), or to factors in general mathematical systems, we have a type of theory which reduces probability to mathematical manipulations— either simple arithmetical, algebraic, or more complex analytic processes. Indeed the proponents of this theory have adopted the calculus of classical theory and added frequency as a substitute for the subjective interpretations. In other words, coin tossing, dice throwing, or some sort of fixed collective is used as a paragon of, if not the exclusive guide to, probabilities. Though the proponents of this theory may believe that only by trial can probability ratios be ascertained, the fundamental principle is that the factors involved approximate fixed limits, whether finite or infinite.

An illustration is von Mises' argument that probability involves stochastic, random, or casual variations. In coin tossing, for example, if a certain characteristic, say, heads, occurs with definite regularity, no probability is involved. On the other hand, every sample selected from the series must show the same probability. The probability is, of course, one half, and the larger the number of throws the nearer the frequency approaches this probability fraction. Despite the randomness, the same result is obtained when we number or order the throws. We may select (a) all even or odd numbered throws, (b) all those the number of which is a prime, (c) all throws after a head, or (d) those following two tails.

The mathematical theory consists of two subtypes. The first begins with natural happenings, say, biological data as in the case of much of Pearson's work, or economic materials, which are then connected with the mathematical theory. The technique is, of course, to apply a probability calculus. The second type is framed by a mathematical setting. Examples are all those probabilities stated in terms of collectives or infinite series.

Calculation Rather than Probability. An objection to a theory of this sort is that at most it merely recognizes the existence of problematic events. Its main emphasis is on numerical manipulation, which is believed to be best achieved by the probability calculus. But since this is a rigid instrument, based upon given premises, the total result is not completely satisfactory. Even the stress of series or numbers becomes an emphasis upon numbers, rather than upon characteristics of events.

To overstress the repetitive and serial character of happenings may lead to the emasculation of a good principle. It may be carried so far as to conceal genuine events and make probability entirely a matter of the manipulation of mathematical variables. Accordingly, the best check is to ask: Whence are the variables derived, and how closely do our probability calculations keep in touch with the data calculated and with the original problems basic to the calculation?

Certainly, empiricists and positivists like Venn, Jevons, and Pearson adhere to a psychological and philosophical view that enables them to reduce the stimulus objects with which presumably they are dealing to their own calculations. Experience of objects in any case reduces to states of mind. It is therefore only a step from the experience of the numbers of things to the things themselves.

(4) *Probability as Propositional Relations*

Stemming from Leibniz and other rationalists of the 17th century is the theory that makes probability a step in a rational approach to certainty. Probability situations are inconclusive conditions, as compared with mathematical ones where reason holds full demonstrative sway. To probability arguments it is rational to attach some weight, but not as much as to those arguments in which our knowledge is certain. Such situations, however, come within the province of logic which investigates the general principles of valid thought.

Keynes, one of the main proponents of this type of theory, confines his treatment of probability to a "general theory of arguments from premises leading to conclusions which are reasonable but not certain."[21] As we have seen (p. 220), a symbol of this fundamental relation between premises and conclusive propositions is a/h, representing the probability of a conclusion a derived from the premise or hypothesis h.

[21] Treatise, p. 98.

Keynes proposes the theory of propositional relations as a complete theory, presumed to deal with unique events as well as with repetitive ones. It derives this power from its emphasis of propositions, rather than of things or beliefs. According to the logical theory, probability is independent of actual events; it is a unique relation, an indefinable concept. Probability, then, must be treated as an absolute relationship between propositions.

On the same basis Keynes regards probability relations as thoroughly objective. This means that the relations are independent of any observed events. To justify this peculiar doctrine Keynes falls back upon the notion that knowledge is of two sorts: (1) direct—that is, based upon contacts with things, and (2) logical—namely, argument. Though Keynes frequently refers to the occupation of workers with things and with knowledge of things, and though he discusses evidence for propositions, in the final analysis he retreats to a Platonic position.

Since no emphasis is placed upon things, and frequencies of actual occurrences are minimized, the primary technique of dealing with probabilities is a process of intuition or *a priori* reasoning. Furthermore, Keynes forgoes exact numerical statements of probability, satisfying himself merely with the absolute relationship between propositions which state the conclusion and, presumably, represent the evidence. The measurability of probability for Keynes, therefore, has to do with the numerical relation between the degrees of rational belief in one of a pair of conclusions relative to the other. Similarly, the simple comparisons equal to, greater than, and less than are concerned more with comparable rational beliefs than with definitive relations of conclusions and hypotheses.

Logically Intuitive. A fundamental criticism of the intuitive type of probability formulation is that it is impossible to deal with such unavailable processes as intuition. It may be argued, however, that such criticism applies only to the form of Keynes' statements, for in actual practice he himself asserts that what he means by intuition is merely direct recognition of the truth or validity of propositions. These direct intuitions are used as means toward some cognitive end. For example, he uses the illustration of employing trigonometry to determine the position of an object, not by direct observation of it, but by observing some other object together with certain relations. This he regards as a type of indirect method.

Furthermore, one might say for this theory that it does place considerable emphasis upon the expertness of the judge. In other words, more than other theories it gives a place to the reactor in a problematic situation. Of course, to grant this point means to modify its Platonic character and bring it closer to actual problematic situations.

Nonmeasurability. The view that probabilities are not measurable provokes serious critical attacks. In the first place, it has been argued—by Jeffreys,[22] for example—that one may believe probability is a unique indefinable relationship and yet give each probability a numerical value. Other objectors point out that if probabilities are not numerical or measurable there is a complete hiatus between probability and scientific situations—in other words, such probability theory is said to be philosophically abstractive and unrelated to scientific situations, as well as disconnected from statistics.

Noneventual. Another serious objection to the propositional relations theory is that it stands remote from concrete events. For one thing, relations between propositions are independent of any observation, and are presumed to hold regardless of any actual state of affairs.[23]

Propositional Relations are Linguistic. Again, this theory is clearly a system of linguistic items. Presumably the propositions refer to, or stand for, actual events, but there is lacking a safe bridge between the interrelated propositions and events.

A final comment. Despite all the weakness of the proposition-relation system, we must not overlook its merit as a check on other theories. Certainly we may grant its value in demonstrating that the probability domain is large enough to accommodate more than one system. Furthermore, it is of some importance to question the wisdom of exclusively occupying oneself with a frequency system.

(5) *The Truth-Frequency Theory*

The present theory, which may be traced back to Peirce, originally was an outgrowth of Venn's so-called mathematical or sta-

---

[22] Scientific; Theory.

[23] See, Nisbet, Foundations.

tistical doctrine.[24] The claim is made for it that it interrelates objects with propositions concerning objects. Peirce may well be expected to think in terms of scientific situations, even though he occupies himself with abstract systems rather than concrete enterprises. The following represents his more concrete attitude:

The inference from the premiss, A, to the conclusion, B, depends . . . on the guiding principle, that if a fact of the class A is true, a fact of the class B is true. The probability consists of the fraction whose numerator is the number of times in which both A and B are true, and whose denominator is the total number of times in which A is true, whether B is so or not. Instead of speaking of this as the probability of the inference, there is not the slightest objection to calling it the probability that, if A happens, B happens.[25]

Peirce, however, was essentially a mathematical logician. Accordingly, we do not find him cleaving too closely to events, or even to their numerical representation.[26] For this reason he constantly strives to preserve the rational or mathematical factors in probability theory. Both Peirce's empiricism and rationalism appear in the view that probability relates to the future[27] and that great emphasis must be placed upon propositions in the probability situation. His ideas are excellently combined in the definition that probability is the limiting value of the truth frequencies arising from the application of leading principles. Probability propositions are compared on the basis of the relative frequency with which they actually do turn out to be true, and "truth consists in the existence of a real fact corresponding to the true proposition."[28]

Though the truth-frequency theory is undoubtedly an improvement over its Vennian prototype, it has lately been worked over in an appealing way. Nagel[29] especially has attempted to articulate it with recent scientific situations, as well as to free it from some of the objections made against the earlier, or material-frequency, theory.

In particular, it is claimed that the improved truth-frequency

[24] C.P. 2, 651.
[25] Ibid.
[26] C.P. 2, 101.
[27] C.P. 2, 66.
[28] C.P. 2, 652.
[29] Nagel, Frequency.

theory is less restricted than other frequency theories. While it can take over the mathematical method and apparatus of the statistical and mathematical frequency theories it can also deal with inde-terminate cases. Again, it is not restricted to the future, but can also treat of the past. And, finally, because the emphasis is upon propositions instead of events, it can handle the probability of single events on the basis of the relative truth-frequency of propo-sitions concerning the evidence for the original proposition. On the whole, the truth-frequency theory approximates an opera-tional viewpoint.

Not Operational Enough. Nevertheless it does not go far enough in an operational direction. Even though it assimilates several originally independent theories, it does not escape the stigma that attaches to a doctrine presumed to be universal and complete. To be sufficiently operational a theory must be able to handle specific situations as they occur. No matter how inclusive and comprehen-sive the description of a process must be, it is not permissible to dissipate the original referents in the descriptive or referential process.

The criticism, it will be said, is admitted and hence of no force. For at bottom the truth-frequency theory deals with inferences. But how are we to understand inferences? It is our contention that inferences are forms of interbehavior with stimulus objects; con-sequently, one can not get away from specific events. Inferences are not detached propositions, though they must always be lin-guistically referred to or described.

Why Stress Propositions? After all, why should we make proba-bility a matter of propositions rather than of events? Even if we properly distinguish between (a) propositions as intellectual con-structs and (b) sentences as symbolizing or referring instruments there is no advantage in completely bypassing events. And if we are dealing with propositions we are in touch with events, albeit indirectly. Whether or not this is sufficient depends upon specific problems.

When, on the other hand, we are operating with sentences, we run into two different sorts of problems. We may be merely fol-lowing the conventional logical tradition which substitutes lin-guistic factors for various psychic states—for example, (a) con-cepts or ideas (terms), (b) judgments ("propositions"), and (c) inferences (syllogisms). Thus we confuse our propositions with our materials, for the handling of which we construct propositions to begin with.

By no means do we object to the construction of a probability theory covering the testing and comparing of propositions. Such a theory, however, should not be permitted to run over into situations for which it was not designed. In general, it would be concerned with conditions for formulating propositions and applying them to data.

Incidentally, a theory of this nature would be brought heavily to bear on the crippling doctrine that a sentence is a basis for an inference without regard to how it was constructed. This deductibility property of sentences, tied up as it is with syntactistic doctrine, can have no meaning whatever except in mathematical situations. And there the manipulation of symbols in given systems is only possible because the symbols are known to stand for strict relations.

Do Propositions Overcome Subjectivity? In favor of the propositional formulation is the argument that it attempts to overcome subjectivity. But can we by this method hope to avoid the difficulty of subjective probability theory? In the first place, does not the propositional or linguistic theory misinterpret the subject matter of probability by making it exclusively into truth-frequencies, while at the same time it confuses a person's operations upon objects with mental states? Insofar as this is true the theory serves to perpetuate the mentalistic doctrine. In the second place, this theory is contradictory in rejecting psychological processes and at the same time standing as a theory of inference. Only when an interbehavioral view is adopted can this contradiction be resolved. In that case, however, the theory would not constitute exclusively either a frequency or a propositional system.

Inapplicable to Unique Events. The claim that the truth-frequency theory can deal with unique events is not really substantiated. If we are concerned with a specific situation—say, a medical prognosis—in what sense can we test the frequency of application of certain propositions? The attempt to avoid this difficulty involves one or all of three procedures.

First, resort is had to the covert definition of frequency as contact with actual conditions. While frequency is described as the statistics of science and as an objective ground for measurement and prediction, it is still assumed that particular contacts with events are being dealt with. To interbehave with single-occurrence situations is in no scientific sense objectionable, but why stress the frequency construction? There is danger, on the other hand, in emphasizing numbers and repetitions if by so doing one interferes with successive investigative approximations.

A second procedure is to shift from frequency of occurrence to frequency of evidence of a single occurrence. Here, frequency signifies testimony, which may or may not be a record of occurrence. Such conditions are sometimes useful, but note that we are dealing with different kinds of frequency in the two cases. It is an advantage, however, if we observe the necessity of considering different kinds of probability events.

The third procedure is to shift to phenomenal classes so that we can carry over from one event to another. This means an immediate shift from a frequency to an operational theory. Naturally, if there are resemblances we can draw inferences concerning event *a* from observing *b*, *c*, etc. The emphasis, however, is on the possibility and validity of the inferences. On the other hand, when we cease to strive for numerical ratios we are able to deal with various situations as they actually occur, rather than revert to some modified form of rational or *a priori* theory.

Nonnumerical Frequency. A serious question concerning the truth-frequency theory is how it can square with the lack of numerical coefficients, as in the case of propositions concerning events without numerically significant confirmation. This query is especially pertinent when it is admitted that probability propositions are only theoretically capable of being numerically formulated. In some cases it is even granted that only a general confidence in the value of truth frequencies is available.

For this theory numbers, then, turn out to be goals not always attainable. It simply yields to the convention that numbers are important and powerful. But this is to forget that the first elaborate number or calculation techniques were developed by means of the classical theory. Indeed, numbers or calculations are merely techniques and are only necessary and applicable where they can be used. Moreover, numbers are frequencies only by definition. The numbers 0 and 1, or even 2, can hardly be connected with frequencies. Numbers may well be regarded as characteristics, if not qualities, of events or things.

We should not conclude that the lack of numerical probability weakens the theory. On the contrary, if that lack helps to direct it toward the goal of concrete investigation it distinctly gains in value.

(6) Probability as Factorial Coordination

A unique probability theory concerns combinations of field factors without regard to the reactor's observation or formulation of them. This theory deals only with the interbehavior of factors of the sort we may presume to occur in such singular events as the formation of a solar system, the birth or death of an individual, the eventuation of an electron, etc. The emphasis is upon the collocation of factors which in one combination (absence, presence, or pattern) constitutes a different state of affairs from another. Many varying combinations may occur. Probability situations from the present standpoint involve comparative or relative possibilities, and may be associated with experiential and properly interpreted causal circumstances.[30]

A simple illustration of two situations sharing some features and not others, with different results, may be found in life expectancies of different individuals. It may be true that *a* has a greater probability of living to be 75 years old than has *b*. The basis? Given equally favorable biological constitutions, as well as comparable living habits, *a* appears to be heading toward a profession more favorable to a longer life than *b*. At least so the insurance company decides.

Probability Requires Response. The factorial-coordination construction immediately arouses the anomaly objection. Probability theorists are extreme in their predilection for some phase of response as over against the stimulus object. They stress the making of sentences or propositions, counting, evaluating, and believing. This predilection in turn is based upon traditional doctrines concerning the power of knowing to engender things. At least, existence is made to depend upon knowing (p. 308f).

Because probability as an objective set of possibility conditions

---

[30] Cf. chap. 19; also Ducasse, Neglected, and Struik, Foundations.

requires someone to know, count, or evaluate the probability—*if* it is to be known, counted, or evaluated—does it follow that probability does not exist without the responder? Does not our very approach to things and events in order to enumerate, estimate, and evaluate them imply their independent and prior existence? Independent probability events can not be denied on the basis that assertions about them can only be made on the ground of how frequently certain signs have been observed to connect with particular eventualities.[31]

Factorial Coordination not Reducible. To refer to a probability situation suggests that one is responding to an independent occurrence which in no wise depends upon anyone's manipulation or knowledge. Moreover, one's later acquaintance with something happening or not happening need not involve frequencies or even classification, but simply an analysis of field factors. For two reasons we regard as futile the attempt to equate knowledge of, and ability to analyze, a situation with a frequency formula.

First, it is intellectually reprehensible to assert that one has either frequency or nothing; it is quite possible that an individual might have a general acquaintance with events bearing upon a unique case. Even in the form of frequency assertions it is improper to make probability situations into absolutes or certainties. From an objective standpoint, reactions, whether beliefs, assertions, or predictions, constitute definitely occurring events even if they happen only once. As a matter of fact, a probability situation may be similar to other cases and still be unique. One does not attempt to predict a long or short life for an individual upon no basis at all, and this basis can be regarded as an accumulation of observations; thus any present probability situation is part of a collective or series.

In the second place, we must acknowledge the hypothetical character of probability judgments. Because of the uniqueness of the situation the predicter makes a hypothetical statement; in other words, he asserts his belief on the basis of the assumed copresence of certain factors in the situation. He may be wrong. This very fact implies that he is attempting to react to events independent of himself, rather than on the basis that the events, or their probability, exist because of his knowledge or assertion.

[31] Nagel, Frequency, p. 546f.

Factorial Coordination Specific. Not the least appealing feature of this construction is its lack of comprehensiveness. Because it is a formulation with a genuine emphasis of specific events it contrasts with inclusive formulations implying universality of application. We regard it as a distinctive merit of this construction that it stresses probability events which owe their fortuity to their complexity and fluidity. While no probability theory can be inclusive and final it would be a distinct deprivation to probability logic not to have a place for this formulation among the others.

Probability Systems and Logical Multiplexity

Our analysis of probability systems bears out the view that probability is a multiplex domain of system building. Even if we confine ourselves to general formal systems, to the exclusion of specific operational enterprises, there are too many irreducible varieties to warrant any universal formula.

We conclude further that probability systems can not be assimilated to the older conventional formalistic logics. Nor can we construct universal probability systems to replace those logics. In other words, we can not, for example, replace a two-valued logic—true-false—by a single many-valued probability system.

A unique form of logical universalization is to assert that there is a general type of probability logic, though it has a limited field —for example, science. The proponents of this view agree that the logic of science is of the probability sort, in contrast to the logic of truth which reigns in the domain of mathematics and other abstractionistic locales. While this partially universal view is preferable to a completely totalitarian one, it still stops short of a specificity system in that it verbally erases the lines marking off different problems, different subject matter, and different modes of investigation. The defect is not mitigated by proposing the idea of probability deduction. Doubtless, probability may be inferred if not deduced, but neither deduction nor inference constitutes a criterion of logic.

Can probability be assimilated to a universalistic logic on the ground that systems in themselves are problematic? No: In the first place, not all systems are problematic. In an immense number of cases, either because systems are arbitrary or practical, no such question arises. In the second place, the question whether systems are problematic really refers to the *investigation* of system building rather than to system building itself. The investigation, then, is the stimulus object reacted to, and the probability question concerns work upon systems. Such an investigation may well be a nonlogical enterprise. Logic as system building may be sharply distinguished from (1) the investigation of the degree of knowing, (2) the basis for calculation, or (3) the character of events entitling them to a place in a system.

PROBABILITY, EPISTEMOLOGY, AND ONTOLOGY

Every probability theory or system carries within it the philosophical presuppositions influencing the constructor. This is a fact we can not deplore, unless we immediately assume that all philosophy is objectionable. Such an assumption is wholly unwarranted, since the specifications for an acceptable philosophy are available. They may be summarized as follows. (1) Philosophy constitutes a set of attitudes developed by an individual in contact with a considerable area of things and events. (2) Its propositions depart radically from uncontrolled magnification and multiplication. (3) The philosophical system remains rooted in the actual affairs from which the promulgator builds it, and in his measured extrapolations from them.

As it happens, however, most writers who attempt to explain the purpose, power, and scope of probability indicate their entanglement with traditional ontological and epistemological problems[32]—for instance, when they adopt finite and infinite collections as their operational fields. We have already referred to the metaphysical determinism implied in the Laplacian formulations (p. 218).

Acceptable philosophical presuppositions for structuring probability favor systems for handling specific situations and exclude world views such as are implied in the following:

If I have seen just three crows and they were all black, then it is *certain* not only that my next crow will be black but that all the crows I shall ever see will be black.[33]

---

[32] See, in this connection, A Symposium on Probability, in *Philosophy and Phenomenological Research*, Part I, 1944-45, 5, 449-532; Part II, 1945-46, 6, 11-86; Part III, ibid., 590-622.

[33] Williams, Ground, p. 54.

A probability system based on such specifications as we have mentioned above might be set up in the crow situation, but it would lack completely any absoluteness concerning either all the possible animals to be met or the validity duration of the system.

General Philosophical Problems. A few samples of general philosophical problems inherent in probability discussions will be sufficient. We have already had occasion to notice how seriously probability students consider the question of the *a priori* or *a posteriori* character of probability inferences. There are also problems concerning faith in belief and judgment. Such principles as nonsufficient Reason or Indifference are certainly epistemological, while such laws as those of Large Numbers are not only ontologico-metaphysical, but may be mystical as well. Here, too, are located such puzzles as Euler's attempt to account for his firm confidence that the stones in the Magdeburg Church were heavy and would fall unless supported. Jevons[34] quotes with approval Euler's assertion that it would be impossible to fix on any one thing really existing of which we could have so perfect a knowledge as to put us beyond the reach of mistakes.

Special Philosophical Problems. Among the more special issues we number all the attempts to relate probability situations with traditional nominalism, conceptualism, and realism. We include here also those efforts to bring independently developed probability calculations into relation with actual events.

The procedure of philosophizing probability encounters the serious indictment of intellectual treason. All writers pay lip service to the principle that one should above all investigate and systemize events. But as soon as they encounter probability happenings they smother them in philosophical principles. Thus, instead of making authentic probability studies available for philosophical reflection such writers impose illegitimate philosophical notions upon probability events. The result: Events are distorted and misinterpreted.

INTERBEHAVIORAL PROBABILITY VERSUS EPISTEMOLOGY

When a naturalistic probability view is adopted, such problems as how one can have confidence in one's judgments, how to be

[34] *Principles*, p. 238.

satisfied with one's beliefs, and how to develop expertness in prediction are all easily solved in terms of an individual's operation
with stimulus objects. Preoccupation with concrete interbehavior
makes it easy to see which knowledge events have been transformed into epistemological issues. Is not the construct of an
organizing and unifying mind merely a bad description of an individual carrying over judgments from one situation to another?
Is Keynes' intuition anything more than the practical expertness
of one who can estimate the relation of hypothesis to evidence on
the basis of his prior contacts with similar and dissimilar situations?

On an interbehavioral basis inferences are made on the ground
of contacts with things, even though a propositional or linguistic
construction may be necessary in the process. From this standpoint the *a priori* is merely a term for practical expectations employed as a ground for inferring from one behavioral situation
to another.

INTERBEHAVIORAL PROBABILITY VERSUS ONTOLOGY

Similarly, when we eliminate such illicit constructions as metaphysical chance and determinism, ontological questions are
brought down to events. Probability formulae and calculi, for
example, either refer to events or are employed as tools for manipulating them. When we deal with specific happenings we
lack no criteria for distinguishing between (1) stimulus objects,
(2) responses to them, and (3) the interbehavior from which
both are abstracted.

PROBABILITY PROPOSITIONS VERSUS PROBABILITY EVENTS

Like all intellectual enterprises probability studies have borne
their share of damage inflicted by the recent symbolistic revival.
Not only philosophers but scientists have heeded Goethe's injunc-
tion:

> . . . haltet Euch an Worte!
>
> . . . .
>
> Mit Worten lässt sich trefflich streiten,
> Mit Worten ein System bereiten.

And in consequence they have disguised sentences, syntactic symbols, and symbol systems in an effort to make them look like things and events.

Specifically, probability students have been influenced to build ultimate probability systems in order to eliminate events from the probability field. Events are replaced by propositions. Keynes[35] traces back to Ancillon[36] the first suggestion to depart from events. This view is stressed also by Boole,[37] and shared alike by Czuber[38] and Stumpf.[39] Boole, however, regarded the nominalistic substitution of propositions for events as only a procedure for logical purposes. Other writers insist, however, that questions of probability always involve factual, in addition to purely logical, considerations.[40]

Probability studies have suffered greatly from symbology by being thrown into the epistemological arena of Neo-Nominalistic metaphysics. According to linguistic (semantic, syntactic) metaphysics, one transforms things, events, and relations into propositions or sentences. This movement has gone so far as to absorb not only the stimulus events with which scientists operate, but also the scientists' operations upon (interbehavior with) them. Symbolic philosophers overlook the fact that in the end all knowledge and all description of knowledge depend upon the existence of things with which to interact.[41]

Though linguistic philosophers do distinguish between thing language (semantics) and pure language (syntactic formations and transformations), they still substitute descriptions for things described; worse, they overlook that things exist independently of descriptions. To determine the probability or improbability of events is not an epistemological or a linguistic problem, but one of observing and estimating the conditions under which certain events do or do not occur.

At this point we must distinguish sharply between (a) actual probability operations and (b) the linguistic descriptions of, and references to, them. This distinction is tellingly illustrated by a

[35] Treatise, p. 5.
[36] Doutes.
[37] Laws, 7, 167.
[38] Warscheinlichkeitsrechnung, vol. 1, p. 5.
[39] Ueber.
[40] Nagel, Frequency, p. 541.
[41] The shift away from linguism is taking on momentum. See Feigl, Existential.

controversial exchange between two of the participants in the probability symposium mentioned earlier. Whereas Carnap[42] characterizes von Mises' frequency theory as purely mathematical, not physical, the latter[43] is surprised that Carnap, whose whole recent stress has been on empty syntactic sentences, should add an inductive logic to his extremely deductive system.

The importance of the above distinction merits another illustration. When linguistic logicians face probability problems, as they inevitably do, they naturally run into problems of scientific methodology. They make a place for themselves by assuming that their task is to make "rational reconstructions" of scientific procedures. But that they soon identify their rational reconstructions with those scientific procedures is exemplified by their assertions that the constructions they develop are of importance to the methodology of empirical science[44] and to practical life.[45] Observe carefully, however, that no description of, or reference to, a thing absorbs that thing (p. 259). Also we can avoid a "rational reconstruction" when no actual thing is being worked on.[46]

We can not urge too strongly the full consideration of statistical inference and basic elementary manipulations as models of probability situations. A considerable literature is developing which illustrates correct probability operations, though, unfortunately, the metaphysical curse is not entirely lifted.[47] The way to avoid this metaphysics may be to keep close to the kind of statistical operations employed, for example, in quality control or other concrete situations.[48]

Inevitably we return to interbehavioral operations. An excellent analogy is D'Alembert's organization of dynamics by introducing a factor of inertia. This is tantamount to reducing dynamics to statics. The question here is whether some useful scientific purpose is served by this procedure. Since the mathematician does

---

[42] Remarks.
[43] Comment.
[44] Hempel and Oppenheim, Definition.
[45] Carnap, Probability.
[46] Bergmann, Comments.
[47] Churchman, Theory, Probability.
[48] Butterbaugh, Bibliography; Neyman and Pearson, Contributions; Shewhart, Economic, Statistical; Wald, Principles.

not interfere with the dynamic processes, but simply develops a form of reference to them which is useful in further concrete or referential reactions to the original data, a satisfactory relationship exists between the formulation and the thing formalized. In this argument lies justification for setting up probability formulations on the basis of infinite series: one does not thereby interfere with problematic events, nor with the descriptions designed to handle them.

Probability Calculation: Goal or Operation?

The undesirable authoritarianism and universalism which characterizes traditional logic has cast its net over probability logic by means of the probability calculus. Numeralization and calculation have become touchstones, even ends in themselves. Only where there is a calculus is there authentic probability. Not only the proponents of frequency theories, but also those who hold to the classical or Laplacian view, practically define probability in numerical terms. On this basis probability becomes closely integrated with statistics.

Granting that nothing escapes statistics where numbers of things are dealt with, and also that the subject is highly important where it is applicable, it is still necessary to consider whether statistics is identical with probability or merely an essential feature of it. But before going further into this question let us look into the nature of statistics and calculation.

Statistics and Probability. Statistical systems have evolved from something very unlike the calculative manipulation of numerical data. As an enterprise, statistics began as political arithmetic, as the enumeration of vital records. In the form of enumerated items statistics involved no probability problem; the primary purpose was to specify the changing conditions of life. With the accumulation of such records questions of significance inevitably arose. Purely calculative questions concerning the relation and organization of data came to the front. Later, more fundamental problems relating to prediction were precipitated, the outcome of which was the construction and application of probability theories. Thus, influences, correlations, and, if possible, cause-and-effect conditions, have been established as the significant features of statistical data.

We might say that originally statistical data were concerned with the present and past, whereas an interest in the future introduced probability.

With the development of a semitechnical interest in building systems involving, on the one hand, present and past events and, on the other, future contingencies, probability and statistics come together. This coupling of the two disciplines forces to the front a number of their common properties.

Starting from the side of probability as a general enterprise for operating with particular happenings, it is inevitable that the statistical technique in the form of calculation processes should be utilized. The tendency is to depart immediately from actual events and to jump to numerical abstractions as units and quantities. Thus statistics and probability are identified, and probability definitions are made to center around frequencies of various sorts. Probability then becomes a measure of frequency, or, as in the most popular definition, probability is the limit of the relative frequency of events in series.

Undoubtedly, the possibility of being able to calculate more or less accurately the probability of an event, or the probability value of a proposition, adds definiteness and value to a probability situation. But are we interested in the probability, whether or not it yields calculative results, or are we limiting our probabilities to calculative situations? Possibly we can learn more about probability by adhering to probability fields than by restricting ourselves to any sort of defining condition, no matter how attractive the latter condition may be.

Again, we ask that most crucial of questions: Is the operator keeping in touch with actual happenings? Is he expertly summing up and predicting conditions on the basis of his prior contacts with similar situations? A secondary question is whether the situations involved lend themselves to calculative treatment, or whether the probability concerns merely a relationship between a certain type of event and other similar happenings.

The Nature of Calculation. Calculation consists of the manipulation of relations. Now it is possible to emphasize the relations of observed facts or of abstracted and formal relations. In general, calculation consists of such interbehavior with relations as to indicate their similarity or equation. Or it may involve enumerating items or elements in a field—that is, ordering elements on the basis of given criteria—or ascertaining the quantitative determinations of elements.

The question arises, then, whether our calculations are features of concrete situations or whether calculations are the exclusively formal ordering of relations. Calculation is fundamentally a type of interbehavior for particular and definite purposes. Can we, therefore, make calculation a criterion of our interbehavior, or should we regard interbehavior as bounded by certain conditions? To make calculation the criterion of probability immediately prejudices the case. Probability is a condition of facts discoverable by observation, not a result of calculation.

Above all, it is illegitimate to confuse calculative constructions with objects or relations. The latter may be entirely independent of calculative operations. The specificity principle forewarns us to keep such situations distinct from those in which the data or relata are themselves constructions. In the latter type of situation, of course, we may regard calculation as the probability criterion.

Those who make the calculative procedure the criterion of probability frequently rely upon the actuarial situation as their guide, and point out the truth that statistics can not predict anything about a single case. But must we take the insurance or statistical situation as the probability model? In other words, are we required always to deal with collections or series? If we are interested in the nature of probability we shall have to consider that in important circumstances we may want to know the life expectancy of a particular individual—for example, a prospective employer or employee, a company or institution.

Even insurance companies do not limit their investigations to the actuarial department. Nor do they pay attention only to generalized numbers or averages, except possibly to calculate mathematical expectations. For the most part, the acceptance of a risk may be regarded as a scientific investigation of a particular person. The medical examination serves as a biological investigation; an economic and sociological one is made by inquiring into the habits and occupation of the insured individual.

The extensive development of statistical methods suggests their indispensability for achieving certain ends—in other words, for interbehaving with certain happenings. The psychologist, physicist, biologist, or economist who concerns himself with statistics and the laws of probability is primarily interested in psychological, physical, biological, or economic events; and it is an accepted canon that the calculative procedures he employs must be suitable for the ascertainment of the kind of information demanded by his scientific specialty.

Collectives or series, therefore, are constructed, and are not metaphysically unique and autonomous. They may be summaries or organizations of particular kinds of objects, or they may be constructional in the sense of creations more or less arbitrarily and analogically designed.

CHAPTER XXIII

LOGICAL ASPECTS OF MEASUREMENT

THE PLACE OF MEASUREMENT IN LOGIC

MEASUREMENT implies system. Measuring operations typify the entire system-building enterprise. At the very least, mensurational situations require operations to interrelate: (a) things measured, (b) measuring behavior, (c) measuring instruments, and (d) standards of measurement.

Thus the topic of measurement fits perfectly into the logical domain. In fact, metrology as the science of measurement is a phase of systemology, while mensurational practice implies mensurational systems. Even those logicians who make use of measurement materials to justify a metaphysical rather than a system-building theory acknowledge this fact effectively, if not explicitly. Indeed, for many metaphysical logicians mensurational operations provide the only link between their arbitrary constructions and the objective events which alone lend significance to their labors. How an author treats the topic of measurement may well provide a criterion for the appraisal of his logical doctrines.

WHAT IS MEASUREMENT?

Although mensurational operations are readily inspected, few attempts have been made to describe them. Even these few show disagreements and contradictions which can only be explained by the greater influence which traditional philosophical ideas have exerted upon measurement theory as compared with mensurational practice. Measurement described on the basis of what is done in measuring situations consists essentially of a series of systemizing operations for ascertaining precisely the properties and relations of things and events. Formally, measuring operations constitute the organization of criteria, units, and standards, and the observation of the relative positions occupied by items with respect to the scaling instruments. The emphasis must be placed on the systemizing of, or structuring operations upon, things.[1]

[1] In the sense of stimulus objects, cf. vol. I, chap. 5.

We reject both of the following views: Through measuring operations one can (a) discover the "basic" (quantitative) properties of things, and (b) interact with transcendental magnitudes.

IDEOLOGICAL TRENDS IN MEASUREMENT THEORY

Current measurement theories manifest a series of unsatisfactory constructional trends.

First, measurement is assumed to be a single type of fact. As a consequence, whatever things are to be measured are forced to fit one exclusive set of mensuration principles. That this is an unsatisfactory assumption has long been appreciated, as indicated by the metrologist's struggle with the problem of intensive and extensive properties. More recently, the development of microscopic or atomic physics, with its indeterminacies (pp. 311f., 319f.), has precipitated the issue concerning radical differences in measuring situations.

Secondly, measurement theories by being closely assimilated to philosophical views are decidedly colored by Idealistic, Realistic, Conventionalistic, or Pragmatistic ways of thinking. It is not unusual to find measurement theory complicated with the problem of the existence of an external world, and with the belief in the existence of invariable relations independent of those wishing to measure or approximate them. In general, philosophical constructions tend to supplant the actual measuring operations performed in both nonscientific and scientific situations. Philosophic theories, therefore, simply analogize and rationalize measuring operations.

Thirdly, measurement theories for the most part are confused with the descriptive formulations of particular measuring operations (p. 307). Generally, metrological ideas are limited to classical dynamics, even kinematics. Although it is realized that larger-event domains must be taken into account, the ideal pursued is derived from early sources of mensurational ideas. Accordingly, there is little relationship between (1) the theoretical constructions and (2) the measurement operations of everyday life and science. And so, even if the theory does articulate with some features of mensurational behavior, it hardly offers a sufficient coverage of the facts involved.

Finally, most, if not all, mensurational systems imply some sort of dualistic psychological view. When a scientist writes that "our primary data are sensations" and that when we say "we observe an object" we are really saying that we have a series of sensations coordinated by forming the concept of an object, he holds views that carry within them more than mere potentiality for distorting the events handled.[2]

Measurement as Applied Mathematics

The universalistic and philosophical trends just mentioned, as well as the whole procrustean enterprise of forcing mensurational facts to fit a theory, are well illustrated by the popular doctrine that measurement is applied mathematics. Measurement is thus regarded as a process of interrelating numerals or numbers with things. This formulation has a definite historical background in the triumphal achievements of mechanics during the interval from the Renaissance to the 19th century.

Since Helmholtz was an early formulator of the essential principles of this theory, let us briefly review his attitude toward measurement.[3] As an empirical philosopher and experimental scientist he regarded calculation and measurement as the most exact, fruitful, and certain of scientific methods. But these methods themselves must be logically or epistemologically founded. Thus he demanded some metamensurational justification for mensurating operations.

Though to a certain extent, Helmholtz was willing to eschew transcendental intuition, his empiricism did not go so far as to allow him to depart completely from *a priori* laws. Nor could he resist founding measurement on axioms concerning "the fundamental nature of mind." He was an empiricist, relative only to the absolute idealist. For Helmholtz mathematics still comprised a transcendental source of certainty. Consequently he could not really assimilate the idea concerning the cultural development of numbers and number systems.

With the replacement of Kantian intuitive mathematics by the Realistic variety the applied-mathematics doctrine of measurement took on the latter's complexion. Since the revival of Platonic Realism in mathematics, measurement has been defined in

[2] Cf. Jeffreys, Scientific, p. 206.
[3] Zählen.

terms of abstract magnitudes and numbers. For example, Russell writes:

Measurement of magnitude is, in its most general sense, any method by which a unique and reciprocal correspondence is established between all or some of the magnitudes of a kind and all or some of of the numbers, integral, rational or real, as the case may be.[4]

With a lessening of emphasis on abstract, preexisting numbers and magnitudes the applied-mathematics view takes the form that measurement consists of interrelating numbers with things. What these things are considered to be depends upon the auspices under which the proposition is formulated. The philosophical opponents of extreme realism refer to some experiential factor. We quote from Spaier:

La mesure est l'établissement d'un correspondance uni-univoque entre les nombres et les données évaluées.[5]

In connection with experimental investigations Campbell asserts that measurement is the process of assigning numerals to represent qualities[6] or properties[7] in accordance with scientific laws. In debate, however, he varies his position to make measurement "the assignment of numerals to things, so as to represent facts and conventions about them."[8] Writers who adopt Campbell's general viewpoint accept the following phrasing:

Measurement, in the broadest sense, is defined as the assignment of numerals to objects or events according to rules.[9]

To the critical observer it is clear that the applied-mathematics theory of measurement does scant justice to the complex facts in question. Howsoever important numerals and numbers are in measurement situations, they hardly seem to be the center and focus of all the complicated activity comprised under the heading of measurement. True as it may be that the goal of certain mensurational operations is to ascertain the quantity of some thing relative to another, it is not appropriate to reduce all of measure-

---

[4] Principles, p. 176.
[5] La Pensée, p. 34.
[6] Physics, p. 267.
[7] Ibid., p. 295.
[8] Quantitative, p. 340.
[9] Stevens, Theory, p. 677.

ment to this feature. It is a reasonable hypothesis that the applied-mathematics theory stems from the Pythagorean tradition that somehow numbers are the heart of reality. There are definite implications here that require examination if they are not to prejudice measurement theory.

The Power of Mathematical Reasoning. Although the number-assignment theory is really concerned with the concrete conditions of applied mathematics or arithmetic, it harks back to the view of the great power of mathematical reasoning in science. The basic idea is that mathematics purveys certainty and achievement.

Against this unwitting projection of mathematical reasoning into science there are powerful protests. We have quoted Hardy's declaration concerning the inapplicability of mathematical reasoning to the physical world.[10] Similarly, Einstein raises a serious question concerning the relationship between mathematical propositions and events.

Insofern sich die Sätze der Mathematik auf die Wirklichkeit beziehen sind sie nicht sicher, und insofern sie sicher sind, beziehen sie sich nicht auf die Wirklichkeit.[11]

Furthermore, what of the recent developments of mathematical thought which make plain that number is not the basis of mathematics? Mathematics may perhaps be better regarded as a science of order or, even more to the point, as a science of relations. On the latter bases we must modify our views concerning the place of number in measurement.

Numbers as Supreme Universals. Deeply imbedded in our scientific and logical culture is the tradition that numbers constitute the supreme universals. Not only are other universals, such as *things* and *qualities*, placed lower in the scale, but numbers are regarded as the means of transcending things altogether. Even more, through numbers a transcendent realm of certainty and accuracy is considered attainable. As a matter of fact, those who put so much stress on numbers in measurement have in view those transcendentals of infinity, absolute identity, and difference conventionally represented by discrete integers. As superior universals, numbers are abstracted and extrapolated from various

---

[10] Chap. 13, p. 21.
[11] Geometrie.

practical relations of things and made into metaphysical invariants of nature, or, even more frankly, into cosmic essences.

Numbers as Philosophical Abstractions. Most writers who glorify numbers, thus making measurement into the essence of science, do so on the ground that numbers somehow pertain to a higher order of being. Whatever is connected with number is presumed to transcend the humble qualities of things. A paradox found in the writings on measurement is that while the ascertainment of the metrical properties of things is justifiably regarded as an essential feature of scientific method, the characteristics ascribed to metric principles project them out to unreachable metaphysical domains.

Numbers and External Reality. The metaphysics of the "external world" is frankly implied in the stress of number and quantity as basic factors in measurement. To a great extent the emphasis of numerical and metrical properties is predicated on the assumption that numbers as superior entities guarantee the existence of the "external world." Here we run into the perennial ideological convention. Reality can not be found in the evanescent occurrences of sensory experience, but must be sought in the general formulae of abstract relations. Thus numbers and mathematical equations provide the perennially desired tongs with which to grasp and hold *Reality*.

Numbers and Mental States. It is evident that the tradition of psychic processes is basic to the historical quest for reality and for a guarantee of the existence of the external world. The need for guarantees and absolute formulae of relations of things is intimately tied up with the concept of "sensations," and of other psychic elements, implied by traditional notions of experience.

Mensurational Operations and Numeral Assignment

Measurement involves a complex handling of things and events on the basis of particular problems in distinct situations. However, because of the ubiquity of measuring instruments, such as balances, rulers, calipers, thermometers, and galvanometers, measurement is taken to be simply the manipulation of these tools. The nature of the instruments, their derivation and calibration, are usually taken for granted. The assertion that measurement consists of matching the ends of things measured with those of the measuring instrument is a case in point.

Actually, the processes of measurement constitute complex forms of interbehavior in situations involving many things and conditions. We can not neglect what is being measured, nor the use to which the results will be put. Measurement envisaged as a series of systemizing operations does full justice to the process of number assignment. Moreover, when we regard measurement as system making rather than as practical manipulation, we find that number assignment plays two important, but still auxiliary, parts in measurement situations.

(1) Of the two numeral assignment processes the more elaborate and useful consists of calculation and relation structuring, executed by means of various mathematical techniques. However essential these structuring processes may be, they are always subsidiary to the measuring operations which involve definite contacts with things. Even so strong an adherent of the number-assignment theory as Campbell[12] takes account of all sorts of manipulative operations anterior to number assignment.

(2) A less prominent, though still important, numeral-assignment process consists of recording the results of measuring manipulations. By statistically treating mensurational records these second auxiliary operations may take on an importance hardly subsidiary to the mensurational manipulations themselves. The priority of manipulative operations is clear from a number of facts. First, no one would say that any assignment of numbers is measurement.[13] On this ground writers distinguish between counting and measurement. Again, the emphasis upon additive units and processes bespeaks a bias toward things and their qualities as over against the abstract relations of formal arithmetic.

Those theorists who adopt the number-assignment formula do so mainly because they are influenced by symbolic and mathematical logic systems. And this, despite the fact that number assignment may be more closely allied with practical arithmetical operations than with the more abstruse theory of number relations.

Specificity of Measurement

In line with the prevailing universality of logical theories metrological systems are naturally patterned as general and inclusive

---

[12] Physics, Account, Measurement.
[13] Campbell, Physics, et passim; Einstein, Meaning, p. 1.

as possible. Minor theoretical variations are incorporated into a single comprehensive formula.

From an interbehavioral standpoint there is no single law or logic of measurement. On the contrary, there is a range of systems corresponding to: (1) variety of things and events to be measured, (2) available operations—for example, (a) isolating particular materials and fields of operation, (b) constructively analyzing applicable units, and (c) organizing a scale relative to situations more or less distantly removed from the one immediately in view—and, finally, (3) needs and purposes of those performing the measuring operations.

When we describe or formalize measurements we, of course, pounce upon an abstraction, and construct some sort of idol. Either we develop a verbal model very different from our actual operations, or we elevate a part of the measuring situation to the dignity of the whole. By such means anyone can transform all measuring, even all science, into pointer reading. It is such analogical thinking that stimulated the 19th century idea that physics is the basic science because it is essentially the mensurational discipline.

To overlook the contingent and specific character of measurement is to depart from concrete measurement operations. Above all, it is extremely hazardous, as well as scientifically objectionable, to withdraw from the actual things and processes measured. Significant measurement can neither go on in a vacuum nor be reduced to the formal application of instruments to objects. Measurement conceived independently of the things to be measured in specific situations is nothing more than a fetish, whereas indifferent manipulation of instruments glorifies the instruments and the manipulative movements.

(1) *Specificity of Measured Objects.* The stress of operations in measurement is surely justified when one considers the large number of objects requiring precise evaluation. We can do no more at present than list classes of measurable things calling for specific sorts of operative procedures. For convenience we shall differentiate from each other three grand classes of measurable things: (a) objects, qualities, and relations, (b) interactions of things, and (c) interactions of judges and experts with such things as are comprised in (a) and (b).

(a) *Things and relations.* Here we include actual things

and their properties, both relations and qualities. Among the qualitative properties some are of the first order—for example, color, length, area, volume, density, hardness, fragility, malleability, etc. Second-order qualitative properties comprise similarities, contrasts, identities, equalities and equivalences.

(b) *Interactions of things*. In this class there are various sub-classes. For example, measurable interactions of inorganic things require different manipulations and scales from those demanded by organic things. The characteristics to be elicited in the inorganic subclass are relative rates, motions, frequencies, and products. What interests us with respect to organic interactions are effects on organisms, measurable as interferences of behavior, inhibition of growth, immunological warding off of pathological conditions, etc.

(c) *Judging and Evaluating Behavior*. A general interest in measuring systems demands that we consider ways and means of measuring the behavior of judges and experts. Considerable attention has recently been given such mensurational interactions (attitudes) with things. The measurement of judging and evaluating behavior implies no retreat from standards and ideals of accuracy and precision, despite the difference between such events and the things treated by means of the conventional C.G.S. systems.

(2) *Specificity of Operations and Techniques*. Because there are many types of objects to be measured it follows that different mensurational operations must be performed. The following types are selected as illustrative.

(a) *Direct and Indirect Measurements*. The operations here consist in comparing and matching properties, either by applying some direct standard or by means of some indirect device. Stretching a chain between two given points is essentially a direct technique. A good example of an indirect method is Faraday's technique of weighing gold leaves to obtain their thickness (p. 291), or Galileo's weighing water to measure time.

(b) *Simple and Complex Measurements*. Even when operations and instruments have been perfected for mensurational situations their mode of application may be relatively simple or complex. To illustrate, simple measurements require either (1) the application of rules or scales to the objects measured, or (2) some computational procedure. Complex measurements, on the other hand, require both forms of operation.

(c) *Fundamental and derived measurements*. It has become conventional to refer to linear and weight measurements as fundamental. While this is an arbitrary designation, it is presumed to imply some basic mensurational difference from temperature or density determinations. If we regard mensurative operations as processes for achieving a more precise determination of the properties of things, we look upon the "fundamental" and "derived" classes only as items in a series. This is not to deny that from the physicist's standpoint the distinction may be useful and even important. However, the assumptions implied by the distinction should be carefully noted. Unquestionably, for some purposes the conventional fundamental operations are properly named; in other instances this is not the case.

(d) *Status and Construction Measurements*. Most mensurational operations and techniques are bounded by relatively stable circumstances. The status of the things to be measured and the instruments employed are conventional and standardized. But there are other situations in which considerable fluidity prevails. No more striking example can be cited than the circumstances surrounding mensuration processes in the domain of quantum mechanics.[14] Here the mensurational work requires building a practically complete metrological system. One must set up criteria of observability and of scale making and using.

Many are the circumstances leading to constructive procedures and uniquely original instruments. In our quantum-mechanics example we have obvious difficulties in the microscopic character of the things to be measured and in the unavailability of close contact with the units of energy we aim to determine. The constructional nature of the operations is excellently indicated in the development of a wave and a particle model and of the formulae for their successive and simultaneous application in measuring situations. And when the measuring operations lead to probability functions, rather than to numerals representing concrete cardinal magnitudes, we have an even better illustration of constructional measurement.

(3) *Specificity of Mensurative Situations*. When we assert that

[14] See next chapter.

measurement is secondary to some need or purpose we are referring to a specific mensurational situation. Of course, this purpose may be highly abstractive and theoretical, rather than immediately practical. Still, the results achieved, or the numbers attained, serve the needs of a particular investigation. Numbers, in other words, are instruments for measurement.

The basic conclusion is that no type of mensurative product need be rejected as a member of the classes of mensurative systems. Numbers representing a person's reactions in the form of estimations and judgments constitute objective mensurative features in the same degree as quantities of length or weight. Judgments or estimates as events consisting of interactions with things are just as free of arbitrary construction as are interactions between nonhuman objects.

LEVELS OF MEASUREMENT

The mensurational data so far treated may be arranged on a horizontal plane. Weighing, length measuring, scaling, and ordering activities may be set side by side. We have still to consider the variations of measuring situations organized in the vertical dimension. Thus, we survey briefly the continuum ranging from the practical situations of everyday life, through the intervals of technological operations, to the most abstruse ordering procedures of special and general mathematical situations.

Practical Measurement. On this level the operations constitute comparatively simple, sometimes crude, manipulations for ascertaining the values of the things handled. The qualities and properties of objects are measured for some immediate purpose. On the whole, practical measurement implies the mere application of an already-existing measurement system or the simple coordination of means and ends.

The direct handling of objects characterizing the simplest measuring situations may be illustrated by the following process of fitting boards to a surface. The edge of one board is laid against one boundary of the place to be covered, and the length required is marked by matching with the other boundary. Then the strip cut first is used as a standard for sawing as many more strips as are required. When a ruler is used the process is somewhat indirect, and thus the level becomes slightly raised.

How high the practical level rises from the gross handling indicated may be gauged by the amount of labor and ingenuity required to make scales and standards for comparing things. The primary operational emphasis, however, is on the things and their manipulation. Since the things measured, together with their circumstances, are the focal points, we add the following list to suggest the range of practical measurement.

1) Things and properties (size, length, area, volume).
2) Relations (number, quantity, magnitude).
3) Strength or intensity in relation to (a) function (electrical resistance) or (b) effect on other things.
4) Rates (frequency according to various criteria): period, time interval, speed, velocity, acceleration.
5) Behavior (what a thing does under various circumstances).

The primary purpose of this list is to indicate the concrete operations useful or necessary for handling given objects. The operations are as specific and as local as the things and situations demand.

Technological Measurement. When the objects to be measured are small, complex, or extremely important, we reach a measurement level in which the whole situation is no longer focused on the objects. The operations take on a unique importance; the goal of precision assumes a somewhat autonomous character. Technological measurement requires elaborate manipulative processes involving specially designed apparatus. The operations include calculation and sometimes actual research work. The most intricate technological measurements may be said to establish the identity and properties of things whose scientific existence is problematic.

Technological measurement operations are best observed in the behavior of scientists as they construct their mensurational instruments. While devising units and scales considerable research may be needed to establish the existence and value of things and events, as well as ways of dealing with them. As our examples we choose the developments in measuring temperature, and electricity and magnetism.

From the beginning of thermometer making by Galileo and Drebbel in the early years of the 17th century,[15] workers desiring to compare warmth differences had to contend with the problem of bringing into system a series of factors. On the side of things

[15] Grimsehl, vol. II, p. 2, et passim.

measured there were warmth changes to be correlated with expansions of substances like alcohol, air, mercury, and hydrogen gas. Then scale points had to be determined; naturally, the melting point of ice and the boiling point of water were taken as standards. Magnitude and denomination of intervals required the decision whether zero or 32 should mark the melting point of ice. Whether 80, 100, or 212 degrees should be the boiling point became a matter of specific system making.

More complex and more refined temperature systems were developed with the evolution of knowledge concerning light, energy, and the spectrum. Coincident with Ritter's and Herschel's discovery of the ultraviolet and infrared extensions of the energy spectrum was the development of Nobili's thermopile and Langley's bolometer. With the latter instrument:

Measurement of the charge in resistance could be made so precisely that temperature changes of one ten-millionth of a centigrade degree were identifiable.[16]

Perhaps even more informative examples of the development of technological measuring systems are found in the evolution of electrical units and scales. Here we can only mention the complex labors of Ohm which finally resulted in the system for measuring electrical current, resistance, and potential difference, and the work of Oersted, Ampère, Gauss, Weber, and others in establishing the units called ampere, volt, coulomb, farad, etc.

Formal Metrology. When measurement as operation and system becomes interesting in itself, and is thus made an object of study, it attains the level of abstract constructional ordering. Measurement on this level is quite remote from the practical and technological circumstances of the other two levels. Formal metrology stresses a theoretical system-building interest. Accordingly, speculative and general philosophical views are allowed free scope. Stressing measurement systems as the objects of their study, metrologists concern themselves with abstracted relations of formal geometric and analytic consistency structures. More particularly, formal metrology centers about invariant relations which can be comprehended and fixated in deductive systems.

The best illustrations of systems on the present level are found

---

[16] Taylor, Physics, p. 542.

in the abstruse geometries based on the criteria of congruence and coherence. The upper ranges of this level include mensurational speculations concerning subsistential magnitudes and modes of reaching them. The field of formal metrology may be described as the construction of generalizations about measurement as removed from all the concrete factors of specific mensurational situations.

Interrelation of Levels. As we should expect, the numerous gradations in each level extend so far as to interrelate all three types. True, an individual may use rulers, balances, ammeters, even more complicated measuring instruments, without knowing anything about their nature or origin. But the fact that cultural practice extends beyond technical system does not permit an absolute barrier between the manipulations and the creative organization of a system. Even if we reject the notion that measurement presupposes geometry,[17] because only through geometry can the necessary determinations of rigid bodies and straight lines be made, the interrelationship between the use and creation of a mensurational system can not be set aside.

That mensurational levels are interrelated follows from the fact that they all consist of interoperations with things. There is a continuum in human behavior on any point of which mensurational behavior may be represented. Certainly, those who construct measuring systems may proceed either on a humble manipulative level or on one involving elaborate abstractive formulations.

Despite the dense-point continuum, the theory of measurement must be kept distinct from particular mensurational operations. To do so is to respect the differences between diverse kinds of systems, especially those concerned with (a) the relationship between measurable things and (b) the structure of factors in purely descriptive systems.

QUALITY AND QUANTITY

It is a paradox of measuring theory that even when one's primary interest is in quality one comes to stress quantity. On the whole, this paradox is inherent in the fact that discussions of measuring are usually pitched on an extremely abstract level. In actual mensurational situations the paradox does not exist.

---

[17] Russell, Knowledge, p. 282.

Metaphysical writers range themselves on opposite sides of the quality-quantity problem. Some adopt the ancient Pythagorean-Platonic idea of the superiority of numbers as eternal essences, but others look upon the two categories *quality* and *quantity* as at bottom one, or as transformable one into the other.

The sharp differentiation between quantity and quality is, of course, a purely historical accident. Out of the 17th-century dichotomy of nature into thought and extension the conception has evolved that quantity is more fundamental than quality. It is still a prominent feature of our dualistic culture to regard quality as a diaphanous manifestation of quantity.

However, we need no longer be bound by this tradition. We have already achieved an objective psychological view which not only obviates the thought-extension dichotomy, but enables us to consider scientific as well as other kinds of magnitudes as definite products of interbehavioral enterprises. It is interesting to note that the persistence of dualistic dogma has resulted in overlooking the fact that in our century accurate measurements of such events as color, heat, and sound have been achieved. No longer need we abide by the notion that reality is quantitative and that number rules the world.

Though few, there are some writers who protest against the subservience of quality to quantity.[18] The most favorable result of such protest would be a modification of view concerning measurement. The entire enterprise of abstracting qualities and quantities, and using them as elements in the construction of systems, is either a private or a group operation.

Today it is clear that the distinction of primary and secondary properties is only an outcome of operational situations. What were called primary qualities were those that could easily be measured with the simple tools and techniques available. This fact is apparent when we analyze the various aspects or properties of things. On the whole, metrical properties are more stable and simple, or at least more fixable, than qualitative ones. But the point to emphasize is that they are aspects of things. When we break a stick we can put the pieces end to end and regard the operation as adding the parts to make up the total length. The same process does not apply to the hardness of the glue which holds the pieces together. Similar

[18] See, for example, Spaier, La Pensée; Nagel, Measurement; Benjamin, Logic.

variations in operating upon different things yield constructions concerning qualitative and quantitative properties. In each case the basis is type of available manipulation.

Notice how influential the selective operation is in distinguishing between quality and quantity. Such selection is rooted in the processes of describing or referring to things. We may or may not emphasize the fact that the organism is two-sided or bilaterally symmetrical, is two-handed, two-legged, 200 boned, and so on. When we are concerned with these characteristics, however, we surely need not separate quality from quantity. Similarly, the organism's height and weight are metric properties, but where is the sharp line between one kind of metric property and another? All properties are, or can be made, metric.

The relation between qualitative and quantitative aspects of things for measurement theory suggests a differentiation between quantities as: (1) properties of things, (2) products of operating upon things, and (3) more or less independent constructions concerning things.

(1) *Quantity as property of things* consists of all the aspects of any quality or dimension which allow for diversity. The qualitative aspect constitutes primarily that which is uniform and continuous. To look to the limit of spread or relation of color, extension, hardness, or cohesiveness is to select out the quantitative property. In some cases, of course, quality and quantity are so interdependent that we have an indifference point in description or scaling. Analysis of volume illustrates the inseparability of mathematical quantity and any relevant form of quality. When we ask how old a person or thing is, how many revolutions per second or minute, how long a person or thing will live—that is, number of years or time units—we can not distinguish quality from quantity, though we do so in formalized description.[19]

In concrete measurement situations recall that we are always dealing with things, not with abstract quantities or magnitudes. Nor are we interested primarily, certainly not exclusively, in quantity. The extension, difference, and relation of things exist within the limits of what we ordinarily call one thing or within the connection between several. In the latter case we may describe the properties of things as relatively extrinsic.

[19] Concerning some identities of quality and quantity, see Benjamin, Logic.

(2) *Quantity as measure* constitutes a highly selective aspect of things complicated by measuring processes and instruments. The intrinsically quantitative and relationally numerative properties have been rendered a bit more remote from the things of which they are a part. Measured, recorded, and described quantities include effects based upon (a) the interaction of the measurer, as well as of (b) the measuring conditions; in this sense quantities are contrived and are thus more or less artificial.

The contrived character of quantity is best illustrated by the varying qualities of numbers in the sense of relations, as these qualities depend upon measuring or other situations. For example, the conventional over-evaluation of simple additive quantities reflects the operator's domination of the things he operates upon. By contrast, operation with vector or tensor quantities suggests a sensitivity to the qualities and properties of the things.

(3) *Quantity as constructions* are best illustrated by various averages, coefficients, and other products such as numerical laws or equations. The important criterion here is the initiative and degree of independence in manipulating the results of measuring operations. The types of product developed reflect the influence of the operator's adherence to some sort of theory or philosophy of number, as well as his proficiency in handling calculative techniques.

Variety and Specificity of Magnitudes

The fact that measuring operations are specific with respect to objects measured means there must be as many different kinds of magnitudes as there are kinds of measurable things. The tradition that dichotomizes all magnitudes into intensive and extensive types appears therefore to be wide of the mark. This bipartition of magnitudes is not, however, without some advantage. Since extensive magnitude is presumed to be based upon the prototypical operation of comparing straight lines, it has historically been regarded as the basic, even exclusive, type. Thus, to insist that there is also a nonadditive type indicates a need for further descriptive terms.

The most serious objection to the twofold classification lies in overstressing additive properties. Why should we be overwhelmed by such things as can be heaped up or laid end to end, as in the case of primary additive things yielding weights and linear measure?[20]

[20] Stevens, Theory; Churchman, Materialist; Comrey, Operational.

In what sense are hardness, density, color, elasticity, and temperature less important or less fundamental?

Aside from harking back to the dichotomy of primary and secondary qualities the two-fold classification stresses illegitimate analogies in the sense of reducing measuring operations to the manipulation of rulers and balances. Moreover, the assumption that there are certain fundamental properties results in overlooking the variety of things to be measured. We ask: Should the systematic consideration of measurement stress abstract structures, or rather the process of systemizing operational procedures?

The farther one departs from metaphysical constructions the greater the number and variety of magnitudes. The very purpose of measurement operations is to work out as many magnitudes and dimensions as are necessary to provide the required information for the task at hand. It is fatal, therefore, to measurement theory to make metaphysical or mathematical systems the criteria for measurement systems. Is it proper to regard a thing's length as more basic than its hardness or compressibility merely because one has available an obvious and simple tool to facilitate mensurational operations?

That some things and events are difficult to appraise constitutes no more than a challenge to those who regard investigation and measurement as techniques for discovery and experimentation. Surely it is contrary to scientific behavior to make the novelties of inquiry conform to established rules. Such behavior is inimical to intellectual advancement. It is the most appealing feature of scientific history that the unknown becomes discovered and the unmeasurable becomes determined and subsumed under rule through the effective action of the unbiased worker.

MEASURING SYSTEMS

Measuring systems constitute the most practical and manipulative of logical structures. On the whole, they are not constructed except for some purpose beyond themselves, a fact which probably accounts for the paucity of attempts to describe them explicitly. Still, a formalizing description is of considerable importance, even though for the moment it means disregarding the fact that measuring operations are always specific. According to our plan, therefore, of treating measuring systems by means of a generalized model[21] we propose the following five-factor description, based on many simple and complex situations.

A. Acts of assumption and postulation.
B. Choosing and refining units.
C. Instruments and manipulations.
  How many scales?
  Scales and scale construction.
  Bias in scale making.
  Scale application (mensuration).
  Scale fitting operations.
  Extrapolation and interpolation.
D. Recording.
E. Statistical treatment.

A. *Assumptions and Postulates of Measurement.* In practical situations the assumptions usually concern immediate operational details—for example, the sufficiency and trueness of the devices used, whether levers, rulers, galvanometers or other electrical instruments.

When, as in the case of more theoretical measuring systems, assumptions are examined and evaluated, they become authentic and sometimes significant postulates. Such is the assumption that mathematical relations are somehow ultimate features not only of measuring processes, but of the nature of nature itself. Because all measurement involves comparison of relations, we expect numbers to play a part in all measuring systems. It is a crucial question, however, whether to regard such numbers as metaphysical elements, rather than as operational factors in actual situations. We must not overlook the inevitable postulate that the development of number systems, as well as of mathematics in general, consists of a complex cultural evolution, and consequently involves the activities of individuals. Among the interbehavioral implications we list the relatively arbitrary nature of scales. In other words, units and degrees, or their variation, are selectively constructed. A competing postulate regards all measuring devices as instruments for achieving cer-

---

[21] The effectiveness of this model is determined by the amount of necessary detail that can be included without overcrowding the exposition or overemphasizing any element.

tain purposes; thus the kinds of things worked with are kept well in view. Whether or not mathematical relations constitute the fundamental nature of these things is a problem to be determined, not an absolute assumption from which we must make our departure.

Though mensurational postulates are factors in a system, they are nonetheless susceptible to scrutiny and estimation. When ranking assumptions we place at the metaphysical pole the view mentioned above concerning the relational essence of things. At a somewhat lower point is the popular attitude that science consists of measuring behavior, and that scientific data therefore comprise nothing but the products of such behavior irrespective of what is originally measured. On still lower levels, which approach more closely the interbehavioral operations themselves, are the assumptions (a) that what is measured is a fair sample of the total sample, and (b) that there is or is not a population or a universe beyond the larger sample.

B. *Choosing and Refining Units.* Within specific systems units vary on the basis of the sort of thing measured. Also, the refinement and improvement of units are differentially variable according to the mensurative situations. Probably the simplest and most satisfying systems are those in which the units constitute parts of the things measured, as in the so-called fundamental units—for example, proportions of length and weight. The things measured in these instances possess definite metrical properties which are divided into convenient units.

More analogical are the essentially constructive units; for example, all units derived and compounded from so-called basic dimensions[22]—units of density, temperature, velocity, etc. The units for all derived[23] magnitudes may be regarded as tools of comparison, their primary function being to indicate relative differences of change or proportion between properties of things.

Those whose mensurational horizon is not bounded by the additive constructs of physics, and who therefore have room for estimating, assessing and judging systems, are free to construct other

---

[22] As the most important of the properties that can be fundamentally measured, Campbell (Measurement, p. 127) lists numbers, mass, volume, length, angle, period, force, electrical resistance, current, and voltage.

[23] Campbell, Physics, p. 346f.

types of units. Such freedom is limited only by the exigencies of the problem of ascertaining properties and relations of things and events. In other words, the guiding principle is to carry out a piece of work instead of applying formal and rigid specifications developed and suitable only for another situation.[24]

C. *Instruments and Operations.* Mensurative operations so frequently consist of handling instruments that the occupation with apparatus and things measured constitutes a single complex factor in mensuration systems. The primary instruments comprise scales of which there are many sorts. Measuring involves the problem of making a scale to fit the objects to be measured. Should we emphasize the comparison of things or merely fit objects to arbitrarily chosen scales? Some of these issues, as we have already implied, hark back to philosophical views.

How Many Scales? The general trend of opinion is that there are only a few kinds of scales. The tradition of primary and secondary qualities has influenced scientific writers to divide qualities into additive and nonadditive types. Only the primary are considered fundamentally measurable. Alternate names for these qualities are extensive and intensive. Writers so influenced allow only four scales. On the whole, physicists, in whose province one locates the things capable of addition and subtraction, permit a limited number of scales, while psychologists and social scientists are willing to increase the list to accommodate less palpable items than those of physics.

The physicists' scales, on the whole, are of two types. The first, dealing with extensive or additive properties, is called a ratio scale; the second, concerned with intensive or nonadditive magnitudes, is named an interval scale.[25] Psychologists and sociologists are inclined to add two others—namely, a nominal and an ordinal scale. The former is employed for identifying and classifying things, the latter for arranging things in series.[26]

The standard for setting up this quadruple scale system is the conventional opinion that measurement is the application of numerals to things. Such a scale system can only be justified when

---

[24] Clearly, this sentence suggests that we question the assumption that any science, including physics, is the *scientia scientiarum.*

[25] There is no uniformity, however, in term usage. Cf. Stevens, Theory.

[26] Stevens, Classification.

writers acknowledge that they have set up a range of mensurational scales on the basis of their own fields of investigation. But
there are two problems here. First, the use of scales must be differentiated from theories of scale making. Using certain scales
is a process dictated, for instance, by the kind of magnitudes with
which one works. It is another matter to make one's own scale
the exclusive model of measurements, and thus to limit scale
variation. Secondly, from a logical standpoint we are obliged to
make room for as many scales as mensurational operations indicate.
To fix an arbitrary limit to their number is to adopt an authori-
tarian attitude.

Scales and Scale Construction. Scales as tools for ascertaining the
nature of things must maintain a workable harmony with the
things measured. In order to clarify this point we contrast our
view that (a) scales must conform to the things measured and also
to the problem under inquiry with (b) the numbers conformity
theory. As a basis for this discussion we examine Stevens' four
scales.

I. *Nominal Scale.* Defining measurement as "assignment of
numerals according to rules," Stevens includes the nominal type
among his scales. The operation consists merely of applying numerals to items in a series for differentiating and identifying them.
The numerals serve as ready labels or names, as in the marking
of policemen, prisoners, box cars, football players, and race horses.

The rule here is simply not to assign the same numeral to different items at the same time, or different numerals to members
of the same group when classes are to be distinguished. Stevens
himself questions the nominal scale as a measuring device, but is
influenced to retain it because it conforms to the given definition.
The basic objection to this scale, which is really no measurement
scale at all, is that the operations in no sense yield any information
about the qualities or characteristics of the labeled things. Even
the ordered numerals on state highways are scantily informing unless we already know the marking system.

Despite these criticisms, however, there is justification for including a nominal scale in a scale system. First, the heavy hand of
quantity is lifted. The difference between numerals and numbers
is recognized. But more important is the implied view that measuring scales should not be limited to a few classic types. Tradi-

tional measurement discussions take no account of the tremendous development of technological and scientific domains and of the tools and operations invented to cope with new events.

II. *Ordinal Scale.* Ordinal scales are ranking devices for placing things and properties in relative positions on the basis of a given criterion. The operations are performed to determine the asymmetric relation of greater or less of the compared objects or qualities. Because they are not strictly quantitative, the measurements are not subject to statistical treatment involving means and standard deviations. The classic example of an ordinal scale is Mohs' instrument for differentiating and ordering minerals according to hardness, which is determined by the scratches one mineral makes upon another. This test results in the following order:

(1) talc, (2) gypsum, (3) calcite, (4) fluorite, (5) apatite, (6) feldspar, (7) quartz, (8) topaz, (9) corundum, (10) diamond.

Physicists, for obvious reasons, are less tolerant of such scales than are psychologists. The physicist, interested in and influenced by things that can be handled as independent and additive, can not admit hardness as a measurable property at all. In fact, Campbell admits only money value as equally measurable with the phenomena of physics.[27] To be sure, things vary in their capability for precise determination; it is equally certain that the function of science is better served when arithmetical quantity is not made into a fetish, but maintained as a working ideal. However faulty an ordinal scale like Mohs' may be in the inequality of its intervals,[28] it is still true that mensurational principles call for a multiplication of measuring scales as features of investigative systems.

III. *Interval Scale.* Interval scales, such as the Centigrade and Fahrenheit temperature scales, are regarded by Stevens as genuinely quantitative. Accordingly, the interval scale is presumed to exemplify the isomorphism between what can be done with the aspects of objects and the properties of the numeral series. While the additive principle is absent here, the equality of expansion

[27] Measurement, p. 135.
[28] Spencer, Abrasives.

volume can be accurately matched with equal intervals on the temperature scale.

In many ways the interval scale is an excellent representative of the entire series of mensuration constructs and operations. Not only are many important statistical treatments available—computation of mean, standard deviation, correlation coefficients—but the range of applicability is larger.

IV. *Ratio Scale.* The authority of the physical sciences and the power of numbers are responsible for an irresistible tendency to accord the greatest weight to ratio scales. Such scales are constructed for things that can be added together and grouped in various ways, as well as divided and otherwise manipulated. Further, there is ascertainable a definite zero point to help in comparing things.

An interesting suggestion of Stevens is that the cardinal number itself constitutes a ratio scale. This brings up the important question of the relation between counting and measuring (p. 296). At the least, such a suggestion prompts the consideration of the large range of scales necessary to discover the significant properties of things.

Bias in Scale Making. The impact of philosophical thinking on the logic of measurement is illustrated by the arguments concerning the nature of psychological scales. Since their earliest attempts to measure things psychologists have been assiduously engaged in finding means of scaling psychic as over against physical magnitudes. Because psychic magnitudes were not available for manipulation, the scales devised were presumed to measure relations between "sensations," for example, and the magnitude of the stimulus or the action of the organism. The vigorous discussion concerning the possibility of psychological measurement which started when such measurement was first attempted continues to the present moment.[29]

Doubtless the solution of such problems lies in determining precisely what is to be measured before scales are made and applied. One important suggestion is that psychological scales measure actions of organisms in relation to stimulus objects. Since these ac-

---

[29] The gravitational center of this discussion is the question whether psychic qualities can be measured. Cf. Ferguson, Quantitative; Reese, Application; McGregor, Scientific; Scates, How; Bartlett, Measurement; Wiener, New Theory.

tions vary, the authentic scale problem is to devise instruments with which to assess the values of such mensurative objects for the mode of inquiry.

Scale Application. Juxtaposing a rigid rod with an object is conventionally regarded as the primary mensurational operation. No one can deny that the application of a ruler scale typifies the procedural factor of a measuring system. It is frequently remarked that there are comparatively few measurements which do not resolve themselves into reading off a length on a scale.[30] Still, it is inexcusable to single out linear measurement as illustrating more than a general method. Scale applications vary enormously and always directly with the situations for which scales are designed.

Added to the influence of the above physics-measurement situation is the overemphasis of the fact that most measuring situations constitute scale application, not scale construction. This leads directly to overstressing scales as instruments. Hence one clings to the linear-scale model and disregards the fact that linear values constitute some, but not all, of the results sought and obtained.

The *reductio ad absurdum* of scale application is to assume that mensurational operations may be performed without definitely knowing what is being measured. Mass, it is asserted, was measured before it was clearly appreciated as an inertial property. The development of the formula $F = M \times A$ did not differentiate between force defined in terms of mass and mass defined in terms of force.[31] As this example clearly indicates, all that is involved here are different levels of measurement. It is indeed true that measurement on one level may be very different from measurement on another, and that the earlier may be basic to that performed later. In the present case the measurements were first made on a simpler level by means of observations on bodies differently accelerated. With increased knowledge concerning the factors involved one can better describe the system. We may well assume that all complex mensurational systems are evolved by a step-by-step evolution.

Similar assertions are made by psychologists who accept the view that numerical values are obtainable without knowing what is being measured. A generalized statement of this sort has it that if a

[30] Ritchie, Scientific, p. 125.
[31] Ibid., p. 148.

"structure" is decomposable into countless elements or units, the number obtained by adding such units gives the measure of the structure's magnitude.[32] This attitude has recently been developed in connection with the measurement of intelligence, which has been regarded as an intangible and unobservable entity determining performances. While measuring the performances it was assumed that the imaginary entity *intelligence* was being measured. But why interpret this situation as measuring an unknown entity when one is actually measuring performance? As it happens, when what is measured once becomes known, it turns out that what was originally measured was the performance. Surely this is the case when the measured performances consist of answers given by different individuals to "series of conundrums."[33]

To such an extent have writers emphasized measuring instruments that they have regarded measurement as a guarantee of the existence of a thing. Misconstruing Kelvin's (Thomson's) famous assertion in his lecture on Electrical Units of Measurement:

In physical science a first essential step in the direction of learning any subject is to find principles of numerical reckoning and methods for practicably measuring some quality connected with it. I often say that when you can measure what you are speaking about, and express it in numbers, you know something about it; but when you can not measure it, when you cannot express it in numbers, your knowledge is of a meager and unsatisfactory kind: it may be the beginning of knowledge, but you have scarcely, in your thoughts, advanced to the stage of *science,* whatever the matter may be.[34]

they have translated knowing into being, and misplaced Kelvin's view which was excellent for the circumstances of which he spoke.

How strange that it should ever be necessary to insist upon taking properly into account the quantitative or numerical properties of things! But such is the case whenever one departs from spatiotemporal objects to talk about magnitudes as important abstract entities. Why avoid any quantitative property of things, as long as it is available? As a matter of fact, when we deal with actual things

[32] Horst, Measurement, p. 632f.

[33] Ibid., p. 635.

[34] Thomson, Popular, vol. I, p. 73. Kelvin's statement typifies the attitude that science is measurement and stands in contrast to the view that science is not based upon measurement. See George, Scientist, p. 332.

we find that they may have more than one kind of quantitative property. When liquids can be differentiated as drops they may require counting; when not, they can be treated by weight or volume.

Scale Fitting. Complex mensurational situations usually call for more ingenious procedures than the mere application of scales. Analogizing and transforming operations are required to achieve accurate specifications of properties and relations. An excellent example is the substitution of weighing for linear measurement when the problem concerns the precise determination of the magnitude of a very thin object.

Faraday weighed 2000 leaves of gold, each 3⅜ inches square, and found them equal to 384 grains. From the known specific gravity of gold it was easy to calculate that the average thickness of the leaves was 1/282.000 of an inch.[35]

Jevons offers a wide range of illustrations of what he calls indirect measurement. The most striking instances consist of substituting forces in equilibrium; in other words, substituting static conditions for dynamic or kinematic events, as in the case of D'Alembert's principle.

The latter example, illustrating the more analogical form of transformation, has relatively more to do with constructional operations. Transformations developed during the manipulative processes of measuring may be described as interchanging the ascertainable properties of the measured things with attributes deemed necessary or expedient. The most radical transformations belong to the interpretative phase. For calculative purposes, events or objects become points in a field of coordinates. In more remote cases, numerals representing items become parts of curves representing trend lines.

Interpolation and Extrapolation. Complex measurements involve both calculative and manipulative operations (p. 276). The calculative operations may be equated with judging and estimating activities. In general we may separate measuring situations on the basis of direct or indirect manipulation. In the former the objects to be measured are stressed; in the latter the behavioral strategy necessary to assay the thing in question is emphasized. Prominent

[35] Jevons, Principles, p. 296, from material derived from Faraday, Chemical Researches, p. 393.

among the calculative schemes employed to control objects beyond the range of direct manipulation are the mathematical processes of interpolation and extrapolation.

The substitution, in whole or part, of calculative devices for direct manipulation is analogous to making indirect estimates on the basis of samples. Obviously, the extreme case is that in which no application of a definite scale or other instrument is possible; thus from casual or partial observation one is obliged to build up a complete system of speculative estimates.

D. *Recording.* No inconsiderable part of mensurative operations consists of recording the results obtained. This point is obvious in view of the importance of holding to the basic information secured. Planck[36] asserts that measurement is the recording of answers which nature gives to questions put to it in the form of experiments.

Within the scope of recording lie such operations as tabulating, ordering, and graphing data. The expertness required for dealing with this material in complex situations is directly proportional to the care demanded in building and applying scales and standards. Not only are recording operations integral parts of the total measuring behavior, but they influence the other operational procedures and for this reason are highly important in the all-around measuring situation.

The importance of recording operations reaches down to the very marks and schemes employed. Notice the part played by signs, graphs, and tables in recording results for future treatment. Recall the role of proper notation in the development of effective calculation and theoretical mathematics.[37] On a higher plane we discern at once the advantages and disadvantages of particular techniques in organizing data for summing, averaging, and integrating. Merely to consider the extensive place that tabulating and graphing occupy in the establishment of trends and constants as a basis for scientific laws is to acknowledge the proper value of recording operations in mensurative enterprises.[38]

E. *Statistical Operations.* The statistical factors of the total mensurational system are performed primarily in order to verify and

---

[36] Meaning, p. 235.

[37] Cf. vol. I, p. 213.

[38] We are reminded of Whewell's (Novum) inclusion of the method of curves among his special inductive methods.

test such features as obtaining, identifying, organizing, and comparing data. Whenever computations are included in the system, checks must be selected and applied. To illustrate controls for calculations and correlations we mention merely the method of least squares and similar statistical tests.[39]

A word of caution: The interrelation of the various factors in a mensurative system is symmetrical. While it is true that statistical operations constitute essential checks on the other operations, it is likewise true that statistical operations are conditioned by the other features of the enterprise. The total set of the system's factors constitutes the criterion for the component operations.

How Arbitrary Are Units or Standards?

Expert metrological opinion vacillates between two views: (1) that units and standards are, or ought to be, absolute and (2) that they are completely arbitrary. It is tempting to follow the conventional procedure of declaring that the truth lies somewhere in the mean, but this is not the case. Both views are based on oversimplified premises concerning measurement; and from two wrong notions it is hardly possible to extract a correct one. In neither instance are the many complex features of mensurational system building taken into account.

Although it is obvious that units and standards can not be abstracted so far from the objects and events interacted with as to be made absolute, the attempt is nevertheless made. It is probable that Gauss[40] did not intend his time, length, and mass units to be more than *relatively* absolute and fundamental. Even though metrologists have taken pains to reject the absolutistic construct,[41] there seems to be some notion that such a standard can be approximated.

For one thing, observe the attitude of metrologists in the following statement:

The science of measurement is in practice restricted to mean measurement of the three fundamental quantities, mass, length, and time, from which all other quantities, such, for example, as volume, density, velocity, acceleration, force and power, are derived.[42]

---

[39] Cf. Fisher, Statistical.
[40] Intensitas.
[41] Cf. for example, Runge, Maass; Sears, Measurements.
[42] Sears, Measurements, p. 841.

This not merely reflects the physicist's bias or the influence of mathematical ideals, but implies something beyond the urge to rigor and precision. We might trace it to the cultural assumption of the essentially quantitative character of reality and to the influence of the mechanical domination of science. The latter influence is clearly visible in Gauss' desire to carry electric measurements back to basic mechanical standards.

An interesting speculation is how close the correlation might be between the absolutistic idea and the palpable character of "fundamental" and "absolute" standards. Obviously, units that can be embodied and conserved in platinum and iridium must appear as somewhat ultimate. The physicist's attempt to substitute the wave length of the red cadmium line as a standard[43] may seem to modify this motive; on the other hand, it emphasizes how basic the factor of length is among metrologists.

The importance attached to restricted and relatively absolute standards is evident in the admirable development of dimensional theory. It is undeniable that this theory indicates how well organized mensurational systems can be; nevertheless, there are objections to overstressing certain standards and units, or larger systems made from them.

Length, for example, is important, but it is no more basic than any other dimension. Moreover, we must hold it to the situations where it is appropriate. We have already suggested the cultural influence operating here. Indeed, linear mensuration is historically the first type to be developed. Nor need we question its most precise procedures. Still, by overlooking other important mensurative forms we drift into a false analogy.

Furthermore, we need not be overly influenced by pragmatic conditions. While in practice we are limited by the particular instruments we used and by the practical difficulties in varying them, such circumstances should not be too binding. Because of the fundamental integration of our culture and its impedimenta we are restricted by the gradual evolution of instruments and processes. Automobiles still show their descent from the horse-drawn vehicle, despite the fact that the basic function of instruments of transportation allows for tremendous variation in shape and pattern. The

[43] Michelson, Light.

same thing may be said, of course, for the roads upon which they travel.

Turning now to the notion that measuring units and standards are arbitrary, we observe at once that this is only true within narrow limits. Even though units as features of mensuration systems are constructional products, they are derived from specific situations and are modified by self-correcting operations upon actual things.

No scientist accepts as satisfactory for any serious purpose arbitrary operations with indifferent objects as instruments or tools. Even for historically early units we must presuppose the insight necessary to fit measuring operations to the needs of the situation. The growth of scientific sophistication and of particular kinds of measurement demonstrates an increasing precision in the conformity of measuring instruments and operations to things measured.

As factors in systems, units can not be more arbitrary than the total system. Even writers like Campbell,[44] who regard units as arbitrary, allow for no arbitrariness in any other measuring element. But even the unit's apparent arbitrariness disappears when the measuring system is not taken to be, as in Campbell's case, an arithmetical system, but looked upon as a means to a specific end.

Is it possible that the idea of the arbitrariness of units stems from confusing units with their names or descriptions? The history of the development and adoption of modern electrical units provides some basis for this suggestion.

The Nature of Quantity, Number, and Magnitude

As inveterate apostles of precision, writers on the logic of measurement are confused concerning the referents of such terms as quantity, number, and magnitude. This situation is not simply one of semantic deficiency. It indicates the depth to which such problems penetrate metaphysical foundations.

We have already suggested the orientation of Helmholtz's ideas in philosophical territory. To take a more recent example, Russell,[45] building on an absolute Platonic foundation, contrasts magnitude and quantity on the basis that the former has to do with some-

---

[44] Physics, p. 290ff.
[45] Principles, chap. 19.

thing greater or less but never equal (p. 164). Quantities, however, as the less abstract entities, can be equal in that they possess the same magnitude. Russell illustrates his point by remarking that "an actual footrule is a quantity; its length is a magnitude" (p. 159). Lenzen,[46] who adopts this view, asserts that quantity is a particular, while magnitude is a universal.

Less theoretical writers use the terms *quantity* and *magnitude* interchangeably, but, influenced by mathematical abstractionism, regard them as standing for some entity different from the actual objects measured. Both practical and theoretical writers consider magnitudes as some abstract property of extension and speak of measuring magnitude or quantity. Such a paradox can easily be avoided by taking into account that the measurer is trying to ascertain the size of something, the amount of some quality, or the character of some relation an object bears to another object. One may then use the term *magnitude* for size factors, and *quantity* for amount units. Similarly, the term *number*, also used synonymously with these two, might be reserved for relationship determination. For number, order may also be important. In every case these terms, singly and together, must be associated with dimensions of objects as ascertained through mensurational procedures.

Since upon an operational basis measurement is not simply a matter of constructing an abstract or logical mathematical system, but rather an enterprise carried on for specific purposes, there is a limit to the amount of reduction and elimination of that which is measured.

Admittedly, there exists no accepted standard for the terms *quantity*, *number*, and *magnitude*. Their use depends upon the measuring job. When we abstract from actual things, however, number, quantity, and magnitude become indifferent or equivalent terms, and can be adapted to any sort of metaphysical position.

Measuring and Counting

To clarify the relation between measuring and counting is to cast considerable light upon measurement principles.

For Helmholtz measuring is a counting procedure when the results are denominate or concrete numbers expressing the values of magnitudes. The latter constitute objects, or attributes of ob-

[46] Nature, p. 22.

jects, which upon comparison permit the distinction of greater, equal, or smaller.[47] Here the absorption of measurement by arithmetic is plain, but the empiricistic attitude exhibited does full justice to the auspices under which measuring procedures operate.

On more abstruse grounds rationalistic writers who assimilate measurement to counting do so because of an adherence to some absolutistic logic of number. The numerals attached to things in measuring operations are regarded as symbols for the numbers belonging to a transcendental system of relations. It is for this reason that the properties of addition and independence are made basic to measurement.[48] The statement that "The primary purpose of numerals is to express facts about number"[49] is a clear indication of the great influence abstract relations exert upon ideas concerning measurement. This point is further enforced by the statement:

In order that the measurement shall be really satisfactory, the property measured in this way must obey the rules of arithmetic.[50]

When measurement is approached from a more concrete scientific viewpoint, especially when the difficulties of precise determination of properties are apparent, measuring and counting do not appear so closely related. In fact, the two are sharply separated on the ground that, whereas counting involves cardinal numbers and no manipulation, measurement involves ratios and manipulatory operations.[51] On the surface this differentiation appears reasonable, but unfortunately it is still based upon an insufficient handling of number problems. There is no consideration of actual mensurational work and its relation to counting in concrete situations.

If we turn to specific interbehavior we find that in some cases counting is measuring, while in others it is not. Counting is found to comprise various kinds of operation when we depart from the standpoint of mathematics and approach interbehavior with things.

Granting the interpretation that measuring is a process of ascertaining the properties of things, we must include counting and calculating as measuring actions. Situations demanding knowledge concerning numerical or quantitative properties imply that such

[47] Zählen, p. 35.
[48] Campbell, Measurement, p. 127.
[49] Ibid., p. 122.
[50] Ibid., p. 127.
[51] Ritchie, Scientific, chap. 5.

properties are features of things in the same degree as color, density, length, and area. On the other hand, counting may be merely reciting the progression of the n + 1 relation by means of its conventionally named items. Such counting can be connected with measuring only in a very indirect way. Counting properly associated with measuring may be distinguished by the criterion of facilitating an adjustment to some difficult situation. When dealing with recalcitrant materials measuring may require much complex calculation.

Mensurational operations cover a vast range of specific performances. Counting operations are definitely included. But counting may never be separated from manipulations. In complex situations counting may require moving things about and instrumentally examining small objects. A relevant example is supplied by the work and apparatus required to count blood cells accurately.

Herodotus offers an interesting account of the manner in which Xerxes ascertained that his army at Doriscus had the numerical value of 1,700,000:

A body of ten thousand men was brought to a certain place, and the men were made to stand as close together as possible; after which a circle was drawn around them, and the men were let go: then where the circle had been, a fence was built about the height of a man's middle; and the enclosure was filled continually with fresh troops, till the whole army had in this way been numbered.[52]

---

[52] History, p. 377.

CHAPTER XXIV

METROLOGY AND METASCIENCE

Problems of Mensurational Logic

OUR study of measurement, we believe, has amply justified the suggestion made at the beginning of the preceding chapter that measuring situations illumine every feature of the system-building enterprise. Measurement may thus be regarded as thoroughly integrated with systemology.

This does not mean, however, that mensurational logic is in any sense a static domain. Indeed, it constantly engenders problems just as any other logic does, and in no smaller degree than science itself —the primary environment of mensurational theory.

In the present chapter we are concerned with several problems provoked by the apparent disharmony between modern scientific investigations and traditional mensurational practice. As we shall see, the issues break through the conventional bounds of science to the neighboring metascientific environment. The problems we are to consider arise out of the three following situations.

(1) The influence of modern science, especially microscopic physics (quantology), upon metrology.

Interest in measurement has been keenly intensified by the important issues arising in relativity theory and quantum mechanics. Especially has the Heisenberg indeterminacy principle quickened the study of metrological foundations (p. 309ff.). A significant outcome of the newer developments in physics is the freedom they afford from the fetters of traditional logic of measurement.

(2) The bearing of symbolic logic on the relations between metrology and general systemology.

The development of modern science coincides with that of formal logic. Naturally, then, logicians attempt to harmonize their discipline with the newer scientific developments in measurement. Their success at coordination, we shall discover, depends upon the competence of logic to match concrete mensurational events.

(3) The consequences of microscopic measurement for scientific foundations.

Such fundamental issues as are raised by the mensurational problems of microscopic physics have gone way beyond the bounds of classical science. Measurement problems are intermixed with questions concerning the nature of scientific observation, knowledge, cause, objectivity, even reality itself.

The bridge between metrology and such metascientific problems obviously consists of mensurational systems. To examine briefly a typical series of such systems prepares the way for the analysis of the metrological issues developed in the train of quantum mechanics.

System Type and Metrological Evolution

Our investigation has certainly demonstrated that when we start from measurement situations, rather than from the applied-mathematics theory, we encounter a great number and variety of metrological systems. Up to this point we have stressed chiefly the correspondence between measurement systems and the situations to which they belong. Now we must emphasize the fact that measurement systems occupy distinctive chronological positions in the evolution of science. On the whole, measurement principles, like the term *measurement*, comprise a heritage from the time when geometric mensuration dominated the scientific scene. Today we know that historical mensurational principles belong to but one of many kinds of metrological situations. A comparison of metrological systems throws light on the evolution of science and its mensurational techniques.

As a basis for our comparison we use four variant criteria—namely, (a) things measured, (b) instruments employed, (c) standards used, and (d) operations involved.

(1) *Measuring Systems.* Influenced in part by traditional linguistic usage we place under this heading all mensurational systems involving linear relations. Included are all activities to ascertain lengths or distances between points. Points constitute actual places on or between objects. Though we cannot avoid linguistic habits in referring to the values ascertained and recorded, we repeat that we are concerned not with abstruse geometrical magnitudes but with concrete things and relations. We may say, then, that the values here comprise all lengths, areas, volumes, and distances.

So great is the number and variety of things belonging to the present class of measuring situations that listing is impossible, also unnecessary. Its range extends from everyday objects to astronomical bodies, to radiation of every variety, and to abstract geometric relations as represented by drawn figures and analytic formulae. The instruments used indicate the specific character of mensurating situations. To the conventional rigid body may be added all sorts of optical instruments required for triangulation and other long-distance procedures. In the simplest measuring situations the pertinent operations consist merely of juxtaposing a standard measuring instrument as a workable unit. Sometimes an object to be fitted into a given place is juxtaposed with the place to be covered.

(2) *Weighing Systems.* Weighing systems involve things that can be heaped together or separated. The primary comparison is between (a) one or more bodies and (b) distinct heaps. The typical metrological weighing instrument is the beam balance constructed with equal lever arms, so that an attached pointer in an equilibrium position indicates the symmetry of the system on the basis of the bodies hung from the arms. Approximations to the required results are obtained from various spring arrangements. Aside from the manipulation of balances, weighing operations also include various procedures for determining the homogeneity of the material to be weighed. Scales can be balanced by adding salt or sand to sugar, but the results can not be carried over to situations demanding a more discriminating result than bulk equivalence.

Weighing information can also be obtained by an equivalent form of measuring. Assume that the homogeneous material is available in large heaps; then by arranging a rectangular container the right amount of, say, sand can be determined by linear measurement.

Interesting here is Maxwell's suggestion of measuring substances by the effects they produce:

. . . if we are dealing with sulphuric acid of uniform strength, we may estimate the quantity of a given portion of it in several ways. We may weigh it, we may pour it into a graduated vessel, and so measure its volume, or we may ascertain how much of a standard solution of potash it will neutralize.[1]

(3) *Counting Systems.* When the metrological question is how

[1] Matter, p. 33.

many rather than how far, or how long in duration, or how much, we develop a counting system. Accordingly, the things dealt with consist of unit objects which can be enumerated and added. The operations constitute the behavior of the operator himself, unless some recording machine (manual or electrical registration device— "Geiger pulse counter") is utilized.

In situations in which no apparatus is employed we must still distinguish between the direct interaction with objects and the more or less long-range operations performed in dealing with abstract relations. Behavior such as uttering number names illustrates long-range contacts with things.

(4) *Calculating Systems*. Generally speaking, calculative aspects of metrology concern auxiliary features of gathering information. Operations upon things are substitutive in character, and the instruments consist of mathematical processes applicable to every type of object.

The rules of proper identification and classification of items are determined by the specific interbehavioral fields in which they occur. As substitution operations calculation processes are involved with recorded data specifying lengths, areas, volumes, numbers of things, and so on. More specifically, the operations consist of multiplying, dividing, and the computing of averages, rates, correlations, etc. Perhaps the most definite features of such systems are various ratios—rates of production, motion, and changes of all sorts.

(5) *Ordering Systems*. Too numerous to mention are the kinds of things subject to this type of systemization. In fact there is hardly any sort of object for which an ordering rule or standard can not be contrived. Moving things into certain positions on the basis of previously ascertained information concerning their qualities and properties is the fundamental operation. When things are not sufficiently tangible to be handled in this way they can be indirectly ordered. Recall that among the enormous range of things subject to ordering are traits of every variety—merits, achievements, actions, as well as social and cultural properties.

(6) *Estimating Systems*. Objects belonging to estimating systems are generally characterized as less definite and less manageable than objects in other systems. As a matter of fact, writers who regard the physicist's arithmetical metrology as the only genuine

type discriminate against estimating activities as measuring altogether.[2]

The measurer's operations occupy a unique place, indeed a focal position, in the metrological system. The ability to set up a system depends to a great extent upon his expertness. In a genuine sense, therefore, the operator himself constitutes the metrological instrument. The diagnostician in medical practice, for instance, is a more or less efficient instrument operating like a ruler, galvanometer, or balance. One is reminded here of the early days of electrical science when Cavendish used himself as a more or less sensitive galvanometer. Concerning Cavendish's work, Maxwell wrote:

Cavendish is the first verifier of Ohm's law, for he finds by successive series of experiments that the resistance is as the following power of the velocity, 1.08, 1.03, .980, and concludes that it is as the first power. All this by the physiological galvanometer.[3]

Such incidents in the historical development of science suggest a tolerance toward various as yet unstandardized metrological systems.

A distinctive type of estimating measurement system is that by which the mass of the meson (mesotron) is determined. While cosmic-ray mesons are too energetic to be treated directly by magnetic fields, the mass can be indirectly estimated.[4]

Because of the interrelation of the charge, mass, and velocity values of particles, the cloud-chamber technique furnishes photographs yielding the following quantities which can be employed in a measuring system: (1) curvature of the track, (2) range of the particle, (3) ionization per centimeter of path, and (4) rates of change of these quantities during the passage of the particle.

The character of the measuring system is illustrated by the fact that while ionization does not depend greatly upon the mass it does depend upon the velocity of a particle. To estimate the mass, then, one must invoke the relationship between mass and velocity.

(7) *Evaluating Systems.* The measured things comprised within the present type of system consist of second or higher-order relations. The measurer's interest is in the significance of things,

---

[2] Cf. Johnson, Pseudomathematics.
[3] Campbell and Garnett, Life, p. 402.
[4] Stranathan, "Particles," p. 520.

rather than in such crude surface properties as length and weight. To a great extent his operations amount to imposing a value upon an object, rather than drawing it out of the thing itself. Obviously, the criteria are not as rigid as in other metrological systems, but entail much more viable acts of assumption and postulation. Another way of saying this is that the mensurative standards are not as close to the things measured as to the behavior and behavioral history of the evaluating individual.

A prominent factor here is the influence of the cultural conditions which comprise the immediate milieu of the measurer's activity. Excellent examples are the various axiological techniques (chap. 17) organized in an attempt to measure aesthetic values. Despite the fact that the builders of such systems are excessively imbued by the ideals of measurement in physics, their work plainly shows the large place that the measurer and his cultural traits occupy in the completed structure. These points are well illustrated by the formula $M = O/C$ developed for measurement in the arts.[5] M as aesthetic measure or quantitative index is defined as the ratio of aesthetic association to motor adjustments of the person reacting to or appreciating the comparative pleasantness-producing qualities of aesthetic objects.

(8) *Equating Systems*. To a great extent equating situations, along with the included equating behavior, may be regarded as generalized metrological types. Equating one thing with another appears to be the fundamental comparing activity of all measurement. Nevertheless, under this designation it is possible to isolate a technical mensurating system.

Basically, measurement in equating situations consists of discovering equivalence relations. Mensurational objects in these instances are not directly manipulable. They consist of abstractive and constructive things such as intricately interrelated geometric objects. Metrological systems contrived for such objects lead to the ascertainment of various sorts of congruity relations. In general, equating measurements are involved with a variety of nonmetric mathematical systems and situations. Moreover, there is a decided emphasis on the standards constructed for producing the matches and equivalences.

(9) *Probability Systems*. The most important examples of prob-

5 Birkhoff, Aesthetic.

ability measurements are localizable in the domain of atomic physics. What is dealt with are nonvisible things, such as energy disturbances and energy interchanges. Here the greatest resources of analogy and complementarity must be exploited to accomplish desirable results.[6] Atomic or microscopic measurements must be built up from such elementary and indexical observables as cloud chamber tracks, oil-drop behavior in magnetic fields, and the activation of silver grains on photographic plates.[7]

To measure the behavior of photons or electrons requires the observer to invoke the statistical probability that particles or corpuscles passing through a slit will distribute themselves at calculable terminal points on a screen. In one sense such corpuscular behavior is comparable to statistical or group activities plus the variations provided by the specific field conditions in which the particular group items occur. Among the differences we must note that the probabilities dealt with in quantum mechanics are not derived from generalizations concerning individuals, but directly and immediately from groups and aggregations as such.[8]

Probability measurement differs greatly from other sorts in accordance with the general principle that each situation is unique. It is an error, however, to enlarge the differences between situations to the dimensions of kind rather than of degree. Probability measurements merely involve less directly manipulative operations than other types.

Since probability measurements are most intimately at home in microscopic physics, what are the basic variations from macroscopic situations? Certainly we should disagree that in the former situations causality in the proper sense is excluded. True it is, however, that hierarchies of construction must be relatively more emphasized. The intensification and broadening of knowledge concerning complex and recondite events call for courageous initiative in analytical and constructional work. This implies that the operations in probability measurement are refined and original acts of system building leading to an understanding of things and events on the basis of more elaborate analogical treatment than is given to objects immediately observable and manipulable.

[6] Bohr, Causality.
[7] Margenau, Critical; Jordan, Process.
[8] Einstein and Infeld, Evolution, p. 299f.

Coincident with the growth and transformation of scientific problems, measuring situations also evolve and thus may become enormously complex. Unfortunately, this fact leads those scientists who entertain traditional presuppositions to translate metrological problems into metascientific issues. For this reason clarification of the following measurement problems promises a gain for both science and logic.

Measurement: Abstract and Concrete

Since measuring is a procedure for comparing at least two things —that is, ascertaining relations—it is easy to overstress the relational feature. Moreover, it has become conventional that relations are abstract or formal. The peak of abstractionism is attained when the relation is represented by a numeral.

From an interbehavioral standpoint no numeral or number is apriorily an empty abstraction. This does not mean that we may not differentiate between a numeral and the mensurational operations which engender it. Still, in the interest of effective analysis the operation should be kept in the foreground.

While discussing symbols[9] we pointed out the interdependence of numbers and things. This interdependence can not be overlooked either when we deal with number symbols or with numbers as (a) ascertained relations and (b) numerical qualities.

Jeffreys[10] asks: Is an angle a number in terms of a certain measure? Is a right angle $\frac{1}{2} \pi$ and the angle of a complete circumference of a circle 2π? In each case it must be specified that the numbers of radians are in question. The same writer goes on to show that while 2 sheep + 3 sheep = 5 sheep, 2 sheep + 3 houses $\neq$ 5 of anything. As a matter of fact, both the concreteness of numbers and their instrumental character can be observed in the fact that 2 sheep + 3 houses do make 5 things. Of course, it depends on the situation and on the mensurational postulates how one interprets things. Why exclude even an equation like 2 sheep + 3 houses = 5x in which x symbolizes trouble? To increase one's possessions so far is to increase one's trouble by a factor of 5 as compared with possessing only 1 or no animal.

In addition, we must check the range of allowed abstractionism.

[9] Vol. I, p. 213f.
[10] Scientific, p. 138.

In order to balance a weight on one pan we can heap sugar plus sand on the other. From an abstract standpoint the materials placed on the pan are sufficiently homogeneous. Not so when a specific quantity of sugar is called for. Only extremely abstract situations can be satisfied by simple equality or inequality.

Abstractionizing measurement results from confusing concrete measuring operations with generalized descriptions of them. Measuring operations may be legitimately described as work done to obtain numerals, but then the other features of the measuring situation must not be slurred over. Descriptions constitute verbal analogies to measuring manipulation. However, generalizing and abstracting must not be carried so far as to allow the equating of linear measurement with the measurement of energy, of strength of materials, and of other processes leading to coefficients of expansion, torques, etc.

Thus, when describing measuring situations, it becomes illicit abstraction to overstress the relational factors, so that arithmetic becomes the center and the model. Events are not arithmetic, though arithmetical operations are events. Conventional descriptions of measurement carry relations far beyond actual measurement situations.

The basic point here may be formulated as that oft-repeated warning not to absorb events in descriptions. When quantum mechanical measurements are under consideration the question whether we are dealing with waves or particles suggests that, unlike ordinary physical descriptions made with direct reference to space and time, it is now expedient to resort to the relatively more constructional description in terms of probabilities.[11]

MEASUREMENT: CONSTRUCTION AND OBSERVATION

Problems of construction and observation have become intensified in the scientific measurement situation as a consequence of the evolution of relativity and quantum physics.

Bohr puts the matter concisely. Einstein's relativistic emphasis that:

Every observation or measurement ultimately rests on the coincidence of two independent events at the same space-time point[12]

[11] Einstein and Infeld, Evolution, p. 308f.
[12] Atomic, p. 53f.; also see, p. 97f.

he thinks conflicts with the findings of atomic research showing an interaction of object and measuring instrument:

An independent reality in the ordinary physical sense can neither be ascribed to the phenomena nor to the agencies of observation.[13]

Hence the question has been posed whether measurement in general does not involve a constructive operation creating both the measurement and thing measured.[14] This has led to the juxtaposition of metaphysical and physical problems, and to the physicist's occupation with questions concerning objectivity and reality. A thorough clarification of the nature of observation and construction is called for, with respect not only to measurement but to scientific work in general.

Observation. In its lowest terms observing consists of performing a differential response to something existing independently of the immediate field. The simplest observation involves no instrumental aid (microscope, telescope), although it may require assuming a facilitating position with regard to the object, as in modifying illumination conditions or removing something intervening between the observer and the object. To observe more complex things necessitates instrumental aid, but certainly in the case of macroscopic fields no question arises as to the independent existence of the observed. As Jordan remarks:

We *know* of the planet Pluto only because we possess astronomical observatories; but we believe Pluto to have existed already in the time of homo neandertalensis.[15]

Surely, no one with a "mind" undebauched by Berkeleyan theology believes that Leeuwenhoeck created his animalcules just because he was able to magnify them to 270 times their size. It is a strange circumstance of scientific thought that writers seem to adopt creative epistemology as though they believed that Herschel and Galle are responsible for the existence of Uranus and Neptune, or that Ritter and Herschel created ultraviolet and infrared radiation respectively.

At the bottom of the modern physicist's difficulties with quantum measurements lies his sensationistic-psychological view. Observa-

[13] Ibid., p. 54.
[14] Einstein, Reply, p. 669.
[15] Process, p. 271.

tion as an operation he carries back to sensations. Accordingly, when he can not assume the presence of sensations he questions the existence of events. The literature on quantum mechanics testifies to the difficulties the psychistic view has injected into the problems of cause, scientific objectivity, and reality in physics.

Modern objective psychology allows nowhere for the theory that observation consumes the thing observed. No matter how indirect and remote the act of observation may be from the observed object, the interbehavior is always the rock upon which all descriptions and interpretations are founded. It may be helpful in illustrating this point to indicate a continuum of varying observational interbehaviors.

In the case of macroscopic physics, the existential independence of observed objects need never be questioned. But these objects may be bound up with observation. Objects as perceived are interdependent with the act of perceiving. The perceptive act, however, does not create the perceived object. The psychologist is also concerned with such independent objects as acts of persons—for example, assertions which linguistically produce objects—and with other no less independent objects once they are created, such as the products of assertions—phlogiston, ether, and caloric. Though such things exist only as human inventions they often constitute objects in cultural situations as things talked about or believed in. What is required is to distinguish (a) things whose existence is independent of human behavior but which come to be known, (b) things in knowing relations, and (c) things existing only by human construction.

Construction. Scientific construction consists basically of descriptions or reports of what occurred during observational contacts with events. To record or describe an event by constructing a protocol is to create an index or representation of it. How simple or complex the construction is depends upon the simplicity or complexity of the events treated, the ease or difficulty of getting into contact with things, and the type of interpretation needed. By interpretation is meant, of course, the interrelation of present events with others observed at various previous or contemporaneous periods.

It follows that the measurement problems of modern physics demand more complicated construction than the descriptions of classical mechanics, though the differences are only differences of degree, not of kind. Many of the difficulties which physicists experience with relativity and quanta-measurement problems are traceable to the attempt to treat atomic and electronic events on the same plan as macroscopic events.[16] Obviously, measurements in modern physics call for more spontaneous and original constructions. New and bolder forms of mathematical equations are required. The situation must be clearly faced that microscopic events are less easily approachable, less easily observed. Still, the scientific work and the systems built are directly continuous with each other.

Quantum measurements provide no occasion for the illicit epistemology and ontology with which physicists have recently been struggling. Nothing in the history of atomic physics lends countenance to the confusion of authentic construction with any sort of mysticism. The fact that knowledge concerning energy involves intricate operations upon the type and quantity of energy provides no warrant for assuming that the existence of energy depends upon anything the operator does. The operator's most effective means of controlling energy changes and directing their distribution consist of his interbehavior with events.

In the interest of clarity we must sharply differentiate our view of construction from that of psychistically-oriented writers like Morgan, Pearson, and Margenau. A construct for Morgan and Pearson consists of present and stored sense impressions ("sensations"). These constructs constitute external objects—that is, things known as compared with knowing, mind, or consciousness. Constructs or external objects are projected from consciousness to make up the real world.[17]

Margenau's construct differs from the Morgan-Pearson type in that it includes, besides sense material, also some factors like the Kantian categories—for example, the property of permanence or continuity of existence.[18] Pearson's constructs belong to Humian phenomenological metaphysics, while Margenau's stem from Kant's transcendental realism. Both of these constructs are worlds apart from the descriptive and interpretative products of workers who derive constructs from observational, experimental, and mensurative contacts with the things about which they construct.

[16] Loeb and Adams, Development, p. 627; Menzel and Layzer, Physical, p. 304.
[17] Pearson, Grammar, pp. 40-42, 58, 67f., et passim.
[18] Reality, p. 301; see also Bentley, Physicists.

All constructs pertaining to nonscientific and scientific description and interpretation are built up from such contacts. Thus, "sensations," "sense impressions," and "sense data" are constructed on the basis of contacts with the primarily qualitative characteristics of things, whereas constructs like cause, permanence, and relation arise from more direct contact with relational properties.

We repeat: The retention by writers on quantum measurement of psychistic psychology leads them into an unnecessary and troublesome entanglement with metaphysics. In the following sections we examine this issue with respect to causation, objectivity, and reality.

MEASUREMENT AND CAUSE

Bohr writes:

Causality may be considered as a mode of perception by which we reduce our sense impressions to order.[19]

This Kantian view goes contrary to the observer's actual operations with stimulus objects. Cause is not a mental or subjective principle which unifies psychic qualities to form objects. We find no basis in any fact for such a construction. What observed facts show are individuals operating upon things directly or indirectly. Causal description results from the activity of analyzing events in order to discover or construct a law which refers to the organization or interrelation of the component factors in a field (p. 157f.).

In a similar manner Einstein,[20] who is closer than Bohr[21] to the position that scientific work constitutes contacts with originally independent events, proceeds valiantly on the level of concrete interaction with things, but in the end comes back to impressions.[22]

And so we have the unusual paradox that measurement, which is regarded as so powerful a criterion of precision and validity, brings mysticism into science. At once we must differentiate conclusions concerning free will, indeterminism, vitalism, and other supernaturalistic matters from more legitimate questions concerning the limits of observation and construction. Bohr[23] has indicated

[19] Atomic, p. 116f.
[20] Einstein, Podolsky, Rosen, Can quantum-mechanical.
[21] Bohr, Can quantum-mechanical.
[22] See, Einstein and Infeld, Evolution, p. 310f; Einstein, Reply, Physics, et passim.
[23] Causality.

his recoil from the former problems. But even the more modest involvement with indeterminacies maintains a too-close attachment of science to historical philosophy. What is determinism? The proper answer is suggested by the entire scientific enterprise. The event with which the scientist begins may consist of closely interbehaving factors which he measures and modifies in order to reach descriptions and laws.

No inconsiderable portion of a scientist's activity must be devoted to the elimination of wrong views and badly constructed or unverifiable hypotheses. Many initial problems center in alleged events . To sum up: In quantum measurements the analogical procedures based upon classical mechanics turn out to be unsuitable. As we concluded in our study of causation, the creative doctrine must be discarded in favor of sets of factors in specific fields. This view makes useless any question of indeterminism (172f.).

MEASUREMENT AND OBJECTIVITY

In a similar way the physicist's psychistic premises have brought the problem of objectivity into the quantum-measurement domain by leading to the confusion in different measurement situations of (a) interbehavior with things, (b) visual reactions to things, and (c) the presence of "sensations."

Quantum-mechanical situations obviously present great mensurational difficulty. First, there is the inherent complexity of the situation itself. It has been suggested that such difficulty stems at least in part from an ineptness in adjusting from the technique of classical or material mechanics to that of quantum or energy mechanics. As a consequence of this lag physicists have inferred that by comparison with classical situations there is something irrational and unreal in quantum mechanics. Because in classical mechanics the measuring system could be set up with a looser interrelation of objects, of space-time coordinates, and of instruments, it appeared that the tight interrelation of factors in an energy system made the thing measured inseparable from the measuring apparatus and even from the measurer.

The question has thus been raised whether the data are objective or exist only in the process. Physicists have indicated their belief that a tree or a wave length is a construct or a mental creation.[24] A flower in Berkeleyan fashion is blue only when it is perceived, and in general there is no difference between the world and the knowledge of it.[25] Clearly, on this basis one may either affirm or deny the existence of subatomic events genuinely or allegedly not amenable to accurate estimation.

It is only the psychistic tradition which stands in the way of describing quantum-measuring conditions as they are actually encountered.[26] Once metaphysical constructions are rejected such historical questions as subject-object and reality-illusion will not be dragged into experimental science. Foremost in the situation will be the facts of constructing hypotheses and theories, mathematical or nonmathematical, as the result of interbehavior with things. A measuring problem on this basis has nothing to do with an existence or objectivity problem. The scientist merely has to exert himself to the utmost to discover a means of obtaining the increased precision of knowledge concerning, for example, an electron's simultaneous momentum and position. Such technical difficulties require no new theory of knowledge, no new cognitive principles.

Why should we introduce into any measuring situation, even the most difficult one of quantum mechanics, any occult and spurious factor such as an ego? Despite the futility of dabbling in psychics, atomic and quantum physicists indulge heavily in such theoretical excesses as confounding a scientific observer with (1) an ego observing its brain or retina, (2) a measuring instrument, or (3) the thing with which the ego is interacting.[27]

MEASUREMENT AND REALITY

Scientists accustomed to thinking of themselves as safely protected from the vagaries of metaphysics by the impenetrable curtain of measurement found their complacency shattered by the evolution of quantum mechanics. After long entertaining the dogmas that science is measurement and that physics, because built upon mensurational operations, is the primary science, they have had to face the two following propositions:

[24] Margenau, Reality, p. 294.
[25] Ibid., p. 288; see also Lenzen, Concepts.
[26] See Menzel-Layzer, Physical; Frank, Foundations.
[27] von Neumann, Mathematische, p. 223f.

P(Measurement can not be regarded as operations performed upon isolated things possessing unique autonomous properties).

P(To measure is to create the thing measured).

The most ironical thing about the injection of metaphysics into physics is that there is no basis for it whatsoever. That it occurred is evidence enough that physicists have lacked an objective psychological viewpoint. Consider for a moment what precipitated the difficulty. In terms of measurement or other direct description we can not interpret a photon as an individual particle moving, say, from the sun to the earth. It is impossible to state the precise position and momentum of isolated light particles, as in a classical mechanical system. As Frank says:

A particle by itself without the description of the whole experimental setup is not a physical reality.[28]

Now from an objective psychological standpoint there is no occasion for physicists to be disturbed by the interdependence of things measured and the measuring apparatus, and by the alleged mutual interference of the two. This alleged interference is only relative. In a genuine sense every measurement disturbs the system being measured.[29] In other words, a measuring situation constitutes a different system from the nonmeasuring situation. In the former the object measured does not remain independent of the measuring instrument and the conditions required for the mensurational operations. In the nonmeasuring system the object in question does remain independent of the same list of factors. All technical or precise observation requires the isolation or organization of a system. If one describes the observer's manipulations as interferences, measurement certainly intensifies them. Other interferences are also inevitable. Scale readings must be averaged and calculated; this fact involves considerable transformation.

When we deal with an observer's interbehavior with things, no reality question obtrudes itself into any measuring situation. If it is not possible, as in classical mechanics, to set up a geometric map locating the position and motion of a particle, one can invoke the prediction criterion as proposed by Einstein, Podolsky, and Rosen:

---

[28] Foundations, p. 48.
[29] Menzel-Leyzer, Physical, p. 323; Grimsehl, Textbook, vol. V, p. 275.

If, without in any way disturbing a system, we can predict with certainty (i.e. with probability equal to unity) the value of a physical quantity, then there exists an element of physical reality corresponding to this physical quantity.[30]

The prediction criterion admittedly involves considerable construction, but even if it is not formulated in terms of certainty it emphasizes the continuity of the measurer's contact with events. The measuring system may require the employment of various correspondences; momentum and position may have to be separately determined, but at no point does any metaphysical reality problem come in.

Nor need the observer's and measurer's participation in the measuring system be regarded as introducing a subjective factor. Since objective psychology has liquidated all psychics, the distinction between subjective and objective involves no scientifically detrimental factors. To demonstrate the position or momentum of a subatomic or a light particle it may be necessary for the physicist to arrange a diaphragm either to mark the point passed by the light or the momentum it imparts. All such operations are continuous with those necessary to (a) produce events such as the presence or absence of spectra, electronic-protonic discharges, heat, or (b) accelerate events, as in supplying catalysts or operating instruments like cyclotrons, betatrons, etc.

Only a psychistic background makes physicists wary of the observer's place in the occurrence of a measuring event. In no way does the worker's participation introduce a factor of unreality. There is nothing occult about an observer or about anything he can possibly do. Whether, and how far, events involve such participation are matters concerning specific situations. Also, the reduction of such participation whenever desirable is the problem and challenge of the scientific job.

A number of writers have correctly pointed out that what seems to precipitate reality questions in quantum mechanics is the fact that the visual or pictorial form of descriptive model is lacking.[31] Like the other difficulties, this, too, is based on the traditional psychological doctrine of internal sense qualities and sense data. His-

[30] Can quantum-mechanical, p. 777.
[31] Bohr, Causality; Kaiser, Consequences; Berenda, Note.

torically the question has centered around the relationship of an equation with sensory quality. Because of Mach's prominence in such matters we refer to his views concerning the relation both of mathematical functions and of atoms to "experience."

As an adherent of the Berkeley-Hume-Mill sensation tradition Mach clung to elements or sensations as the only realities. Mathematical functions or equations, accordingly, he regarded as a sort of language or auxiliary mental artifice for facilitating the "mental" reproduction of facts.

Although we represent vibrations by the harmonic formula, the phenomena of cooling by exponentials, falls by squares of times, etc., no one will fancy that vibrations *in themselves* have anything to do with the circular functions, or the motion of falling bodies with squares.[32]

It is this view probably that is reflected in Einstein's remark about the discrepancy between mathematical exactness and reality.[33]

That the sensationistic view prevents a proper attitude toward the relation of construction and observation is apparent from Mach's attitude toward atoms and the atomic theory of his time. Ruark and Urey recount the dramatic scene when Mach rose up after Boltzmann's lecture on molecules to say: "You do not know that molecules exist."[34] Mach rejected the atomic theory because atoms "cannot be perceived by the senses."[35] With all his well-intentioned effort to banish metaphysics from physics he accomplished the opposite. Though Mach retreated from his anti-atomic position, he could not be expected in his time to realize that "sensations," "experience," and "intuitive" items are constructs. Moreover, as we have repeatedly pointed out, they are not helpful in any science, but simply reflect historical inventions in nonscientific situations.[36]

The view held by both physicists and psychologists that "sensations" and "immediate experiences" are basic processes runs back to spiritistic metaphysics which interpreted perception as a process by which a soul or ego creates things, or somehow intuits

[32] Science, p. 492.
[33] Chap. 13, p. 6.
[34] Atoms, p. 1.
[35] Science, p. 492.
[36] See chap. 6.

or absorbs them. Current objective psychology has left far behind all questions related to subject and object, or how mind or thought can be connected with extension and matter. Perception we treat as complex interbehavior between organisms and things. Both organisms and things become behaviorally modified through coordinate conditions surrounding their successive contacts.[37] The history of these contacts viewed as an evolution in a set of situations is the basic feature of objective perception theory. Instead of on a theological basis, the objective view is grounded on the observation of the cultural evolution of the organism's behavior.

At once we obviate all metaphysical questions in quantum mechanics, such as the nature of unobserved objects. This problem is formulated as: "How do things look when we do not look at them,"[38] and is considered in the context of the disturbance of an object while it is being measured. Writers who do not regard such problems as "nonsense," on the ground that perceived objects are not created by the perceiving act or observation,[39] demonstrate the insidious domination of cultural presuppositions over the most competent philosophers of science. Such writers may declare that quantum mechanics, like all other parts of physics, deals with nothing but relations between physical things, and further that all its statements can be made without reference to an observer;[40] still they can not move away from the cultural institution concerning "the existence of an external world."[41]

Such views bypass the fact that all descriptions and interpretations originate in contacts of organisms and objects. From such contacts we derive our information concerning the properties of things and our changing responses to them. These contacts constitute an enormous history, which begins at a time when organisms and objects are autonomous and independent; it continues through a series of reciprocal behavior changes which are constantly being conditioned by circumstances in the interbehavioral field.

The demand that reality in quantum mechanics be established on the basis of experiments and measurements requires no justifi-

---

[37] Kantor, Principles, chap. 9, Survey, chap. 10.
[38] Reichenbach, Philosophic, p. 18.
[39] Ibid.
[40] Ibid.
[41] Reichenbach, Experience.

cation. Experiment and measurement constitute contacts with things; every theory designed to describe those things and predict how they will act must correspond to them.

Decisive for the solution of the reality problem in quantum mechanics is the fact that we are studying the scientist's interbehavior with radiant electromagnetic or electronic energy. Hence all energy values as the products of measuring operations are derived from the events investigated. The prominence of constructional activity in atomic measuring situations should not allow us to lose sight of the events which originally promote the work and which naturally must be represented in the product.

METROLOGY AND LOGIC

Students of the logic and methodology of science appreciate in some degree that measuring enterprises constitute system building. Also, scientists interested in measurement theory have expertly discussed such system components as units, scales, standards, operational techniques, and homogeneity of things measured, in addition to the relation of all these items to their environing framework. Nevertheless, their adherence to formal logic prevents logicians from integrating measurement systems and metrological science with systemology as the general science of logic—that is, system-building theory. We demonstrate this point by considering the reflections of two writers who are sympathetic to metrological and systemological integration, but who do not differentiate between (1) systems of operations upon things and (2) systems of statements or descriptions of those operations.

The first of the two attempts to connect measurement with formal logic is based upon an analysis of measurement into three parts: (a) formal statements, in the sense of numbers in serial or other relations, (b) the measurable experience (or content), and (c) a dictionary of interpretative statements in which the items of (b) are so defined as to exhibit the logical properties of the group in (a). By means of this dictionary the numbers of (a) are assigned to the contents of (b).[42]

But now it turns out that since the dictionary consists of sentences analyzable into (a) logical forms, (b) referring contents, and (c) the assignment of these contents to the variables of the logical

[42] Ballard, Paradox.

forms, a second dictionary is required. With this type of analysis the regress continues endlessly. Measurement is thus inflicted with a serious paradox.[43]

Comment: The paradox is inherent only in the logical theory according to which logic is made into an extraneous system constructed at best to serve a describing or symbolizing function. Consider the enormous contrast with the interbehavioral view according to which logic constitutes an enterprise of constructing systems for ascertaining the values of things and properties. The description of measurement on the formal basis does not even allow for such concrete operations as are required for number-assigning. A measurement is defined as a proposition stating an assignment of numbers to objects, or classes of objects, discriminated in experience.[44] Here is the typical conversion of interbehavior into words.

Our second example has its source in the quantum-mechanics field. In consonance with the common belief that quantum mechanical events present altogether different observational and mensurational problems from the classical mechanical type, it is assumed that quantum mechanics must be less concerned with the structure of the physical world than with the structure of the language in which that world is described.[45] Thus questions concerning the existence of physical entities are transformed into questions concerning the meaning of propositions (language).

Because of the limited measurability of quantum events, and their alleged anomalous character, they can only be described by means of uniquely descriptive languages. The corpuscle language and the wave language each is restricted to some phase of quantum action, and thus is deficient. The neutral language describes what are called interphenomena consisting of energy occurrences when there are no coincidental collisions with matter resulting in a record by a Geiger counter, a photographic film, or a cloud-chamber track. An example is a photon travelling between its source and point of collision.[46]

Now, it is argued that since quantum mechanics can not escape the indeterminacy principle, its language can not be patterned on a

---

[43] Ibid.
[44] Ibid., p. 134.
[45] Reichenbach, Philosophic, p. 136ff.
[46] Ibid., p. 21.

two-valued logic which comports with propositions built on a true-false dichotomy. Instead resort must be had to a probability logic with at least three values, including the indeterminacy value.

Comment: Aside from the issue whether such differences exist between the macroscopic and microscopic fields as to necessitate different types of observation and measurement, some general logical questions come to the surface. In the first place, why attempt to confine scientific situations in the straightjacket of a formalistic system? Not even a three- or n-valued logic can do justice to all mensurational problems. Again, why assume that logic consists of setting up a *language?* To be correct, we ought to say we set up a large number of descriptive systems to deal with the many features of the quantum situation. And what about the motivation for quantum-mechanics system building? Is the logician working with a view to a possible cooperation with the physicist in solving some problem, or is he indulging in arbitrary constructionism? In the latter case one must admit at once the irrelevance of his activity. One can not in either case escape the multiplicity and complexity of the specific conditions involved.

CHAPTER XXV

SYSTEM BUILDING AND METALOGIC

The Continuity of Human Behavior

BOTH psychology and logic point to a direct line connecting system building and logical theory. This continuity extends even beyond these limits. Below system building are interbehaviors of persons with stimulus objects involving only partial structuring of things, as well as completely nonorganizing behavior. Above systemology lies the metalogical domain—the source of the system builder's presuppositions and motivations.

Metalogic, notice, is not confined to the technical definitions and postulates connected with formal system construction.[1] It is concerned also with the background of systems, with logical applications and possible consequences of logical work. Briefly, metalogic comprises the basic philosophy of the logical theorist. It can be no better described than:

. . . an exploration of the periphery of logic, the relations of logic to the rest of the universe, the philosophical presuppositions which give logic its meaning, and the applications which give it importance.[2]

At once we ask: What kind of philosophy? What kind of universe? And precisely how is logic related to both?

We renounce, of course, the absolutistic and supramundane philosophy revealed in the following:

Formal logic is the heart of philosophy precisely because the subject matter of logic is the formal aspect of all being, an aspect not only of objects and events in time and space, but equally of nonspatial and nontemporal relations of objects.[3]

Our universe consists of nothing but our natural habitat plus civilizational artifacts. Logic, then, is inevitably set within the spatio-temporal milieux of individuals and cultural groups. All transcendent and mystical systems built for escapist and sentimental reasons exist only within these behavioral limits.

[1] See p. 93.
[2] Cohen, Preface, p. xi.
[3] Op. cit., p. x.

Nor can we assume that logic is the heart of philosophy. Revealed here is the presupposition that philosophy delivers a complete and fixed cosmic system and that logic is exclusively an instrument for constructing the system. However, the study of philosophizing behavior discloses no necessity for building such a philosophical system. Again, if we reject such cosmic philosophy, logic takes on a different aspect. Throughout this treatise we have emphasized that logic constitutes a concrete kind of work resulting in specific system products. Logic belongs to every department of human behavior. Moreover, though system building is exceedingly important for effective adaptation to life conditions, logical behavior is still only one type of behavior, systems but one kind of behavioral product.

The application of logic brings up another important issue. If logic is not a single inclusive entity which is profitably exploited by being applied to all types of situations, it loses its key or dominant character. Logic pervades all human situations precisely because it constitutes system-building behavior complementary to other sorts.

Logicians who find our philosophical presuppositions too narrow because restricted to human behavior and to the human scene can not escape the fact that their dissatisfaction, after all, can only have significance within such a boundary. What they object to are restrictions placed on their invention of transcendent systems. But, surely, to overlook the continuity of interbehavior with one's natural and cultural environs when constructing a system of universals, when inventing nonspatial and nontemporal objects, and when creating a transcendental universe or logos is to prevent logic from becoming a datum for study. Interbehavioral continuity alone makes logical study vital and urgent.

METALOGIC AND LOGICAL PRACTICE

The interplay of philosophical presuppositions and system-building practice provides a treasury of source material for observing and evaluating system-building behavior. Transcendent systems are based on non-naturalistic philosophical presuppositions. Naturalistic systems are constructed from specific and concrete materials. But are not all systems, both transcendent and naturalistic, products developed by particular persons having particular backgrounds and interests? Not the least important advantage of keeping logic exclusively within the interbehavioral range is the restraint it places on irresponsible system construction. Thus in the system builder's life conditions we have a touchstone for evaluating his system. From the standpoint of logic as a tangible pervasive discipline we consider the potentialities and limitations of logic on three levels: (A) affairs of everyday life, (B) science, and (C) philosophy.

A. *Logic and Living*

System as order or structure in everyday situations makes for perspective and convenience; it aids in appreciating relationships, fitness, and cogency. Such factors are basic for orderly and effective adaptation to a vast variety of things and situations. Even the child very early in life begins to systemize his reactions with respect to the objects and persons about him. Elementary as such structuring of behavior is at this level it nonetheless is continuous with logical system. Order and system are also definite aids in all effective thinking, judging, reasoning, and debating behavior. The fact that systemizing things is a prerequisite for achieving proof, inference, and prediction, and for gaining self-assurance and securing conviction means that logic becomes an intimate part of our daily-life situations.

Unfortunately our innumerable system-building operations are frequently overshadowed by finished structural products handed down as cultural heritages—for example, the syllogism. The basis for the syllogism's appeal as the model of reasoning lies in its systemic properties. The perfect system is the circle without corners or loose ends. What is fitted into it is uniquely localized and firmly fixed. Of course, to achieve perfect systemization one has to resort to an emptying and formalizing procedure. System, however, should not be confused with the empty form, as has traditionally been done.

One of the most important functions of logic in everyday activities is that it enables us to separate (a) systems of things from (b) systems which are sheerly verbal. Systems of things are of two types: (1) those existing *in rerum natura* without human or other animal agency and (2) those previously structured through an organism's contrivance. Purely verbal systems include linguistic descriptions of things howsoever fashioned. The most marked contrast between (a) and (b) types of system arises when the latter consists of word structures which do not correspond to existing objects.

To be able to differentiate between (1) acts, (2) objects acted upon, and (3) products of action is to achieve considerable orientational power. It likewise does away with the perennial problem of *knower* and *known*. Knowing is interbehavior with (a) natural things, (b) contrived things, and (c) statements concerning things actually or allegedly existing. Interbehavioral logic is useful in finding one's way among these various situations.

Similarly, the system-building view of logic is of use in clarifying traditional fallacies. For the most part these fallacies concern improper or incomplete systems. The parts do not hold together, as in the fallacy of the consequent or *non sequitur*, or the system is not rounded out—that is, it is left incomplete, as in the classical *petitio principii* illustration.

B. *Logic and Science*

System-building finds its most significant scope in the scientific domain. Even though science is not merely an enterprise of systemization, classification and organization are important features of scientific work. Here we recall Poincaré's classic allusion to science as essentially systemization.

Science is built up with facts, as a house is with stones. But a collection of facts is no more a science than a heap of stones is a house.[4]

The importance of system and order in science constitutes the *raison d'etre* of the methodistic logics. Indeed, classical inductive logics are mainly sets of critical suggestions concerning scientific systematics—prescriptions how grand-scale systems should be built.

Overemphasis of system, however, may be detrimental to scientific work. The task of science, after all, is to resolve problems concerning events. Can these events be reduced to generalized happenings? Can single methods be devised to solve scientific issues? How often the history of science reveals the fallacy of reducing many things to one, a reduction made in order to achieve universality. Has it helped, for instance, to reduce astronomy and

[4] Foundations, p. 127.

physics to mechanics, mechanics to geometry?[5] The neatness and order obtained by single comprehensive systems hardly do justice to the events for the investigation of which science exists.

The advancement of knowledge and the success of investigation point effectively to the futility of totalitarian systems. Generalized systems restrict research, repress the claim of events for the attention of scientific workers. Systemization must be instrumental to the work of science. But this means limiting systems, keeping them down to specific data and problems. Certainly the closer one stays to actual events the more specific systems will be. Conversely, the more comprehensive systems are, the more they are involved with formulae and words, with linguistic or symbolic elements.[6]

The growth of geometry, for instance, reduces the self-contained and universal Euclidean system to *one* of the systems. Geometries are multiplied by a large factor. The development of knowledge concerning heat, electricity, and optics increases the number of scientific systems. The rise of biology, geology, and psychology calls for far more systems than were allowed by those who stressed the system maker's constructive products to the exclusion of the materials conditioning his system-building work.

An instructive example of an all-encompassing system is furnished by an eminent physicist who wants to reach out to the living cell and "life," to weld together into a whole the sum-total of all that is known. Schrödinger writes:

> We have inherited from our forefathers the keen longing for unified, all-embracing knowledge. The very name given to the highest institutions of learning reminds us, that from antiquity and throughout many centuries the *universal* aspect has been the only one to be given full credit.[7]

The outcome is that each individual is God, a result which universalists want and believe in, but have not the courage to proclaim. Schrödinger himself shrinks from this final conclusion and escapes by adopting the Indian Athman-Brahman doctrine—

[5] Cf. Nagel, Meaning.
[6] Interesting here is Reichenbach's proposal. "Instead of speaking of the structure of the physical world, we may consider the structure of the languages in which this world can be described; such analysis expresses the structure of the world indirectly, but in a more precise way." Philosophic, p. 177.
[7] What is Life? p. vii.

namely, the personal self equals the omnipresent, all-compre-hending eternal self.[8]

The product is no more instructive than the procedure leading to it, since it is a scientist who turns the wheels. The classical regu-larities of nature are statistical. But even the genes of biology, which, on this basis, can not be regarded as stable because of the fewness of the atoms in their composition, can be reduced to deter-ministic mechanisms by a quantum theory of molecular structure. Admittedly this is an extreme example. But even if Schrödinger's freedom of creation is not completely attained by other univer-salists, even if comprehensiveness of achievement is not aspired to by other scientists, the difference is one of degree only. When the urge to universalization is present, an improper emphasis is somehow impressed upon investigation. At the least, the specificity of the job, the influence of data, and the tentative and probable characteristics of the work done are minimized. The present example therefore recommends itself as a model precisely because it shows us the power of verbal and imaginative behavior to create the appearance of exalted system.

Scientific system building has definite boundaries. Astronomy, which is potentially limitless in its scale, stops short on the basis of its observational and calculative materials. Though a figure like 3,500,000,000 light years as an estimate of the diameter of the universe lacks familiarity, it is still well within the range of arith-metical operations. Similarly, the science of thermodynamics speci-fies definite limits to the generalizations it establishes. The first law reminds us of the boundaries placed upon complex and intense processes; there are optimal probabilities to be observed. The second law limits the temporal interval of the energy interchanges, such that perpetual motion is ruled out. And if we allow Nernst's heat theorem[9] to pose as the third law, it asserts the impossibility of attaining absolute zero by any process whatsoever.[10] As another example of scientific limitation and checking we may mention the Le Chatelier principle, as formulated by Braun.

Every process caused by an external influence or by a primary proc-ess in a system takes place in such a direction that it tends to oppose

[8] Ibid., p. 88.
[9] New Heat Theorem.
[10] See Grimsehl, Textbook, vol. II, p. 150f.

the alteration of the system produced by the external influence or primary process.[11]

The state of equilibrium which the Le Chatelier principle indicates is a warning supplied by natural events against arbitrary extrapolations of observed results.

If scientific systems are to be significant, limitations must also be placed upon their unit constructs. To be valid and workable, hierarchies of constructs must plainly show their derivation from events and from observation of the latter. We plainly see the work of the individual abstractor and system builder throughout the continuum of word descriptions, pointer records, averages and other statistical constructs, and formulae and equations.

Constructing an External World

An interesting system-building convention harbored by philosophically inclined scientists concerns the creation of an external world. How created and from what? From "sensations," is the traditional answer:

In the first instance the elements of the physical order are given in sensation. In physical science one constructs the fundamental concepts of the things, characters and processes revealed by sensation. A physical theory is the systematic representation of certain characters of the physical order. The goal of physical science is a unitary system of physical theory.[12]

What seems to be overlooked is that "sensations" are constructs, as indeed are all descriptions and interpretations of things. Strange that scientists wish to create objects of physics out of products previously constructed by traditional theology and psychology. Sensation constructs are in no sense derived from any investigation; they are therefore not scientific constructs. If physics, psychology, or any other science is to produce constructs with descriptive and predictive value, it must create them on the basis of relevant contacts with things.

The notion of constructing a world is utterly misleading. Actually what is constructed is a description of events and of the operation of things, such as the interrelations of masses—planets, terrestrial objects, and so on. Such a large-scale system as our objective world goes far beyond the scientist's scope or competence. The primary objection to such ungoverned and futile system building is that the scientist neglects his proper work. What he is qualified to do is to investigate events and the problems they suggest. Whatever system he builds in his capacity of scientist can be done only on the basis of such investigation. Going beyond this work he assumes a role other than scientist.

Evidence is not lacking that all notions of the construction of a world[13] are based upon a confusion of constructs with the things stimulating the construction. Descriptions are confounded with events described, quite in the Berkeleyan obfuscation tradition. That the descriptions are made in terms of words, sentences, mathematical or logical symbols instead of in terms of sensations constitutes no palliation.

C. *Logic and Philosophy*

The philosophic level of logical activity is essentially that of systems. Philosophers consider their work as, above all, the building of knowledge or world structures. For this reason logic is regarded as intrinsically a philosophical enterprise or as identical with all philosophy.[14]

What constitutes a philosophical system? For the most part, systems constructed on a philosophical level are as expansive as speculative imagination can make them. A considerable portion of traditional philosophy consists of method systems to transcend the actual world. That these systems turn out to be fragile collocations of words is a pathetic fact of philosophical history.

Methodistically inclined builders of philosophic systems seek to construct absolute techniques for achieving equally absolute certainty; they aim to give laws to nature or to develop omnipotent reason. Thus they create powers to extend their own powers. By comparison the ontologists attempt to achieve some transexperiential realm, an elysium to which they can escape from the actual world, and thereby transform every observable thing according to a scale of ultimate values. In some form or other all content

---

[13] Russell, External World; Reichenbach, Experience.
[14] Russell, Mysticism, p. 111f.

philosophies aim to prove there is a god, that man is free and at least partially immortal.

Even sceptical philosophers do not wholly relinquish commerce with such supramundane inventions. Although they question the work and achievement of their opponents, they fail to touch the nerve of the difficulty—namely, to provide an adequate basis for checking such extravagant performances.

TOWERS AND SYSTEMS

Traditional philosophy supports Wilde's *mot* that man does not live by bread alone but by catchwords. He might have added, too, that man the philosopher lives also by building towers. Not only towers of ivory to enable him to withdraw from the affairs of everyday life, but also towers of babel to transcend the concrete world. From this tower:

The free intellect will see as God might see, without a *here* and *now*, without hopes and fears, without the trammels of customary beliefs and traditional prejudices, calmly, dispassionately, in the sole and exclusive desire of knowledge—knowledge as impersonal, as purely contemplative, as it is possible for man to attain. Hence also the free intellect will value more the abstract and universal knowledge into which the accidents of private history do not enter, than the knowledge brought by the senses, and dependent, as such knowledge must be, upon an exclusive and personal point of view and a body whose sense-organs distort as much as they reveal.[15]

The value of philosophy for the tower-dweller is:

. . . through the greatness of the universe which philosophy contemplates, the mind also is rendered great, and becomes capable of that union with the universe which constitutes the highest good.[16]

Doubtless the higher the tower the more pristine the good achieved from union with the universe; also the farther man transcends the world of which he is a part. He neither profits from Antaeus or the biblical tower builders, nor does he consider the lesson implicit in concrete system building.

Tower construction as the unrestricted system building of absolutistic philosophers goes on in reckless disregard of the kind of

[15] Russell, *Problems*, p. 248.
[16] Ibid., p. 250.

acts performed and the means employed. The egoism displayed completely masks the fact that the builder lacks any transcendent powers by which to get beyond himself and his world. Support for the production of such mystic and supernatural systems the absolutist finds in his alleged ideals. Reason, to deserve the name, for most philosophic system builders must be mystical.

Techniques of Unrestricted System Building

Prominent among the techniques of unrestrained system building are (1) obeisance to utterance and (2) projection and fixation of verbal creations.

(1) *Obeisance to Utterance.* More than whimsy is implied in the theory that myths are diseases of utterance. Utterance as reference to things and events constitutes, to begin with, reliable description. But linguistic behavior may easily become unruly even in the presence of fact. References and descriptions are distorted; extrapolations are made way beyond anything observed or legitimately inferred. The end point is to create the *utterness* of the supernatural.

Submission to utterance involves accepting and preserving verbal creations. Upon such behavior depend the power and evil of myth making. Probably the most effective mechanism to preserve the products of verbal creation is argumentation for and against their acceptance.

(2) *Projection and Fixation of Utterance.* By hypostatizing and fixating utterances men establish what they wish or what they blindly draw from the well of folkbelief. In this way the great mysteries of philosophy and religion are created and maintained. Systems are built up without limit in number, without bound in rationality.

Abnegation Motive in Philosophy

A primary condition for the self-expanding exercise of building supramundane systems is renunciation of kinship with concrete things and events. To harp upon a real world beyond the things observed in nature is behavior stemming from primitive theological sources. Discernible, too, in such statements as we have quoted from Russell is the theological view of man's sin and corruption, the devaluation of knowledge "brought by the senses" because dependent upon a "body whose sense-organs distort as much as they reveal." On what ground can anyone favor knowledge verbalized in abstraction from a purely rational source to the original domain of things and events?

It is an eloquent comment upon the hold that ancient theological traditions exert upon modern thought when a writer is compelled to urge an appreciation of the "infinite beauty of our natural world" in support of a naturalistic philosophy.[17]

What is it but a folkway to regard the speculative construction of hypotheses concerning the integration of knowledge as inevitably concerned with supramundane things? Such construction is really centered in the activities of persons as they interbehave with their surroundings.

The Problem of the Inductive System

Ever since David Hume made popular the notion that from past and present data or knowledge we can not deduce any future datum, philosophers have been disturbed by this limitation. Thus has arisen the futile attempt to justify inductive inference. Inductive theory has been dubbed the despair of philosophy;[18] many writers have agonized over it, argued about it, only to leave the problem where it has always been.

The conviction that there is no *a priori* foundation for induction:

. . . will slowly shatter civilized life and thought, to a degree which will make the modernist's loss of confidence in Christian supernaturalism, so often cited as the ultimate in spiritual cataclysms, seem a minor vicissitude.[19]

So writes a philosopher with the anguish of one who is being deprived of a cherished hope. He continues:

To dispute the rational validity of induction, however, is to deny that reason and good-will have a purchase on reality, to deny mind's hope of acclimating itself to any world whatever, natural or supernatural.[20]

---

[17] Lamont, Naturalism, p. 597. Notice Lamont's comparison of the Christian with Chinese and Indian attitudes toward nature. It is suggested that appreciation of nature is a cultural trait.

[18] Whitehead, Science, p. 35.

[19] Williams, Ground, p. 16.

[20] Ibid.

Here is a demand for an all-embracing system capable of enchaining all events occurring and to occur. Is not this craving for cosmic mastery entirely out of harmony with any specific or significant human problem or enterprise?

The assimilation of induction to deduction is circle squaring in reverse. Those who wish to subject concrete events to the absoluteness and imperiousness of *a priori* principles wish to transform the squareness, hence the incompleteness, of the inductive system into the completely rounded-out circle of deduction. Inevitably those concerned with the problem of justifying the inductive principle are dominated by the quest for supernatural knowledge and absolute reason. Though the inductive problem is said to be an issue of science and derived from contact with concrete things, actually those who deal with it do not build systems for scientific purposes.

It is encouraging that even philosophers who are not altogether free from the quest for certainty, and who regard the systems they build as inherent in the nature of things, suggest abandoning the inductive problem.[21] But something more than logical policy is called for. We must take into account the specific system-building enterprise. Whether or not the procedure is inductive or deductive depends upon the kind of materials used.

Statistical Procedures and Absolute Systems

A most interesting metalogical item concerns the absolutistic system builder's assimilation of scientific techniques. So persistent are aprioristic presuppositions and motivations that statistical methods, which can hardly deviate from concrete events, have been invoked to establish absolute systems. Thus the instruments constructed in order to facilitate adjustments to events by predicting their future occurrences are made into tools for extrapolating beyond events and our reactions to them. We can not too strongly object to the fallacious belief that somehow statistical and arithmetical procedures can transform contingent events into absolute things.

Philosophical system builders regard any means as justified if only it helps to attain some absolutistic end. They further their activities by using the intricacies of statistical arithmetic to obscure

[21] Cf. for example, Ambrose, Problem; Will, Problem, Future; Black, Language; Jeffreys, Theory; Bergmann, Comments; Wang, Notes.

plain and definite issues. Accordingly, when we find a logician making use of a statistical or proportional syllogism we must inquire into his presuppositions and motivations, as well as into his procedures. In this way we can understand perfectly the flat failure to achieve knowledge-less knowledge, and also observe the confusion regarding the actual things about which knowledge is desired. *Apriorists* start with the valid principle that predictive propositions are subject to probability calculation; they end with the assertion that induction possesses jurisdiction over all branches of philosophy, as well as over the natural sciences.[22]

Logic and the Plenum

On the whole we have stressed the magnification of the systemizer's appetite and emphasized the checks that should be placed upon his ambitions. There is another and reciprocal impropriety to be avoided—namely, limiting systems to abstractions.

In order to magnify himself and his work the system builder minimizes his world. He stresses simplicity, vacuousness, and quantity. All this in order to reduce the universe to a manageable system by means of signs and symbols.

Paradoxically the emphasis of specific things and operations allows for a more comprehensive system coverage. Obviously more things can be dealt with if systems are made for things and things not reduced to elements of systems.

For logic cosmos is system; it is the organization and ordering of the systemizer's field of interest. But systemizing means creative operations. Systems imply selection, the application of criteria of use or of completeness. Under no circumstances must we lose sight of the operational field. There is always a plenum—a set of events, things, and entities—which can never be exhausted by the structuring operations.

[22] Williams, Ground, p. 202.

BIBLIOGRAPHY

Aiken, H. Notes on the categories of naturalism. *Journal of Philosophy*, 1946, 43, 517-523.

Ambrose, A. The problem of justifying inductive inference. *Journal of Philosophy*, 1947, 44, 253-272.

Ancillon, J. P. F. Doutes sur les bases du calcul des probabilités. In *Mémoires de l'Académie Royale des Sciences et Belles-Lettres*, Classe de Philosophie Spéculative, Berlin, Decker, 1794-1795, 3-32.

Aristotle, The Works of. Translated into English (J. A. Smith and W. D. Ross eds.) vol. I, Oxford, Oxford Univ. Press, 1928.

Avey, A. E. The law of contradiction: its logical status. *Journal of Philosophy*, 1929, 26, 519-526.

Bain, A. Logic: Deductive and Inductive. London, Longmans, 1870.

Ballard, E. G. The paradox of measurement. *Philosophy of Science*, 1949, 16, 134-136.

Balmer, J. J. Notiz über die Spectrallinien des Wasserstoffs. *Annalen der Physik und Chemie*, 1885, 25, 80-87.

Bartlett, R. J. Measurement in psychology. *The Advancement of Science*, 1939-1940, 1, 422-441.

Beck, L. W. Constructions and inferred entities. *Philosophy of Science*, 1950, 17, 74-86.

Becker, O. Mathematische Existenz; Untersuchung zur Logic und Ontologie Mathematischen Phänomene. Halle, Niemeyer, 1927.

Bell, E. T. The Development of Mathematics. New York, McGraw-Hill, 1940.

Benjamin, A. C. Logic of measurement. *Journal of Philosophy*, 1933, 26, 701-710.

Bentley, A. F. Physicists and fairies. *Philosophy of Science*, 1938, 5, 132-165.

Berenda, C. W. A note on quantum theory and metaphysics. *Journal of Philosophy*, 1942, 39, 608-611.

Bergmann, G. Some comments on Carnap's logic of induction. *Philosophy of Science*, 1946, 13, 71-78.

Birkhoff, G. D. Aesthetic Measure. Cambridge, Harvard Univ. Press, 1933.

——— Intuition, reason, and faith in science. *Science*, 1938, 88, 601-609.

Black, M. The Nature of Mathematics: A Critical Survey. New York, Harcourt, Brace, 1935.

——— Language and Philosophy. Ithaca, Cornell Univ. Press, 1949.

Bogoslovsky, B. B. The Technique of Controversy: Principles of Dynamic Logic. New York, Harcourt, Brace, 1928.

Bohr, N. Atomic Theory and the Description of Nature. Cambridge, Cambridge Univ. Press, 1934.

——— Can quantum-mechanical description of physical reality be considered complete? *Physical Review,* 1935, 48, 696-702.

——— Causality and complementarity. *Philosophy of Science,* 1937, 4, 289-298.

Boole, G. An Investigation of the Laws of Thought, on which are Founded the Mathematical Theories of Logic and Probabilities. London, Walton and Maberly, 1854.

Born, M. The Restless Universe. New York, Harper, 1936.

Brewster, D. Memoirs of the Life, Writings, and Discoveries of Sir Isaac Newton. Edinburgh, Murray, 1855, 2 vols.

Bridgman, P. W. Logic of Modern Physics. New York, Macmillan, 1927.

——— Statistical mechanics and the second law of thermodynamics. *Bulletin, American Mathematical Society,* 1932, 38, 225-245.

——— The nature and limitations of cosmical inquiries. *Scientific Monthly,* 1933, 37, 385-397.

——— The Nature of Physical Theory. Princeton, Princeton Univ. Press, 1936.

——— Some general principles of operational analysis. *Psychological Review,* 1945, 52, 246-249.

Broad, C. D. On the relation between induction and probability. *Mind,* 1918, 27, 389-404; 1920, 29, 11-45.

Burks, A. W. Empiricism and vagueness. *Journal of Philosophy,* 1946, 43, 477-486.

Burtt, E. A. Value and existence. *Journal of Philosophy,* 1947, 44, 169-179.

Butler, J. The Analogy of Religion, Natural and Revealed, to the Constitution and Course of Nature. London, Bell, 1878.

Butterbaugh, G. I. A Bibliography of Statistical Quality Control. Seattle, Univ. of Washington Press, 1946.

Campbell, L., and Garnett, W. Life of James Clerk Maxwell. London, Macmillan, 1882.

Campbell, N. R. Physics: The Elements. Cambridge, Cambridge Univ. Press, 1920.

——— An Account of the Principles of Measurement and Calculation. London, Longmans, 1928.

——— Measurement and its importance for philosophy. *Aristotelian Society,* Supplementary vol. XVII, London, Harrison, 1938.

——— Quantitative estimates of sensory events (Final Report). *The Advancement of Science,* 1939-1940, 1, 331-349.

Carmichael, R. C. The Logic of Discovery. Chicago, Open Court, 1930.

Carnap, R. Testability and meaning. *Philosophy of Science,* 1936, 3, 419-471; 1937, 4, 1-40.

——— The two concepts of probability. *Philosophy and Phenomenological Research,* 1945, 5, 513-532.

——— Remarks on induction and truth. *Philosophy and Phenomenological Research,* 1945-1946, 5, 590-602.

———— Probability as a guide to life. *Journal of Philosophy*, 1947, 44, 141-148.

Carus, P. The problem of causality. *Open Court*, 1888, 2, 1200-1204.

Cassirer, E. Substanzbegriff und Functionsbegriff. Berlin, Cassirer, 1910.

Child, A. On the theory of the categories. *Philosophy and Phenomenological Research*, 1947, 7, 316-335.

Churchman, C. W. Probability theory, I, II, III. *Philosophy of Science*, 1945, 12, 147-173.

———— Theory of Experimental Inference. New York, Macmillan, 1948.

———— A materialist theory of measurement. In *Philosophy for the Future* (R. W. Sellars, V. J. McGill, M. Farber eds.) New York, Macmillan, 1949.

Cohen, M. R. Reason and Nature. New York, Harcourt, Brace, 1931.

———— A Preface to Logic. New York, Holt, 1944.

Cohen, M. R., and Nagel, E. An Introduction to Logic and Scientific Method. New York, Harcourt, Brace, 1934.

Comrey, A. L. An operational approach to some problems in psychological measurement. *Psychological Review*, 1950, 57, 217-228.

Costello, H. T. The naturalism of Woodbridge. In *Naturalism and the Human Spirit* (Y. H. Krikorian ed.) New York, Columbia Univ. Press, 1944.

Cournot, A. A. Exposition de la Théorie des Chances et des Probabilités. Paris, Hachette, 1843.

Couturat, L. The principles of logic. In *Encyclopaedia of the Philosophical Sciences*, vol. I, *Logic*, London, Macmillan, 1913.

Crookshank, F. C. The importance of a theory of signs and a critique of language in the study of medicine. In *The Meaning of Meaning* by C. K. Ogden and I. A. Richards, Supplement II, London, Kegan Paul, 1923.

Czuber, E. Warscheinlichkeitsrechnung und ihre Anwendung auf Fehlerausgleichung, Statistik und Lebensversicherung. Vol. I, Leipzig, Teubner, 1903.

Dadourian, H. M. Force in mechanics. *Science*, 1939, 87, 388-389.

Dantzig, T. Number: The Language of Science. New York, Macmillan, 1939.

Darwin, C. G. Logic and probability in physics. *Philosophy of Science*, 1939, 6, 48-64.

Davis, H. T., and Nelson, W. F. C. Elements of Statistics, with Applications to Economic Data. Bloomington, Principia Press, 1935.

Dennes, W. T. The categories of naturalism. *In Naturalism and the Human Spirit* (Y. H. Krikorian ed.) New York, Columbia Univ. Press, 1944.

Descartes, R. See Haldane and Ross.

Dewey, J. Logic: The Theory of Inquiry. New York, Holt, 1938.

Dewey, J., and Bentley, A. F. Definition. *Journal of Philosophy*, 1947, 44, 281-306.

———— Knowing and the Known. Boston, Beacon Press, 1949.

Diels, H. Die Fragmente der Vorsokratiker Griechisch und Deutsch. Berlin, Weidmann, 1922, 3 vols.

Dingle, H. Science and Human Experience. New York, Macmillan, 1932.

———— Through Science to Philosophy. Oxford, Clarendon, 1937.

Dubislav, W. Die Definition. Leipzig, Meiner (3rd. ed.), 1931.

Dubs, H. H. Rational Induction. Chicago, Univ. of Chicago Press, 1930.

———— Definition and its problems. *Philosophical Review*, 1943, 52, 566-577.

Ducasse, C. J. On the nature and the observability of the causal relation. *Journal of Philosophy*, 1926, 23, 57-68.

———— A neglected meaning of probability. *Proceedings, Sixth International Congress of Philosophy*, New York, Longmans, 1927, 343-347.

Eaton, R. M. General Logic: An Introductory Survey. New York, Scribners, 1931.

Eddington, A. S. Space, Time and Gravitation: an Outline of the General Relativity Theory. Cambridge, Cambridge Univ. Press, 1920.

———— The Philosophy of Physical Science. New York, Macmillan, 1939.

Edgeworth, F. Y. Probability. In *Encyclopaedia Britannica,* vol. XXII, New York, Encyclopaedia Britannica, Inc. (13th ed.), 1926.

Einstein, A. Geometrie und Erfahrung, erweiterte Fassung des Festvortrages gehalten an der Preussischen Akademie der Wissenschaften zu Berlin am 27 Januar 1921. Berlin, Springer 1921.

———— The Meaning of Relativity. Princeton, Princeton Univ. Press, 1923.

———— Physics and reality. *Journal of the Franklin Institute*, 1936, 221, 348-382.

———— Autobiographical notes. In *Albert Einstein: Philosopher-Scientist* (P. A. Schilpp ed.) Evanston, Library of Living Philosophers, 1949.

———— Reply to criticisms. In *Albert Einstein: Philosopher-Scientist* (P. A. Schilpp ed.) Evanston, Library of Living Philosophers, 1949.

Einstein, A., and Infeld, L. The Evolution of Physics. New York, Simon and Schuster, 1938.

Einstein, A., Podolsky, B., and Rosen, N. Can quantum-mechanical description of physical reality be considered complete? *Physical Review,* 1935, 47, 777-780.

Ellis, R. L. On the foundations of the theory of probability. *Transactions, Cambridge Philosophical Society,* 1843, 8, 1-6.

Enriques, F. The Historic Development of Logic. (J. Rosenthal trans.) New York, Holt, 1929.

Eve, A. S. Rutherford; Being the Life and Letters of the Rt. Hon. Lord Rutherford, O. M. New York, Macmillan, 1939.

Fairbanks, A. The First Philosophers of Greece. New York, Scribners, 1898.

Faraday, M. Experimental Researches in Chemistry and Physics. London, Taylor and Francis, 1859.

Feigl, H. Operationism and scientific method. *Psychological Review*, 1945, 52, 250-259.

———— Existential hypotheses. *Philosophy of Science*, 1950, 17, 35-62.

Ferguson, A., et al. Quantitative estimates of sensory events. *Report of the British Association for the Advancement of Science*, London, British Association, 1938.

Fisher, R. A. Statistical Methods for Research Workers. London, Oliver and Boyd, 1942.

Fourier, J. B. J. The Analytical Theory of Heat. (A. Freeman trans.) Cambridge, Cambridge Univ. Press, 1878.

Frank, P. Foundations of Physics. In *International Encyclopedia of Unified Science*, vol. I, No. 7, Chicago, Univ. of Chicago Press, 1946.

Frege, F. L. G. Die Grundlagen der Arithmetik, begriffsschriftlich abgeleitet. Vol. I, Jena, Pohle, 1893; vol. II, 1903.

Gauss, C. F. Intensitas vis magneticas terrestris ad mensuram absolutam revocata. In *Werke*, vol. V, Leipzig, Teubner, 1863-1903.

George, W. H. The Scientist in Action: Scientific Study of His Methods. London, Williams and Norgate, 1936.

Ginsburg, B. The finite universe and scientific extrapolation. *Journal of Philosophy*, 1935, 32, 85-92.

Goldenweiser, A. History, Psychology, and Culture. New York, Knopf, 1933.

Gotschalk, D. W. Of the nature and definition of a cause. *Philosophical Review*, 1931, 40, 469-477.

Greenwood, T. Probability. In *The Dictionary of Philosophy* (D. D. Runes ed.) New York, Philosophical Library, 1942.

Grimsehl, E. A Textbook of Physics. (Translated from 7th German edition. L. A. Woodward, ed.) London and Glasgow, Blackie, 1932-1935, 5 vols.

Haldane, E. S. and Ross, G. R. T. (eds.) The Philosophical Work of Descartes. Vol. I, Cambridge, Cambridge Univ. Press, 1911.

Harding, T. S. Science at the tower of Babel. *Philosophy of Science*, 1938, 5, 338-353.

Hardy, G. H. The theory of numbers. *Science*, 1922, 56, 402-405.

von Hartmann, E. Kategorienlehre. Leipzig, Haacke, 1896.

Hawkins, D. Existential and epistemic probability. *Philosophy of Science*, 1943, 10, 255-261.

Heath, T. L. The Thirteen Books of Euclid's Elements. (Translated from the Text of Heiberg with Introduction and Commentary.) Cambridge, Cambridge Univ. Press (2nd ed.), 1926, 3 vols.

Hedrick, E. R. Tendencies in the logic of mathematics. *Science*, 1933, 77, 335-343.

Helmholtz, H. Zählen und Messen. In *Philosophische Aufsätze, Edward Zeller zu seinem fünftzigjährigen Doctor-Jubiläum*, Leipzig, Fues's Verlag (Reisland), 1887.

Hempel, C. G., and Oppenheim, P. A definition of "degree of confirmation." *Philosophy of Science*, 1945, 12, 98-115.

———— Studies in the logic of explanation. *Philosophy of Science*, 1948, 15, 135-175.

Herodotus. History. (G. Rawlinson trans.) New York, Dial Press, 1928.

Hobbes, T. See Molesworth.

Hoffman, J. J. I. Der Pythagorische Lehrsatz mit 32 teils bekannten, teils neuen Beweisen versehen. Mainz, Kupferberg (2nd ed.), 1821.

Hofstadter, A. Causality and necessity. *Journal of Philosophy*, 1949, 56, 257-270.

Horst, P. Measurement, relationship, and correlation. *Journal of Philosophy*, 1932, 29, 631-637.

Houston, W. V. Philosophy of physics. *Science*, 1937, 45, 413-419.

Hume, D. A Treatise on Human Nature. (L. A. Selby-Bigge ed.) Oxford, Clarendon, 1896.

James, W. Principles of Psychology. Vol. I, New York, Holt, 1890-1905.

Jäsche, G. B. Immanuel Kant's Logik. Leipzig, Meiner (3rd ed.), 1920.

Jeffreys, H. Scientific Inference. Cambridge, Cambridge Univ. Press, 1937.

———— Theory of Probability. Oxford, Clarendon (2nd ed.), 1948.

Jevons, W. S. Elementary Lessons in Logic. New York, Macmillan, 1912.

———— Principles of Science. London, Macmillan, 1924.

Johnson, H. M. Pseudomathematics in the mental and social sciences. *American Journal of Psychology*, 1936, 48, 342-351.

Johnson, W. E. Logic. Cambridge, Cambridge Univ. Press, 1921.

Jones, P. C. Kant, Euclid and the non-Euclidians. *Philosophy of Science*, 1946, 13, 137-143.

Jordan, P. On the process of measurement in quantum mechanics. *Philosophy of Science*, 1949, 16, 269-278.

Joseph, H. W. B. An Introduction to Logic. Oxford, Clarendon (2nd ed.), 1916.

Kaiser, C. H. The consequences for metaphysics of quantum mechanics. 1940, 37, 337-348.

Kantor, J. R. Principles of Psychology. New York, Knopf, 1924-26, 2 vols.

———— A Survey of the Science of Psychology. Bloomington, Principia, 1933.

———— An Objective Psychology of Grammar. Blomington, Indiana Univ. Publications, Science Series, no. 1, 1936.

———— The operational principle in the physical and psychological sciences. *Psychological Record*, 1938, 2, 1-32.

———— An interbehavioral analysis of propositions. *Psychological Record*, 1943, 5, 309-339.

———— Problems of Physiological Psychology. Bloomington, Principia, 1947.

Kaplan, A. Definition and specification of meaning. *Journal of Philosophy*, 1946, 43, 281-288.

Kemble, E. C. The probability concept. *Philosophy of Science*, 1941, 8, 204-232.

Keynes, J. M. A Treatise on Probability. London, Macmillan, 1921.

Keynes, J. N. Studies and Exercises in Formal Logic. London, Macmillan (4th ed.), 1906.

Klein, F. Elementary Mathematics from an Advanced Standpoint. (E. R. Hedrick and C. A. Noble trans.) vol. I, New York, Dover, 1945.

Kneale, W. Probability and Induction. Oxford, Clarendon, 1949.

Lamont, C. Naturalism and the appreciation of nature. *Journal of Philosophy*, 1947, 44, 597-608.

Laplace, P. S. Théorie Analytique des Probabilités. Paris, Courcier (3rd ed.), 1820.

Larmor, J. Dimensions of units. In *Encyclopaedia Britannica*, vol. XXVII, New York, Encyclopaedia Brittannica, Inc. (13th ed.), 1926.

Leibniz, G. W. Monadology. Chicago, Open Court, 1902.

Lenzen, V. F. The Nature of Physical Theory: Study in Theory of Knowledge. New York, Wiley, 1931.

———— Indeterminism and the concept of physical reality. *Journal of Philosophy*, 1933, 30, 281-288.

———— Concepts and reality in quantum mechanics. *Philosophy of Science*, 1949, 16, 279-286.

Lewis, C. I. Mind and the World-Order. New York, Scribners, 1929.

———— Alternative systems of logic. *Monist*, 1932, 42, 481-507.

———— Some logical considerations concerning the mental. *Journal of Philosophy*, 1941, 38, 225-233.

Lillie, R. S. Transmission of activation in passive metals as a model of the protoplasmic or nervous type of transmission. *Science*, 1918, 48, 51-60.

———— Transmission of physiological influence in protoplasmic systems, especially nerve. *Physiological Reviews*, 1922, 2, 1-37.

———— The physical nature of nervous action. *American Journal of Psychiatry*, 1929, 9, 461-479.

Lindsay, R. B., and Margenau, H. Foundations of Physics. New York, Wiley, 1936.

Locke, J. An Essay Concerning Human Understanding. London, Johnson, 1801.

Loeb, L. B., and Adams, A. S. The Development of Physical Thought, A Survey Course of Modern Physics. New York, Wiley, 1933.

Lotka, H. J. Probability —increase in shuffling, and the asymmetry of time. *Science*, 1924, 59, 532-536.

Lotze, H. Logik, Drei Bücher vom Denken, vom Untersuchung und vom Erkennen. Leipzig, Hirzel (2nd ed.), 1880.

McGill, V. J. Concerning the laws of contradiction and excluded middle. *Philosophy of Science*, 1939, 6, 196-211.

McGilvary, E. B. Relations in general and universals in particular. *Journal of Philosophy*, 1939, 36, 5-15, 29-40.

McGregor, D. Scientific measurement and psychology. *Psychological Review*, 1935, 42, 246-266.

Mach, E. Space and Geometry in the Light of Physiological, Psychological, and Physical Inquiry. Chicago, Open Court, 1906.

—— The Science of Mechanics. Chicago, Open Court, 1907.

Mansel, W. L. Prolegomena Logica: An Inquiry into the Psychological Character of Logical Processes. London, Livingston (1851), 1862.

Margenau, H. Critical points in modern physical theory. *Philosophy of Science*, 1937, 4, 337-370.

—— Reality in quantum mechanics. *Philosophy of Science*, 1949, 16, 287-302.

Maxwell, J. C. Matter and Motion. (J. Larmor ed.) New York, Macmillan, 1920.

Meldrum, W. B. and Daggett, A. F. A Textbook of Qualitative Analysis (Using the Semimicro Methods). New York, American Book Co., 1946.

Menzel, D. H. and Layzer, D. The physical principles of the quantum theory. *Philosophy of Science*, 1949, 16, 303-324.

Mercier, C. A. On Causation, with a Chapter on Belief. London, George, 1919.

Merz, J. T. A History of European Thought in the Nineteenth Century. Edinburgh, Blackwood, 1903-1923, 4 vols.

Michelson, A. A. Light Waves and Their Uses. Chicago, University of Chicago Press, 1903.

Mill, J. S. A System of Logic, Ratiocinative and Inductive. London, Parker, 1862.

—— An Examination of Sir William Hamilton's Philosophy. New York, Holt, 1884, 2 vols.

von Mises, R. Probability, Statistics, and Truth. (J. Newman, D. Sholl, and E. Rabinowitsch trans.) New York, Macmillan, 1939.

—— Comment on Donald Williams' reply. *Philosophy and Phenomenological Research*, 1945-1946, 6, 611-613.

Molesworth, W. The English Works of Thomas Hobbes of Malmesbury. London, Bohn, 1839-1845, 11 vols.

Moore, G. E. Principia Ethica. Cambridge, Cambridge Univ. Press, 1922.

Moore, J. S. Why a realism of universals? *Journal of Philosophy*, 1939, 36, 884-888.

Murray, G. Five Stages of Greek Religion. New York, Columbia Univ. Press, 1925.

Nagel, E. A. Can logic be divorced from ontology? *Journal of Philosophy*, 1929, 26, 705-712.

—— On the Logic of Measurement. Doctoral Dissertation, New York, Columbia University, 1930.

—— A frequency theory of probability. *Journal of Philosophy*, 1933, 30, 533-554.

———— The formation of modern conceptions of formal logic in the development of geometry. *Osiris*, 1939, 7, 142-224.

———— Principles of the Theory of Probability. In *International Encyclopedia of Unified Science*, vol. I, no. 6, Chicago, Univ. of Chicago Press, 1939.

———— Logic without ontology. In *Naturalism and the Human Spirit* (Y. H. Krikorian ed.) New York, Columbia Univ. Press, 1944.

———— Some reflections on the use of language in the natural sciences. *Journal of Philosophy*, 1945, 42, 617-630.

———— The meaning of reduction in the natural sciences. In *Science and Civilization* (R. C. Stauffer ed.) Madison, Univ. of Wisconsin Press, 1949.

Needham, J. A biologist's view of Whitehead's philosophy. In *The Philosophy of Whitehead*. (P. A. Schilpp ed.) Evanston, Northwestern University, 1941.

Nernst, W. The New Heat Theorem, its Foundations in Theory and Experiment. London, Methuen, 1926.

von Neumann, J. Mathematische Grundlagen der Quantenmechanik. Berlin, Springer, 1932.

Newton, I. Philosophiae Naturalis Principia Mathematica. (Cajori revision) Berkeley, Univ. of California Press (1934), 1946.

Neyman, J., and Pearson, E. Contributions to the theory of testing Statistical Hypotheses. *Statistical Research Memoirs*, 1936, 1, 1-37; 1937, 2, 25-57.

Nicod, J. Foundations of Geometry and Induction. New York, Harcourt, Brace, 1930.

Nisbet, R. H. The foundations of probability. *Mind*, 1926, 35, 1-27.

Oliver, W. D. Logic and necessity. *Journal of Philosophy*, 1950, 47, 69-73.

Pap, A. On the meaning of necessity. *Journal of Philosophy*, 1943, 40, 449-458.

Pearson, K. The Grammar of Science. London, Dent (Everyman ed.), 1937.

Peirce, C. S. Collected Papers. (C. S. Hartshorne and P. Weiss eds.) Cambridge, Harvard Univ. Press, 1931-1935, 6 vols.

Pepper, S. C. How to look for causality. In *Univ. of California Publications in Philosophy* (G. P. Adams, J. Lowenberg, and S. C. Pepper eds.) vol. XV, Berkeley, Univ. of California Press, 1932.

———— Definition. In *Univ. of California Publications in Philosophy* (G. P. Adams, J. Lowenberg, and S. C. Pepper eds.), vol. XXI, Berkeley, Univ. of California Press, 1939.

———— The descriptive definition. *Journal of Philosophy*, 1946, 43, 29-36.

———— What are categories for? *Journal of Philosophy*, 1947, 44, 546-556.

Planck, M. The meaning and limits of exact science. *Science*, 1949, 110, 319-327.

Poincaré, H. The Foundations of Science. New York, Science Press, 1921.
Polya, G. Heuristic reasoning and the theory of probability. *American Mathematical Monthly*, 1941, 48, 450-465.
Popper, K. Logik der Forschung, zur Erkenntnistheorie der modernen Naturwissenschaft. Vienna, Springer, 1935.
Ramsey, F. P. The Foundations of Mathematics, and other Logical Essays. New York, Harcourt, Brace, 1931.
Rankine, W. J. M. Miscellaneous Scientific Papers. London, Griffin, 1880.
Reese, T. W. The application of the theory of physical measurement to the measurement of psychological magnitudes, with three experimental examples. *Psychological Monographs*, 1943, 55, no. 3.
Reichenbach, H. Wahrscheinlichkeitslehre. Leiden, Sijthoff, 1935.
———— Experience and Prediction. Chicago, Univ. of Chicago Press, 1938.
———— Philosophic Foundations of Quantum Mechanics. Berkeley and Los Angeles, Univ. of California Press, 1944.
Reid, T. Essays on the Intellectual Powers of Man. Edinburgh, Bell, 1785.
Rickert, H. Zur Lehre von der Definition. Tübingen, Mohr (2nd ed.), 1915.
Ritchie, A. D. Scientific Method, an Inquiry into the Character and Validity of Natural Laws. London, Kegan Paul, 1923.
Robinson, R. Definition. Oxford, Clarendon, 1950.
Robson, W. A. Civilization and the Growth of Law. New York, Macmillan, 1935.
Rosenblueth, A. and Wiener, N. The role of models in science. *Philosophy of Science*, 1945, 12, 316-321.
Royce, J. The Principles of Logic. In *Encyclopaedia of the Philosophical Sciences*, vol. I (A. Ruge ed.) London, Macmillan, 1913.
Ruark, A. E., and Urey, H. C. Atoms, Molecules, and Quanta. New York, McGraw-Hill, 1930.
Runes, D. D. The Dictionary of Philosophy. New York, Philosophical Library, 1942.
Runge, C. Maass und Messen. In *Encyclopädie der Mathematischen Wissenschaften mit Einschluss ihrer Anwendungen*, 1903-1921, 5, 3-24.
Russell, B. The Problems of Philosophy. New York, Holt, 1912.
———— On the notion of cause. *Proceedings, Aristotelian Society*, New Series, vol. XIII, London, Williams and Norgate, 1913.
———— Our Knowledge of the External World as a Field for Scientific Method in Philosophy. London, Allen and Unwin, 1914.
———— Logical Atomism. In *Contemporary British Philosophy*. (J. H. Muirhead ed.) London, Allen and Unwin; New York, Macmillan, 1924.
———— Introduction to Mathematical Philosophy. London, Allen and Unwin (1919), 1924.
———— Analysis of Matter. London, Kegan Paul, 1927.
———— Mysticism and Logic. New York, Norton, 1929.

———— Principles of Mathematics. Cambridge, Cambridge Univ. Press, 1903; (Reissue) New York, Norton, 1938.

———— An Inquiry into Meaning and Truth. New York, Norton, 1940.

———— My Mental Development. In *The Philosophy of Bertrand Russell* (P. A. Schilpp ed.) Evanston, Northwestern University, 1944.

———— Reply to Criticisms. In *The Philosophy of Bertrand Russell* (P. A. Schilpp ed.) Evanston, Northwestern University, 1944.

———— Human Knowledge, Its Scope and Limits. New York, Simon and Schuster, 1948.

Ryle, G. Induction and hypothesis. *Aristotelian Society*, Supplementary vol. XVI, London, Harrison, 1937.

Scates, D. E. How science measures. *Journal of Experimental Education*, 1937, 5, 296-312.

Schiller, F. C. S. Formal Logic. London, Macmillan, 1912.

Schlick, M. Causality in everyday life and in recent science. In *University of California Publications in Philosophy*, vol. XV, no. 15 (G. P. Adams, J. Lowenberg, and S. C. Pepper eds.), Berkeley, Univ. of California Press, 1932.

Schopenhauer, A. On the Fourfold Root of the Principle of Sufficient Reason, and On the Will of Nature, London, Bell, 1891.

Schrödinger, E. What Is Life? The Physical Aspects of the Living Cell. Cambridge, Univ. Press, 1944.

Sears, J. E. Measurements. In *Encyclopaedia Britannica*, vol. XXX, New York, Encyclopaedia Britannica, Inc. (13th ed.), 1926.

Sellars, R. W. The Philosophy of Physical Realism. New York, Macmillan, 1932.

Semat, H. Fundamentals of Physics. New York, Rinehart, 1945.

Sheppard, W. F. Probability. In *Encyclopaedia Britannica*, vol. XXXI, New York, Encyclopaedia Britannica, Inc., 1926.

Shewhart, W. A. Economic Control of Quality of Manufactured Product. New York, Van Nostrand, 1931.

———— Statistical Method from the Standpoint of Quality Control. Washington, Graduate School, Dept. of Agriculture, 1939.

Sommerfeld, A. Atomic Structure and Spectral Lines. (H. L. Brase trans.) vol. I, New York, Dutton (3rd ed.), 1934.

Spaier, A. La Pensée et la Quantité: Essai sur la Signification et la Réalité des Grandeurs. Paris, Alcan, 1928.

Spencer, L. J. Abrasives. In *Encyclopaedia Britannica*, vol. I, New York, Encylopaedia Britannica, Inc. (14th ed.), 1929.

Spinney, L. B. A Textbook of Physics. New York, Macmillan (3rd ed.), 1925.

Spinoza, B. Ethics. London, Dent (Everyman ed.), 1910.

Stebbing, L. S. A Modern Introduction to Logic. London, Methuen (3rd ed.), 1942.

Stevens, S. S. A classification of scales of measurement. Paper read before *The International Congress for the Unity of Science*, September, 1941.

——— On the theory of scales of measurement. *Science,* 1946, 103, 677-680.

Stranathan, J. D. The "Particles" of Modern Physics. Philadelphia and Toronto, Blakiston, 1942.

Strong, E. W. Procedures and Metaphysics: a Study in the Philosophy of Mathematical-Physical Sciences in the 16th and 17th Centuries. Berkeley, Univ. of California Press, 1936.

Struik, D. J. On the foundations of the theory of probability. *Philosophy of Science,* 1934, 1, 50-70.

Stumpf, C. Neben den Begriff der Mathematischen Wahrscheinlichkeit. Berlin Bayr, Academie (phil. class.), 1892, 37-120.

Taylor, L. W. Physics, the Pioneer Science. Boston, Houghton, Mifflin, 1941.

Thomson, W. (Lord Kelvin) Popular Lectures and Addresses. London, Macmillan, 1889, 3 vols.

Todhunter, I. A History of the Mathematical Theory of Probability from the Time of Pascal to that of Laplace. Cambridge and London, Macmillan, 1865.

Toms, E. The law of excluded middle. *Philosophy of Science,* 1941, 8, 33-38.

Vaihinger, H. Die Philosophie des als ob: System der Theoretischen, Praktischen und Religiosen Fiktionen der Menschheit auf Grund eines Idealistischen Positivismus. Leipzig, Meiner (7th ed.), 1922.

Veblen, O. Problems and solutions. *American Mathematical Monthly,* 1922, 29, 357-358.

Veblen, O. and Young, J. W. Projective Geometry. Vol. I, Boston, Ginn, 1910.

Venn, J. The Logic of Chance: an Essay on the Foundations and Province of the Theory of Probability with Special Reference to its logical Changes and its Application to Moral and Social Science, and to Statistics. London, Macmillan, 1888.

Waismann, F. Are there alternative logics? *Proceedings Aristotelian Society,* 1945-1946, 46, 77-104.

Wald, A. On the Principle of Statistical Inference. South Bend, Notre Dame Univ., 1942.

Wallace, W. The Logic of Hegel. (Translated from the *Encyclopaedia of the Philosophical Sciences*) Oxford, Clarendon, 1892.

Wang, H. Notes on the justification of induction. *Journal of Philosophy,* 1947, 44, 701-710.

Webster, D. L., Farwell, H. W., and Drew, E. G. General Physics for Colleges. New York, Century, 1923.

Weitz, M. Philosophy and the abuse of language. *Journal of Philosophy,* 1947, 44, 533-546.

Whewell, W. History of Scientific Ideas. London, Parker, 1858, 2 vols.

——— Novum Organum Renovatum. London, Parker, 1858.

Whitehead, A. N. The Concept of Nature. Cambridge, Cambridge Univ. Press, 1920.

———— Science and the Modern World. New York, Macmillan, 1925.

Whitehead, A. N., and Russell, B. Principia Mathematica. Cambridge, Cambridge Univ. Press, 1910-1912, 3 vols.; (2nd ed.) 1925-1927.

Wiener, N. A new theory of measurement. *Proceedings, London Mathematical Society,* 1921, 19, 181-205.

Will, F. Is there a problem of induction? *Journal of Philosophy,* 1942, 39.

———— Will the future be like the past? *Mind,* 1947, 332-347.

Williams, D. C. The definition of yellow and of good. *Journal of Philosophy,* 1930, 27, 515-527.

———— The Ground of Induction. Cambridge, Harvard Univ. Press, 1947.

Windelband, W. Vom System der Kategorien. In *Philosophischen Abhandlungen (Christoph Sigwart zu seinem siebzigsten Geburtstage.)* Tübingen, Mohr, 1900.

Winderlich, R. Das Ding: Eine Einführung in das Substanzproblem; Teil I, Die Dinge der Naturwissenschaft. Karlsruhe, Braun, 1924.

Winn, R. B. The nature of causation. *Philosophy of Science,* 1940, 7, 192-204.

Wittgenstein, L. Tractatus Logico-Philosophicus. New York, Harcourt, Brace, 1922.

Wolff, K. H. The unique and the general: toward a philosophy of sociology. *Philosophy of Science,* 1948, 15, 192-210.

Wundt, W. Logik. Stuttgart, Enke, (3rd ed.) 1906-1908, 3 vols.

Young, J. W. Lectures on Fundamental Concepts of Algebra and Geometry. New York, Macmillan, 1911.

SUBJECT INDEX

Absolutism (see Universalism), in abstracting, 15; in definition, 33f., 46; in formal systems, 82; in philosophical systems, 76, 82f., 332f.; in categorization, 128; in causation, 147, 152f., 154, 159; in laws of thought, 175f., 181; by means of language, 194; in mathematics, 196f.; in probability theory, 206, 215f., 226f., in measurement theory, 293ff.; and statistical procedures, 332f.

Abstracting, in system building, 1, 7, 26f., 80, 106f., 333; as interbehavioral operation, 1f., 7, 10f.; field character of, 1; in mathematics, 1ff., 23f.; logical forms as products of, 2ff., 138ff.; and symbolic logic, 2ff.; constructional principles in, 4ff.; in Euclidean geometry, 4ff.; individual and cultural operations of, 7ff.; and quantum mechanics, 8, 12; and the existence problem, 8, 9f., 188ff.; of numbers, 8f., 10, 25, 26, 306; interrelated with generalizing, 9f.; and perception, 9; means formalizing, 10; specific characteristics of, 10f.; in measurement, 10, 306f.; symbols as products of, 10f.; divisive, 11f.; multiplicative, 12f.; and atomism, 12; in psychology, 12f.; role of language in, 18ff., 27; criteria for, 20f.; specificity principle in, 20f., 24; limits of, 21f.; illicit, 21ff.; extrapolation in, 24; and universals, 132, 138, 143; in science, 189.

Action sources, of logical forms, 141.

Acts, as system materials, 73; fixated, 98.

Actuality, a probability factor, 225.

Aesthetics, categories in, 129; measurement in, 304.

Algorithms, as mathematical instruments, 101.

Ambiguity, in definition, 46ff.

Analogizing, as generalizing interbehavior, 15f.; in mathematics, 15; and scientific models, 15f.; definition by, 51.

Analytical logics, 144.

Analyzing, definition by, 50f.

Antigenetic fallacy, 2.

Atomic physics, 266, 305ff., 309ff.

Atomism, and abstracting, 12.

Axiological categories, 124f.

Behavior, largely abstractional, 10f.; source of logical forms, 140; systemological, and logical laws, 202f.; measurement of judging, 273; continuity of, 321f.

Belief, probability as degree of, 208f., 212, 218, 223f., 238ff.

Biology, instrument construction in, 103; and ontology, 103; categories in, 126f.

Calculating systems, 302.

Calculation, in probability theory, 206ff., 210, 239, 245f., 261ff.; operational character of, 220; in measurement, 271, 291f., 302.

Calculus, probability (see Probability calculus), 210, 220, 243.

Categories, necessary in logic, 108; misinterpretations of, 108; are systembuilding instruments, 108f.; basic intellectual tools, 109; Aristotelian, 109f., 129; Kantian, 109; Hegelian, 109; historical evolution of, 109ff.; reflect cultural background, 112f., 116, 122, 129; current attitudes toward, 112; different sources of, 113; and knowledge, 113; as psychic entities, 114; related to classes and universals, 114f.; connect logic with language, 115, 128; and symbols, 115; technique of creating, 115; interbehavioral origin of, 115ff.; space and time as, 116; abstract continuous with concrete, 116f.; specific functions of, 117f.; range of, 118f.; in mechanics, 119f.; in electricity, 120; in geometry, 120; everyday, 121; religious, 121f.; in dimensional analysis, 122ff.; value, 124f.; in thermodynamics, 125f.; in biology, 126f.; ethical, 127f.; logical, 128; grammatical, 128f.; philosophical, 129; and ontology, 129; aesthetic, 129.

Causation, as a logical problem, 145f., 167; as an ontological problem, 145f., 149ff.; influence of deductive mathematics on, 146f.; in methodistic logic, 146f.; cultural background of, 147ff., 159, 167; naturalistic Greek conception of, 148; and mysticism, 148; classical theories of, 149ff.; substituted for, by sentences, 150, 154, 162; as

NAME INDEX